How to Set Up and Run a Successful Law Enforcement Sting Operation

JOHN F. SMITH
Detective (Retired)
Albuquerque Police Department

JAMES R. SHERIDAN
Detective (Retired)
Albuquerque Police Department

DENNIS F. YURCISIN
Detective
Albuquerque Police Department

PRENTICE HALL
Englewood Cliffs, New Jersey 07632

Prentice-Hall International (UK) Limited, *London*
Prentice-Hall of Australia Pty. Limited, *Sydney*
Prentice-Hall Canada Inc., *Toronto*
Prentice-Hall Hispanoamericana, S.A., *Mexico*
Prentice-Hall of India Private Limited, *New Delhi*
Prentice-Hall of Japan, Inc., *Tokyo*
Simon & Schuster Asia Pte. Ltd., *Singapore*
Editora Prentice-Hall do Brasil, Ltda., *Rio de Janeiro*

© 1991 *by*

Prentice Hall, Inc.
Englewood Cliffs, New Jersey

10 9 8 7 6 5 4 3 2 1

This publication is designed to provide accurate and authoritative information in regard to the subject matter covered. It is sold with the understanding that the publisher is not engaged in rendering legal, accounting, or other professional service. If legal advice or other expert assistance is required, the services of a competent professional person should be sought.
. . .from the Declaration of Principles jointly adopted by a Committee of the American Bar Association and a Committee of Publishers and Associations.

The material in this book is intended solely for use by trained law enforcement officers and agencies. The publisher disclaims any liability, loss or risk incurred as a consequence, directly or indirectly, of the use and application of any of the techniques, information or advice contained in this book.

Library of Congress Cataloging-in-Publication Data

Smith, John F. (John Frank)
    How to set up and run a successful law enforcement sting operation
/ John F. Smith, James R. Sheridan, Dennis F. Yurcisin.
      p. cm.
    Includes index.
    1. Undercover operations—United States—Handbooks, manuals, etc.
2. Receiving stolen goods—United States—Prevention—Handbooks,
manuals, etc. I. Sheridan, James R. (James Richard) II. Yurcisin,
Dennis F., 1944–   . III. Title.
HV8080.U5S65 1991   91–17371
363.2′52—dc20   CIP

ISBN 0-13-431065-9

PRENTICE HALL
Business Information & Publishing Division
Englewood Cliffs, NJ 07632
Simon & Schuster. A Paramount Communications Company

Printed in the United States of America

About the Authors

JOHN F. SMITH began his law enforcement career on patrol, assigned to a walking beat. The Albuquerque Police Department soon recognized his enthusiastic and professional approach and named him Officer of the Month. Other acknowledgments he received while in uniform include the Albuquerque Jaycees Outstanding Young Police Officer; Fraternal Order of Eagles Meritorious Service Award, and the Kiwanis Club Exemplary Police Officer Award.

The majority of his time in service, however, was spent as a detective assigned to the Criminal Investigations Division. His primary responsibility there was to organize and operate undercover sting operations. He was named Outstanding Detective by the department, in addition to receiving many other commendations from outside agencies, including the FBI, the Alcohol, Tobacco, and Firearms Division; the IRS (Criminal Investigations Division); the U.S. Department of Agriculture (Enforcement Division); and the U.S. Attorney General's Office. He has instructed on pro-active criminal investigation in the New Mexico Law Enforcement Academy and the Albuquerque Police Academy.

Now retired after twenty years of service, the knowledge John F. Smith acquired during his career is still being shared with law enforcement officers today.

JAMES R. SHERIDAN, JR., is also recently retired after twenty years of service to the Albuquerque Police Department. Sheridan spent his last eight years as a detective in special investigations. During this time he was involved in four storefront operations in which he was assigned as the case agent or undercover agent. During these operations Sheridan was responsible for the recovery of over one million dollars in stolen property and narcotics. During his last two years with the Albuquerque Police Department, Sheridan worked in narcotics, responsible for the interdiction of narcotics that are smuggled by air, rail, and land to and through the state of New Mexico. During this time Sheridan seized in excess of two million dollars in contraband cash and narcotics. He has also instructed at the Albuquerque Police Academy.

DENNIS F. YURCISIN is currently a member of the Albuquerque Police Department and has fourteen years of law enforcement experience, seven years in Albuquerque and seven years in the state of Maryland (Hagerstown P.D. and Prince George's County Sheriff's Department). During his law enforcement career he has worked in uniform patrol, organized crime, and narcotics. He has worked undercover on many occasions and has been responsible for the recovery of stolen property and narcotics in excess of one million dollars. Yurcisin has also worked as an aerial observer during his assignment to narcotics. Yurcisin currently instructs narcotics recognition and the controlled substance act at the Albuquerque Police Academy. In addition, he teaches the basic drug course for Northwestern University Traffic Institute.

All three officers have worked together on more than one occasion and have purchased illegal items that include firearms, explosive devices, cars, tractor trailers, and narcotics. In addition, all three officers have worked closely with other local and state agencies in these operations, along with the following federal agencies: FBI, DEA, ATF, IRS, U.S. Department of Agriculture, U.S. Immigration and Naturalization Service, and the Bureau of Land Management.

Preface

Periodically a news story will hit the nation describing the culmination of a police undercover storefront (or sting) operation. These news stories, whether reported by television anchorpersons or newspaper journalists, usually focus on the unorthodox methods law enforcement used to investigate a certain criminal activity, the mass arrests made, and the vast amounts of contraband and/or stolen property confiscated. To the uninitiated, the storefront seems to be a fairly simple operation. However, it is far more complex than it first may appear.

What exactly is an undercover law enforcement storefront, and what are its benefits? It is a cost-effective, proactive technique that uses a business facade to attract, infiltrate, and gain the confidence of the criminal element. The storefront will enable you to do the following:

- Identify the perpetrators.
- Secure undisputable evidence for a successful prosecution.
- Remove contraband from illicit markets.
- Recover stolen property and return it to its rightful owners.
- Develop contacts with cooperating individuals.
- Immobilize the criminal element.
- Instill confidence in the community that law enforcement has progressive and effective means to combat today's increasing crime problem.

So how do you organize and take advantage of a storefront operation? This book, written by police officers for police officers, takes you through the process step by step, from the initiation of the operation to court presentation. It describes how to:

- Identify and document the problem.
- Formulate the data collected.
- Establish the objectives for the operation.
- Determine the feasibility of the investigation.

Armed with this information, you are ready for the next step, in which you

- Determine the most appropriate type of storefront.
- Recognize the liabilities of each type of investigation.

Next is the preoperational phase, in which you:

- Write and present your proposal for the storefront.
- Select storefront personnel.
- Lay a foundation for a successful prosecution with a preoperational briefing with the prosecutor.

The legal aspects of entrapment, interviews, arrest raids, and case preparation are also covered throughout this book. The authors have used examples from first-hand experience, so you do not have to be a scholar to understand crucial legal issues pertaining to storefront operations.

To set up a storefront, you must

- Select a site and prepare it for the investigation.
- Develop an operational proposal for administering the storefront.
- Operate the storefront (that is, perform administrative duties).
- Utilize surveillance techniques to their full potential.
- Utilize cooperating individuals.

Before the doors are open for "business," you must develop a tactical operation plan:

- Develop a cover story for operatives.
- Arrange a meeting with the targets.
- Identify the "sellers"; that is, the persons you will buy from.
- Determine what to buy.
- Establish rules for the sellers.
- Schedule a first-buy debriefing with the prosecutor.

When the investigation nears its conclusion, culminate the operation with arrest raids and in-custody interviews, and work with the prosecutor to prepare the case and present the evidence in court.

The appendix to this book includes work sheets and forms that will assist you in conducting a storefront operation.

Since the structure of law enforcement entities varies widely, the authors have covered a wide range of material. Likewise, experience and expertise will vary among readers. This book enables small departments, large departments, newcomers, and experienced officers to obtain a comprehensive understanding of an undercover storefront.

Why should you spend the time and energy to learn more about this approach? Storefronts have proven time and time again that they are a productive, cost-effective, and proactive tool for combating crime. They can address a variety of criminal activity. The facades you can utilize for a storefront are limited only by your imagination. The storefront can be adapted to investigate the illegal activity of an individual or the illicit activities of a group. An operation that is carefully organized and administered by enthusiastic, enterprising, and competent personnel will be economical and fruitful. When utilized properly and within current departmental and judicial guidelines, only one thing can be said about storefronts: *"They work!"*

Contents

CHAPTER 6 / COMPILING AND PRESENTING A STOREFRONT PROPOSAL 101

CHAPTER 7 / CRITERIA FOR SELECTING STOREFRONT OFFICERS 113

CHAPTER 8 / PREOPERATIONAL BRIEFING WITH THE PROSECUTING ATTORNEY   125

CHAPTER 14 / TACTICAL OPERATION OF THE STOREFRONT   263

CHAPTER 1

How to Determine If the Criteria Exist to Initiate an Undercover Storefront

Establishing the criteria needed to initiate a law enforcement undercover storefront consists of several different phases:

1. Receipt and verification of information, or documentation of information
2. Analysis and evaluation of documented information
3. Determination of the objectives of the undercover operation
4. Determination of the feasibility of a storefront to meet the objectives.

The complexity of the criminal activity to be addressed will determine the extent to which any or all of these phases are utilized.

Many of the investigative techniques that are, or should be, instrumental in initiating any criminal investigation are involved in implementing a storefront. As with any criminal investigation, establishing a solid foundation is crucial. This is especially important with a storefront. A storefront, before becoming operational, requires administration approval. Proper documentation is essential to demonstrate the adverse impact of the criminal activity on the community. The documentation shows the value of the proposed storefront in combating this problem.

DOCUMENTATION: KNOW WHERE TO LOOK

Information can originate from a multitude of sources, such as (1) personal experience, (2) ongoing criminal investigations, (3) interviews with other members of your department or an outside department, (4) debriefing sources or informants, (5) in-custody interviews of suspects, (6) surveillance, and (7) other undercover operations. Once this information is received, it must be independently verified. This can be accomplished using four primary methods.

1. Use any number of information sources within your own department, or information sources from an outside law enforcement agency. These may include
   a. Offense reports
   b. Warrant files
   c. Arrest records
   d. Modus operandi files
   e. Prosecutor records.

2. Develop a source or informant who will be able to corroborate the information received. This source does not have to be involved in the criminal activity being documented. He or she can be a "good citizen" or a victim of the criminal activity who will respond to questions. This information may be classified as confidential or nonconfidential.

3. Use information obtained from private organizations and businesses.

4. Use surveillance. By closely monitoring the suspected individual or individuals, you attempt to verify information received.

Once you have verified the information, you must analyze and evaluate it and determine the feasibility of utilizing an undercover storefront to engage the criminal activity.

In this chapter we discuss in detail

Receipt and verification of information or documentation

How to analyze and evaluate the documented information pertaining to the storefront

How to determine the objectives of the storefront

How to determine the feasibility of using a storefront to confront criminal activity.

Receipt of Information

Any criminal investigation begins with the receipt of information. This is when you learn that a particular individual or individuals are participating in criminal activity or that specific criminal activity is occurring. After you receive the information on illicit activity, you must make a tentative evaluation of the information and its source.

Information can come from many sources. Your personal experiences are a valuable source of information that is often overlooked. What you see, hear, smell, feel, or taste is often all you need to initiate an investigation. However, try to verify or corroborate the information. In addition, you must document it. You can do so using one or more of the methods discussed in this chapter.

The investigation of criminal activity using a storefront must be planned carefully and thoroughly. Remember that the need for a storefront must be demonstrated to the administration. The success or failure of this presentation is often a direct result of preparation. The success of the operation often depends on seemingly insignificant procedural details which must be considered during initial planning.

Crime Reports: Know What to Look For

You have received information that may be best addressed by using a storefront. How do you determine the extent of the criminal activity and its impact on the community? How do you decide that a storefront is the most desirable approach to the problem?

First you must identify and document the information received. Identifying and documenting a problem enables you to show others that the problem does indeed exist. Researching crime reports is one method of identifying and documenting. Although a dull and tedious task, it is necessary in building a strong foundation to justify a storefront. Examining departmental records and reports is fundamental to any investigation. You can frequently find many investigative leads within your own police department's records.

Time Frame

First establish a time frame to be researched. In doing so, keep in mind what your research is attempting to demonstrate. Six months to one year may be long enough if you are trying to learn the magnitude of an illicit activity within the community. When attempting to show that a certain individual or individuals have a history of criminal dealings, more time may be needed. The type of activity to be investigated determines the time needed. However, there must be sufficient time to demonstrate the adverse influence the criminal activity is having on the community.

Crime Category

Once you have established a time frame, you must determine the category (auto theft, burglary, larceny) of the crime. Try to narrow the scope of the category. With too broad a scope, the documentation process can become overwhelming. With too narrow a scope, the documentation becomes limiting.

Determining the category of the crime(s) to be researched is usually obvious. You receive information that a certain area is plagued by residential burglaries. The category to be documented would obviously be residential burglaries. However, when you receive information that a particular area is being devastated by a crime wave, determining a category becomes more complex. You must make a tentative evaluation of the problem and choose the category(s) to be documented. The criminal activity that was not researched can still be attacked using a storefront. By limiting the categories to document, you can still obtain a solid foundation, and the documentation does not become cumbersome and overwhelming.

FOR EXAMPLE

The crime rate in a certain geographical area is increasing at an alarming pace. Property crimes, rapes, assaults, and homicides are on the rise. The investigator has received and independently verified information that a small gang of criminals is responsible for this dramatic increase.

To prevent the process from becoming unwieldy, the investigator could focus on the members of the gang and any illicit activity that can be directly attributed to them.

If the activity is of such a magnitude, the investigator may wish to limit the process even further. The investigator can concentrate documentation on the leaders of the gang and a specific criminal offense. Even though documentation has been limited in this way, all aspects of the criminal activity and all members of the gang can be investigated once the storefront is operational.

The investigator has been able to narrow the scope of the documentation without jeopardizing the foundation of the investigation. The investigator has made the process manageable.

Offense and Incident Reports

When you have determined a time frame and category(s) of crime, there are two types of crime reports to be researched.

1. The offense or incident report. These are initial reports completed by a responding police officer. In some jurisdictions, the victim is allowed to file his or her own report. In either case, the reports are maintained by the police records division.

2. The investigative supplementary, or follow-up, report. These reports contain all additional information obtained after the offense or incident report was filed. These reports are often compiled by someone other

than the responding officer. The supplementary report may also contain an investigative summary if the case has been cleared or closed.

Most law enforcement records divisions today are computerized. This speeds up the process of obtaining desired information. However, if your crime records are not computerized, you must hand search reports for the necessary data.

When using computerized records, obtain a printout of the desired reports. These printouts usually contain most of the information that is on the original report. After you evaluate the printout, you can obtain a copy of the original crime report if necessary. This method saves you time and the department money. If your department's records are computerized, learn how to access that information.

Uniform Crime Report

Your records division can also compile a Uniform Crime Report (UCR). This report is sent to the FBI so they can determine national crime statistics. The UCR is a good reference to show trends in criminal activity. It was established in 1930 to compile summary statistics from participating agencies. Today there are over 16,000 law enforcement agencies that submit information to the system. Agencies submit data on all significant events occurring during a criminal incident, not just the most serious. Additional information is reported, including time of day, the relationship of victim to offender, and any weapons used. The UCR reveals much more information than merely numbers. It is capable of analyzing crime trends, showing when and where different crimes are occurring, and assisting in developing strategies to combat criminal activity.

Remember, each storefront has its own special requirements. You must establish what data you want to obtain from the crime reports to best suit your particular investigation.

Outside Law Enforcement Agencies

Do not forget the records divisions of other law enforcement agencies in your area. They, too, can contain valuable information needed for your documentation. The interchange of information from one department to another usually leaves a lot to be desired. Do not assume that your records division has all the information from the other law enforcement agencies in your area. The records divisions of other departments can provide you with that one piece of information that is lacking. You will never know unless you ask. Other departments are usually more than willing to help, but they do not know you need the information unless you ask for it.

Helpful Tip: Before visiting any records division to obtain the information you need, *call first*. Talk to the person in charge of the records division, or to a subordinate, explaining what you need. That person will often have you contact someone they have designated to assist in the research. When you call this designated person, explain what you need, and find out approximately how long it will take to retrieve this information. Arrange a time to obtain this information that is convenient for both of you. This method is usually better received than walking in without an appointment and demanding that records personnel retrieve fifty reports immediately. Doing so can cause hostilities and keep you waiting a long time for the reports you need.

Local Law Enforcement Officers

Interviewing field officers and detectives to help document criminal activity can be advantageous. These people are a viable, but often overlooked, source of information. They have a vast quantity of knowledge. The only way to tap this information is to inquire. Often, officers notice things while performing their duties that do not seem important at the time. Instead of filing a report, they make a mental note and store it away. They may have noticed trends or patterns that seemed insignificant. They may have observed people or places that appeared a little out of the ordinary, but not enough to generate an offense report. That seemingly unimportant piece of information could be the missing piece of the puzzle you are looking for. Do not limit yourself in who you interview. A narcotics detective may have information on a burglar or a fence. The burglary detective may have information on a drug dealer or an auto thief.

Shifts of Information

Do not forget the officers or detectives who work different shifts. The officer who works a certain area on day shift might describe the beat as relatively calm and crime free. The night officer on the same beat may describe it as a war zone. Criminal activity can fluctuate widely in the same area depending on time of day and day of the week. One old-timer's analogy of this fluctuation is that perpetrators are like raccoons: They come out at night and steal shiny things.

Field Contact Cards

Field contact cards or field interrogation reports are another source of information. These informal cards or reports contain information about minor or incidental activities observed by field officers or detectives. They can reveal when a suspect was stopped or seen, the current description of the suspect, the time and location the suspect was stopped or observed, the description of the vehicle or associates, and suspicious activity at a certain location. These cards are often maintained by an intelligence unit within the department.

Intelligence Unit

Intelligence units can provide valuable information needed for documentation. They may also have contacts with various other intelligence units. One such unit is the Law Enforcement Intelligence Unit (LEIU), a fraternity of intelligence officers from over 225 state and local police departments that gather and exchange information.

RISS Projects

Throughout the United States, there is a network of six Regional Information Sharing Systems (RISS). RISS projects are multistate agencies designed and funded by the U.S. Department of Justice. RISS projects support state and local law enforcement agencies' efforts to combat criminal conspiracies. The two primary services provided by RISS projects are a centralized computerized law enforcement data base and investigative analysis products. The RISS database contains entries on major criminals that member agencies are willing to share with other member agencies. RISS investigative analysis products include link charts for telephone toll analysis assessments of criminal activity and other analytical products. In addition to the two primary services, RISS projects provide

Investigative equipment on loan

Confidential funding

Timely bulletins of criminal information

Training

Technical assistance

Referrals

Access to a telecommunications system.

Agencies across the nation have access to a number of projects which provide information to support documentation. However, there have been recent court challenges to the legality of law enforcement maintaining such intelligence files. Know your department's guidelines for maintaining and using such files. (For further information on RISS, see chapter 5.)

Performance Logs

Different units within a department usually maintain some type of log or performance record. These logs usually contain the information you are seeking, such as the following:

How many cases of a specific type crime the unit has been assigned
Clearance rate
Dollar value of property stolen
Recovery information
Suspect information
Associates
Past criminal investigations
Modus operandi.

Modus Operandi Files

The modus operandi file contains detailed descriptions of characteristic patterns of criminal activity associated with individuals. Do not overlook these logs and/or files when doing research, and do not forget the other law enforcement agencies in your area. Their specialized units also maintain logs. These logs are a potential gold mine of information.

Arrest Records

Arrest records completed at the time of arrest may also contain valuable information pertaining to

Aliases
A suspect's current residence
A suspect's employer
A suspect's present description including scars, marks, or tattoos
A suspect's criminal history
Other information that would be useful in the documentation.

You should also obtain a rap sheet to show if the suspect has a history of criminal activity outside your jurisdiction. Additional information can include

Identification photographs: Also known as mug shots. These are usually taken at the time of incarceration. They can provide visual details of a person's appearance at the time the photograph was taken. They can be filed with a limited criminal history, details of past residence, and employment. Storefront personnel should see the mug shots of suspected criminals before the storefront begins, and when planning for apprehension of suspects at the conclusion of the operation.

Fingerprint files: A fingerprint file is usually maintained along with the identification photographs. The fingerprint file provides final identification verification. It might include other pertinent information needed for documentation.

Arrest warrant files: Arrest warrant files and wanted bulletins can also be helpful. Warrant files can reveal if a suspect has a warrant outstanding. They may contain information on previous warrants issued, location at which the suspect was arrested, who was present at the time of arrest, criminal nature of the warrant, and subsequent judicial action. Wanted bulletins can contain photographs of the offender, details of personal appearance, modus operandi, personal details, and types of known criminal activity and associates.

Juvenile records: With the alarming increase of juveniles perpetrating felonies, it is often necessary to examine their police records. Juvenile records are usually maintained separately from adult records. They may include

The arrest record

Family history

Present and past school attendance

Personal details

Photographs

Fingerprints

Associates

Modus operandi

Name of the juvenile probation officer.

Access to and use of juvenile criminal history may be restricted in some jurisdictions. Determine if there are any departmental or judicial restrictions concerning the use of this information before incorporating it into your documentation.

Traffic Reports

Traffic accident reports, traffic records, or traffic violation history can divulge needed information. Traffic records are usually maintained separately from general police records. They may include

Information on the type of violation

Time and location of the violation

Type of vehicle
Insurance company
Passenger(s) in the vehicle when cited
Traffic violation history

Traffic accident reports are usually maintained in the departmental general records division and may contain the same information as traffic records. However, they may contain additional information, such as vehicle description, passenger information, insurance company, location and time of accident, names of witnesses, and statements given by parties involved.

Police Dispatch Records

Records maintained by police dispatchers can also be a valuable asset. They are usually kept in chronological order and can be useful in establishing a comprehensive view of police reaction to a type of incident. These records also include names of responding officers and can be a good source in determining which officers to interview.

Firearm File

Depending on the size of the department and local ordinances, a firearm registration file may be maintained. The registration files often contain the names of registered owners, residence, employer, criminal history, and type of firearm permit.

Crime-stoppers Reports

Most law enforcement agencies now have a crime-stoppers program. Such programs go by many different names but are all basically the same. They pay cash to callers who supply useful information on criminal activity. The information received by a crime-stoppers program can be a valuable documentation tool that is often overlooked. This information usually cannot be retrieved through your records division. Speak with the personnel assigned to crime-stoppers to determine what information they may have that would be helpful to you.

Outside Agencies: A Further Source of Information

When compiling documentation for a storefront, do not overlook the records and files that are maintained by outside law enforcement agencies. State and county law enforcement agencies maintain many of the same types of records and files as a local police department. However, inquiries to an outside agency can provide needed additional information. With today's criminal element utilizing motor vehicles for ready mobility, you should routinely check with other law enforcement agencies in your area. As with any criminal investigation, the type of criminal activity and criminal element investigated will determine the extent of outside documentation needed. The amount of time and effort spent on this documentation will be roughly proportional to the importance of the anticipated outcome.

If you plan on using the resources of an outside agency, establish a friendly working relationship with the individuals at that agency. Considerable time can be wasted going from one agency to another and then waiting for needed material. Developing a contact within the agency can allow you to obtain the information over the phone, or to request the data and arrange a time for pickup.

Statutes often govern the types of information that can be divulged. It is your responsibility to be familiar with what information can be legally obtained from an outside agency.

Non-Law Enforcement

Non-law enforcement agencies can provide needed assistance. They, too, may be governed by statutes limiting the information that they can furnish. In addition, they could require a court order or other formal request before they can divulge information. Knowing what is required before seeking material can prevent an unpleasant experience.

The following nonpolice agencies maintain records or files that could be useful in documentation:

Court records: Criminal, juvenile, probate, and civil proceedings in both state and federal courts. Often in a civil proceeding the petitioner may agree not to press criminal charges in favor of a monetary settlement. Probation and parole officers can supply information on the parole or probation status of individuals, record of employment, current residence, criminal history, associates, and comments of parole or probation officers.

Social services: Also known as public welfare agencies. They may have information concerning employment, dependents, current residence, and vehicle information.

Motor vehicle departments: State motor vehicle administrations or bureaus have information on operator's license, certificates of title, motor or vehicle identification number (VIN), license plates, and, in some instances, photographs.

Licensing bureaus: Usually within city, county, or state. These agencies issue licenses or permits for businesses, contractors, pets, work permits, etc. They may have information on an applicant's name, date of application, disposition of request, financial information, and other pertinent information.

Coroner's office: The medical examiner's office has information on relatives of a deceased person, any witnesses who might have testified at a coroner's inquest, and cause of death.

Bureau of Vital Statistics: The bureau maintains birth, marriage, and death records.

Board of Education: Schools have personal records, student records, lists of associates, and teacher's comments on students' behavior.

Board of Elections: Maintains a list of registered voters and residence information.

Attorney General: May have information on past or present investigation of criminal activity. Could also provide legal assistance.

Department of Corrections: This department has information on criminal history, photographs, list of associates, visitors' information, and dates of incarceration.

Alcohol beverage or liquor control boards: Have names of applicants, residential and business address, list of associates, and financial reports.

Gambling board or commission: When applicable in your jurisdiction, this agency can supply names and financial background of those holding or applying for a license.

Public libraries: These are a source of information that is often overlooked. They can supply needed technical data and information on a suspect or criminal element that has been reported in periodicals or newspapers. Most libraries maintain a large collection of periodicals and local and major newspapers. These sources are often indexed, making information retrieval much easier.

Private Organizations and Businesses

Private organizations and businesses can also be helpful in documentation. Remember, when requesting information from any source, especially the private sector, the manner in which you request assistance is important. The old adage, "You can attract more flies with honey than with vinegar" applies here. You can obtain more information and assistance with a pleasant, understanding, and professional approach than with an arrogant, demanding, and unprofessional approach. Cooperation on the part of any source is voluntary. Yes, there are certain agencies which are required to give you assistance. Be assured, however, that if your attitude is unpleasant, obtaining information, even from an agency that is required to supply it, can be impossible. The agency will use any excuse possible to keep the desired information from you just because of your unprofessional approach; also be assured that when the information is released it will be scarcely sufficient. When soliciting information from any source, a tactful approach will produce the desired results. Remember, you may have to return to the source for further assistance in the future.

When seeking information, always use a cautious approach. Explain carefully exactly what information or assistance you need, and why the information is important, without relaying too much information about the proposed storefront. Assure the source that the information will only be used in accordance with departmental and judicial guidelines, and that you will do everything within your power to maintain confidentiality. If you need the information at a later time for court, you should obtain it with a subpoena. The subpoena will direct the organization to make accessible specific records for the court. This allows the business organization, or a representative, to testify as a custodian of the records or files without having to comment on their content.

The following private organizations and businesses may be useful in the documentation process:

Telephone companies
Insurance companies
Gas companies
Banks
Electric companies
Savings and loans
Water companies
Trade unions
Telegraph companies
Professional associations
Transportation companies
Laundries
Churches
Credit card companies
Credit agencies
Private investigators
News media
Private libraries.

Federal Agencies

As of 1980, there had been over 100 federally assisted sting operations in forty-seven cities throughout the United States. What type of assistance can a federal agency supply? They can supply you with a wide range of information and services, anything from a fragment of information, technical advise, expert personnel, specialized equipment, or funding, to an abundance of information that can be invaluable in the documentation process. The most frequently contacted federal agencies and the assistance they can provide are as follows:

Federal Bureau of Investigation, U.S. Department of Justice: Maintains comprehensive identification files; crime laboratory analyses; expert testimony; investigative files; National Crime Information Center (NCIC); training programs; and investigative advice and guidance.

Drug Enforcement Administration, U.S. Department of Justice: The most direct source of assistance for narcotics investigations; compiles and maintains files and records of narcotics' law violators and other investigative files; maintains the El Paso Intelligence Center (EPIC)/Narcotics and Dangerous Drugs Information System (NADDIS) computerized intelligence system; laboratory analysis of drugs; can also provide legal assistance and expert testimony.

Alcohol, Tobacco, and Firearms Division, U.S. Department of the Treasury: Information on firearm sales, ammunition sales, and firearm registration; information on distillers, brewers, and companies dealing in the sale and handling of alcoholic beverages; information on certain companies dealing in tobacco products.

Compliance and Investigations Branch, U.S. Department of Agriculture: Permits and applications submitted by meat packers, food canners, and other food handlers; results of inspections conducted under the Pure Food and Drug Acts; food-stamp fraud.

Immigration and Naturalization Service, U.S. Department of Justice: Records of alien registration, immigration, and naturalization; lists of passengers and crew members of foreign vessels; information on those involved in alien smuggling.

United States Attorney's Office, U.S. Department of Justice: Files on past and present judicial proceedings; defendant information; ongoing investigations; legal assistance.

Bureau of Customs, U.S. Department of the Treasury: Information on importers and exporters; international shippers; registry and licensing of vessels; information related to smuggling.

Visa Division, U.S. Department of State: Responsible for alien visa control; controls immigration quotas and departure of aliens from the United States.

Passport Division, U.S. Department of State: Determines the eligibility of applicants for passports; determines eligibility of people registered in American consulates as citizens of the United States.

United States Postal Service: Can provide names of people receiving mail at an address; limited information pertaining to postal money orders; mail fraud; forwarding address; mail trace; mail covers.

Interstate Commerce Commission: Maintains route and rate data pertaining to interstate shipments and common carriers engaged in commercial transport.

United States Coast Guard, U.S. Department of Transportation: Maintains records of ship movements within United States waters; background information on all U.S. merchant seamen; performs coastal patrol; some information on smugglers through interdiction program.

United States Maritime Commission: Maintains files on crew members of all U.S. vessels; lists common carriers engaged in foreign commerce; people engaged in freight forwarding, docking, warehouse facilities; other freight terminal facilities.

Social Security Administration: Identification numbers can be traced to place of issuance.

Internal Revenue Service: Investigations of income tax violation; money laundering; seizures of assets for tax violations.

United States Secret Service, U.S. Department of the Treasury: Maintains files on counterfeiters; thefts and/or forgery of government checks and bonds.

Some federal agencies are restricted by law pertaining to the amount of information and/or assistance they can provide. You should determine what restrictions apply before inquiring at the agency in question.

The Use of Cooperating Individuals: Confidential Sources

Information can be received and/or documented through a cooperating individual (CI). Cooperating individuals include all people who contribute information as a result of personal contact with you: people on the fringes of crime, criminals, "good citizens," and fellow officers. The information they give may be classified as confidential or nonconfidential. Information is usually classified as confidential to protect the identity of the source. Maintaining source confidentiality can be desirable in

Protecting the source's personal welfare

Ensuring that the source will be able to supply information in the future

Protecting the source's loved ones
Protecting the source's employment.

Cooperating individuals have been labeled with many different names such as snitch, informant, rat, stool pigeon, fink, blabber, squealer, Judas, and canary. These terms conjure a despicable image and should not be used by law enforcement personnel. The person who contributes information to you should be referred to as a cooperating individual, source, confidential source, or other term that does not convey a derogatory image.

Motivation

While using to the fullest any information provided by cooperating individuals, you must stay alert to the motivation that prompts the assistance. In many cases, the noncriminal cooperating individual merely wants to be helpful. The criminal cooperating individual may have other motives—monetary gain, revenge, culling the competition, among others. You must remain attentive to these motives and know when exaggeration replaces fact and when an eyewitness report deteriorates into embellishment and speculation. The information received must be evaluated relative to the source and the circumstances of its receipt.

Reliability and Credibility

Establishing the reliability of the source is key to establishing the credibility of the cooperating individual's information. Here are some of the ways you can establish the source's credibility.

1. Determine if the source has given credible information in the past.
2. Independently verify all or part of the information given.
3. Determine if the information given was obtained by firsthand knowledge or hearsay.
4. Establish what the motives for giving the information were.
5. Know the source's standing in the community.

Remember, a source's information is only as good as the source. (Chapter 13 discusses cooperating individuals in greater detail.)

Prosecutor

The case reports maintained by the prosecutor's office can be another source of information. Remember, you are concerned with the same time frame and specific criminal activity identified earlier. Prosecutor's reports can show if there is an increase or decrease in the number of cases being submitted to the prosecutor's office, as well as the prosecution, or lack of it, in these types of cases. Cases may not be prosecuted because of a particular problem inherent to this type of investigation—a problem you can possibly overcome using a storefront.

Suspect Information

The prosecutor's office usually handles cases submitted by different departments in or around your jurisdiction. These cases can contain valuable information that other avenues of research have not revealed. Suspect information submitted to the prosecutor's office is often more complete than that found on the original crime report.

Often, in a plea bargain, offenders must give information on criminal activity that they are aware of, such as who their "fence" is, their nonindicted co-conspirators, suspects they are aware of who are committing crimes, etc. The prosecutor will be able to tell you to which law enforcement personnel this information was forwarded.

Other Information from the Prosecutor

The prosecutor's office may also be aware of repeat offenders and their co-conspirators. They can reveal the status of these offenders—whether they are in prison, on parole, on probation, or out on bail awaiting trial. They may also be aware of the method of operation used by these offenders. Does the method established through your documentation fit with any of the offenders they have prosecuted or are prosecuting?

Checklist/Work Sheet

One method of ensuring that all possible avenues are investigated is to use a checklist or work sheet. List all the appropriate sources to contact that may have information needed for documentation. Often more than one person is involved in this process. To prevent duplication of efforts, indicate the following on the work sheet: who made contact; date of contact; was information obtained; and from whom. The work sheet gives everyone involved a quick reference to the progress of the documentation procedure. An example of a work sheet you may wish to use is included in the appendix (see work sheet 1).

SUMMARY OF DOCUMENTATION

Obviously, you will not need to use all the sources of documentation discussed. The sources you use should be expanded as far as imagination and good judgment allow. Remember, the documentation process will be used to show

1. The extent of criminal activity
2. Adverse impact on the community
3. Target of the storefront
4. The capability of the storefront to address the problem.

The target of the investigation should determine the appropriate level of documentation needed. So carefully choose the steps that will be appropriate for adequate documentation of the storefront.

FORMATTING THE DATA COLLECTED

Now that you have received and documented the information, it must condensed into an easily understood format. Choose a format that will best illustrate the magnitude of the criminal activity. The format may contain any of the following applicable information:

Specific criminal activity: Burglary, auto theft, drug violations, etc. (the criminal activity to be addressed by the storefront)

Total number of incidents reported: Number of police reports taken on specific criminal activity

Clearance rate: Percentage of incidents reported that have been cleared

Recovery rate: Percentage of stolen property that have been recovered

Frequency rate: Is criminal activity on the increase or decrease?

Monetary loss to the community: Dollar amount of property stolen, damage to property, or estimated economic impact on the community

Suspect information: Any and all information obtained on suspect(s)

Modus operandi: Any pattern that has been established that may be useful in combating the criminal activity

Time of day and day of week: When criminal activity is most prevalent

Geographical area: Where the criminal activity occurs most often.

A work sheet may assist you in the formulation of data collected. (An example of this type of work sheet is included in the appendix; see work sheet 2.)

The crime analysis unit of your department can be useful in obtaining some of the information you need. Most units use a format that contains information similar to the foregoing list. They may also be able to project frequency rates, geographical area of next occurrence, and date and time the activity is most likely to occur. The Uniform Crime Report (UCR) can also be used to obtain some of the information desired.

Many departments may have computer equipment and trained personnel to assist you in developing a computer program to formulate the information. In the documentation process, one problem you may encounter is an abundance of information that becomes unmanageable. A computer may help to place the information in a manageable and easily understood format.

ANALYZING THE DATA COLLECTED: READING BETWEEN THE LINES

Once the documentation has been completed and placed into an easily understood format, it needs to be analyzed. The raw data listed in the format often does not project a realistic representation of the criminal activity. Frequently, a more in-depth look at the data is required to reveal the true picture. Trends, frequency rates, and clearance rates, among other aspects, may need to be compared to show the true effect of the problem. In the following segment, examples of how to analyze the data and what benefits can be gained from doing so are discussed. The extent of the analysis needed will depend on the nature and complexity of the criminal activity to be addressed by the storefront.

Calculating the Crime Rate

Calculating the total number of crimes reported can help show the magnitude of the problem, but remember, you are analyzing the criminal activity. Just saying there were so many of this type of crime reported in a certain time period is not enough. Compare the number of crimes reported in the two previous time periods. If you have chosen a six-month period to study, show the comparison between the two previous six-month periods. The raw data on the number of crimes reported is easily accessible through the records division, crime analysis unit, or UCR reports. These figures are kept by every department. You do not have to obtain all the crime reports for the previous year and calculate the figures by hand. The goal is to see if the total number of crimes reported is increasing, decreasing, or remaining the same.

The Clearance Rate

An important piece of data is the clearance rate of the criminal activity being studied. If the clearance rate is 90 percent, even though there has been a large increase in the number of crimes reported, the problem might not be as bad as first perceived. Check the clearance rate of the two previous time periods being studied. This information is easily accessible through the records division. Determine if the clearance rate has increased, decreased, or remained the same. If the analyzed crime reports indicate a problem, what is the increase, what is the clearance rate, and what impact has it had on the problem?

FOR EXAMPLE ―――――――――――――――――――――――――

The first time period studied has a clearance rate of 55 percent, the second 20 percent, and the most recent time period 22 percent. Those comparing the second and most recent time period would say that the clearance rate is up by 2 percent. But by comparing the three time periods you can show the overall picture, that the clearance rate has dropped significantly.

The Clearance Rate and the Facade

Another advantage of analyzing the clearance rate is that this information may assist in the selection of the appropriate facade and location for the storefront. This could mean the difference between the success or failure of the operation. A majority of storefronts are designed, in part, to retrieve stolen property. By examining the clearance rate, a more informed decision can be made regarding the type and location of the storefront. This breakdown can indicate a geographical area and/or type of business where recoveries have taken place.

FOR EXAMPLE ―――――――――――――――――――――――――

Home electronic equipment is stolen at an alarming rate. Recoveries have been made at two secondhand stores within two blocks of each other.

Armed with this knowledge, the investigator may want to use the facade of a secondhand store and locate the storefront in this area.

Analyzing the clearance data will not always yield such revealing factors as shown in the preceding examples. Often, bits and pieces of a pattern are established. You must combine this information with experience to make an informed decision.

The Recovery Rate and What to Look For

The condition in which stolen property is recovered can also be an important factor, as shown by the following examples.

Example 1: In cases of auto theft, determine if the vehicles being recovered are in approximately the same condition as when they were stolen. One thousand vehicles have been stolen in the past six months. Say that 900 of the stolen vehicles have been recovered. That is a recovery rate of 90 percent. Presenting this information on face value, you will probably have a difficult time in convincing superiors of the need for a storefront.

But analysis of the crime reports shows that 600 of the recovered stolen vehicles were recovered stripped. That gives an entirely different meaning to the 90 percent recovery rate.

This type of analysis can also be applied to other types of property. The home electronic equipment that was recovered had all the components removed. All that remained were the cabinets. With this information, you can show a more realistic overview of the actual recovery rate.

Example 2: One thousand vehicles were reported stolen in the last six months. Of the 1,000, 600 were recovered in the same condition as when stolen. But, in analyzing the reports, you see that of the 1,000 vehicles reported stolen, 400 were pickup trucks and no pickup trucks have been recovered. Realizing this, you design a storefront to target the theft of pickup trucks. When presenting the idea for the operation the raw data indicates a respectable 60 percent overall recovery rate for auto thefts. The need for such an operation may not be evident. However, since you have analyzed the recoveries, you can show that the rate of recovery for pickup trucks is zero percent.

The Frequency Rate

The frequency at which crimes have occurred can also be a significant factor. Is the frequency increasing or diminishing?

FOR EXAMPLE _____

In the data gathered, there were 1,000 reported auto thefts in the last six months. There were 850 in the first three months, 100 in the fourth month, 40 in the fifth month, and 10 in the most recent month. This shows that the frequency is declining. If reversed, this would show that the problem is growing and a storefront could be a viable option. There may also be a reason for the increase or decrease that was discovered in analyzing the data.

FOR EXAMPLE _____

A large labor force comes into the area during certain times of the year. When the labor force is present, residential burglaries increase. When the labor force is gone, the residential burglaries decrease. This could explain the drop in the frequency rate and help in determining the most appropriate operating period for the proposed storefront.

Monetary Loss

Monetary loss to the public is also a meaningful factor to consider in showing how the criminal activity is placing a financial drain on the community. This expense can be shown in several forms.

The direct loss to individual victims

The loss to the community

The financial strain the criminal activity places on police budgets in terms of labor, equipment, and salaries used to combat the problem with conventional methods.

Remember, eventually you may want to show how the storefront can help reduce the monetary loss suffered by the community, and how the storefront can ease the burden this activity has placed on the department's budget.

Some crimes do not have an easily determined monetary factor. Crimes dealing with moral turpitude, such as pornography, are an example. The corruption of society's morals is more readily apparent than the monetary loss. In some areas, just showing that the moral consciousness of society is being threatened is enough to raise a public uproar. But to show the monetary loss to the public, you may have to analyze this type of crime more carefully. You may need to show that the money gained from this type of activity historically goes to finance other types of illicit undertakings, such as the distribution of controlled substances, prostitution, and gambling. Then you will be able to show the monetary loss suffered by the community because of these crimes.

Suspect Information

Suspect or target information sometimes requires a little more leg work. Most computer printouts received from the records division indicate that there is suspect information in the crime report, but do not give the suspect information. Other printouts give only partial suspect information. To obtain the complete information, you need a copy of the crime report. Even if the printouts contain full suspect information, it is good practice to obtain the needed crime report. The information on the printout is usually entered into the computer by a data entry clerk in the records division. With the vast amount of entries each clerk has to enter each day, the possibility exists for error or incomplete information. Also, by having a copy of all the police reports containing suspect information, you will be able to piece together partial descriptions from the different reports and develop a more complete suspect description. Often suspect information is contained in the narrative portion of the crime report. The narrative portions of the crime reports are not contained on most printouts. Obtaining the crime report and reading the narrative section is the only way to retrieve this information.

Time of Operation

Determine the time(s) of the day and day(s) of the week that the crimes occur most frequently. This can be beneficial in deciding the hours of operation and days of the week the storefront should be open. If the research shows that the criminal activity does not occur on Monday or Tuesday, being closed on these days might be advantageous. If most of the criminal activity occurs between noon and 6 P.M., being open from noon to 8 P.M., may be most fruitful. Since most storefront operations are not open twenty-four hours a day, seven days a week, you must choose carefully the times and days of operation.

Modus Operandi

Establishing modus operandi (MO), method of operation, may help to determine if a single individual, a group of individuals, or several groups of individuals are conducting the criminal activity. It may also reveal the possible identity of these suspects. The information obtained so far will help to establish the MO(s). Was there a particular method used to gain entry into a structure? Does the suspect(s) leave a calling card such as graffiti on the walls, enjoy a meal while burglarizing a home, or defecate in the structure being burglarized? Is a particular type of item always taken while other valuable items are left behind? Is something taken from the scene of the crime, such as a pillowcase, garbage can, or bag that the suspect uses to carry the stolen property? Is there any other peculiarity you have discovered that the suspect(s) has demonstrated? Is this specific eccentric behavior connected with the criminal activity being analyzed?

THE OBJECTIVES OF THE STOREFRONT

The objectives of a storefront are usually multifaceted and in some aspects are unique to the operation. The more objectives a storefront can meet, the more successful it is. Here are some of the objectives a storefront can accomplish:

Identification of the target: Naming the individual or individuals responsible for the criminal activity

Collection of evidence: For the arrest, prosecution, and convictions of those identified as being responsible for the criminal activity. This can be for crimes culminating at the storefront, and/or prior criminal dealings. Once the targets become comfortable with the undercover officers, they will have a tendency to boast about their past criminal activities and may unintentionally give needed evidence that can be used in solving previous criminal acts.

Recovery of stolen property: The retrieval and return of stolen property to the rightful owner. This tends to have a positive impact on public relations.

Seizure of contraband: The removal of contraband from the criminal element such as weapons, narcotics, and explosives

Intelligence: Information gathered from and concerning the criminal element. Conversations with the criminal element who frequent the storefront will often reveal that they are involved in, or are aware of, a wide range of criminal activity. They may also disclose who else is perpetrating these crimes.

Public relations: Favorable media coverage upon the conclusion of the storefront. This could improve the department's public relations within the community.

Reduction of criminal activity: Giving the citizens of the community a safer atmosphere in which to live

Easing monetary loss: The loss suffered by the public; reduction of the strain placed on departmental budgets in combating the criminal activity addressed by the storefront

Spinoffs: The criminal activity the storefront encounters that it was not designed to investigate

Spinoffs

Often, you can adapt and investigate spinoffs along with the targeted activity, a big plus for the operation. Sometimes, however, the illicit undertaking is of such a nature that it cannot be investigated by the storefront. For instance, the probe is designed and budgeted to investigate property crimes. During its course, undercover agents befriend a major drug dealer. To conduct the "buys" needed, the budget of the storefront would be completely depleted. Does the investigation discontinue because of budgetary constraints, or is the investigation turned over to another agency that is properly funded to conduct the inquiry? Too often, because of petty jealousies and power struggles between agencies, the criminal wins. The sharing of information and co-investigations between agencies can be the most beneficial and often overlooked benefits of a storefront. With a little understanding and cooperation between agencies, the only loser is the criminal.

Finally, the objective most often overlooked is the improvement of relationships between law enforcement agencies. As we know, relations with other departments are not always what they should be. The storefront often uncovers criminal activity occurring in other jurisdictions. The offenders who have been identified through the operation are possibly committing their unscrupulous deeds in more than one jurisdiction. The sharing of this information with other agencies can lead to a more cooperative atmosphere. In this day and age, we need all the cooperation between agencies we can get.

DETERMINING THE FEASIBILITY OF A STOREFRONT: STOREFRONT VERSUS CONVENTIONAL METHODS

Criminal activity is diverse, and each type presents its own unique set of circumstances. Therefore, there is no secret formula to determining the feasibility of a storefront. A determination must be made by a thorough understanding of the problem—knowing what objectives can be accomplished and how best to accomplish the objectives.

The target of the investigation will help in determining the need for a storefront. The target can be a single individual, a group of individuals, or specific criminal activity. The magnitude of the criminal activity being committed and its effect on the community is an important factor in determining feasibility.

Compare the storefront method with conventional law enforcement methods. Conventional methods are usually designed to be reactive. A crime is committed and the police are dispatched to investigate. The storefront is designed to be proactive. It is used to infiltrate the criminal element, identify those responsible for the criminal activity, and obtain evidence necessary for successful prosecution. It must be decided which approach is the most feasible and will yield the most dramatic results. Will the reactive approach enable you to address the problem and accomplish the objectives, or is a more proactive approach needed to obtain the desired results?

Have conventional law enforcement techniques dealt with the problem, and are they capable of dealing with the target? The documentation that has been compiled should supply that answer, but a guess would be, no. If these conventional techniques had dealt with the problem, you would not have perceived a problem. If conventional techniques were capable of dealing with the target, you would not be considering a storefront.

Determining Factors

Departmental resources are an unavoidable factor in determining the feasibility of the storefront. You can only work with the tools that are available or that can be acquired for the operation. Alternative sources of funding will be discussed in more detail in chapter 5. Some of the critical factors to consider, however, are as follows:

Labor: The labor available through the department must be determined. If the proposed storefront requires ten investigators and twenty support staff and the department can supply two investigators and two support staff, the proposed storefront is not feasible. You can not ignore a realistic appraisal of labor needs and availability.

Length of investigation: Time considerations will vary depending on the target chosen. It may take considerable time to obtain confidence, and then to gather the necessary evidence for prosecution. The anticipated length of the operation, as it relates to the department, must be considered.

Equipment: You must determine what equipment is available within the department and what can be reasonably utilized for the storefront. The equipment can include such items as video cameras, video recorders, audio recorders, microphones, body transmitters and/or recorders, and any special equipment indigenous to the nature of the operation. When surveillance will be a part of the storefront, investigators may need binoculars, night scopes, cameras, and vehicles. You may also want to determine what equipment can be obtained from outside sources.

Funding: You must be aware of available funds within the department and/or funds that can be acquired from an outside source. This must be a realistic appraisal. With an unlimited budget, we all could do just about anything, but in the realm of law enforcement the constraints of funding are a reality.

Legal assistance: This should be an intricate part of the planning for any storefront. The complexity of the law and numerous legal points that govern many aspects of this type of investigation must be understood and followed. Legal assistance will help you avoid the nullification of many months of hard work due to a legal technicality. Establishing a good working relationship with the prosecutor's office is important for any law enforcement officer, especially those involved in a storefront operation.

Departmental Objections

The attitude of your individual department may be an additional hurdle to overcome. Some administrators have an aversion to this type of investigation, fearing that some indiscretion may occur which would create an unfavorable reaction. The storefront operation can often be misunderstood by the general public and focus unwanted attention on the administrator. If this antiquated attitude exists, you must show the administrators that with proper documentation and preparation the storefront is a proven, productive, and cost-effective law enforcement technique.

Benefits

Stress the benefits that a law enforcement agency can expect from a storefront operation, such as

An increase in felony arrests

An increase in stolen property recovered and returned to its rightful owner

Higher conviction rates

Development of additional intelligence on criminal activity that is not the target of the storefront (spinoffs)

Improved interagency relations

Increased public morale

Confidence in the criminal justice system

Community recognition that the police have the ability to successfully address the criminal activity in the community.

Storefronts historically attract career and professional thieves who are responsible for committing a disproportionate number of crimes, especially property-related crimes. UCR statistics indicate that approximately 60 percent of the people arrested for property crimes using conventional law enforcement techniques are convicted, while approximately 90 percent of those arrested for property crimes as a result of a storefront investigation are convicted. Our experience in conducting other types of criminal investigations using storefronts resulted in the same high conviction rate. Not only was the conviction rate higher, but more of the convictions were accompanied by prison sentences when they were obtained with evidence gathered from a storefront. Approximately 20 percent of those convicted of property crimes when arrested as a result of conventional methods received prison sentences. Approximately 90 percent of those arrested and convicted with evidence obtained using a storefront received prison sentences.

SUMMARY

When a solid foundation is built using proper documentation, and when departmental and judicial guidelines are followed, a storefront is a cost-effective and successful method in combating today's growing crime problem. You must to take into account the limitations of your department when considering this proactive law enforcement technique. A proposed operation that exceeds these limits will surely fail. The feasibility of the storefront investigation will depend on your investigative skills, good judgment, and common sense.

CHAPTER 2

Types of Storefronts

In light of the definition of a police undercover storefront—a proactive law enforcement technique that uses a business facade to attract, infiltrate, and gain the confidence of a criminal element—the possible types and facades for an operation are limitless. There have been many different types of storefronts. Budgetary restrictions, departmental policies, judicial guidelines, and your imagination are the only limiting factors.

A majority of storefronts are established to combat property crimes. This type of criminal activity is becoming more prevalent. According to a UCR report released by the FBI, there were over 3.2 million burglaries in 1986, which accounted for an estimated loss of $3.3 billion. One of every 128 registered motor vehicles will be stolen, causing an additional loss of over $7 billion. There were 7.7 million larceny-thefts, resulting in an additional loss of $3.4 billion.

Alarming as these figures are, property crimes (burglary, larceny, and theft) are increasing at a staggering rate. The storefront is a proven cost-efficient tool which can be used to engage this type of lawlessness. In addition, the versatility of storefronts allows other types of criminal behavior to be addressed. The police undercover storefront can be used to combat and deter many types of transgressions. We have used storefronts to investigate

1. White-collar crimes
2. Murder
3. Arson
4. Controlled substance violations
5. Crimes of moral turpitude.

With proper planning, the storefront is not only an effective and productive law enforcement technique, but it has many potential applications.

The degree to which law enforcement prevents criminal activity is very subjective. How much crime does any law enforcement technique prevent? There is no definitive answer. We all know that the presence of law enforcement officers deters crime, but to what degree? There are some people who would engage in criminal activity no matter what the circumstances might be. Then there is the opportunist who takes advantage of law enforcement's inability to be at all places at all times. A storefront, when properly utilized and publicized, can project the illusion that law enforcement is or could be anywhere, at any time. When opportunists are unsure where the police may be, or what disguise they may be using, they are less likely to seize the opportunity.

As stated, budgetary constraints are a reality we all must face. A storefront, however, can be very cost effective and produce dramatic results while placing little or no strain on the departmental budget. The storefront is being used more frequently due to the need for an innovative, proactive, cost-efficient method to combat crime. We are all familiar with the ongoing monetary constraints that are placed on law enforcement. Political candidate after political candidate runs for office on the platform of law and order. Once elected, however, they state that the funds are not available to support the police to the degree they should be. Knowing how the public feels about higher taxes, law enforcement is faced with the dilemma of accomplishing more with less monetary resources. This dilemma may seem unsurmountable at first; it has, however, created at least one positive aspect. Officers have had to become more creative in their war on crime. The storefront is one method to combat criminal activity creatively, thus accomplishing more with today's restrictive budgets.

THE FACADE: LOOKING THE PART

The facade used to mislead the criminal is critical. The offender must be convinced that a business exists and that the opportunity to conduct illicit activity at this location is likely. This applies to whatever type of storefront is chosen. Using creativity and imagination will enable you to meet this challenge. But there are certain types of ventures that seem to attract the criminal element more frequently than others. This does not mean that these types of undertakings are operated by, or patronized by, only the lawbreaker. Honest citizens toil many hours to make a living operating these types of businesses. It is just that in our professional experience and in discussions with others in our profession, certain types of businesses seem to attract good citizens along with the bad citizens. Some of these businesses are

1. Secondhand stores
2. Used furniture stores
3. Salvage yards
4. Paint and body shops
5. Used car lots
6. Pawn shops
7. Liquor establishments
8. Head shops
9. Automobile repair stores
10. Scrap yards
11. Gold and silver exchanges.

Our firsthand knowledge has also shown that almost anyone can be a fence either knowingly or unknowingly if the opportunity is right. A theory among law enforcement professionals is that if the activity of the fence could be curtailed, property crimes would diminish significantly. If there were no one to purchase stolen property, there would be no reason to steal. In our observations, and in many discussions with other law enforcement professionals, this theory seems to have one major flaw. We used to think that there was a limited number of fences who purchased the vast majority of stolen property, thereby creating an unlimited number of thieves. In interviewing hundreds upon hundreds of property crime offenders, we have found the opposite to be true. Only a small portion of society has the mental makeup to burglarize a business or home. But a large portion of society is capable of fencing, if only for a single time, to take advantage of that unbelievable, once-in-a- lifetime deal. "It was a deal too good to pass up" is a phrase often heard while investigating those who have purchased stolen property.

FOR EXAMPLE

A thief steals a color television from a business and takes it to a local bar. The thief asks if any of the patrons would be interested in buying the television set. One of the patrons, whose television has just broken, purchases the television even though he suspects it is stolen. The patron would never consider burglarizing a home or business for any reason, and under other circumstances would never purchase property which he suspects is stolen. But when this opportunity presented itself, "It was too good a deal to pass up."

It is because of the unlimited outlets for stolen property that a small segment of society commits felonious thefts. This does not mean that there are no major fences— there are and they should be of primary concern for any storefront dealing with property crimes. However, understanding that the criminal element is always seeking new outlets to dispose of stolen property will assist you in choosing the type of storefront most likely to attract the criminal element.

Periodicals: The Written Review

In chapter 1, periodicals were listed as a possible source of information for the documentation process. Periodicals can also assist you in choosing the type of storefront. Many investigators overlook or are not aware of the information available in periodicals. One reason may be that the type of publications containing the desired subject matter are not a mainstay of reading material. Many of the desired titles are not easily obtained and are not found on the magazine racks at the neighborhood store. Some of the desired periodicals are not available on *any* magazine rack. They are not widely publicized and have a small and specific clientele. A few of the publications would cause most citizens embarrassment if the mail carrier delivered them to their home. Imagine if a neighbor or a friend saw one lying on your coffee table. When we would pick up our mail from the post office box used for our undercover operations, the postal personnel would often point at us and then whisper to each other. We did not blame them; we would probably have done the same thing. Our mail consisted of many, let's say, unusual magazines and news letters.

What Is Available

Periodicals can be found that deal with the interests of almost every segment of our society, however small that segment may be. If the proposed storefront is to combat crimes of moral turpitude in the community and you need more information on the type of storefront that would be most attractive to prospective customers, there are publications that can provide the needed information. In addition to the information gathered from within your department (vice unit, intelligence unit, etc.) and appropriate units outside the department, there are periodicals dealing with the subject that may contain useful information. Pornography is the topic of numerous publications covering such controversial interests as kiddy porn, blue movies, snuff flicks, and other deviant pursuits. In addition to broadening your knowledge of the subject and subsequently enabling you to conduct an informed conversation with suspects, these publications can assist you in deciding which type of storefront would attract the desired patrons. The periodicals also contain advertisements for supplies and materials that may be needed for the storefront. Many discuss the potential legal problems one may encounter in operating this type of business and how to overcome these problems using deception and legal loopholes— very helpful information when investigating this type of crime. In addition, many have articles on which areas of the community would be most profitable and what decor and type of building will attract the most customers. All of this would assist you in making an informed decision. Do not worry, most of the risqué publications will mail the periodical in a plain brown wrapper to avoid embarrassment to the subscriber.

If you are contemplating using a storefront to combat today's increasingly disturbing drug problem and you need further information on the drug culture in our society, there are periodicals that can help. These are not periodicals designed for law enforcement use—just the opposite. These periodicals contain information that can be very helpful. They deal with many aspects of the drug culture.

> Want to know the latest street price for cocaine in New York, Miami, Detroit, Los Angeles, and many other cities?
>
> What is the newest fad or "in" street jargon used by dealers or users?
>
> What methods are the drug purchasers using to test the quality of the product?
>
> What are the legal defenses this illicit community is advocating?

All the answers to these questions can be found in various publications. These periodicals also supply information on the products in demand, what type business is selling these products, and the type of establishment that could attract your target.

Concerned about the influx of firearms and other deadly weapons into your community? Want to initiate a storefront to combat this problem? Need more knowledge in reference to this subject? There are many periodicals on the topic that can be of assistance. Many of these publications can be found on the newsstands and are considered to be in the mainstream, but others are intended for a very select readership with interests and views considered outside the mainstream. Some of these publications cover such subjects as

> The weapon of choice when conducting a hit
>
> Which firearms are most easily converted from semi-automatic to full automatic, and how to accomplish this task
>
> Guns for hire or mercenaries that can be contacted through the publications
>
> Information on how to obtain almost any weapon
>
> How to make special-purpose weapons
>
> Weapons or ammunition that will penetrate body armor.

Much of the information found in or available through these publications is frightening for those of us involved in law enforcement. But it can be very helpful in deciding the type of storefront that would be best for addressing this problem.

Right or Left: The Controversial Periodical

There are other controversial periodicals that contain information on topics that may be the focus of a storefront. Outlaw motorcycle gangs and radical groups from both the left and right have news letters and publications that cover their activities and advocate their philosophy. There are groups that operate under the disguise of religion, who methodically spread information or ideas which promote destruction to all who do not follow the doctrine of the group. Often, these groups use illegal activity to advance their cause. They also publish news letters and periodicals.

The Technical Periodical: Simple to Complex

Do not overlook the technical periodicals that are available. Although these publications are written to assist legitimate technicians in a particular field, some of the information contained in them can be very helpful for illegitimate technicians—the ones the storefront wants to attract. These periodicals have information on how to

1. Circumvent alarm systems
2. Disengage security devices on automobiles (locking steering wheels, code key doors, door locks, etc.)
3. Open locked windows, doors, safes, etc. at home and/or business.

If you are armed with this knowledge, you are better able to communicate with the targets; however, do not give away trade secrets. You want to use this knowledge in evaluating what the target says, not to inform the target of a more efficient method to conduct illegal activities.

Where to Look

Where do you find the periodicals that will assist in the storefront operation? Because of the controversy that could arise from listing the names of some of these publications and stating their purpose, we will rely on your initiative to obtain the publications desired. Here are some suggestions on how to find the desired publications.

1. Determine what subject matter you want to study and then start the search in house. Contact

    a. The vice unit

    b. The narcotics unit

    c. The firearms section of either the shooting range or criminalistic's unit

    d. The violent crimes unit

    e. The burglary or property crimes unit

    f. The auto theft unit.

Many units within your department may have the information needed or know how to obtain the desired periodicals.

    2. Check with outside law enforcement agencies.

If the desired periodicals are of a technical nature, check

    1. Trade unions

    2. Locksmiths

    3. Gunsmiths

    4. Automotive shops

    5. A head shop, dirty book store, or adult movie theater

    6. The public library and large book stores. These usually contain a large selection of periodicals and a catalog of the types of periodicals available and where to subscribe.

Many magazines that deal with a topic on a more acceptable or general level contain advertisements for the more explicit publications. These more explicit publications have advertisements for even more explicit publications. With a little initiative, you can find any type periodical desired.

Propping Up the Facade

When applicable, you should obtain copies of periodicals that may be of interest to the target. Not only will they supply useful information, but they contain advertisements of different businesses—possibly an enterprise that may be advantageous to use as a facade. These publications also make good props—having them visible in the storefront may help the criminal element become relaxed and less suspicious. They can be *valuable* reading material for the customers who frequent your business.

You must consider all available information in determining the appropriate type of storefront. The selection must be conducive to meeting the objectives established for the operation, and it must be compatible with current budgetary constraints. Facade is the cover for the operation, e.g., a used car lot, a printing company, or a video game room. The facade must be of such a nature to attract the type of criminal targeted. The storefront is the physical structure and type of operation. The facade chosen must be harmonious with the type of storefront selected. The following are some of the types of storefronts you may consider:

Mobile

Stationary

Telephone.

THE MOBILE STOREFRONT

The term *mobile storefront* may sound contradictory at first. When you think of a storefront, it is usually a business located in a building. With the demands placed on today's businesses for more and more convenience, the mobile storefront is more common. Many businesses have adopted the strategy, if the customer won't come to us, we will go to the customer.

The Moving Advantage

This strategy has certain advantages for a storefront operation. The first and most obvious is mobility. The storefront can easily be moved to operate in different areas of the community. Operational costs are usually lower with a mobile operation than with a conventional business location. When it's not utilized, the mobile storefront can be concealed, reducing the risk of burglary and the need for extensive security measures.

The Portable Disguise

There are may facades that can be used with the mobile storefront. Vans and other types of vehicles sit on vacant lots, empty corners, or any other suitable space within a community, displaying a large variety of merchandise—everything from velvet portraits of Elvis to pottery imported from exotic lands. Mobile automotive repair vehicles are able to fix everything from dead batteries to broken windshields. Handymen often drive around with advertising on the side of their vehicles calling the public's attention to their skills. Lunch wagons, affectionately given the nickname "roach coaches," move from site to site serving a wide assortment of meals. Large vans make the rounds selling a variety of tools. Sign painters tour the city seeking prospective customers. Vehicles that contain a check-cashing service are often visible outside factories, office complexes, and large industrial work yards. Pest control vehicles are present in almost every city. Locksmiths often take to the road to increase their clientele. Limousine services are obviously very mobile, and with the advent of the mobile phone almost any type business can be packaged into a vehicle.

Moving while You Speak

The mobile phone allows clients easier access to your storefront. They can contact the storefront no matter where the operation may be. They do not have to wait for the operation to return to a certain location before business can be conducted. Also, recording these telephone conversations, when permitted, can yield valuable evidence. Beware, however, of the ease with which some of these conversations can be intercepted. Remember, the conversation is being transmitted over the airways.

Mobile Phone Cautions

When using mobile phones, do not discuss police business. When police personnel make contact through the mobile phone, a prearranged code should be used to relay any information. If the information is of such a nature that the prearranged code cannot be used to convey the message, the calling party should be contacted via a public phone. To ensure the protection of the personnel operating the mobile storefront, the mobile phone should be used only for conversations with suspects and for emergencies. You may be unpleasantly surprised at who else may be intercepting the phone conversations.

The Transaction Area

In establishing a mobile storefront, if at all possible, have an area within the vehicle that can be used for transactions with offenders. If permitted, this area should be wired to allow for audio and/or video recording. Often, due to the location and subsequent background noise, the mobile storefront's recordings can be of poor quality.

FOR EXAMPLE

We had a mobile storefront which was located on a vacant lot adjacent to a busy thoroughfare. The operation had been underway for a relatively short time when one of the targets approached. The conversation with the target was recorded. The suspect stood outside the van talking to us while we sat inside the van. After the transaction, we were all excited and anxious for the shift to end so we could return to the offsite and play back the conversation for the supervisor. When this opportunity finally arrived, our excitement soon turned to dismay. The start of the conversation was of such fine quality that it sounded as if the conversation were taking place in the same room. Soon the customary greetings and chit-chat were over and the transaction was discussed. There was a traffic light approximately two blocks from the storefront. The light must have changed to green just as the transaction was discussed. The conversation on the tape became inaudible.

The traffic noise was all that could be heard. We were aware of the traffic on the thoroughfare but did not anticipate what affect it would have on the recording. Before the operation continued, we allocated a space inside the mobile storefront for transactions, thus eliminating much of the background noise.

The Area Is the Obstacle

Space can become a problem for a mobile storefront. This type operation often has limited space. Not only is space required for conducting transactions, but it is needed for storing

Evidence

Display items

Recording equipment.

One method of alleviating some of the problem is to attach a trailer to the main vehicle. Display items and evidence can be stored there along with other appropriate material.

Home on the Move

A motor home makes an excellent mobile storefront. There is usually much more space available than in a van or similar type of vehicle. A motor home can also provide a more comfortable working atmosphere. The extra space also allows for transactions to take place in a secluded area, which could give the target a more secure feeling about dealing with you. This is one of the main objectives of a storefront: to gain the confidence of the criminal element.

Eating on the Job

Another mobile storefront our department operated was a lunch wagon. Through documentation, it was established that the theft of construction equipment had reached an alarming rate. In analyzing the limited amount of construction equipment recovered, it was discovered that the recovered property had been located at other construction sites. A lunch wagon was selected to combat this problem. The lunch wagon would travel from construction site to construction site serving breakfast, lunch, and snacks. With the assistance of a cooperating individual, the word went out that the people who operated the mobile bistro might be interested in buying construction equipment. We had to put up with a lot of verbal abuse in reference to our culinary skills, but we accomplished our objectives.

THE STATIONARY STOREFRONT

This type of storefront is more customary. It can consist of anything from a stand at a flea market or swap meet, to a large warehouse. Some advantages of this type of storefront include the following:

Space—there is usually much more room to conduct business.

The protection of undercover officers may be easier to maintain.

Larger items of stolen property can be taken into the storefront.

Some of the targets may feel more at ease dealing in this type of setting rather than a mobile storefront.

The specific needs of the investigation will assist you in determining the type of storefront needed to accomplish stated objectives.

Type of Business

The facades that can be used by a stationary storefront are limited only by your common sense and creativity. With any type of storefront chosen, you must determine if the facade will be a functioning or non-functioning business.

The Functional Business

Will the business be organized to function as a legitimate business, or just appear to be a legitimate business? The functioning business storefront has more inherent problems to overcome, but it also has advantages. The basic layout for many storefronts is not conducive to making the targets feel at ease. There can be visible external security, buzzers on doors for entrance and exit requirements, the presence of armed body guards, a physical barrier between counter persons and customers, no admittance without an appointment, and no appearance that a legitimate business is being conducted. This type of storefront has been widely publicized both by the media and word of mouth. A portion of the criminal element is very aware of this type of disguise. We have dealt with customers who had been arrested as a result of dealing with a storefront that used this strategy. If we had used the same technique, the repeat offenders would not have dealt with us. You can also be assured that their cohorts have been made aware of how they met their demise by dealing with this type of business.

An automotive detail shop was a functioning business we used for a storefront. The shop had legitimate customers as well as the criminal element. Some of the targets of this storefront were repeat offenders who had been arrested for previous dealings with other storefronts. Conversations with the targets revealed that they had conducted extensive surveillance of the detail shop before making contact. They conducted surveillance in an attempt to uncover the true identity of the operatives. They were very suspicious about dealing with another business that could be run by the police. What put them at ease was the coming and going of customers and seeing the investigators doing the work one would customarily expect to see the operators of such a business involved in. We must admit, however, that more legitimate business was turned away than accepted. It seemed that as the number of cars detailed rose, the easier it was to find excuses not to accept any new legitimate customers. Although some of the security measures previously discussed were used to protect us as well as the customers, they were sufficiently concealed by the business activity being conducted. This, in turn, created an atmosphere in which the targets were less apprehensive about conducting their business at the storefront.

The Nonfunctional Business

The same type of atmosphere can be created by either the functional or nonfunctional business. The latter, however, can be a more difficult undertaking. When targets enter a storefront time after time and observe the operators just sitting around watching television or doing some other type of activity not associated with a normally functioning business, they may become suspicious. New targets will also feel suspicious when they enter the storefront. The facade and activity of the storefront will lessen suspects' uneasiness.

We once used a print shop as a facade. It was a nonfunctioning business. However, this did not mean the business would not appear to be functional. We went to great lengths to create the illusion that the shop was a functioning business. Printing equipment was obtained for the storefront through private sector donations. The props necessary for this type of business were obtained, including

Ink

Paper

Work aprons

Business cards

Price lists

Signs.

When the storefront was open for business, the printing equipment was churning out the product. Paper was streaming off the press—of course, nothing was being printed and the same paper was used over and over. We donned our work aprons and always had ink on our hands. Bundles of printing packages, as if to be sent out to clients, were strategically placed so they would be easily seen by those coming into the storefront. When appropriate and properly timed, to create the desired illusion, customers (other undercover investigators) would enter the business and place or pick up an order. If legitimate customers did enter the storefront, they were simply told we could not handle any more business and they were directed to a competitor. When targets entered the storefront, they were truly under the impression that this was a functioning business. The undercover operatives had to do much more than just sit around to create the desired illusion. The illusion paid off by creating an atmosphere in which the targets were comfortable and confident that they were dealing with businesspeople and not law enforcement officers.

Residential Storefronts: Living with the Business

The residential storefront can pose significantly different challenges. The facade created can be of a business conducted out of a house or apartment lived in by the undercover officers or just used as a meeting place to conduct business transactions. There is a great deal of difference between the two. The challenges you will have to overcome using the latter approach are significantly different from the first technique. You must make the distinction clear to the offenders.

The House of Business Is Not a Home

There are many types of businesses that can be operated out of a house or apartment. We have all seen the advertisements in magazines and on television. They tell the reader or viewer of the vast wealth that can be obtained from operating their business out of their house or apartment. These include

Envelope stuffing

Mail-order merchandise

Demonstrations of products.

More traditional ventures can also take place in a house or apartment, such as

Accounting offices

A beauty shop

Furniture making or repair

Used book store

Distributor of merchandise.

As with any type of storefront, the business conducted does not have to be a legitimate one. You may want to create the illusion that an illegitimate business is conducted, that is or is not separate from the transactions conducted with the target. You may also want to create the visual impression that the house or apartment is just a hideaway—a place in which to conduct transactions away from unwanted intrusions. No matter how you decide to use the house or apartment, it should be made clear to the targets that it is not your dwelling: It is a place to conduct business.

The Home Is a Business

The second type of residential storefront, though it may contain some of the same characteristics as the first, has one significant difference: You give the impression that the house or apartment is also a dwelling rather than merely a structure in which to conduct business. This type of storefront has been used successfully, but it does pose unique challenges. The offenders may expect and/or assume an entirely different set of circumstances. When the storefront is also a dwelling, the targets may expect to find you home at any given day or hour. Even when they are given explicit instructions on how and when they can come to the dwelling, they do not always follow these instructions. As the targets become more accustomed to you, they may come to believe you are their friends, even if you have done everything in your power to convey just the opposite. The suspects may want to drop by at different times and/or days just to visit. They may want to use the storefront as a crash pad—and why not, you are their friend. When the targets realize that the only time you are home is Monday through Friday from 8 to 5, the consequences to the investigation and/or you could be disastrous.

In a storefront of this type that we were involved with, we lived in an apartment for six months. During this time, we conducted transactions with over sixty targets. As the number of targets grew and they became more and more comfortable with the surroundings and us, more and more visits were made just to talk. Some of these visits turned out to be very beneficial. The conversations provided much-needed intelligence information on criminal activity throughout the city. Other conversations, however, were hard to endure, time consuming, and unproductive. At one point in the investigation there was a suspect or suspects at the apartment eighteen hours a day. With steadfast perseverance that the rules for coming to the storefront be followed we curtailed the visits to only twelve hours a day. Even at this reduced rate, you can understand the additional stress placed on us.

Another such storefront involved the investigation of one target. The target came to the apartment to conduct transactions, visit, and even for an occasional dinner. The visits were regulated, and we had ample time to be away from the apartment. Our protection was much easier to maintain, as was the security of the apartment. In the aforementioned storefront, it was not at all unusual to have small items taken from the apartment. Some items were stolen and others just borrowed without permission. In the first circumstance, we were always scrambling to replace stolen video and audio tapes. The paperwork concerning the activity at the first apartment was considerably more complex than at the second just because of the sheer numbers of visitors. The unending visits to the first apartment made the keeping of logs, account reports, incident reports, etc. almost impossible. Both types of residential storefronts can be utilized successfully, but pay attention to the expected activity and any undue stress it may place on the undercover operatives.

THE TELEPHONE STOREFRONT

With convenience being the prerequisite of today's shoppers, many businesses allow their customers to shop by phone. The variety of merchandise one can purchase via the telephone and then have delivered is unending. There is also a myriad of other services offered over the telephone. You can talk to your favorite sports figure, hear from the newest television or movie teen idol, rap with rock and roll's latest phenomenon, cure all your ails by conversing with a guru from some exotic land, and chat with the woman of your dreams. Many more opportunities await the caller who is adventurous and does not mind paying a small fortune in telephone bills. The facades you can employ with a telephone storefront are almost unlimited. This type of storefront can also be inexpensive to operate. The telephones and recording devices needed can be installed in an area already occupied by the department.

FOR EXAMPLE _____

We operated a telephone storefront that used the facade of a wholesale import mail-order house. We had business cards printed with the business name, telephone number, and our names—of course we gave ourselves impressive titles. We made arrangements with a wholesale importer to supply us with merchandise if and when the need arose. We familiarized ourselves with the import business and the merchandise we were selling. We had a price list printed using the company name and logo. The telephones and recording devices were installed in our office. There was an answering machine connected to the phones that relayed a message to the caller in reference to the wisdom of doing business with our company. The business cards and price lists were a one-time expense of approximately $60. The average monthly telephone bill was $70.

The storefront, which was originated to investigate a single individual, resulted in the arrest and conviction of six individuals. Those arrested included an ex-Attorney General of our state; two Colombian drug smugglers; a Mexican drug smuggler with ties to the Federal Police in Mexico; and a minister who was laundering money through his church. The storefront was initiated by our department; however, as the investigation grew in scope it involved the cooperation of the FBI and the IRS.

As you can see, a storefront does not necessarily have to be an elaborate and expensive undertaking. A simple and inexpensive facade can often result in dramatic results. You must choose the type of storefront and facade that will best allow you to accomplish your stated objectives while minimizing expense.

Phone Problems

The telephone storefront can, however, create a dilemma for you when the crook being investigated wants to visit the business. When planning this type of storefront, this problem must be addressed. We often told those who wanted to visit our business that it was located in a complex that contained many other inquisitive tenants, and for their protection they should not come to the location. Of course, this type of storefront can also be used in conjunction with one of the other types of storefronts. Not wanting to jeopardize the security of your new-found friends by taking them to an office complex filled with inquisitive tenants, you take them to a residential storefront. You may want to rent a small office in a business complex for a storefront and, after becoming more familiar with the criminal element, invite them to the residential storefront to conduct business in a more relaxed and secure atmosphere. Many combinations can be used to obtain the desired results. Remember, the purpose of any storefront is to create a facade that will attract the criminal element. Once the criminal element is attracted to the storefront, the business must be sufficiently convincing to put the target at ease.

One Machine to Another

Transactions with the target should be recorded to aid in prosecution. When using a telephone storefront in conjunction with another type of storefront or meeting place, this can be accomplished with little expense and dramatic results.

CREATING THE ILLUSION

Late one afternoon my partner and I were on our way to meet with Miss Zola. We were having a difficult time interpreting the directions Miss Zola's assistant had given us. We were on a narrow, winding road lined by large cottonwood trees on the outskirts of the city. There was supposed to be a sign indicating the dirt road which led to Miss Zola's. My partner had me stop alongside the road, and she got out of the vehicle. Then she kicked some fallen leaves away from a board that was on the side of the road. To our relief, it was the sign for Miss Zola's.

We drove down the road and suddenly Miss Zola's appeared through the mist. It was a small house trailer wedged between two large cottonwood trees. The leafless branches appeared menacing as they draped down around the trailer. We got out of the vehicle and walked slowly toward the trailer. As we approached the door, we both stopped. Something on the windowsill had startled us. It was a large black crow. As we cautiously approached, we realized the bird was stuffed. We looked at each other and smiled. I know we were thinking the same thing, two big bad cops startled by a stuffed bird.

We knocked on the door and a young female answered. She invited us in and asked us to be seated. She then walked behind a curtain that covered a doorway and announced our presence. After a short time the young female reappeared. She asked us to follow her; Miss Zola would see us now. We were led to a small room. In the middle of the room was Miss Zola.

Miss Zola was seated behind a low round table. She had jet black hair which stuck out from her pale yellow scarf. An old, deep-blue sweater with some kind of reflective thread in it kept her warm. The deep-blue sweater was the perfect background to show off all her shimmering jewelry. A white lace tablecloth covered the table, and in the middle of the table was a large crystal ball. There were dark rugs hanging from the walls, and from behind them came soft rays of light. Music was played at a very low volume. It reminded us of the music in a funeral home.

Miss Zola asked in a deep, soft voice who had come to see her. My partner said "I did." Miss Zola then said it was quite evident what the crisis was. She told my partner to lie on the floor and expose her abdomen. Miss Zola then brought out a gold box and placed it on the table. She opened the box and took out a white lace handkerchief. Inside the handkerchief was a pure white egg, the whitest egg I had ever seen. Miss Zola told my partner that the egg was a conduit for Miss Zola's special powers. She then rubbed the egg over my partner's abdomen and made incomprehensible guttural sounds and grimaces as if she were in excruciating pain. After a short time she gently collapsed to the floor. Then, slowly gaining back her strength, she sat up. She gave us the egg and the handkerchief with these instructions: The egg was to be wrapped in the handkerchief and placed in a refrigerator for twenty-four hours. It was very important that the doors to the refrigerator not be opened during the twenty-four hours. At the end of the required time, the egg was to be taken out of the refrigerator and rubbed over my partner's abdomen while chanting the secret phrase supplied by Miss Zola. This ritual had to be performed every four hours for fifteen minutes. If any of the instructions were not followed exactly the cure wouldn't work.

Miss Zola then asked if we could find it in our hearts to make a small donation. She explained that she never charged for her services since the powers she possessed were a gift given to her by a supreme being, and she would not abuse the powers by using them for personal gain. However, a small donation to allow her to continue her work would be appreciated. After negotiating, it was agreed that one hundred dollars in food stamps would do nicely. We left Miss Zola's and returned to our vehicle. As we drove back, I congratulated my partner on the buy and performance. My partner was uncharacteristically quiet. Then, very softly, she said, "Did you hear what Miss Zola said my crisis was?" She then yelled, "I'm going on a diet right now! How can anyone think I'm pregnant? I'm not that fat, am I?" I said no, and she called me a liar, insisting she was going to lose weight. She then took the egg and white lace handkerchief and was about to throw it out the window. I told her she couldn't do that—they were evidence. She yelled again, "Oh no, I don't want to go to court and tell everyone what Miss Zola said." I promised I would keep her "pregnancy" a secret. She didn't appreciate my feeble attempt at humor, and it was a very quiet ride back to the office. Miss Zola may have had some kind of special power after all—she inspired my partner to lose a lot of weight.

What does this story have to do with types of storefronts? Miss Zola, even though she may not have realized it, understood a portion of the concept of a storefront operation. The illusion she was trying to create was an essential part of her performance and, in turn, the success of her business. The same performance in a high-rise with modern decor would not have lent itself to the desired illusion. The location of Miss Zola's establishment, the decor, the props, and Miss Zola's dress all were designed to create a certain mystique, which was intended to make her business more profitable. The facade created by Miss Zola was an intricate part of the scam.

SUMMARY

You must decide which type of storefront would be most advantageous in creating the desired illusion and enabling you to meet your stated objectives. This decision must take into account

Departmental budgetary constraints
Departmental guidelines
Judicial guidelines

Labor restrictions

Availability of the desired location

Ability of investigators to utilize the type of storefront chosen

Any other particular requirements of the individual storefront.

Each storefront investigation will pose its own unique problems. No one type storefront will work for all investigations. Choose the type of operation that will

Be the most cost effective to operate

Afford maximum protection for its investigators

Be organized most effectively and swiftly

Create the desired facade

Be the most advantageous in meeting stated objectives.

With a little forethought, imagination, and planning, you will easily accomplish this task.

CHAPTER 3

Recognizing the Liabilities of a Storefront

You have documented the criminal activity to be addressed. Through analyzing this and other available information, you have determined the feasibility of a storefront. You have stated your objectives. You have considered the type or types of storefronts to best accomplish your stated objectives. Now you must consider what liabilities the proposed investigation may encounter, including

1. Criminal
2. Civil
3. Financial
4. Public opinion.

In this chapter we discuss some of the liabilities that are inherent to most storefronts and how to recognize the liabilities of a particular type of storefront.

VICARIOUS LIABILITY

Vicarious liability: Those two words make the ears of any law enforcement administrator perk up, as well they should. What is vicarious liability? Simply stated, it is when you screw up and someone else pays for it. Within law enforcement, it is usually when an administrator suffers for the acts of a subordinate.

FOR EXAMPLE

The patrol officer is sued for using unreasonable force in making an arrest. The officers, sergeant, lieutenant, captain, and so on up the chain of command are named as codefendants in the civil suit even if they were not present during the alleged impropriety. The chain continues even past superiors. Their boss (mayor, city manager) can also be named in the litigation. It does not stop there—when you finally reach the top, the governing body itself (city, county, etc.), the "deep pocket" will be included on the guest list. Lawyers know if they are rewarded a judgment against you for a million dollars, the chance of collecting even a small portion is slim. However, including the governing body in the suit enables them to collect the judgment.

"Deep pocket" is based on an economic theory of reaching the optimum resource. Its reasoning is that a governing body cannot justly disclaim responsibility for activity which may reasonably be said to be characteristic of its activities. The governing body and the supervisor can be held civilly liable for your actions.

Why should this concern you? One reason some police administrators are overly apprehensive when presented with a proposal for a proactive law enforcement technique is fear of vicarious liability. Being unfamiliar with this type of operation can create unreasonable anxiety. You can defuse this anxiety by recognizing what liabilities the proposed storefront may encounter. Once the liabilities are recognized, you will be able to address the potential problems and thus ease administration's fears.

Innate Liabilities

Police work has many innate liabilities. This is evident in the cumbersome and forever-changing standard operational procedures that most law enforcement agencies employ. These SOPs, or rules and regulations, are published by most departments to inform their members of acceptable procedures and conduct. Most SOPs contain vast areas of information on almost every aspect of police work except that which is used in a proactive technique. Due to the lack of formal guidelines for this type of operation, many administrators are leery when it comes time to approve such a venture.

You must remember that administrators can be drawn into a civil lawsuit through vicarious liability. Anyone operating the storefront may be liable for the conduct of each investigator involved in the operation. So each investigator must be able to recognize any potential liabilities of the proposed storefront. These potential liabilities must be satisfactorily addressed, not only to protect you but to demonstrate to the administration that the necessary precautions are being taken.

Avoiding Potential Liabilities

Fear of potential liabilities the storefront may encounter should not be the determining factor in quashing the investigation. Such fear could be the reason to reconsider one aspect of the operation or to revamp the entire operation, but it should not deter you from using a storefront. With proper planning and forethought, you will be able to anticipate potential liabilities and take the appropriate measures to reduce or eliminate these problems.

Each type of storefront will encounter a variety of potential liabilities. The type chosen and how it is to be operated will determine the liabilities to be addressed.

FIRST AND FOREMOST, INVESTIGATOR SAFETY

Any storefront should be organized to maximize the investigators' safety. The safety of the police personnel who are conducting the day-to-day activity at the site must be of paramount importance. Police work in itself has many innate dangers. These dangers and those not usually associated with police work can be increased considerably while operating a storefront.

Decreasing the Danger to Investigators

The storefront must be organized to limit or preferably eliminate these dangers, not to increase them. Make the site an unattractive victim for criminals.

An armed robbery occurring at a police storefront may sound preposterous. Who in their right mind would try to rob the police? If the site has been organized properly, the unscrupulous segment of society is not going to be aware that it is a police operation. To them it's just another business, an illegitimate business at that. Armed robberies do occur at storefronts. You must recognize this liability and take steps to discourage it.

FOR EXAMPLE _____

We had established a secondhand store as one of our storefronts. It had been in operation for approximately three months when it became the victim of an armed robbery.

The offender had been conducting business at the storefront for six weeks. He had been using an alias and was completely unaware that we knew who he was. He came into the store one day with a load of property he wanted us to buy. The investigator conducting the transaction refused to buy the property, and an argument erupted. The offender then pulled a small revolver and demanded all the money. The investigator placed a small amount of money on the counter. The investigator then ducked into a small, bullet-proof square which had been built into the counter for just this purpose and activated an audible alarm. The offender appeared to be startled by the disappearing act and the alarm. With a bewildered expression on his face, he looked around the store and then fled, leaving the money on the counter.

Unbeknown to the offender, a second investigator was in the storefront conducting surveillance of the transaction and acting as backup. Both investigators carried out their duties as described in the guidelines we had established for the storefront. These guidelines were established because we had recognized this liability. The robbery was recorded on video tape, and the offender was eventually captured and successfully prosecuted.

Administration's Fear: The Worst Case Scenario

The administration was concerned with the additional liabilities an armed robbery attempt could place on the investigation. They were worried not only about officer safety but about the loss of departmental funds. They also did not want any public perception that the operation was organized to lure in armed robbery suspects, thus enabling officers to gun them down. Recognizing this liability enabled us to establish an acceptable plan of action. This plan of action assured the investigators' safety by providing a safe place for concealment and backup. It limited the funds that would be lost by providing that only a small amount of marked bills could be taken. If the offender did meet his demise as a result of this criminal act, the public would not see it as a set up. The integrity of the storefront could be maintained, and it could remain functional until its planned conclusion.

Officer Recognition

While working in a storefront, you must be aware of the possibility of being recognized by the criminal element. If this should occur, what liabilities will the operation face? The most grievous would be the death of an investigator. The most obvious is the premature closure of the storefront. Many labor hours have been spent organizing the operation, not to mention the expenditures incurred. Another liability is the potential jeopardy of ongoing criminal investigations. These are liabilities that must be considered and properly planned for.

Minimizing the Risk to Investigators

How can these liabilities be minimized or eliminated? Try to arrange the entrance to the storefront so any potential customers can be screened before contact is made. If you recognize a likely patron and know there is a possibility that he or she will recognize you as a law enforcement officer, you can take appropriate action before contact is made. This can be more difficult than it first appears. The use of buzzers on doors, peepholes, video scanners, and other such devices is not always possible for every type of storefront. When analyzing potential customers for a storefront, look into any possible past contact between clients and the investigators who will be operating or frequenting the site. If contact has occurred, will the customer be capable of revealing your true identity? If the identity of potential clients is not known, you may wish to use disguises such as

A pair of glasses
Facial hair

A fake scar

A phony mole

A wig.

Disguises can make all the difference. With a little imagination, you can overcome the liability of being recognized.

Match the Names to Vehicles

The license plates on your vehicles can also reveal your true identity. The vehicles of those investigators who only frequent the site are also a potential hazard if not properly attended to.

FOR EXAMPLE _____

A group of suspects who had been conducting business at a storefront we operated shocked us one day. They revealed a department of motor vehicle printout they had obtained on our license plates, and then proudly read to us who our vehicles were registered to. Luckily, our police vehicles were not registered to the police department. They then informed us that for a small fee they could obtain motor vehicle printouts on any license plate we wanted. This would prevent us from doing business with the cops.

Would surveillance of the storefront by the criminal element reveal the existence of police activity? Who is allowed to come to the site, and what vehicles do they drive? Could legitimate customers recognize a member of the storefront as being a law enforcement officer and inadvertently give this information to the criminal element? The administration may have the same concerns with these liabilities as you. With proper planning, you can take the necessary precautions and minimize these liabilities.

Hazardous Machinery and Chemicals

Will the personnel working at the storefront have to deal with hazardous machinery or materials? If so, the small amount of time needed for training in proper operation and usage is a wise investment. Those not trained should *not* be permitted to operate the machinery or use any hazardous materials. Consider the following examples:

1. A print shop is the facade that has been chosen. The machinery necessary to complete the illusion can pose potential hazards. Fingers, hands, and/or arms could become entangled in the machinery. Negligently operating the machinery could result in projectiles being thrown, causing disfigurement or blindness. The acids used for cleaning the machinery could alter facial

features. If these cleaning materials are improperly disposed of, they could create many unforeseen complications.

2. A buy is arranged to purchase explosives at the print shop. If the investigators who will conduct the buy have no training in the proper handling of explosives, the potential hazard is obvious.

These types of liabilities may have not been evident when initiating the operation. However, hazards may exist in creating the facade chosen for the storefront. There are many aspects to consider when contemplating liabilities relating to investigator safety. Each type of storefront will pose its own unique liabilities. Time spent determining the possible drawbacks and how to address them successfully is advantageous and necessary.

SAFETY OF NON-LAW ENFORCEMENT PERSONNEL

When a storefront is operated as a legitimate, functioning business, other liabilities may become a factor. Take precautions to ensure that legitimate customers will not be injured while at the site. We have all seen signs posted at automotive garages or other businesses where a potential hazard exists in a work area. The signs are posted to keep customers away from the hazards. They are usually written in a polite style such as, "Our insurance company will not allow us to admit unauthorized personnel into the work area." But they mean, "Keep out unless you work here." If the storefront has a work area that may pose a potential hazard, take precautions to limit this possible liability.

A service the storefront is performing may have hidden liabilities. For example, an automotive garage is to be used as a facade. Will it be functional or nonfunctional? In dealing with the repairs of automobiles and other such facades, there are hidden liabilities that must be considered.

Will the storefront be able to obtain insurance to cover these liabilities?

Would it be advantageous to do only repairs that are less likely to create a liability?

Could the same results be obtained if the storefront only appeared to be operational, thus eliminating hidden liabilities?

Will officers be properly protected while doing repairs?

Are customers likely to be injured in the work area?

Are offenders likely to be injured in the work area? Like it or not, we are responsible for them when they are at the site.

These are questions that must be answered. Every storefront poses its own unique challenges. Only when you are aware of these challenges can proper planning occur.

Having legitimate customers come to the storefront may create unnecessary liabilities. You must decide if this is essential for the success of the operation. The disguise of a legitimate, functioning business can be effective in creating the desired illusion. When the success of the storefront hinges on this aspect, you must take every precaution to ensure the safety of the legitimate customer. However, these possible liabilities need not cause undue concern. Through careful planning and preparation, they can become insignificant.

EFFECT ON OTHER BUSINESSES

What effect is the storefront having on similar businesses in the community? Civil suits have been filed alleging that a storefront conducting a similar business caused the plaintiff to lose customers and income. The loss of customers resulted in the business closing. The storefront was able to operate without the customary cost of doing business. Therefore, it was able to undersell the competitor, which resulted in the store having to go out of business.

Monetary Compensation

When using a functioning business, ensure that prices are equal to or higher than other businesses of this type. For instance: The facade chosen is a functional automotive detail shop. Monetary compensation for services rendered should be comparable with those of competitors. You determine what price to charge by visiting the other businesses in the community that offer this type service and documenting prices. When we operated a storefront using an automotive detail shop as a facade, the fees for our services were the highest in the city. One factor was to stem any possible complaints or retribution from competitors. The other factor, and most important to us, was to keep legitimate customers away—we got tired of detailing cars!

Surrounding Businesses

Do not allow the storefront to create an atmosphere that will cause customers to shun other businesses in the neighborhood. If there is a group of thugs always hanging out, it could intimidate customers into staying away from other businesses in the area. Targets (customers) should be informed to be on their best behavior whenever they are at the storefront. They are to conduct their business and then leave the area.

If a disruptive atmosphere is allowed to exist, unwanted attention will be drawn to the investigation. The result could be premature closure of the operation. The more anonymous the storefront is to the citizenry, the more able it will be to function successfully. It should blend into the neighborhood without having a detrimental impact.

When locating a site in a residential area, determine what adverse effects it might have on the surrounding neighborhood. Then determine how to minimize these effects. Again, do not allow the criminal element to hang out if this activity causes a disruption. Insist that your customers conduct themselves in a way that does not attract attention to themselves or to you. Limiting the hours of operation may be necessary. Do not have people arriving at all hours of the night if this will disturb the neighborhood.

Danger: Transaction in Progress

Any activity being conducted should not endanger the neighborhood in which the storefront is located. For instance,

1. A customer wants to deliver a large amount of explosives. Not wanting to endanger the neighborhood, make arrangements for delivery to take place in an isolated area, thus eliminating the possible danger. Allowing the storefront to be used to manufacture any explosive substances could create an unreasonable liability.

2. A customer wants to use the site to manufacture speed, methamphetamine. Make other arrangements with the customer if property damage and/or physical harm could result to the surrounding neighborhood if an explosion did occur. A mobile storefront or other option should be used to remove the possible danger to an unpopulated area.

INHERENT LIABILITIES

The type of storefront you operate may have inherent liabilities that must be addressed. These liabilities will exist as a permanent and inseparable characteristic. Liquor establishments, pool halls, used car lots, adult book stores, gun shops, and repair shops are examples of these types of businesses. If utilizing a liquor establishment as a facade, be aware that the operators can be held accountable for the conduct of patrons. For instance,

1. Someone consumes liquor at the business and then leaves to drive home. En route, the patron is involved in a major traffic accident. Alcohol is determined to be a contributing factor. The injured parties, including the intoxicated patron, could conceivably seek damages from the storefront.

2. If a patron leaves the bar and commits another type of crime, the liquor establishment may also be held accountable.

3. If a fight breaks out at the pool hall and someone is injured, the operators could be held responsible for not maintaining control in the business.

4. A prospective customer takes a used car for a test drive and the brakes fail, causing an accident. The used car lot may be held responsible.

5. A gun shop used as a front sells a gun to a subject who then uses the firearm to commit murder.

6. A small appliance is repaired by the storefront. The customer takes the appliance home. When it is plugged in, it explodes, causing the home to burn to the ground.

The liabilities a storefront may incur are not always of a financial nature. Imagine the outcry when the public learns that the bar who served the liquor to the drunk that hit the school bus and killed those innocent children was operated by the police.

The preceding examples are exaggerated for a purpose. You must consider all the liabilities the storefront could be confronted with.

Determining Liabilities: Be a Pessimist

One method to use in determining the disadvantages of a particular storefront is to have a "what if" meeting. Those involved in the preparation of the operation meet and ask, "What if?" While the possibilities are discussed, someone makes a list of the drawbacks. If the group cannot satisfactorily resolve the hypothetical situations, it should seek assistance from the department's legal advisor. If a legal advisor is not available, the prosecutor can assist in resolving any questions. Using this method, you are better equipped to minimize any liabilities.

The liabilities a storefront may encounter should not be a source of apprehension. Apprehension only becomes a factor if the liabilities are not properly addressed. An example is an operation we conducted with the FBI to gather information on the theft of semitractor and trailer rigs. Certain inherent liabilities existed. We knew that there was a chance of purchasing one or more of these stolen rigs. When this opportunity presented itself, how were we going to move the rig once we purchased it? The use of a towing company did not seem practical. We needed someone to drive the rig. The logical driver would be the purchasers, us. No one assigned to the investigation had ever driven a semitractor and trailer before. In moving these rigs, the liability that would be placed on the department would be great. How could this inherent liability be lessened? Those involved in the operation went to school to learn how to operate a semitractor and trailer. They took the tests and obtained the necessary licenses before the storefront was operational. The inherent liabilities were still present, but they had been reduced to an acceptable level.

COOPERATING INDIVIDUAL (CI) LIABILITIES

There are many advantages to using a CI in the investigation. However, there are some potential disadvantages. Under *posse comitatus* (power of the county), each person engaged in the performance of active law enforcement service assisting any peace officer at his or her request can be deemed an employee of the public entity. What does that mean? They could receive the same compensation you receive if they are injured while performing their duty. In addition, they could file suit against you if their injury was caused by your omission or neglect of duty. Wrongful acts committed by the CI while under your direction could also be a liability. Those harmed could—you guessed it—file suit against you. There is a great deal to consider when utilizing a CI. (This is discussed at length in chapter 13.) When contemplating use of a CI, consider the risks in the planning stage.

SUMMARY

Trying to list all the liabilities one could encounter in a storefront operation is next to impossible. That was not our intent in this chapter. However, this aspect of the investigation is often overlooked. Usually it does not come to light until it is too late. The civil suit has already been filed or the neighbors of the storefront are beating down the door at city hall demanding you be closed down. This chapter showed the importance of considering liabilities in the early stages of planning.

Possible liabilities should not deter the start of a storefront. Law enforcement contains many inherent liabilities. Merely pinning on the badge opens law enforcement personnel to a myriad of possible civil suits. These, however, do not keep us from completing our appointed duties. We overcome them by understanding what they are and how to avoid or minimize the risk. The same principle applies to a storefront. Knowing what drawbacks a particular operation could encounter will allow for proper training and planning, and thus avoidance of a problem.

CHAPTER 4

How to Project the Cost
of a Storefront

You must be able to project the operational cost of the proposed storefront. No one in law enforcement today has the luxury of an unlimited budget. Many expenditures associated with a storefront operation are easily overlooked if you are not diligent when projecting operational costs. These inconspicuous expenses, if not properly forecasted, could prevent the storefront from meeting its stated objectives. Therefore, it is of utmost importance that you examine comprehensively the possible expenditures of the storefront. If the projected cost of operation is inadequate, the investigation may be doomed. If the projected cost is exorbitant, the storefront will never get off the ground. We must all face and plan for the constraints of funding. Each type of operation will differ in expense. This chapter explores the possible expenses different storefronts may encounter and how to reduce or eliminate these expenses.

THE MOBILE STOREFRONT

The most obvious expenditure of the mobile storefront is the vehicle. First determine the type of vehicle required to meet the operation's needs. We would all like to cruise around town in a brand new, top-of-the-line vehicle which contains all the latest creature comforts. But is this absolutely necessary for the success of the storefront, and is it cost effective? If an older, 20-foot motor home could be utilized successfully, that would be more practical than a new, 40-foot motor home costing twice as much and producing the same results.

Obtaining the Vehicle through a Government Agency

Once you have chosen the type of vehicle, you must determine how to obtain it. First check within your department. Often, the department has or can acquire the type of vehicle desired. Most police departments have a wide variety of vehicles at their disposal.

FOR EXAMPLE ───────────────────────────────────────

We needed a tow truck for one of our storefronts. We approached an automobile dealer with whom we had a good working relationship. He was willing to lease us a wrecker for $1,500 per month. We knew $1,500 a month would not be compatible with our budget. In desperation, we checked within our department. The police garage had a wrecker and would loan it to us, but the stipulations they placed on the loan would not have been conducive to our investigation. Who else had a wrecker? The tactical unit of our department also had one. They were receptive to our proposal, and their stipulations did not interfere with our storefront.

───

Other agencies in your municipality are accessible through your department, including

Refuse department

Parks and recreation department

Water and sewer department

Family planning unit

Health and environment department.

There are others, of course. Some of them you may never have realized existed in your municipality. Keep in mind, however, that any stipulations on the loan must be compatible with your objectives. Your department or other departments may have confiscated the type of vehicle you need. Seized vehicles often come in a surprisingly wide variety. Check with other law enforcement agencies in your area. They may have or be able to obtain the vehicle you need. They also have connections with other organizations that may have what you need.

Ensuring the Integrity of the Vehicle

With any vehicle obtained from any government source, take the necessary steps to ensure the undercover integrity of the vehicle. License plates may need to be changed, and decals and/or stickers may have to be removed.

FOR EXAMPLE _____

Our city has a clean-air ordinance. When a vehicle is examined and passes the emissions test, it gets a sticker on the windshield. The stickers for civilian vehicles are a different color from those on government vehicles. The sticker is very small and hard to notice, but be assured, the offender will notice it, and at the most inconvenient time.

There may also be maintenance stickers or other documents in the glove compartment or trunk that could reveal the true owner of the vehicle. Don't forget to check between and under the seats. It's the little things that are easily overlooked but can lead to dramatic consequences.

Private Sector

If departmental policy permits, inquire within the civilian sector. Often, people who are friends of the department can assist. When using this approach, there must be a written agreement signed by all parties involved. This will ensure that everyone understands their responsibility and/or liability. Friends of the department are a valuable resource. Don't jeopardize this asset by assuming that they already know the details of an agreement.

When approaching the civilian sector, you must realize the possibility of compromising the storefront by divulging too much information. Only general information on what the vehicle is to be used for should be made available: The vehicle will be used in a police operation. No other information should be necessary. This not only protects you, but also the donor. In this way, donors cannot unwittingly impart information. Detailed information on the storefront can be released at the conclusion of the operation. *Helpful hint:* Do not forget a heartfelt thank you. This simple gesture goes a long way in solidifying a relationship.

Leasing and Renting

When you cannot obtain the vehicle through one of the aforementioned avenues, consider leasing or renting the vehicle. A vehicle can be leased or rented for almost any length of time and with proper planning can be very cost effective.

FOR EXAMPLE _____

We needed a semitractor and trailer rig as a prop for one of our storefronts. We could not locate one through our department or an outside agency. Purchasing a rig was out of our budget. Renting was the most cost-effective option. We could rent the rig for only the times we needed it. The insurance and maintenance for the rig were covered in the price of rental.

Purchasing

Purchasing the vehicle is usually the last resort. In a few rare instances this may be necessary. When a vehicle is purchased there may be hurdles to overcome in addition to budgetary constraints.

How can the vehicle be used once the storefront has ended?

Are there any departmental restrictions on the sale of a vehicle?

What are the guidelines concerning this type of purchase?

There are often state and/or departmental policies regulating the purchase and sale of governmental vehicles. Be familiar with any departmental policies before considering this option.

Operational Expense of the Vehicle

You must consider the operational expense of the vehicle. Is the police garage able to perform the necessary maintenance on the vehicle? If the police garage performs the necessary maintenance, could the storefront be compromised? If the police garage cannot do the maintenance or the storefront would be placed in peril if it did, you must locate someone who can maintain the vehicle. Once you find an acceptable garage, determine what, if any, repairs are necessary to make the vehicle safe to operate. Does the vehicle need tires, a windshield, a new paint job, windshield wipers, or a muffler? Once you have determined this expense, calculate the expense for preventive maintenance, oil changes, air filters, lubrications, etc. This is not as difficult as it may first appear. The owner's manual or any competent garage can furnish the preventive maintenance schedule. Determine the approximate number of miles the vehicle will be driven in a given length of time and divide by the maintenance cost.

FOR EXAMPLE _____

The vehicle selected for the storefront needs preventive maintenance every 3,000 miles. The preventive maintenance expense is $60. The vehicle will be driven approximately 1,000 miles per month. The anticipated length of the operation is six months. The cost for preventive maintenance would be $20 per month.

The vehicle may also need insurance. Who insures the department? If the department purchases insurance, determine if the vehicle will be covered by the department's policy. Most departments today are self-insured. If the department is self-insured, ask the administration if you must obtain additional insurance for the storefront vehicle.

Training, Licensing, and Equipment

Do not forget the cost of special training, if needed, to enable investigators to operate the vehicle safely. A mobile storefront can consist of many different types of vehicles. In addition, you may never have operated the type of vehicle best suited for the storefront. Will you need special training to prepare yourself and your staff to operate the vehicle safely? If special training is required, calculate the expense of training in the projected cost of operation.

Special licenses may also be necessary. A business license may be needed if the mobile storefront is a legitimate operational business on wheels. Even if it is not legitimate, a business license can be a helpful prop in creating the illusion. Some vehicles require additional licenses or permits before they can be driven. The operator of these vehicles may also need a special type of license or permit. Any of these expenditures must be added to the projected cost.

Special equipment needed for the mobile storefront must also be taken into consideration. This special equipment may include any of the following items:

Mobile phone

Alarm system

Audio recording device

Video recorder

Cameras

Additional battery power for the vehicle

Trailer for additional storage

CB radio

Concealed police radio

Window tinting

Portable toilet

Exhaust fan

Portable refrigerator

Additional air conditioning

Small safe or strong box.

You must obtain anything needed to convey the desired illusion of the storefront and/or maintain the safety and supply the basic creature comforts of the investigators. In addition, you must include installation, repair, or maintenance expenses in your projected costs.

Mobile Storefront Operational Cost Work Sheet

In projecting the cost of a mobile storefront, you may find it helpful to use a work sheet. Allow a work sheet for each option available in obtaining the vehicle. If the vehicle is available through the department, that would be the first work sheet. Leased or rented is the second work sheet. Purchased is the third work sheet. Then list all the components we've discussed on each work sheet. Note any stipulations that may apply to one or all of the options. Compare each work sheet and make an informed decision on which option is the most cost effective and likely to meet the objectives of the storefront. (See work sheet 3 in the appendix.)

THE STATIONARY STOREFRONT

The expense of the site is the most conspicuous expenditure when dealing with the stationary storefront. All available options must be explored.

Governmental Properties for the Site

First, can a desired site be obtained through the department? Does the department have a suitable location that the criminal element would not perceive as police related? Some departments have warehouses that are used for storage that could be converted to a storefront with a minimum of cost. Our department had an old warehouse it had leased and was not using. We were able to use the warehouse and were not required to pay rent. Property that has been confiscated by the department may also be available for a storefront.

Properties the municipality may have control of can also be used. One option we investigated was an office complex that the city had seized. The city allowed us to use the complex for our storefront. In return, we agreed to maintain the grounds of the complex. For a little yard work, the building was ours rent free. Municipalities often have vacant land that can be utilized. A mobile home or portable office building can be placed on the land and be a cost-effective and productive storefront. Be sure to check the zoning on the land—it may not be zoned for commercial use or for mobile homes. Do not forget the other law enforcement agencies in your area. They may have just what you need.

Renting or Leasing the Site

Leasing or renting a site is the option most frequently considered. Find out your department's policy on leasing or renting property. You must also consider other precautions along with any departmental guidelines. The lease secured must ensure the availability of the desired property for the anticipated duration of the storefront. At the same time, the lease must contain a stipulation by which you may terminate the lease and/or an option to extend the lease. Leasing a building for an extended period of time can be very expensive if there are no provisions negotiated for breaking the agreement.

FOR EXAMPLE _____

The anticipated duration of the storefront is twelve months. A lease is obtained for the desired location for that length of time. Six months into the operation, the stated objectives are accomplished. There were no stipulations for early departure incorporated into the lease at the time it was negotiated. The storefront has concluded, but rent must be paid for six more months.

The lack of an option to extend the lease can be just as devastating. Trying to locate another suitable site for the storefront in the middle of the operation is not an easy task.

FOR EXAMPLE _____

The anticipated duration of the storefront is six months. As the end of the sixth months approaches, the storefront just starts to hit its zenith. The lease must be extended to accomplish the stated objectives. An option to extend the lease was not incorporated at the time it was negotiated. The owner has already leased the building to another party. The storefront must move or close, and the stated objectives may not be met.

Before you seek a location to rent or lease, consider what conditions you need as part of the agreement. List the departmental guidelines that must be adhered to and any specific needs of the operation. For example, you want to make month-to-month rent payments with as little advance payment as possible. Many landlords want first and last months' rent along with cleaning and/or damage deposits as the first payment. This type of arrangement escalates the initial monetary outlay. If these expenditures can be spread out over the length of the agreement, the cost to start the storefront will be lowered. The expense over the length of the investigation is the same, but the initial outlay is reduced. The lower the initial outlay, the more likely the storefront is to gain administrative approval. Of course, the ability to break or extend the lease can be vital. Knowing what is needed in a rental agreement before negotiating the contract will eliminate the headaches of entering negotiations ill prepared.

Purchasing the Site

Outright purchase of a site is not common. Departmental policy and/or budget constraints may prohibit it. Be aware of departmental policies before you consider this option. The big question when purchasing property is what to do with it once the operation is concluded. If you can arrive at a satisfactory answer to this question and there are no departmental guidelines or budget restrictions prohibiting purchase, you should consider this option, but only after all other options are exhausted.

Donation of the Site

Donation of a site is another option. Again, be aware of your department's policy on this. Businesspeople will frequently allow one of their properties to be used for a nominal charge or no charge. We have had friends of the department donate the use of a vacant office or building for a storefront. In many areas today, with the real estate market as it is, businesspeople are receptive to donating a site. They can use such donations as a tax write-off. They also have someone in the site who will take care of it instead of leaving the building vacant and a target for vandals.

Projecting the Cost of the Site

Now that you have explored the available options, how do you project the cost? Obviously, if the site is going to be obtained through the department or another agency, the cost will be readily available. The same applies for donated sites. But what if the site must be leased or rented? The cost may not be so apparent. Check the newspaper(s) in your area. They will have classified ads listing the available properties. In reading these ads, list the properties that may meet your needs. Then make arrangements to view the property after determining the rental expense. There is no need to view the rental if you are aware beforehand that the cost will not meet your budget. As you are viewing the property, ask about the possibility of obtaining a rental agreement that is suitable to the requirements of the department and the storefront.

You can also drive through the area in which it would be advantageous to locate the storefront. Look for signs indicating the availability of property, and determine price if you can. Make arrangements to view the property and discuss rental requirements with the owner or agent.

Ask fellow officers if they know of a location for rent or lease. Talk to real estate brokers about the availability of a desired site. Locating a storefront site takes leg work. You have to get out and look; it will not come to you. Do not be in a hurry; allow enough time to review a number of locations. The location can be vital to the investigation's success, so take the time necessary to explore as many options as available.

Site Utility Costs

As you are viewing the property, you should also discuss with the landlord the cost of utilities. Will they be included in the rental price? If they are not, what will they cost? Usually, a landlord is aware of the approximate cost of utilities for the property. If there are tenants still occupying the property, ask them how much their utility bills have been. Check with other businesses in the area who occupy a similar structure and ask them about their utility costs. Check with the utility companies. They can often supply a computer printout of the utility costs in that particular building for a period up to one year.

Do not forget to check on the availability of utilities. If natural gas is needed to operate machinery that will be part of the facade, be sure natural gas is available. Will there be any special electrical requirements?

FOR EXAMPLE _____

We needed 220-volt outlets for certain machinery in one of our storefronts. The location we liked had electricity, but it did not have 220 outlets. The prospective landlord advised us he would install the 220 outlets at no charge if we rented the building

Examine the telephone system while viewing the prospective site. Is telephone service available at the location, or will it have to be installed? Where are the phone jacks, and how many are there? After answering these questions, determine the cost to install what is needed. Do not be fooled into thinking that your phone bill at home is about the same as a business phone. Business rates in most areas are at least 50 percent higher. Ask who will pay the water bill. Often, the landlord pays for water. But don't assume! It is easier to deal with this expense if you know it is your responsibility. Don't be embarrassed at the conclusion of the storefront by an overdue water bill.

Many utility companies require a deposit. Find out what these deposits are and when they are to be returned. Some utility companies return the deposit after the user has established a reliable payment history. Determine what the practice is. If the time period is short enough, the deposits can be returned to the storefront's operational fund to be used at a later date. Often, no deposit is required for a law enforcement operation. Will revealing this information compromise the storefront? If so, do not take the chance; pay the deposit.

Additional Site Costs

Will the prospective site be furnished or unfurnished? Furnishings will be needed for a convincing storefront. If the prospective site is unfurnished, check secondhand stores for suitable furniture. Costs are usually reasonable there, and the variety is unlimited. If you have not visited a secondhand store lately, you will be astonished at what is available. Often, fellow officers or friends have furniture they will donate or loan. With a little ingenuity, a storefront can be furnished at very little expense.

Determine if the prospective landlord will require insurance on the property. Ask what insurance the owner may carry on the property. If departmental policy requires certain insurance coverage, find out if the property owner carries it. If the insurance is not provided and is required, visit several insurance companies and obtain estimates.

When talking to the prospective landlord, discuss what remodeling will be allowed and to what extent, if any, the landlord will pay for or allow remodeling expenses to be deducted from the rent. Suppose the building is in the right area, the rental price is acceptable, and all the utilities required are available. However, one room needs to be remodeled for the recording equipment. If remodeling has not been discussed with the prospective landlord before signing the rental agreement, do not be surprised if the owner says no to the remodeling after the agreement has been signed.

Determine the security measures of the prospective site. Are there

Dead bolts on the doors?

Wrought iron on the windows?

Fencing?

Alarms?

Remember there will be expensive recording and video equipment in most storefronts. Having to remove the equipment every time you leave the site is reason enough to consider security measures. Decide what additional security devices are required. Then establish if the prospective landlord will allow the installation that is required for the additional security devices. Also determine what portion of this expense the prospective landlord is willing to incur. If the security measures are to become a permanent improvement to the building, the landlord may be willing to pay for improvements or split the cost. You must negotiate this.

Site Expense Work Sheet

As with the mobile storefront, designing a work sheet to assist in locating a site for the stationary storefront is helpful. List the sites available. If there is a site available through the department, that would be the first work sheet. Any property that is available through donations would be the second, third, or fourth work sheet. Property for rent, lease, or sale would be the next work sheets, and so on. On the work sheet, indicate the expense and any stipulations that come with acquiring the site. Then indicate the estimated cost of utilities, including any deposits or installation charges. Then list insurance premiums, if applicable. List the anticipated expenditures for remodeling and any security installations needed. Also consider any of these expenses the landlord will partially or fully incur. Include on the work sheet a list of questions for the prospective landlord—questions concerning the rental agreement, remodeling, security devices, and anything else necessary in obtaining the proper site. Phrase the questions to obtain a simple yes or no response. In calculating cost, determine cost per month and the total cost for the period the storefront will be in operation. Then compare the work sheets and consider the total cost of each option. This will enable you to consider all the options and choose the best site for the storefront. (See work sheet 4 in the appendix.)

Props for the Site

In projecting the cost of the storefront, you must include the cost of any props that may be needed to make the storefront convincing. *Prop* is defined by *Webster's Unabridged Dictionary* as: "To support, hold in place or prevent from falling by placing something under or against." This is exactly what props for a storefront do. They support or hold in place the illusion you are creating with the storefront. They prevent the collapse of the storefront's facade.

We have had to buy very few props for our storefronts. Check with the department's evidence unit. Many evidence units auction off property that has been in their custody for a specific length of time and cannot be returned to its rightful owner. The property that is available for auction is usually varied, and often the props needed can be located there. Furniture is often available, as well as radios, clocks, rugs, tables, trophies, curtains, and any number of props. Determine the departmental policy on the use of this property ready for auction, and follow all the guidelines that have been established when obtaining this property.

PROJECTING OPERATIONAL COSTS

These are expenses you might overlook when projecting the cost of the storefront. You must determine the outlay for personnel required to carry on the investigation. Consider the number of personnel needed, salaries, overtime, and any special training the investigators may require to enable them to conduct a competent investigation. This may appear easy at first. There are the investigators who will be the undercover officers operating the storefront. No special training will be required. You know their salaries and projected overtime. But have you considered all the possibilities?

Case Agent and Supervisor

Will there be a case agent(s) assigned to the storefront? Many storefronts use a case agent(s) who is assigned to the operation full time. A case agent will be invaluable to an investigation that has a large case load (as discussed in chapter 10). The storefront may also require a full-time supervisor. His or her salary must be calculated into the projected cost. If the supervisor is assigned on a part-time basis, calculate that portion of his or her salary.

Clerical Personnel

The need for additional clerical personnel is often overlooked when projecting the operational cost of a storefront. However, this expense must be properly addressed. Additional paperwork created by a storefront can be staggering if not properly planned for. The lack of clerical personnel can cause an otherwise productive investigation to be unsuccessful. What additional paperwork can a storefront create? Documentation in the form of written reports is an example. These reports may include weekly and/or monthly progress reports, financial reports, various logs kept by investigators, and reports in reference to your contacts with the criminal element. There may also be additional reports from the case agent, supervisor, technician, and surveillance officers which all must be typed. This paperwork is in addition to the paperwork generated by the day-to-day routine of the department. You must determine if the clerical personnel available will be sufficient to cope with this additional work load in a timely manner. Prompt typing of these reports is necessary to ensure a successful storefront.

FOR EXAMPLE ——————————————————————————————

We operated a storefront with an outside agency. In establishing the storefront, we determined that the outside agency would be responsible for supplying the clerical personnel needed and for typing reports pertaining to the investigation. The paperwork generated by the storefront overwhelmed the assigned clerical personnel. In planning the storefront, we did not consider the additional clerical personnel that would be needed or the expense of this additional help. Four months after the storefront had ceased operations, we were still having reports and transcripts typed. Because of our oversight, the prosecution of the offenders was jeopardized. Luckily we had established a good working relationship with the prosecutor. We did a lot of typing along with the clerical personnel, and we were able to supply the reports needed for successful prosecution. These reports, however, were not supplied in the timely manner they should have been. Our poor planning created this problem. In organizing future storefronts, we paid particular attention to the clerical personnel that might be needed and projected this cost into the budget.

Transcribing Recorded Conversations

Another function the clerical personnel may have to perform is transcribing recorded conversations. Many jurisdictions require a typed transcript of recorded conversations in addition to the tape itself. If you have ever had to transcribe a tape, you know how time consuming and tedious it can be. A twenty-minute conversation between the investigator and a suspect can take hours to transcribe. A twenty-minute conversation between the investigator and two or more suspects can take many more hours to transcribe. If you anticipate many recorded conversations in the life of the storefront, you can understand why projecting the expense of needed clerical personnel is so important.

Ask about the availability of transcribing machines within the department or other agencies. These machines make it much easier to transcribe tapes. If the machines are not available, determine the cost of leasing. The cost of leasing will be far less than the labor hours needed to transcribe tapes without them. If you lease or rent these machines, project that expense into the operational cost.

Alternatives for Acquiring Additional Clerical Personnel

Hiring additional clerical personnel may not be feasible because of department policies. It may also be damaging to the security of the storefront. In planning for additional clerical personnel, there are several methods that can be used to overcome these potential problems.

Many municipalities and school districts have work-study programs. The student spends a specified amount of time in class and a specified amount of time at work. This employment goes toward credits needed for graduation. Our department used many such students. The students relieved clerical personnel of the day-to-day routine. This enabled the permanent clerical staff to devote more time to the needs of the storefront. If your department has such a program, it is an inexpensive means to ensure adequate clerical personnel. Contracting typing is also an option. The people contracted should be known to the department and cleared as a possible security risk. They can be used to transcribe the recorded conversations or perform other clerical tasks.

Technicians

Technicians may also be needed to install, maintain, and/or repair recording and video equipment. Installation of recording and video equipment can be accomplished by you or a member of the department. However, if there is any question about the competency of the installer, do not hesitate to seek help. The few dollars spent for a trained installer or for any training needed to make you capable is worth the expense. The recordings made at the storefront will be of paramount importance in the successful prosecution of offenders. Do not jeopardize this valuable evidence by trying to save a few dollars. Repair of this equipment usually requires the services of someone outside the department. In projecting the cost of the storefront, include any anticipated cost for technical assistance.

Often, if the equipment needed is not available it can be leased or rented. When leasing or renting equipment, it is a good idea to obtain a service contract as part of the lease or rental agreement. This gives you a fixed cost for maintenance. The maintenance agreement should also include replacement of equipment. If the recording equipment needs repairs that will take a week, the storefront could be out of operation for the week. With a replacement clause as part of the maintenance agreement, the storefront can be operational while the equipment is being repaired.

Surveillance Officers

Surveillance officers may also need to be part of the projected cost. The exact amount of time and number of surveillance officers needed is sometimes difficult to project. A full-time surveillance team is seldom needed. But most storefronts use a surveillance team. Determine the approximate hours per week and number of surveillance officers that may be needed. Then determine the salaries. Most departments have an escalating pay scale, so trying to determine the individual salaries of the officers who may or may not be on a surveillance team could be next to impossible. Use a figure from the middle of the pay scale in calculating the projected cost. Then multiply the salary chosen by the number of surveillance officers you expect will be required. Multiply this figure by the number of hours you anticipate the surveillance team will be utilized. This will enable a reasonable projection of the cost of the surveillance team.

Relief Officers

The need for a relief officer(s), in most storefronts, should be included when projecting the cost of operation. To project this expense, determine the number of hours anticipated for a relief officer, and then simply multiply that by the median salary you have chosen to work with. This will give the projected cost.

There are many reasons a relief officer may be necessary. The duration of the storefront operation and the hours it is to be opened are two factors to consider. If you plan on being operational for a six-month period and being open seven days a week, the necessity for a relief officer is apparent. Even when the storefront is to be functional for a maximum of forty hours per week, there may be many occasions when a relief officer is needed. Court, sickness, vacations, and family emergencies are just a few of the reasons a relief officer may be necessary. Trying to project when the relief officer will be required for these situations is very difficult. We calculated into our projections a minimum of eight hours per week for a relief officer. That way, the relief officer could be at the storefront, even if not needed, and be seen by the criminal element who were dealing with us. The crooks became accustomed to the relief officer's presence, and if the relief officer was needed they would not be hesitant to conduct their business because a new face was present.

The guidelines of the department or other agencies that may be involved in organizing and operating the storefront will determine the extent to which you must project personnel costs. Some storefronts we have organized with outside agencies required us to include all the personnel costs we have discussed here. Others were only concerned with the expense of the undercover officers. Still others wanted to know the projected cost of the undercover officers and any additional clerical personnel. The target of the storefront will also aid in determining what personnel costs should be projected. If the storefront is organized to investigate the criminal activity of a single individual, a case agent might not be required; nor would additional clerical personnel or relief officers. You must determine what is needed and/or required in projecting the operational budget of your storefront. Include these figures in the projected cost of operation.

Evidence Expenditures: Buy Money

Buy money, or funds used for evidence expenditures, is difficult to project. No matter how much buy money is available, it never seems to be enough. In projecting the funds needed for evidence expenditures, consider the following: What does the storefront intend to purchase as evidence? If the storefront is organized to investigate a burglary ring, what has the documentation shown as the contraband most likely to be brought to the storefront? Is this burglary ring stealing household appliances or state-of-the-art medical equipment? Purchasing household appliances may require less funding than purchasing state-of-the-art medical equipment.

The frequency of these purchases also must be considered. Televisions are likely to be brought to a storefront on a more frequent basis than a computerized tomography scanning machine, better known as a CAT scan. Don't laugh, we had a subject who was going to deliver a CAT scan to one of our storefronts. Through negotiations with the subject, we were able to learn when and where the subject planned on stealing this machine. Surveillance was arranged, and the subject's burglary attempt was foiled. Not only does the frequency of buys need to be considered, but how many buys from each suspect are necessary to ensure a successful prosecution. As a general rule, we wanted at least three buys from the same offender. That does not mean the more buys the more successful the prosecution. Making five, ten, or fifteen buys from the same subject is seldom necessary and usually frowned on by the department as well as the courts. The storefront is not organized to squander funds by overkill.

Calculate the anticipated cost to purchase the desired contraband and then multiply it by the optimum number of buys. Multiply that by the frequency rate—the number of suspects you anticipate buying from. This will give you a general idea of the funds needed for evidence expenditures.

FOR EXAMPLE ───

With a storefront we established to combat auto thefts, we calculated buy money in the following manner. Our documentation had shown that the purchase of fifty stolen vehicles in a six-month storefront operation was a realistic goal. The average cost of the vehicles that we wanted to target was $18,000 each. In our particular circumstances, evidence expenditures of 2.5 to 3 percent of the vehicles' value would allow us to be competitive with the criminal element already buying the stolen vehicles.

We multiplied fifty, the number of vehicles we expected to purchase over the life of the storefront, by $495 (the average between 2.5 and 3 percent of the value of each vehicle). The projected cost for evidence expenditures was $24,750.

The projected cost of evidence expenditures may vary drastically from storefront to storefront. Remember that the evidence expenditures are calculated based on

The type of contraband that is expected to be purchased

The frequency of these purchases

The optimum number of buys

Being compatible with competitors' prices

The particular circumstances of the geographical area in which the storefront is to be located.

The price a stolen television commands in your area may be vastly different from the price a stolen television commands in another area. The documentation for the storefront and professional experience should determine this figure. But, as a general rule, new merchandise commands 10 percent of its value and used merchandise commands between 3 and 5 percent of its value. However, these prices are always negotiable.

CI and Information Expenditures

Source expenditures may need to be projected into the cost of operating the storefront if a CI is going to be used. We have operated several storefronts using cooperating individuals and several without; both methods have proved to be successful. Most departments have guidelines on the documentation process required for paying a source. (There is a detailed discussion on this procedure in chapter 13.) But how much is a source paid for a deal? Different units within the department utilize sources more frequently than others. Visit with these units and determine what guidelines they have established on monetary rewards. There is usually a predetermined amount paid for the "typical deal."

FOR EXAMPLE _____

For the introduction of an offender to an investigator which results in a buy, the source receives $100, which breaks down to $50 for the introduction and $50 for the buy. For each subsequent buy, from the same offender, the source receives an additional $50. This compensation schedule is for the typical deal.

_____

Then ask how compensation is determined for the nontypical deal. This is usually determined by the investigator's communication with superiors and a comparison of payments made for similar deals. The important thing to keep in mind when paying a source is to stay within the parameters that have been established by the units within your department. You do not want to initiate a bidding war between units for CI information.

Being familiar with customary amounts paid to CIs by the department and other law enforcement agencies in the area will help you determine the projected cost of source expenditures. There is a great deal to consider when using a source and how a source can be compensated. (This is discussed in more detail in chapter 13.) Knowing the predetermined compensation and the expected frequency at which a source(s) may be used will allow you to calculate a reasonable monetary amount in projecting CI and information expenditures.

Equipment and Props

The cost of equipment or props may also need to be considered in the projection. Earlier we discussed the possible need to rent or lease transcribers that may not be available through your department. Does the storefront need a typewriter, copying machine, or other office equipment? Do these items need to be leased or purchased? Will the storefront require any other special equipment to enhance its facade? You must determine the equipment needed for the storefront, and then determine the expense, if any, in obtaining this equipment. Equipment or props usually do not need to be functional; they just need to appear that way. Therefore, purchasing new equipment or props is seldom required. First try to secure any equipment or props needed through the department or an outside agency. Then check with other members of the department—you would be amazed at what they may have accumulated over the years. Secondhand stores, junkyards, and flea markets can be other good sources for needed equipment or props. Remember, the evidence unit of the department and of other law enforcement agencies may have what you need. If the department's policy allows the use of evidence that has been readied for auction, it can be a valuable asset to the storefront. Using any of these methods will help defray operational costs.

Evidentiary Storage Costs

Evidentiary storage costs may need to be considered for the storefront. If this expenditure applies, it must be part of the projected operational cost. It is ideal if the investigators don't have to worry about evidentiary storage costs. The department has an evidence unit, and the storage of evidence is their concern. All the investigator must do is obtain the evidence and then turn it over to the evidence unit. If only it were always that easy!

FOR EXAMPLE ————————————————————————————————————

We operated a storefront that purchased heavy machinery. We obtained as evidence bulldozers, road graders, scrapers, and the vehicles used to transport this equipment. Knowing the limitations of storage space for our evidence unit, we knew we would not be able to deliver this type of evidence to them and then say store it! Arrangements had to be made to secure a site to store this evidence. The expense of the site had to be a part of the projected operational cost.

If departmental policy permits you to secure an evidence storage site, you may want to do so. With most of our storefronts that is just what we did. It was far more convenient and one less avenue by which the storefront could be compromised. The cost was usually insignificant and well worth the extra expense. Just be sure to follow all departmental and judicial guidelines.

Inventory and Supply Costs

Any furniture, inventory, or supplies the storefront may require must be projected into the operational cost. We discussed some of the different ways to obtain the furniture and other items that may be needed earlier in this chapter. For one of our first storefronts, we had been comparison shopping in the different secondhand stores. We were trying to get an idea of the expense of the furniture needed. We had spent half a day going from store to store. On our way to the final stores, we drove by an apartment complex. There, next to the trash dumpster, were couches, chairs, tables, lamps, and rugs. I said to my partner, "we have been looking for furniture half the day, and they are throwing it away." My partner suggested that we ask what they planned to do with it. If they were going to throw it away, maybe they would give to us. I laughed and kept driving. My partner then suggested it again, and I kept laughing. The third time he suggested it more sternly. I gave in and turned the truck around and went back to the apartment complex. We got out and went searching for the owner. As we searched, I grumbled about what a crazy idea this was. To our surprise, we found the owner in one of the apartments that was being refurbished. We asked about the fate of the furnishings next to the dumpster. The owner was ecstatic to learn that we were willing to cart off his "trash" for free. We loaded up what could be used in the storefront and drove away. En route to our destination, I had to endure my partner's gloating about his brilliant idea. I would never admit this to my partner, but his insistence that we ask about the furnishings was brilliant. Okay, maybe not brilliant, but very clever and, as it turned out, cost effective. The storefront had been furnished and the only expense was having the furnishings cleaned. We rented a steam cleaner and cleaned it ourselves—more money saved.

Inventory and supply costs may also need to be considered. What type of storefront is being planned? What type of inventory or supplies will be needed? We utilized a car lot as one of our facades. What inventory would we need? Cars! In projecting the cost of operation, we had to determine the expense of obtaining the cars which were to be used as props and hopefully sold. You are not going to have a convincing car lot if there are no cars for sale. Cars were not the only expense to consider. A battery charger, jack, tools, polish, and any number of other items to maintain the inventory and complete the illusion were needed. Drive-away stickers or temporary license plates, contracts, display stickers, and other such supplies had to be obtained to make the storefront functional. If you are not sure about what inventory or supplies a specific type of business may need, there is an easy and often overlooked way to find out. Locate a similar business and go snoop. It's usually not advisable to tell the owner or employees about your intentions unless you are absolutely convinced this would not compromise the investigation.

Other supplies to consider may be pens, paper, staplers, tape, paperclips, etc. With some of our storefronts these supplies were obtained through the department at no cost. With others we were required to purchase these items. Depending on the particular circumstances, these items may need to be included in the projected operational cost.

Advertising

Advertising is a reality of doing business. Even if the storefront is not going to be a legitimately functional business, there may be a need to advertise. It could be as simple as a sign or as complex as having an ad on television. Signs, business cards, television ads all add to the illusion you are creating. We used business cards extensively in our operations. Many of the offenders arrested as a result of one of our storefronts still had our business card in their possession when incarcerated. The cards were inexpensive and a good way to advertise and get the word out. We have also used newspaper ads, magazine ads, ads in the yellow pages, posters, giveaways, billboards, and flyers. Knowing the sophistication of the criminal element you plan on attracting to the storefront will help you determine the amount of advertising needed to help create the desired illusion.

FOR EXAMPLE _____

We established a storefront to attract a large family that had been involved in criminal activity in our area for over two decades. They all had been in and out of prison over this time span. By some ironic quirk, they were all free at the same time and were raising havoc in our city. Some of the family members had been arrested in the past as a result of dealing with other storefronts. They were a sophisticated criminal element—not because of their intellectual capacity, it was just that they had collectively learned so much from their past mistakes. Due to the consequences of these mistakes, they were leery about doing business with any strangers.

The storefront had been open for several months when we made our first transaction with a member of the family. Near the end of the investigation, we learned why it had taken so long for the family to start doing business with the storefront and what finally convinced them it was safe. They had seen our signs and even been into the site to get a business card. They checked the telephone book for our listing and our ad in the yellow pages. The ad was reassuring because it contained more than the name of the business and a phone number. We had purchased a small ad in the telephone book that listed this customary information and a description of services offered. Along with this information there was a snappy slogan for the business. The cost was approximately $100 more to place this type of ad than the cost for the standard listing.

Even though the ad in the telephone book was reassuring to the family, they were not convinced we were a legitimate business. Then they saw our ad in a magazine. Being familiar with the family, since the department had been doing business with them for over twenty years, we knew of their interests. A regional magazine was published monthly in our area. It listed available salvage for many different types of vehicles. We knew the family subscribed to this magazine. When they saw our ad, they were convinced we were safe to do business with. The price of the ad was minimal compared to the eventual outcome.

Promotional Gimmicks

Give-aways are inexpensive trinkets that are given away by businesses as promotional gimmicks, usually in the hope of improving customer relations. Get a fill-up from the man who wears the star and you will get a free miniature plastic truck with the company's logo on it. Open an account at your local savings and loan and get a free calendar for your wallet. Pens, pencils, plastic letter openers, bookmarks, plastic cups, and any other inexpensive item that the company's name can be placed on are used as give-aways.

FOR EXAMPLE ———————————————————————————

We had a give-away that worked great for us. It was a small plastic folder. On the outside was the name and telephone number of the business. Open the folder and on one side was a small plastic comb and a piece of shiny metal that almost resembled a mirror—we were not sure if it was a mirror or some sort of survival device. On the other side was a small pad of paper and a pencil. For some reason, the criminal element loved these folders. They would bring in their cohorts and the first thing they wanted us to do was give them a folder. When a transaction was about to take place and it required the suspects to call, we would ask if they had the telephone number. They would proudly pull out this plastic folder and say "right here."

———————————————————————————

These give-aways and other advertising devices can be used to enhance the facade of the storefront. So consider the potential benefits of advertising and, if appropriate, include this expense in the projection.

Licensing and Bonding

Licensing and bonding is an expense that may need to be included into the operation's projected cost. Determine if the storefront will require any special licenses or bonds. A business license is usually required in most areas. Even if the storefront is not going to conduct any legitimate business, a business license may be desirable. The license hanging from the wall for all to see is just another way to enhance the illusion of the storefront. The cost is usually of no consequence and could provide that little extra detail to complete the facade. Also, ascertain if the type of storefront will require special licenses or bonds. With the car lot we operated, we were required to obtain a bond before the business license would be issued. Obtaining a bond or a license takes little effort, but it is an expense not to be overlooked.

Technical Operational Expenses

Technical operational expenses may encompass such items as audio and/or video recording equipment and the hardware needed to make them functional. This hardware can include

Tapes

Batteries

Lenses

Filters

Coaxial cable

Amplifiers

Adapters

Mikes

Remote on and off switches

Date/time indicator

Playback equipment.

Before calculating this expense, become familiar with the equipment available through the department. Does the department maintain the equipment? Is the hardware available to make this equipment functional? Outside agencies may have part or all the technical equipment desired. When contacting these outside agencies, first determine what their policy is in reference to loaning this type of equipment. Many agencies are restricted by law and/or agency policy. Some are allowed to supply the hardware needed to make the equipment functional, but are restricted in loaning the actual equipment. Some are permitted to do neither. Understand the policy of the outside agency before requesting equipment or hardware. Storefronts are organized to collect electronic evidence, which is then used for the successful prosecution of the offenders. So calculating the expense for obtaining this electronic evidence is of utmost importance.

Other Avenues to Explore

Schools, libraries, and the news media may be other sources. They may have the equipment and/or hardware you need. We worked hard to establish a good working relationship with the school district and the news media. Our efforts were not always rewarded, but when they were, we reaped valuable dividends. We were able to secure both the equipment and the hardware needed for storefront operations from both sources. Don't overlook this possible asset. In addition, businesses in the area may be able to help you get technical equipment. They often use the same type of equipment in the preparation and presentation of audio and/or video material.

Securing the Equipment

If you are not familiar with the type of equipment and hardware that may be required, seek out someone who is. From all the possible sources we have discussed so far, there may be someone who specializes in this field. They may not be able to obtain the technical equipment needed, but they can be helpful in explaining what is required and the most appropriate avenue to pursue in securing this equipment. They may be able to prevent you from acquiring expensive and/or inappropriate equipment. (Chapter 9 discusses electronic equipment in more detail.)

Projecting the Operational Costs Work Sheet

A work sheet may assist you in projecting operational costs (see work sheet 5 in the appendix). If you decide to use the work sheets provided in the appendix, you can easily determine a preliminary cost of operating the storefront. Using work sheets or other such aids will also help you review specific costs. When reviewing the specific costs, determine if a less expensive alternative is available. If there are no less expensive alternatives, decide if this expense can be reduced or eliminated without jeopardizing the investigation. After an objective evaluation has been made of each specific cost, the final totals can be compiled to reveal the total projected cost of the operation.

SUMMARY

The projected cost of operating the storefront will be one of the most important components in gaining administration approval. Consider all the possible expenses your operation may encounter. Then investigate all alternatives available to reduce or eliminate these expenditures. A storefront does not require an unlimited budget to be successful. A storefront does, however, require a realistic budget to be productive. Do not jeopardize the approval of the investigation by having an unrealistic projection of operational costs. On the other hand, do not hinder the investigation's performance by projecting a budget that will not allow it to function. There is only one way to obtain this middle ground: careful deliberation on what expense the storefront will encounter and what alternatives are available to alleviate these expenses.

CHAPTER 5

Sources of Funding

You have made a great deal of preparations and many decisions to reach this point. You had to complete documentation to determine if the criteria existed to initiate the investigation. You had to consider the feasibility of the operation and determine the objectives of the storefront. You had to choose the type of business best suited to the objectives of the investigation while at the same time being cost effective. You had to understand any additional liabilities the operation could impose on you and/or the department, in addition to the numerous liabilities already confronting law enforcement. You had to decide what procedures must be implemented to overcome these additional liabilities. Furthermore, you had to project an operational budget. Now you must obtain the funds to operate the storefront. The process seems to go on and on. There must be an easier way!

While it is true that the amount of preparation needed will vary for each storefront, every storefront investigation must take certain steps. These steps ensure a proper foundation for a competent investigation. Whenever we started to grumble about all the preparation required to begin a storefront operation, our crusty old sergeant always had the same reply. He would glare at us with those cold blue eyes and softly but forcefully say, "Proper planning prevents piss-poor performance!" Okay, perhaps he expressed himself a little crudely and could have been more eloquent, but he made his point. You are asking the department and possibly other outside agencies to fund and approve your storefront. In return for placing their confidence in you, they expect a competent investigation. How are you going to demonstrate to the department or an outside agency that the investigation will be competent unless you can first demonstrate that proper preparation has taken place?

Critics of storefront operations cite a common concern—that law enforcement is offering citizens an opportunity to commit crimes even though there is no reasonable suspicion that they are engaged in violations of the law. The ABSCAM case is often cited, specifically Senator Larry Pressler of South Dakota. The senator became a target of the investigation when he was approached and offered a bribe. He made it perfectly clear during the investigation that he would not accept a bribe. The mere fact that the senator was a target of the investigation caused him harm. There was no reasonable suspicion that the senator was engaged in any criminal activity at the time he became a target. Some critics contend that he was clearly an innocent man who was made a target of the investigation even though agents had no reason to suspect him.

We do not wish to endorse or denounce these claims or to use this example to discredit storefront investigations. We just want you to be aware of some of the criticism in reference to this type operation and, for that matter, all undercover operations. Through proper preparation and planning, the storefront can overcome these criticisms. So do not get discouraged and grumble about all the preparation that is necessary to initiate a storefront. Remember, the first time is always the most cumbersome, and it gets easier as you become more familiar with the intricate preparation process. Keep in mind that the storefront is an effective law enforcement technique when a proper foundation is formed and all established departmental and judicial guidelines are followed.

Now that your enthusiasm to pursue this type of investigation has been renewed, let's discuss perhaps one of the most difficult aspects of any storefront: funding. Is your restored enthusiasm waning? We hope not, because you can also overcome this hurdle. We are all familiar with the budget crunch facing all publicly funded entities. The public is demanding that more be accomplished with less expense. As law enforcement officers, we have two options: Insist that additional funding is necessary, or create new and innovative techniques using the available funds in a productive, cost-effective, and proactive approach. One such technique, of course, is the undercover law enforcement storefront. What avenues are available for funding such an operation?

IN-HOUSE FUNDING

Departments receive funding annually from their governing body. These resources are appropriated to fund all facets of law enforcement that the governing body has authorized. A vast diversity of services within the department must be budgeted from this allocation, including

Basic police patrol
Investigative units
Public relations units
Planning units
Motor transport units

Dispatch units

Other branches within the department

Records sections

Recruiting units

Training units.

How do you gain a portion of this allocation for the storefront? First, you must demonstrate to the administration the need for the storefront. The documentation that you have so carefully prepared will help you here. The administration is acutely aware that crime is a problem in its jurisdiction. You must graphically illustrate the extent of the particular criminal activity that is to be addressed by the storefront and its impact on the community. You must then expound on the advantages of using this proactive approach as opposed to conventional law enforcement techniques. The advantages include the following:

Storefronts are an economical method to investigate certain types of criminal activity—much cheaper than many other forms of investigation and often more successful.

The potential to curtail the criminal activity investigated is far greater with this type of investigation.

The depletion of departmental personnel can be greatly reduced with this method of police activity compared to other techniques.

The sharing of intelligence gained through the storefront with other law enforcement agencies will help to strengthen a relationship of interagency cooperation.

A successful storefront operation will increase the public's confidence that law enforcement does have effective techniques to combat criminal activity.

Knowledge of Current Events

Your awareness of current events pertaining to your locality can play an important role in successful fund seeking. When the news media focuses on a certain aspect of criminal activity in the community, citizens may demand that action be taken. When this public outcry is directed toward criminal activity that can be confronted using a storefront, it may be advantageous for you to present the proposal for the operation at this opportune time.

FOR EXAMPLE _____

Auto theft was a scourge that had devastated our city for an extended period of time. Many conventional methods were used to alleviate the problem, but with limited success. We had presented a proposal for the initiation of a storefront to investigate this criminal activity on numerous occasions. The documentation was more than adequate to demonstrate the magnitude of the problem. Everyone agreed on the favorable impact of the storefront on the criminal element. However, we received the same response time after time. There were just no funds available to implement the operation. Then, the news media began a series of articles on the alarming rate at which auto thefts had been occurring in our community.

As these articles continued, the public became more and more aware of the extent of the problem. The public then voiced its concern to the elected officials, who coincidentally control the purse strings. As more and more public attention was focused on the problem, the elected officials sensed an urgency to demonstrate to the electorate that something was being done. Seizing this opportunity, we resubmitted the proposal for the storefront. The funding to conduct the storefront was provided. The subsequent investigation had a favorable impact on the problem and the community.

Budget Awareness

Realizing when the departmental budget is presented for approval to the governing body could assist you in obtaining funding. When the department is aware of pending operations, it can incorporate them into new resources rather than trying to accommodate them within an existing allotment. In larger departments, individual units submit their budget requests to the department, which in turn submits a departmental budget request to the governing body. When the storefront operation can be planned for in an upcoming budget, it is more likely to gain funding approval. Most storefront investigations concentrate on criminal activity that has existed over a period of time, and the duration of the operation is usually longer than the conventional investigation. But with a little forethought and planning, funding approval is more likely.

Grants

You must also be aware of the vast variety of government grants available to the department and allotted for the war on crime. Many departments employ a coordinator to oversee the availability of such funds, which are issued by different government agencies. If the department does not maintain such a position, check with your local or county governments. If neither of these governing bodies employs such a person, surely the state government does. The coordinator will be able to inform you of what grants are available and the proper procedure in applying for these grants. The coordinator can also explain in detail any stipulations that are attached to receiving such funding. Most grants are very specific on how and what the monies can be used for. In addition to the documentation that you must submit for approval, there are often stringent reporting requirements you must satisfy during the duration of the grant. This requirement ensures the grantor that the allocation is used in accordance with the guidelines of the grant. These periodic reports must often be completed before you receive a continuance of the grant.

Helpful tip: Do not overlook another significant resource within the department: Determine if a member of the department may have secured a grant in the past. Their assistance could prove to be an invaluable source of information.

Accountability for Grant Funds

The grant(s) can provide the sole financial support of the storefront or be used in conjunction with other funding. When used in conjunction with other funding, ensure that your accounting records show the grant is being used for its intended purpose. Do not be misled into believing that once this type of funding is secured, you can use the allocated funds for purposes other than those intended, even if the purpose is to combat another type of criminal activity. Remember, most grants are very specific about the area of criminal activity the grant money can be used to combat, and you must follow every condition of the agreement. Serious consequences to you and/or the department can result from misrepresentation.

Equipment Purchase through Grants

Not only may there be grants available to combat the criminal activity the storefront is to address; there may also be grants available to purchase the equipment necessary to operate the storefront. When a grant can be used to purchase necessary equipment, department expenditure is greatly reduced or eliminated. This may also reduce the projected cost of operation. The reduced projected cost of operation could enable an otherwise financially doomed storefront to gain approval. The lower the projected cost of an operation and the less financial demands the storefront places on the department, the more likely it is to gain approval.

Time Considerations

In attempting to secure a grant, do not assume that just because one may be available the storefront will be operational in a short time. Even if the storefront proposal meets all the stipulations that have been placed on receiving the grant, there is a menagerie of governmental bureaucracy to overcome and endure. The process of obtaining a grant, when available, can take anywhere from a couple of months to a year or more. You must keep this in mind when planning the investigation. If a grant *can* be acquired, however, the benefits could far outweigh any inconvenience.

FUNDING THROUGH AN OUTSIDE AGENCY

Unfortunately, even if you are privy to all the inner workings of the department and have a firm grasp of its financial dealings, there simply may not be enough money in the departmental budget to fund a storefront investigation—no matter what the justification for this operation may be. You do not have to give up hope, however. There are alternative means to obtain funding. One of these alternatives is to seek partial or total funding through an outside agency.

Monetary funding is not the only asset an outside agency can provide. There are other assets to consider.

Additional personnel: This could help ease the burden on your department.

Expertise: Members of an outside agency could assist you in conducting a competent investigation.

Sharing of information: You can benefit from information which is not available through your department but could be vital to your operation.

Availability of equipment: An outside agency may have equipment not available within your department.

Improved working relationship: You will establish better interagency relations.

Some law enforcement agencies' desire for jurisdictional independence and sovereignty has resulted in a lack of cooperation between jurisdictions. This results in a duplication of tasks and a random coordination of law enforcement efforts. This nonproductive situation is often complicated by unhealthy competition, dissention, and petty bickering, which result in unwarranted conflicts among agencies. The criminal element, on the other hand, is not affected by jurisdictional borders or disputes between agencies. In fact, they are able to thrive because of them. Their illegal activity often occurs within several law enforcement jurisdictions and can affect many more. They have total disregard to jurisdictional borders.

Multijurisdictional Storefronts

All these factors have limited law enforcement's ability to combat the growing criminal element. One way to combat criminal activity more effectively is through multijurisdictional storefront investigations.

Advantages of Combining Resources

This approach allows law enforcement to apply its combined resources to fight the war on crime. Using this method, law enforcement can

Coordinate investigative efforts.

Establish more uniform enforcement priorities.

Participate in joint investigations that are beneficial to all.

Assist in the efforts of smaller jurisdictions.

Conduct transjurisdictional investigations.

Multijurisdictional units' function, structure, and operational methods address the criminal activity in a way that fits the unique characteristics of their respective communities. This is one of the primary reasons that this concept works so effectively in combating criminal activity.

Designed to Meet Everyone's Needs

That multijurisdictional units can be designed to meet the needs of all involved is demonstrated by the following:

Multijurisdictional units can range in size from two investigators to as many as labor limitations permit.

The investigators are assigned from departments within the multijurisdictional area.

The unit can operate in metropolitan, rural, industrialized, and/or suburban areas.

The unit can encompass one metropolitan community, a county, or as large an area as necessary. Some may even operate interstate.

The unit can be organized to operate in jurisdictions with widely varying populations.

The unit can investigate a wide variety of criminal activity.

The unit can contain members from local, county, state, and federal law enforcement agencies.

The unit can be separated physically from the jurisdictions or incorporated with existing vice, intelligence, narcotics, and/or organized crime sections within an agency.

The unit can operate alone or in conjunction with a statewide coordinating agency.

Common Law Enforcement Problems

Multijurisdictional units are developed to overcome the alarming rise in criminal activity that has taken place in most jurisdictions. Some of the common problems faced by law enforcement today include the following:

The increased publicity in reference to the criminal activity, which in turn heightens public awareness and places more demands on the jurisdiction

The inability of some jurisdictions to pursue investigations outside their respective jurisdictions, even when these investigations would have a direct impact on the criminal activity affecting their community

The increase in criminal activity in the region that is affecting or will soon affect the jurisdiction

The lack of understanding and cooperation between law enforcement agencies

The inability of some local investigators to undertake undercover assignments because they are too easily recognized within their own jurisdiction

The lack of uniformity between jurisdictions in establishing priorities to investigate criminal activity

The inability of smaller jurisdictions to assign investigators to specialize in this type of law enforcement technique

The lack of needed personnel for proactive investigative techniques

The lack of distribution of areawide intelligence and a system to accumulate it

The unlikelihood that a single jurisdiction can obtain state and/or federal funds to assist in the investigation of the criminal activity

The inability to train investigators uniformly so they can more effectively address the criminal activity.

How Multijurisdictional Units Can Resolve Common Problems

Resolving these problems becomes the focus of the multi-jurisdictional unit. The unit strives to attain the primary objective of reducing or eliminating the targeted criminal activity in the area. Specifically, the multi-jurisdictional unit may focus on the following objectives:

Allow investigators assigned to the unit to conduct their investigations throughout the designated jurisdiction regardless of individual jurisdictions.

Coordinate the investigative efforts of all involved against the targeted criminal activity.

Strengthen cooperation between law enforcement agencies by establishing a unit in which agencies will invest personnel and resources. Ensure interaction of the jurisdictions in supervising the unit.

Combine efforts in obtaining funding for the investigation. Also, combine efforts in acquiring equipment necessary for the investigation that can then be shared with all jurisdictions involved and loaned to other jurisdictions when needed.

Enable investigators who are too well known in their own jurisdiction to participate in the undercover investigation.

Establish priorities for the unit and the participating jurisdictions which will direct efforts toward the target of the investigation.

Supply personnel and equipment to those departments which cannot allocate them.

Supplement the investigative efforts of the jurisdictions that lack the personnel to attack the problem adequately.

Establish an areawide intelligence network to gather and disseminate information.

Expedite the use of state and/or federal funds in combating the problem.

Simplify the exchange of information between jurisdictions.

Augment jurisdictional investigations by providing formal and informal training for investigators.

If circumstances warrant the use of a multijurisdictional storefront, it is an excellent option. This approach can enhance the efforts of investigators through combined resources and personnel. It can also strengthen trans-jurisdictional investigations, initiate healthy competition between jurisdictions, and coordinate investigative efforts. Even though many multijurisdictional units are organized to fight the ever-increasing drug problem, they are also an effective force in combating various types of criminal activity.

Establishing a Legal Basis for the Unit

Do not assume, however, that if a multijurisdictional unit is organized all problems are solved. The creation of the unit in itself can pose many challenges. The legal basis of the unit must be established. This can usually be accomplished by

A formal agreement signed by the participating departments

The swearing in of investigators from the various departments as deputies of the counties where the unit will have jurisdiction

State legislation, if necessary, which authorizes the creation of the unit and the agents' operation throughout a region or state.

A formal agreement between the cooperating departments will give the unit a sound legal basis for its operation. Such an agreement formally recognizes that the investigators of the unit have jurisdictional authority. The agreement also formally provides the investigators with life, health, and liability insurance along with other personal benefits of employment while they are engaged in their duties outside their jurisdiction. In addition, using a formal written agreement will require the cooperating departments to consider and plan various aspects of the unit's administration and operation.

Commissioning investigators ensures them the authority to conduct investigations in the different jurisdictions. Investigators are usually sworn in as deputies by the sheriff's office of the county or counties the unit will be operating within. If the unit is to conduct investigations in two or more states, additional steps may be necessary. The attorney general's office of the respective states may waive the residency requirement of the unit's investigators. This ensures that the investigators receive employment benefits from their respective departments, regardless of the state in which they are conducting their duties. Waiving state residency requirements facilitates the swearing in of investigators in different state(s) and ensures the legality of the unit's operation within the different states.

State law makers may enact legislation that authorizes the municipalities and other communities within the state to form such cooperative units. Such legislation may also authorize investigators within the unit to conduct investigations in any jurisdiction with the same powers, privileges, and immunities. Such legislation is often the result of lobbying by law enforcement agencies through the state attorney general's office, legislative representatives, law enforcement associations, and/or sheriff or police chief associations.

Summary of Multijurisdictional Units

The use of this multijurisdictional approach is obviously not required for every storefront. Need will be dictated by the scope of the investigation. However, if the need does exist, this is an excellent law enforcement technique. Don't allow egos, prejudice, and/or petty squabbles among participants to interfere with the appointed task. These counterproductive factors have hindered law enforcement long enough. The multijurisdictional concept offers law enforcement agencies of different jurisdictions and of all sizes to concentrate their full effort on the criminal element without the loss of agency sovereignty and independence.

Funding State and Federal Law Enforcement Agencies

State law enforcement agencies to consider for funding are as follows:

Municipal police departments
Sheriff departments
State police departments
Departments of public safety
Attorney General's office
Organized crime commission
Gambling or gaming commissions

Game and fish departments
Bureau of Land Management.

Federal sources include the following:

Federal Bureau of Investigation

Drug Enforcement Administration

Alcohol, tobacco, and firearms agencies

Department of Agriculture; compliance and investigations branch

Immigration and Naturalization Service

Bureau of Customs

United States Postal Inspector

Internal Revenue Service

United States Secret Service

United States Fish and Wildlife Service

Department of Defense

United States Border Patrol

Bureau of Land Management.

You should be familiar with the responsibilities of the aforementioned law enforcement agencies. If not, a visit to the agency in question would be appropriate. Remember, each agency is regulated by legislative and/or judicial guidelines regarding the amount and type of assistance it can provide. Each agency faces budget constraints. Establishing a friendly working relationship with any law enforcement agency will be beneficial to you, but this becomes even more important when you are seeking assistance. Understanding the agency's responsibilities, restrictions, and constraints can only improve your prospects of obtaining the help you need.

THE RISS PROJECTS

The RISS projects (Regional Information Sharing Systems) are multistate agencies designed by the United States Department of Justice to support state and local law enforcement efforts to combat major criminal conspiracies. The projects form a partnership between the federal government and local law enforcement. There are six RISS projects:

Regional Organized Crime Information Center (ROCIC)

Rocky Mountain Information Center (RMIN)

Western States Information Network (WSIN)

Middle Atlantic-Great Lakes Organized Crime Law Enforcement Network (MAGLOCLEN)

Mid-States Organized Crime Information Center (MOCIC)

New England State Police Information Network (NESPIN).

These six RISS projects provide services to over 150,000 sworn law enforcement officers in 1,658 criminal justice agencies.

Congress makes a yearly appropriation of funds to the RISS project as part of the Department of Justice budget. While the majority of projects became funded in 1980, one was in operation as early as 1974 and another began in 1977. The projects submit annual grant applications to the Bureau of Justice Assistance. These applications detail the projected activities and funding needs of each project for the coming year. The Bureau of Justice Assistance administers the RISS program and has established guidelines for provision of services to member agencies. The projects are subject to monitoring and audits by that office, the General Accounting Office (GAO), a federally funded program evaluation office, the Department of Justice, and local governmental units.

Each RISS project is unique in that it was designed by its members to serve their needs. Yet there are several common services that are required by the Department of Justice. The two primary services RISS projects provide are a centralized computerized law enforcement database and investigative analysis products. The database contains entries made by member agencies on major criminals they have information about and are willing to share with member agencies. The investigative analysis products are provided to members on an as-needed basis and include link charts for telephone toll analysis, assessments of criminal activity, and other analytical products. In addition to the two primary services, the RISS projects provide

Investigative equipment (on loan)

Confidential funds

Bulletins on criminal information

Training

Technical assistance

Referrals

Access to a telecommunications system.

Each project is headed by a project director who has experience in law enforcement. The director answers to the executive group of the project, which is composed of member agency representatives. The project directors gather quarterly to discuss programs, share ideas, and plan long-range goals.

Through this interaction, the projects coordinate their activities to provide the most complete and innovative services to members.

Mid-States Organized Crime Information Center (MOCIC)

MOCIC is located in Springfield, Missouri. It has been funded since 1980 and its grantee agency is the Missouri Attorney General's Office. MOCIC encompasses a nine-state area: Wisconsin, Illinois, Missouri, Iowa, Minnesota, Kansas, Nebraska, and South and North Dakota. It services approximately 295 member agencies.

In addition to information sharing and analysis, MOCIC offers several other services. It distributes a bimonthly intelligence digest which consists of articles on criminal subjects, current types of criminal activities, and other intelligence appropriate to the nine-state region.

MOCIC analysts operate as working partners in member agency multijurisdictional task forces. They provide a wide range of analytical products to members upon request. The project also conducts training for member agencies on subjects including criminal intelligence techniques and intelligence management. Member agencies are also provided with various types of investigative equipment on a loan basis. MOCIC offers a toll-free WATS line and can patch incoming calls through to other agencies to aid information sharing. Technical assistance is also available to member agencies on a request basis. MOCIC has given individualized help on such topics as informant control principles and how to accomplish a buy of contraband under controlled circumstances. Referrals to other law enforcement agencies are provided, and members can obtain funding for investigative operations.

Many law enforcement agencies throughout the Midwest have benefitted from MOCIC services. A multicity task force operating against narcotics in St. Louis County received investigative funding from MOCIC. Thirty-four people were arrested as a result. It was the first time investigators in that area formally banded together to investigate criminal activity. MOCIC also supported a reverse-sting operation in Kansas City. Undercover investigators sold purportedly stolen jewelry and clothing to a number of organized criminals. As a result, information was developed relating to narcotics and illegal firearms distribution. This led the DEA, ATF, FBI, and other agencies to join the case. Over twenty people were arrested as a result. The investigation utilized MOCIC equipment, analytical services, and confidential funds. Another department aided by MOCIC seized the highest quality and quantity of cocaine ever in that area. Burglary groups, fencing rings, and organized prostitution operations have also been dealt serious blows with the help of MOCIC.

New England State Police Information Network (NESPIN)

NESPIN began late in 1979 under the auspices of the New England State Police Administrator's Conference (NESPAC). It is located in Randolph, Massachusetts, a suburb of Boston. The agency responsible for administering NESPIN is the Massachusetts Department of Public Safety. NESPAC was an ideal vehicle to begin the project, as it is a legislatively mandated mutual aid agreement among the state police agencies in Maine, Vermont, New Hampshire, Rhode Island, Connecticut, and Massachusetts.

NESPIN began with only the state police agencies but has since expanded to include local law enforcement. Membership is expected to grow to over sixty agencies. NESPIN offers similar services as those provided by MOCIC.

NESPIN has enhanced many member agency investigations since its inception. In one instance, it provided investigative funds to several member agencies which were conducting an investigation of narcotics smuggling. The member agencies, along with the DEA, seized one aircraft valued at $400,000 and 44 pounds of cocaine valued at over $1 million. Two separate international smuggling operations were smashed. Intelligence gathered from this case was instrumental in the confiscation of 60,000 pounds of marijuana valued at $43,200,000. This load was intercepted off the coast of New England. Intelligence gathered from this case was also given to Florida authorities. Law enforcement officers acted on this information and made two arrests and confiscated 11 pounds of cocaine valued at $440,000.

In another case, a member agency executed three search warrants which were issued as a result of NESPIN-funded investigations. These search warrants yielded approximately 2,000 pounds of marijuana, 72 pounds of cocaine, and other contraband. Of equal importance, the investigation resulted in the identification of individuals from at least seven other states who were involved and who are the subjects of ongoing investigations. NESPIN believes cases of this type continue to document the value of the use of confidential investigative funds as an aid to the exchange of timely, relevant information on criminal activity.

Middle Atlantic—Great Lakes Organized Crime Law Enforcement Network (MAGLOCLEN)

MAGLOCLEN is located in Malvern, Pennsylvania, a suburb of Philadelphia, and its grantee agency is the Pennsylvania Crime Commission. The project received its planning grant in July of 1980 and became operational in June, 1981. It covers eight states: New York, New Jersey, Delaware, Maryland, Pennsylvania, Ohio, Indiana, Michigan, and the District of Columbia. It serves approximately fifty-eight state and local law enforcement agencies, which include over 40,000 sworn law enforcement officers. It provides services similar to MOCIC and NESPIN, including direct funding to support investigations. MAGLOCLEN provided funding and other aid in the investigation of a homicide case. It assisted in setting up the first satellite-transmitted live lineup from coast to coast. It also compiled and distributed a publication on record thieves to all its members which resulted in a decrease in losses suffered as a result of these thefts. Several million dollars in one department store chain alone was saved. With the aid of MAGLOCLEN, three member agencies in three states undertook a major investigation which, individually, they could have never accomplished. MAGLOCLEN provided analytical products, investigative equipment, and investigative funding to this investigation.

Regional Organized Crime Information Center (ROCIC)

ROCIC is the prototype of the RISS project and was founded in 1973, receiving federal funding since 1974. Its grantee is the city of Nashville, Tennessee, where it is located. ROCIC includes the states of Oklahoma, Texas, Arkansas, Louisiana, Mississippi, Florida, Georgia, Alabama, North and South Carolina, Tennessee, Kentucky, Virginia, and West Virginia. It serves approximately 176 municipal, county, parish, and state agencies. It covers the largest land area of any RISS project. ROCIC provides services which are similar to MOCIC, NESPIN, and MAGLOCLEN.

ROCIC aided in the apprehension of James Mitchel Debardelaben, who has been convicted on numerous counterfeiting charges. It did so by piecing together composites submitted by its member agencies in two seemingly unrelated cases. In another case, a number of burglaries in Jackson, Mississippi, went unsolved until ROCIC connected information it received to two burglars from Missouri. Agencies from seven areas were called together for an intelligence-sharing conference, which resulted in the arrest, indictment, and conviction of these traveling criminals on several counts of burglary. ROCIC also provided a compilation of information on serial murderers Otis Toole and Henry Lee Lucas which was used by agencies around the country. Using this publication, local law enforcement agencies have been able to confirm 175 homicides perpetrated by these individuals over a six-year period. ROCIC can also financially support other specific investigations of members.

Rocky Mountain Information Network (RMIN)

RMIN began in 1977 as an outgrowth of the Arizona Drug Control District, or what was later called ACISA. That organization was the grantee for RMIN until early 1983, when the project moved to Albuquerque, New

Mexico, and its grantee became the New Mexico Attorney General's Office. RMIN covers eight states: Montana, Idaho, Wyoming, Nevada, Utah, Colorado, Arizona, and New Mexico. It has approximately 423 members, including municipal, county, state, federal, and prosecutorial law enforcement agencies. One unique problem of RMIN's region is that it covers 24 percent of the geographic area of the continental United States but only 5 percent of the population. This creates an enormous communications problem for law enforcement agencies in the region. The coordination and communication benefits of RMIN members enhance the capabilities of small agencies to meet the challenge of organized and highly mobile criminals.

Of particular importance to RMIN members has been the availability of investigative equipment and funding of specific member agency investigations. In one case, equipment was loaned to a Utah agency investigating racketeering. As a result, several thousand dollars of stolen property was recovered and more than a dozen burglaries were solved. In another case, RMIN loaned equipment to a federal agency involved in a narcotics investigation. The case resulted in nineteen arrests for heroin distribution, the seizure of over $100,000 in narcotics and the additional arrest of a fugitive wanted in three states.

A Nevada agency used RMIN equipment and confidential funds. This case resulted in fourteen indictments, the recovery of $77,000 in illicit drugs, numerous seized vehicles, and over $2 million worth of seized heavy equipment. After utilizing RMIN services, the Gila County, Arizona, sheriff's office uncovered 1,680 pounds of pure cocaine with a street value of $716 million. The additional funding of another Arizona narcotics investigation, which would not have been initiated without financial assistance, resulted in the arrest of eighteen people and the seizure of drugs, weapons, and stolen property. An additional result was the identification and apprehension of a fugitive wanted for murder.

Western States Information Network (WSIN)

WSIN was established in 1981. It is located in Sacramento, California, and its grantee agency is the California Department of Justice. WSIN encompasses five states: Alaska, Hawaii, Oregon, Washington, and California. It has approximately 649 member agencies. WSIN provides services similar to the other five members of RISS.

WSIN has been instrumental in the successful prosecution of many cases in the region it serves. The DEA in Seattle requested analytical assistance from WSIN. The case involved an international narcotic trafficking organization importing cocaine from Bolivia and heroin from India. Law enforcement agencies in eight states and five foreign countries took part in the investigation. Prior to its culmination, an estimated $5 million worth of heroin and nearly $1 million worth of cocaine had been seized. Sixteen subjects were indicted. In another case, WSIN coordination led to the identification of a drug lab. Information separately gathered and received from various California agencies was pieced together by WSIN. The information led to a search warrant served on an 80-acre ranch in Mendocino County. Officers made five arrests and seized chemicals that would have produced 100 pounds of methamphetamine valued at $104 million.

THE PRIVATE SECTOR

The private sector can also be a source of funding if departmental guidelines permit this type of solicitation. Criminal activity that is to be addressed by the storefront may have a direct adverse effect on a specific business or group of businesses. Often, in the interest of the community and self-preservation, these businesses will contribute funding. We have had varying degrees of success with this method of funding.

As with any source of funding there are numerous aspects to consider other than a monetary contribution. Many other private sector contributions can assist you in conducting a successful storefront operation. These contributions can alleviate a portion of the financial burden of initiating the storefront. Site locations, equipment, props, supplies, technical assistance, vehicles, expertise, and much more can be donated by the private sector. These contributions will help ease the expense of the storefront operation.

Helpful tip: When approaching the private sector, be forthright in expressing the anticipated outcome of the investigation. Do not promise more than can be delivered. Present a realistic scenario of the anticipated outcome of the storefront operation. If too much is promised, too much is expected. When expectations rise to an unrealistic level, all that can result is disappointment and distrust.

Warning: Don't organize the storefront to benefit one particular portion of the private sector while excluding others. This is especially true if the particular interest has donated to the storefront effort. This will only lead to unfavorable criticism of the department and the operation. The private sector should not have to contribute to the storefront to reap its benefits.

When seeking funds from the private sector, be cautious, and do not reveal too much information about the storefront investigation. The old adage "loose lips sink ships" applies in undercover police work. When you reveal explicit details of the operation, adversity can follow. This oversight could endanger the physical well-being of the investigators involved in the operation.

SUMMARY

When trying to secure funding, it is essential that you be prepared. You must graphically demonstrate the need for the storefront, expectations of the investigation, and the anticipated cost. You can only do this with proper documentation and preparation.

To be properly prepared, you must be able to demonstrate the following:

A complete understanding of the documentation compiled

The feasibility of the investigation

The primary objectives of the operation

The adverse impact the storefront will have on the criminal element

The beneficial impact the storefront will have on the community

The projected cost of the operation

The benefits to the financing party

Compiling this data into a comprehensive and easily understood format will enable you to present a clear and concise request.

As with most aspects of a storefront investigation, your resourcefulness and initiative will play a large role in determining your success in obtaining funding. Remember, you cannot convince anyone of the need for funding unless you are totally convinced of the need. Finally, do not become discouraged; securing the funding needed to operate a storefront investigation is often the most difficult aspect of the organizing process.

CHAPTER 6

Compiling and Presenting a Storefront Proposal

At this point in your reading you have probably done one of three things. If you are less than motivated about the job and find research something you'd rather not do, you have probably deep-sixed this book and the storefront idea. Or maybe you've put it back on the shelf and hope that someone else will do the leg work and you can come in later and collect your medal. However, if you're still interested and believe it takes hard work and dedication to produce quality work, and you're not prone to making snap judgments, let's look at some successful storefronts that will reinforce these principles. You can draw from these examples to convince your boss to use an unconventional law enforcement technique to catch the conventional criminal. These examples were carried out in different cities throughout the United States, using officers from different backgrounds and using different storefront covers, but they all have one thing in common: They all used cops portraying crooks to catch crooks.

FOOD STAMPS FOR PROFIT

The headline reads "Undercover Police Operation Nets a Total of Thirty-Three Suspects." Depending on the size and type of your jurisdiction, this may or may not be the largest bust in the world. However, the number of arrests in this case, which actually reached into the eighties, is impressive when you realize that these offenders were career criminals for the most part and were each responsible for two to three major crimes involving thousands of dollars in stolen property and contraband. This article went on to say that undercover officers traded food stamps for stolen property, drugs, and cash. The property purchased included cars, trucks, assorted firearms, explosives, oil drilling equipment, assorted tools, heroin, cocaine, marijuana, and U.S. currency. This storefront operation, like others, was researched and executed using guidelines, tactics, and strategies that are the foundation for this book.

The news media sensationalized the mass arrest. However, a mass arrest won't sell your boss on a storefront operation. In fact, in the real world, what's going to sell your boss is the bottom line—cost! So we'll give you the facts behind the headlines.

During a six-month period, it was determined that over 1,400 firearms, 500 vehicles, and 200 pieces of heavy equipment were stolen in the Albuquerque area, and the amount of narcotics on the street was at an all-time high. To combat this problem, law enforcement decided to open an undercover storefront. The storefront opened as a legitimate, functioning used-car lot and auto detailing shop. The operation was a joint effort combining local (Albuquerque police) and federal (FBI) law enforcement. The storefront's initial operating budget for a six-month period was projected at $28,000. Two things occurred to change this figure during the operation. First, the U.S. Department of Agriculture approached us and volunteered two agents and a quantity of food stamps to purchase evidentiary items for an ongoing investigation involving food stamp frauds. Second, because of this welcome addition to the storefront's operating budget and personnel allotment, the operation ran eleven months instead of six.

Throughout this period, this storefront proved to be a lucrative venture in terms of property recovered, evidence obtained, offenders identified, cases made, and intelligence gathered. The operational used-car lot and detailing shop also did well. The officers (operation) made approximately $1,800 on sales of used cars (which were obtained on consignment from a pro-law enforcement used-car dealer) and from the undercover officers' hard work on detailing cars. These proceeds were put back into the operation. There were many times investigators had to turn away legitimate customers to carry on their undercover work.

After eleven months of investigation, the following statistics were tallied. Undercover officers bought

$833,725 in stolen vehicles

$101,000 in stolen electronics

$15,720 in narcotics

$6,100 in stolen or illegal firearms

$700 in stolen or illegal explosives (eighty-four sticks of dynamite and detonators)

$23,642 in cash traded for food stamps, two for the price of one

$980,887 total recovery.

Undercover officers spent

$35,393 in U.S. currency

$50,150 in USDA food stamps

$85,543 total expenditure.

In terms we can all understand, the undercover officers were buying stolen property, contraband, and cash for approximately nine cents on the dollar, on average. No matter where you're from or how skilled your superiors are in mathematics, you'll have to agree that armed with that bottom line you can make a positive point for the use of a storefront. Additionally, all the defendants who were indicted were convicted, and some were convicted in both state and federal court.

YOUR FRIENDLY NEIGHBORHOOD BAR

In another operation carried out in a southern California jurisdiction, undercover officers (local and federal) operated a neighborhood bar that was known for selling more than just booze. By word of mouth, the news spread that the guys who ran the bar would buy stolen goods.

During the nine months the bar was in operation, investigators made in excess of 250 transactions. They bought everything from dancing shoes to machine guns. The officers made it known that they were interested in guns, credit cards, and anything else that could be readily traced. However, as you will find out when you go into business, anything and everything will be brought to you for sale. These officers were particularly surprised at the amount of high-tech property they received. Several thousand dollars in computer chips, microprocessor parts, and hard disk drives were purchased. The operation recovered $1.5 million in property, which included half a million dollars in negotiable securities and travelers' checks.

An impressive total amount of stolen property was recovered for the amount of money that was actually expended. By their own admission, the officers were cheapskates and didn't pay top price for anything. You should follow this example for two reasons. First, if you're too easy, too willing to pay an outrageous price for an item, the crook is going to figure you for a cop or a fool. Second, if you readily pay top dollar, you're going to run out of money fast with few prosecutable cases to show for it.

It is not known exactly how much money the officers spent on purchasing the stolen property in the aforementioned case, but if they were the cheapskates they said they were, the amount of property purchased outweighs the amount spent ten to one. The initial cost of setting up the bar for operation was $39,000.

A key point to be brought to your superiors' attention is the conviction rate. In this particular storefront, the agency had a 100 percent conviction rate. You will find that this is the norm rather than the exception in storefront

cases. The reason for this high conviction rate is fairly simple. All transactions between offender and cop are audio and video recorded, and once
the offender and his or her attorney view the taped transaction, there's not
much of a defense to offer. In fact, you should hear this famous phrase
often: "Your Honor, my client will plead guilty."

THRIFT SHOP IS AN UNDERSTATEMENT

In a Southern jurisdiction, undercover officers purchased 113 automobiles, four motorcycles, firearms, musical instruments, vacuum cleaners,
window fans, chain saws, space heaters, clocks, credit cards, shoes, boots,
digital weighing scales, and an American flag a thief used to wrap his
ill-gotten booty. They paid as little as $500 for a brand-new $15,000
Oldsmobile and $700 for a Buick Skylark. The Skylark was taken directly
off a dealer's lot in another state—however, the thief was kind enough to
leave his name and telephone number. You'll find, in most cases, that once
you have gained the crook's confidence, he or she is willing to give up
necessary information without too much trouble.

The aforementioned storefront, using a thrift shop as a cover, expended
$67,000 in 235 transactions. This amount recovered $2 million in stolen
property, which amounts to spending three and one-half cents on the dollar.
The sixty-five suspects who engaged in business with the storefront officers
let a well-known adage come into play: They let greed outweigh wisdom.

BIG BANG FOR YOUR BUCK

At the intersection of two interstate highways in the Southwest, there
is a truck stop. In this truck stop, not unlike any other truck stop across
the country, a certain subculture thrives. People exist on legal and illegal
activities that are associated with the interstate transportation of goods.
Narcotics, prostitution, theft, and receiving and transferring stolen property
are a few of the illegal activities that take place on a daily basis.

In this jurisdiction, the theft of fully loaded tractor trailers was a
problem. A storefront was established to combat the problem. Its facade
was a salvage office located at the truck stop that bought wrecked trucks
and excess freight. The major go-between was a group of people called
"lumpers," who hang around truck stops and hire out to load and unload
trucks and do anything else to make a quick buck. In time, the word got
out that the salvage office was interested in buying trucks, loaded or un-
loaded, and any freight for a fair price. As it turned out, that fair price was
between $3,000 and $4,000 for a fully loaded tractor and trailer, with the
price varying depending on the freight. The sellers were either truck thieves
or truck drivers who needed some quick cash and were willing to notify

their companies that their truck was stolen. The freight bought, as you can guess, varied from lettuce to a nuclear warhead on a flatbed ready for delivery, destination unknown. The warhead was purchased for a mere $3,500. After this unique purchase, to keep the storefront operational, the truck and its cargo were driven to an isolated area and the proper authorities were notified anonymously. The driver reported it stolen and collected his payoff, the cash on the spot, and some time in one of our federal penitentiaries at a later date. The final result of this sting operation was ninety trucks recovered and eighty-six arrests.

PUTTING IT IN WRITING

Okay, now the hard part: taking all this information and putting it on paper in a clear and concise format that portrays the true advantages of using an undercover storefront. The following format is what we have used in proposing several of our storefronts. We have found it to be successful in explaining our intentions to administrators. Discussing your proposal over coffee with your immediate supervisor is fine and may be a good way to test the waters. However, if your supervisor likes the idea, he or she will probably tell you to put it on paper—that is, prepare a proposal.

Overview

Start with an overview of the operation. This is a statement of the who, what, where, how, why, and when of the operation, just like any other investigative narrative you might write. Basically, you're telling readers that there's a problem and you're going to fix it using a storefront. The readers will be in an investigative branch of your department and/or other agencies that might assist.

In this overview, spell out the problem in detail. If you've done the painstaking research, this section will open some eyes. However, if you have not put in the effort and cannot relay the problem in detail, you may quash the operation.

Objective

This section conveys what major result or results you expect from this operation. You have to be realistic, but your expectations must be worthwhile. You're not going to sell your idea if you say, for instance, that you're going to solve the burglary problem in your jurisdiction by putting all burglars behind bars. More realistically, you might say that your objective is to recover stolen property and identify and prosecute as many individuals as possible who are involved.

This section will also address how you intend to handle cases that arise that are not in the scope of your objectives. For example, are you or your investigative unit going to handle narcotics cases if you are running a property storefront, or are you going to farm out these cases to your narcotics unit? Most likely, depending on the nature of the case, you'll want to hand such cases to narcotics.

Another problem inherent to storefronts, which can be addressed in this section, is what to do with the overly active criminal who may cause critics and lawyers to question whether the storefront created a market for this person. If you have an offender who has sold to you three to four times in a relatively short time frame, then it's time to take him or her off the street. To do this and not "burn" the storefront is a delicate task. We used our repeat offender unit to initiate a surveillance operation in hopes of catching an offender in a crime. Once this is done, and after the offender gets out of jail, storefront officers tell him that because of his arrest it's not safe for him to come to the storefront—because he might bring the police with him and jeopardize the operation. Depending on his character, he might also be told (to appease him) to turn some of his criminal friends on to the operation.

Each operation will have unique circumstances that must be addressed. They should be addressed in this section if they affect the objectives of the storefront. Remember, make your objectives worthwhile but realistic.

Purpose

If you look at the objectives of the storefront as your specific goal, such as putting one individual in jail for making machine guns or putting a group into jail for operating a chop shop, then the purpose of the storefront is to carry on the basic mission of the police department, which is to enforce the laws of the city, county, and state. The only difference is that this enforcement is going to be accomplished using an unconventional method that is proactive in nature as opposed to conventional, reactive methods. In your purpose section, you state that the purpose of the storefront is to infiltrate the targeted criminal element in an undercover capacity to gather intelligence and develop high-quality cases for prosecution.

Feasibility

This section relates that the use of undercover storefronts has a proven track record in successfully identifying, arresting, and prosecuting criminals. You want to brag about your unit's past sting operation results. If this is your first attempt at such an operation, you may want to draw from some of the examples discussed in this book. You also want to let it be known that your unit has the ability to carry out such an operation.

Beneficiaries

As with all law enforcement operations the public is the major beneficiary. Regardless of how the criminal is taken off the street, the victim of the crime benefits as do any people that this offender would have victimized in the future. The total number of people affected by an undercover storefront depend on many variables. However, based on past track records, a successful operation will benefit not only the citizens of the jurisdiction and surrounding jurisdictions but will benefit the departments involved. By using one of the most cost-effective law enforcement tools ever developed, departments will realize a maximum output in regards to quality and quantity of cases developed and prosecuted, with a minimum use of personnel, equipment, and monetary expenditures compared to conventional, reactive law enforcement methods.

Current Progress

This section of the proposal may seem out of place or not belong at all. However, you must accomplish some tasks even before you write up the proposal. The type of unit you work in and what kind of handle your immediate supervisors have on their operating budget will determine how far along you can be in executing the plan to open an undercover storefront.

In the unit we operated most of our storefronts from, the unit, along with supervisors up to the rank of captain, were segregated from the rest of the department, housed in an offsite. This allowed us to know in advance whether the monies were available for a storefront and if the administration would buy the idea. So, by the time we were ready to write the proposal for the higher-ups, we had already picked a site, put down a deposit, obtained furnishings, and collected materials for the undercover facade.

You may or may not have this advantage. If you don't, there are still things that must be accomplished. One of these is the selection of the site. You don't have to go as far as putting down a deposit, but you must have several possible sites selected and know what each is going to cost. You can also start scrounging for materials and props. You'll understand this strategy a little better when you see what is needed in the next section on budget and personnel and what is involved in the selection of a site (chapter 9).

Personnel and Budget

Who and how much? These are two important questions that administrators ask. This section of your proposal should answer the following questions:

1. How many undercover officers are going to work the storefront?
2. What sort of support personnel are needed? (case agent or agents, relief officers, technical support, and surveillance teams)
3. Where is the personnel going to come from—inside the unit, or will we have to draw from other units?
4. What other agencies will be actively involved, and how many agents will they supply?
5. What administrative assistance (clerk/typist) will be required?

In addition to personnel, the operating budget must be addressed. The best way to do this is to list expenditures for a period of six months. This list may include, but is not limited to, the following items (each storefront may have unique expenses):

Building rental (purchase/lease)

Utilities

Telephone

Insurance

Bonding

Supplies, equipment, and materials

Inventory (items for sale)

Evidence expense (buy money)

Overtime (may be covered by department's operating budget).

If there is some other circumstance that affects the budget, this must be stated in this section. For example, if the storefront is a joint operation, the breakdown of how the expenses are going to be shared must be included.

Although this is an estimated budget for a six-month period, or whatever period you decide, it is important that the figures are as accurate as possible and you can back up each figure with documentation. In this age of tight budget restraints, cost overruns are unacceptable.

Undercover Storefront Proposal (Sample)

OVERVIEW

The investigative function of this special investigations unit is a primary focal point of this proposal, the quality of which can make a substantial difference in crime reduction. Law enforcement officials have long recognized the seriousness of the problems of auto theft, burglary, and narcotics violations and the need for constant innovative techniques to combat these problems. The quality of the undercover and support personnel of this unit will make the difference between success and failure of this operation.

Statistical information has been obtained covering a period of approximately eighteen months. In this period, it has been determined that there is a substantial overall percent increase in loss of property through larcenies and burglaries. During the last six months of this period, it has been determined that 1,500 firearms, 650 vehicles, and 225 pieces of heavy construction equipment were stolen in our jurisdiction. Additionally, the amount of narcotics on the street is at an all-time high.

This operation will be a joint effort between our department and the FBI, with our department acting as the lead agency. Because we are going to be working with a federal agency that at times works under a different set of guidelines, it is important that an open line of communications be maintained. It is in the best interest of the ultimate goals of the storefront that the operation be as flexible as possible.

Any problems that arise will be brought to the attention of the immediate supervisor of the department or the FBI so the problem can be addressed in a timely manner.

OBJECTIVE

The primary objective of this proposal is the recovery of stolen property and the identification and prosecution of as many individuals as possible who are involved in the stolen property distribution system. Under this proposal, the property that will be purchased will be primarily limited to firearms, vehicles (preferably four-wheel drives), and construction equipment, which includes heavy motorized equipment, welders, air compressors, etc.

Narcotics violations will be addressed, if applicable, but will usually be referred to another unit or individual for investigation.

The storefront will use the repeat offender squad when an active thief has been identified. The purpose for using this unit is twofold: (1) It will take the suspect off the street, and (2) it will prevent the storefront of being accused of creating a market for the suspects to dispose of stolen property.

PURPOSE

This proposal has three mutually supportive and interrelated elements: the enforcement of related property crimes, narcotics law violations, and intelligence gathering. Criminals, whether they are thieves, narcotics dealers, or fences, are more often than not career criminals. Their organizations or group(s) contain highly skilled, motivated, predator professional individuals.

A majority of law enforcement is reactive in nature; however, this proposal is a proactive approach to the entire scope of the stolen property distribution system. The primary focus of this operation would be to infiltrate this system in an undercover capacity and develop high-quality cases for prosecution.

FEASIBILITY

The special investigations unit has a proven track record of successfully initiating and completing sting operations. The methods used have been adapted by many other law enforcement agencies throughout the nation. The quality of cases presented for prosecution not only to the U.S. attorney, but to many local district attorneys, is evidence of the expertise of the unit. The storefront will be an essential vehicle to enable the unit to infiltrate the stolen property distribution system.

BENEFICIARIES

The total number of people affected by this proposal would depend on several variables, including but are not limited to the number of defendants, the number of crimes committed by each defendant, and the potential number of crimes that will not occur because of this sting operation. Historically, the number of defendants prosecuted in a successful sting operation ranges from fifty to seventy. Usually these defendants are responsible for victimizing between 150 and 300 people. The actual number of crimes prevented through the successful prosecution of these people cannot be accurately assessed. Therefore, the primary beneficiaries of this operation will be the 500,000 plus citizens of the metropolitan area.

PERSONNEL AND BUDGET

In addition to the two full-time undercover agents, at least one FBI undercover agent will be assigned on a part-time basis to operate the storefront. Other special investigations unit personnel and FBI agents will be able to provide technical and surveillance assistance as needed. A full-time case agent will also be assigned.

The following is an estimate of the cost of operation for a six-month period. This length of operation is a variable that may be extended or decreased depending on the actual progress of the storefront.

Building rental	$ 5,400
Utilities @$100/mo.	$ 600
Telephone @$80/mo.	$ 480
Insurance	$ 585
Bonding	$ 200
Supplies (equip./materials)	$ 1,500
Inventory (items for sale)	$ 3,000
Evidence expense	$16,235
Total	$28,000
Overtime	$ 6,000
(Current budget for over-time will cover this amount.)	

The operation expense of the proposal will be shared equally between the special investigations unit and the FBI.

CURRENT PROGRESS

Undercover personnel have rented a building and completed furnishing the premises with materials and equipment. Arrangements have been made with an automobile dealer to take a certain number of vehicles on consignment, and the other aspects of the business are in full operation.

Note: In regard to this proposal, the only other information you may want to add is a copy of the operational guidelines that you will find discussed in chapter 10.

SELLING THE IDEA UP THE CHAIN

If you're like us, the word *sell* makes you cringe. Your first thoughts are of the last used-car salesperson you dealt with, and you don't want anything to do with selling. However, there is one big difference between you and the used-car salesperson. If you've come this far and put the long, hard hours into this project, you must believe in what you're doing and what you're selling—and that's the difference. You can sell what you believe in. But if you have all your facts and figures straight, if you have a plan that is feasible, and if you can show the higher-ups the problem and a solution that will benefit the public and the police department, your idea will sell itself.

CHAPTER 7

Criteria for Selecting Storefront Officers

No matter the size or complexity of a storefront, the personnel selected is critical to the overall success of the operation. When a storefront fails to meet its objectives, nine times out of ten this failure can be directly attributed to the personnel chosen to operate it.

A storefront with all the advantages—unlimited budget, most advantageous location, elaborate cover story, and state-of-the-art electronic surveillance equipment—is more likely to fail when operated by unqualified personnel; whereas the storefront not possessing all these advantages is more likely to succeed when qualified personnel are chosen. In short, the success or failure of your storefront hinges on the personnel selected.

Of all assignments in law enforcement, undercover police work is probably the one job that is least understood. Many may glorify this role as the superagent portrayed on television or in the movies. Others view undercover officers as self-sacrificing people who separate themselves from family and friends for extended periods of time, living within the criminal environment until the conclusion of the investigation. These viewpoints are distorted and unrealistic.

This chapter places you in the hot seat. You may be the person with the ultimate task of selecting the undercover officer(s) who will carry the investigation to a successful conclusion.

THE SELECTION PROCESS

When the storefront operation has been approved by your department or agency, the selection process must begin; you must choose the undercover officer(s). If you are to achieve any degree of success using a storefront technique, you must be able to select personnel who are qualified and capable of carrying out the assignment.

Police work of this nature often does not require any special type of person in terms of appearance or personality, but there are exceptions, and they are discussed later in this chapter. The criteria discussed in this chapter will assist you in the selection of the officer(s) best suited for the operation.

Regardless of the storefront's length of operation, you must look for a certain number of traits in the candidate(s). Along with experience, the candidate must be resourceful and cunning. Good work habits and other characteristics such as maturity, stability, and general attitude must be assessed. Remember, an operative cannot work in an environment alien to his or her personality. Belonging to a certain ethnic group does not automatically guarantee successful performance among these groups.

The Screening Process

As part of the selection process, you may choose to use a screening system to identify the officer(s) most likely to succeed in undercover work. The use of experienced undercover officers in an interview session or an assessment team is desirable. They should possess practical knowledge of department resources, understand the legal responsibilities associated with undercover operations, and be familiar with the personal sacrifices of people who operate in an undercover capacity. This screening process will indicate candidates with potential as well as those who don't have it. The interview should answer the following questions:

1. Has the candidate volunteered for the assignment?
2. What talents or background is required for the assignment, and do this candidate's experiences fit the criteria?
3. How far does the cover story need to go to fit the candidate?
4. What type of environment is best suited to the candidate's personal characteristics?
5. What problems may the candidate encounter during the operation?
6. What is the candidate's current family situation and what effects would the operation have on it?
7. Does the candidate possess common sense?

Posting the Opening

The procedure for selecting your operative(s) should be thorough and equitable. One option is to post a request within the unit or department and specify the qualifications desired, duration of assignment, and method to be used in the selection process.

An Objective and Accurate Process

It is important to provide an objective and accurate method of selecting personnel for assignment as undercover operatives. A formal selection process should be used wherein operatives are selected on a combined basis of previous performance, written test scores, and an oral interview.

The best test of ability to perform is the actual performance itself. However, considerations of morale, time, and the number of potential candidates for the assignment must be considered. Thus, a combination of a written test, past performance, and oral interview is perhaps the most practical and fair method to determine who will be chosen for the assignment.

The Written Test

You may feel that this testing process could exclude candidates who are not able to display their proficiency in writing and that a written test is not without error in identifying prospective candidates who may meet the predetermined requirements. However, if one cannot perform in an objective testing process which requires one to read and observe, analyze and express thoughts in writing under stressful conditions, one lacks some of the qualities needed as an undercover operative.

The testing process is designed to measure ability to reason and to assess the level of knowledge a candidate may have in this field on the basis of comparison with accepted standards. The testing process also requires candidates to study investigative techniques, laws, criminalistics, and other fields related to storefront operations. In this manner, candidates' overall knowledge of investigative procedures is increased.

An effective operative must be able to identify factors that will contribute to the successful conclusion of the operation and be able to write reports that are accurate, complete, and concise. Therefore, the written test should be a standard portion of the selection process.

Previous Performance

One of the initial decisions is the choice between experienced and inexperienced candidates. Whenever possible, experience should prevail, but sometimes it is advantageous to select new personnel because they are unknown to the local community and the criminal element. Remember, however, that the new operative does not yet know the ropes and must be given on-the-job training. Since the operative is inexperienced, closer supervision will be required.

Selecting an officer with too much experience can also create problems. This officer might be too well known, and this could blow the cover story.

In these cases, the officer could be used in a supporting role and on certain occasions could be a buyer or money man.

In either case, it is necessary to consider the candidate's past performance. Of course, inexperienced candidates will not have been involved in undercover operations, but if they have produced quality work in their present assignment or past assignments and meet some of the other criteria, such as confidence, motivation, and common sense, maybe they can fit the role. From personal experience, we have found that many good street cops become excellent undercover cops.

The past performance of a potential undercover operative is usually assessed on the basis of supervisors' evaluations. An in-depth examination of personnel records will reveal strengths and weaknesses of the candidate. Because the success of the operation depends on the candidate's ability to get along with people and win their confidence, negative comments regarding interpersonal relationships should be disqualifying. The personnel record will also provide a measure of the candidate's judgment and reactions under stressful conditions. The more positive the evaluation, the greater the probability that the candidate can accomplish the task with a high degree of success and minimize or avoid unnecessary risk.

Attitude about the Job

Commitment to the particular job and to law enforcement in general should be assessed. Determine if the candidate is willing to make sacrifices in terms of time and effort to get a job done. This factor may seem minor now, but when a storefront is a long-term effort, it will become very important in the operative's life. While commitment is important, the undercover should not be overzealous, but controllable.

For example, the operative may want to pursue a case further than his supervisor feels is appropriate. He must be objective enough to see that regardless of his personal feelings, the supervisor has sound reasons for discontinuing a certain line of investigation. In effect, the undercover officer has to balance commitment and dedication with ability to perceive the job objectively.

Investigative Ability

Examine the cases that the candidate has investigated and the case reports he or she has compiled. Specifically, you are looking for capabilities in interviewing, interrogating, and report writing. Consider ability in clearing cases, perseverance in pursuing investigations, and willingness to participate as a team member.

Decision-Making Ability

The ability to make sound decisions should be expected of the successful candidate. An undercover operative must make split-second decisions based on limited information. An operative working in a storefront making a purchase of weapons, for example, is making decisions that not only pertain to the success of a case but also to his own safety. At the same time, he must be prepared for unforeseen circumstances. Remember that many undercover circumstances cannot be pre-planned, so officers must use a considerable amount of discretion and common sense.

Interest

Select the candidate(s) who has shown an interest in undercover work, but realize that there is sometimes little opportunity to demonstrate this interest. Some of the questions that you may ask during the interview include the following:

1. During the investigation of cases, did the candidate make some effort to dig a little deeper?
2. Has the candidate made an extra effort to assist other officers assigned to case(s) on follow-up?
3. Has the candidate developed intelligence and/or information which has proven useful to other officers or cases and, most important, was that intelligence or information passed on in a timely manner?

Candidates are not going to know everything about acting in an undercover role, but their responses to such questions give an indication of their interest or lack of interest in this line of police work.

Oral Interview

Much of the preceding information can be verified in an oral interview. This demonstrates candidates' ability to respond to spontaneous questioning, much the same as they will encounter at the storefront. It also provides a measure of how well candidates can improvise.

Personality

Versatility in undercover operatives is important. They must be able to shift from one role to another and be able to discard certain idiosyncracies of a police officer and adopt the characteristics of the type of person whose role they are portraying. Undercover operatives should preferably have a variety of life experiences—mixing with different crowds and working varied jobs prior to entering police work. They will have to get along and communicate well with people from various backgrounds. If they never worked, played, or lived around other ethnic groups, they will find it difficult to interact with them and gain their confidence.

Operatives will be effective if they have the ability to be flexible and adaptable. Targets tend to gravitate to their own kind (i.e., burglars, Spanish, Jewish); however, the very nature of their criminal activities frequently causes temporary interfacing of various criminal groups. An operative having assumed one type of role which has achieved acceptance should be able to adapt to a new target if a reevaluation establishes a new group as the primary targets. Once again, experience has shown that conditions at the storefront often change rapidly, and the operative must be able to change with them.

Appearance

The physical appearance of the candidate(s) is important insofar as they should resemble, as much as possible, the type of character being portrayed.

Every department or unit has members who don't fit the public's idea of what a cop should look like. This, along with the ability to cloak oneself in a role, makes a very effective operative. How many times have you watched an individual and, although that person was not wearing a uniform, you knew you were watching a cop? Many police officers behave like the stereotype of a police officer and are not suitable as undercover operatives. Even though physical appearance in itself will not make a good operative, at times it must be considered. It must be compatible with the target group. A storefront designed to infiltrate the KKK would not select black officers; similarly, one designed to infiltrate the "blood" would not select white officers. Using officers whose physical appearance is not compatible with the target group increases the probability that they will not be accepted.

The ideal situation is to use an officer of the same nationality as the role he or she is to assume, especially when the nationality is the same as the target group. This is not absolutely necessary with all operations, but it does provide the operative with something in common with the target. This can be the basis for building credibility with offenders. Experience has shown that the greater the number of things the operative has in common with the target, the easier it is to gain access.

Foreign Language

The need to speak and understand a foreign language will be dictated by the target group. If they exclusively use Spanish as the primary means of communication, it is obvious that the candidate must have a command of that language. However, there are other instances when having a comprehensive knowledge of a foreign language is not necessary. Simply knowing a few social phrases or idioms of that language can be enough to enhance the operative's credibility.

FOR EXAMPLE

If the investigator is to assume an Italian identity, it would behoove him or her to extend greetings in Italian when introduced to someone of that extraction.

Educational Background

Sometimes special education beyond the basic educational requirements to become a police officer is necessary.

FOR EXAMPLE

If the targets are involved in computer program pirating or stocks and bonds conspiracies, the operative should be educated in computer programming and systems development or stock market operations.

Personal Stability

Considering the personal life of the candidate is a very important factor in selection, especially if the operation is long term. Should a candidate's family life be unstable, the stress involved in an extended operation could further deteriorate it. By the same token, a solid family life can be a source of strength.

You must recognize that problems at home may affect job performance. In role-playing during an operation, especially one of any length, officers could change appearance, change the way they talk, and spend a lot of waking hours with the criminal element while becoming adept at being devious. These factors can have a detrimental effect on officers and their family life. A long-term undercover storefront can bring a tremendous amount of stress to bear on the operative. You must consider this issue.

Indebtedness and Integrity

When possible, examine the financial status of candidates. This will reveal those who are clearly living beyond their means and/or determine the extent of indebtedness. It is not necessary or desirable to eliminate a candidate who has financial obligations. However, it is necessary to know the extent of those obligations. The potential for corruption exists in many aspects of storefront investigation. Therefore, it is foolish to select an officer who is so financially burdened that even a small amount of money may be tempting. A storefront officer will be continually handling money. There will always be opportunities to cheat on expense reports, undercover buys, or the purchase of information. The point here is not that corruption or dishonesty is prevalent, just that it could be unwise to place a heavily indebted officer in a tempting situation. Similarly, a candidate whose background indicates questionable integrity should be eliminated. These candidates can be a greater risk than the debt-ridden individual.

The Female Undercover Officer

You must consider female officers as potential candidates. There has been much controversy concerning females and law enforcement work, but experience in our storefronts has proven the value of a female undercover operative. The criminal element becomes very complacent when dealing with a female on a daily basis—they simply do not expect a female to be an undercover agent. The problem, however, is the tendency of male officers to overprotect female officers. Female officers resent this. Again, the time you spend in selecting undercover officers is of utmost importance in reducing such problems, whether you choose men or women.

SUPPORT PERSONNEL

Your need for support personnel in a storefront will vary, but again, the selection process is basically the same as for undercover operatives. The support personnel will be involved with the operation from beginning to end, and in most cases actually will do more than the undercover officer.

In almost all storefronts, you will need at least a technical officer, a case officer, and an evidence officer.

Technical Officer

The tech officer will handle all phases of audio and video surveillance equipment, photography (if required), and, in some cases, hard wiring the site selected. The tech officer *must* be experienced. You cannot afford to waste time once the operation has been approved looking for someone who can capture the evidence needed for successful prosecution.

The tech officer must be someone you can trust not to talk about the job. He or she must know what is expected by the judicial system in your area for successful prosecution of storefront cases. Additionally, the tech officer must be available at the most inopportune times should the need arise for repair and/or replacement of the equipment.

Case Officer

The case officer will, once the purchase or deal is made, do a background investigation on the target. The purpose of this investigation is to identify the target positively. It can and should include past involvement with law enforcement and anything that will assist in the eventual apprehension and prosecution of the target (associates, addresses, phone numbers, etc.).

The case officer will also prepare, as completely as possible, the written case, documenting the daily events in a timely manner. This will reduce the amount of time spent doing documentation at the conclusion of the operation. He or she will also maintain audio and visual tapes and the undercover officer's reports concerning transactions.

Evidence Officer

The evidence officer will collect, preserve, and maintain the chain of evidence obtained during the operation. The evidence officer can do research regarding possible victims and owners of items.

The evidence officer can also return items that are impossible to hold as evidence due to size, value, quantity, etc. to the rightful owners, following agencies' guidelines for later prosecution.

In some instances, case and evidence officers can be used to relieve undercover operatives for needed time off, but this must be done with discretion since new faces are sometimes a hindrance to storefront operations. You may also find that your case and evidence officers' duties will have to be combined due to personnel restrictions in your department or unit. This is a situation you will have to live with.

A VOLUNTEER'S JOB

Assignment as one of the officers in an undercover operation should be voluntary. This ensures the candidate's willingness to participate and desire to make the storefront succeed. Using individuals who do not want to be involved will hamper the successful completion of the operation. Consider the candidates' personal lives, emotional stability, and maturity. They must be able to understand and react to stressful situations in a mature manner and understand the burnout that can occur if one is involved in a long-term operation.

Self-confidence in one's ability to carry out a role to successful completion is another asset, along with the capacity to make a decision and to understand the legal aspects, personal aspects, and agency policy as they relate to the decision.

Specific criteria established by your agency or department, such as commitment, experience, resourcefulness, and specialized skills, should determine those chosen for the job. Candidates' work backgrounds are a critical element of selection. Thus, volunteers with experience as sworn officers are excellent selections. Hopefully you will be able to select officers with a minimum of five years' experience, but this depends on things like department size, background of your officers, and the type of operation.

Remember that difficulties may arise due to the storefront's length of operation. A short-term operation will give more latitude in selection, since few individuals possess the necessary traits to assume a role for long periods of time.

INDOCTRINATION OF THE UNDERCOVER OFFICER

After selecting the candidate, arrange a meeting between the unit supervisor, investigators, and the undercover selectee. This meeting is best conducted away from any police facility and in a place closed to the public. Brief the selectee on the nature of the investigation. At first, speak in generalities and include a description of the role the officer will be expected to play. Then give the selectee the chance to accept or decline the assignment. When the selectee has committed to the storefront investigation, you can reveal additional detailed information.

This does not mean that the operative must know every detail about the target or the operation. Depending on the sophistication of the probe, providing too much information to an operative can jeopardize long-range and/or short-range objectives if the operative is compromised. However, it is important for operatives to know everything about their assignments. Any information beyond the scope of their specific duties should be provided only on a need-to-know basis.

After defining the problem to be addressed and establishing objectives and parameters, you will have a clear idea of who needs to know what. Supply the operative with relevant photographs, physical descriptions, and criminal backgrounds of the target individuals and their associates, when available. Also provide other available information in reference to

1. Hang-outs
2. Residences
3. Vehicles
4. Personal interest
5. Hang-ups

   6. Fringe people.

Provide any information that will enable the undercover officer to better understand the target.

   Give the new member time to study the photos, criminal records, and relationships between the targets. This will provide for immediate recall ability when the operative sees a car, a face, an associate of the target's, etc. Much of this ability will be developed after deployment to the storefront. However, being supplied with available information prior to deployment enables the operative to be effective almost immediately in contributing to the investigation. This will also enable the operative to develop a personal strategy designed to penetrate the target at the most ideal level. This strategy must be compatible with those used by the storefront.

   Before deployment, the operative may need to learn local jargon or the lingo of the target group. Learning after deployment wastes time. Even worse, ignorance may cause the operative to be classified as a square or outsider and could hinder the success of the investigation. You may want to prepare a glossary of appropriate street terms for the new member to study before deployment.

How to Dress

   It may also be necessary during this indoctrination process to discuss dress. The operative must dress and groom in conformance with the facade chosen for the storefront and target environment. Nothing is more contradictory than assuming the role of a high-roller but dressing in a $30 leisure suit. First impressions are often derived from appearance. However, do not expect operatives to buy thousand-dollar suits. When circumstances dictate this kind of appearance, include it in the operational budget. Not many of us have the funds available to purchase expensive wardrobes.

   Nothing can stop the operation or the operative faster than the tell-tale signs of a police officer. These include the following:

   1. Short haircut

   2. Black uniform shoes with civilian clothes

   3. White socks with a dark blue suit

   4. An FOP medallion hanging from a key chain

   5. Uniform belt worn with civilian attire

   6. Departmental standard-issue weapon

   7. Old army clothes (in some groups it means *cop*)

   8. Handcuff key on key chain

   9. Carrying undercover ID in a wallet that has the imprint of a badge.

Do not assume that the new team member knows everything there is to know about undercover work. Expressing what is expected in a friendly, noncondescending fashion will ensure that there are no slip-ups and ensure a productive, cooperative working relationship.

SUMMARY

Without the proper personnel, the storefront will surely flop. So choose a selection process that is objective and accurate. When there are many prospective candidates, you may want to use a prescreening process to identify those most likely to succeed. The selection procedure should include a written test, an oral test, and a previous performance record review. It should examine the following:

1. Job attitude
2. Investigative ability
3. Decision-making ability
4. Personality
5. Physical appearance
6. Personal stability
7. Indebtedness and integrity.

Once the new member(s) of the team is selected, he or she must be indoctrinated into the world of undercover work and the objectives of the storefront. Those participating in this type of investigation should be volunteers. This will allow for a more cohesive team striving for the same results. Remember, most important is that team members be dedicated, hardworking cops who still enjoy the excitement of the chase.

CHAPTER 8

Preoperational Briefing with the Prosecuting Attorney

Legal assistance is an invaluable component of the storefront investigation because the law is complex and there are numerous technical points that could nullify the efforts of the operation. Pleading ignorance will not alter the eventual undesirable outcome. Therefore, avail yourself of legal counsel when possible.

Rapport with the prosecutor's office is indispensable. You should view the prosecutor as a significant member of the storefront team. When the prosecutor provides investigative guidelines, study them carefully and follow them. If you have any concerns about the legality of a particular tactic, consult with the prosecutor's office and obtain legal advice before proceeding.

We have often overheard investigators boast that no lawyer is going to tell them how to conduct their operation. The investigator who makes such a statement is ignorant of the role the prosecutor plays in a law enforcement investigation. Prosecutors are not there to dictate how the investigation is to be managed. They are there to provide legal counsel to ensure that the operation is proceeding in accordance with established judicial guidelines. This guidance contributes to the desired outcome of the storefront and helps you avoid undue criticism.

Before you can conduct an informative and productive preoperational briefing with the prosecutor, you must understand the criticisms of storefront operations. Therefore, in this chapter we discuss:

1. Criticism of other sting operations
2. Critical comments of undercover work in general
3. How to respond to criticism with the help of the prosecutor.

Without being aware of these criticisms, you cannot take the appropriate steps to curtail them.

After you have outlined how to deal with the aforementioned complaints, you can concentrate on specific aspects of the law concerning the storefront, including

1. Entrapment of the target
2. Predisposition of the target
3. Affording opportunity to the target
4. Egregious government conduct.

Again, without a basic knowledge of these legal facets and how they can affect you, you cannot conduct an informative conversation with the prosecutor. How are these crucial legal issues to be reviewed if you are unaware of their importance?

This chapter also includes an example of the instructions given to a jury concerning these legal points. Officers are seldom familiar with the instructions given to a jury deliberating these questions. Recognizing what these issues are will better enable you to conduct the investigation in such a fashion that these technicalities will not affect the outcome.

Finally, we discuss an option that many storefront investigations overlook: the reversal. Fear of using this strategy is caused by misunderstanding its purpose and the legal unknowns. Most storefronts will have the opportunity to use this technique, so do not let it pass by. Discuss with the prosecutor how you can pull off such a sting when the chance presents itself. Then you can demonstrate to supervisors your grasp of the legal aspects involved. Remember, the more aware you are of the criticism and legal issues confronting the storefront, the more meaningful and informative the preoperational briefing with the prosecutor will be.

UNDERSTANDING THE CRITICISM OF STING OPERATIONS

Undesirable public attention is often focused on all types of sting operations, including the storefront, because of the widely publicized shortcomings of a small number of sting investigations. To better understand the criticism, we discuss several examples. ABSCAM and the John Delorean case are probably the two most infamous examples. Unfortunately, there are others:

Operation Grey Lord was a sting operation in which agents attempted to divulge the suspected massive corruption in the Cook County courts. Subsequent to the investigation, a Chicago judge was acquitted on bribery charges.

Operation Colcor, critics claim, influenced voters in a North Carolina town to conduct a referendum which resulted in the legalizing of liquor sales. This was achieved through bribes given to suspect politicians by agents.

Operation Recoup, was an attempt to apprehend auto thieves in Illinois. The FBI conducted an undercover sting which assisted the alleged culprits in legitimizing stolen vehicles. The vehicles were then placed on the market for resale. Agents reportedly knew this activity would result in unsuspecting auto buyers incurring monetary loses.

Operation White Wash was a sting operation in which California agents organized a painting establishment to probe kickbacks to labor unions. No criminal charges were filed in connection with this investigation. However, legitimate businesses maintain that they endured considerable financial strain as a direct consequence of this operation.

Operation Corkscrew was a five-year probe of Cleveland judges who were suspected of corruption. Critics cite this operation as a textbook example of the dangers inherent to such undercover operations. Agents were deceived by a bailiff who they assumed would try to bribe judges with funds provided by them. However, the bailiff retained the funds for his own personal use. No judges were indicted, but the integrity of the entire court system may have been damaged, according to a subcommittee of the House Judiciary Committee.

Operation Falcon involved agents from both the United States and Canada. It was designed to reveal those involved in an alleged worldwide black market dealing in birds of prey. Detractors claim the probe violated sections of the Endangered Species Act that prohibits this sort of activity. Section 9(g), which is in question, states, "It is unlawful for any persons subject to the jurisdiction of the United States to attempt to commit, or cause to be committed, any offense defined in this Section." Critics point out that even though the most notorious offenders were found guilty, the minor penalties imposed on them and the willingness of the prosecutors to settle for these lenient plea bargains demonstrate the true nature of the operation. Critics also say the United States Fish and Wildlife Service was not truly concerned with the criminal activity—they merely used the sting to bolster their conviction record. The confidential source employed by the operation also met with many of the same disparaging remarks as did the source used in the Delorean case.

Criticism of Undercover Work in General

Never mind the good that might have come from these operations; the focus has been on their misfortunes. Some other criticism that we have encountered includes the following:

1. Undercover work, even though it is very effective, is a dangerous technique that has suddenly become too pervasive in law enforcement. With the current inadequate guidelines, someone can be offered an opportunity to commit a crime even though no reasonable suspicion has been established that the person is already engaged in such activity.

2. There must be more focus on the conduct of undercover agents since they often engage in activity that causes ordinary, law-abiding citizens to commit a crime. Under current guidelines, once there is evidence that a defendant was induced to commit an offense, the prosecution must prove that the defendant was predisposed. This focuses on the defendant's state of mind, which is often difficult to establish. It allows people to be convicted who should not be.

3. People are being coaxed into committing crimes by agents threatening harm, manipulating personal circumstances, and providing otherwise unavailable opportunities for crime.

4. Innocent people are being harmed by monetary losses incurred as a direct result of undercover activity.

5. Personal rights are likely to be violated when agents act on information that is received from an informant who has a criminal record and unclear motives.

6. Undercover probes are not cost effective. Taxpayers are burdened with the high price of these investigations and the prosecution of innocent people who just happened to be caught up in one of these overzealous probes.

7. The present regulations governing entrapment allow law enforcement to lure law-abiding citizens into criminal activity.

8. Law enforcement has gone too far in its attempt to combat crime. Undercover operations are more suspect than the supposed criminals they are pursuing.

9. Law enforcement uses undercover techniques to test the honesty of apparently innocent citizens. Undercover techniques should not be used to tempt the community.

10. Undercover operations, with their lack of operational guidelines, haphazard selection of operatives, and inadequate supervision, place the safety of officers and the rights of citizens in danger.

We cannot stick our heads in the sand and pretend this type of disapproval doesn't exist, or assume that the elimination of undercover operations will stem the flow of unfavorable remarks. Much of the criticism aimed at undercover activity could also apply to the more conventional methods—for example, the use of radar or airplanes to catch speeders. Fooling ourselves into thinking that all critical comments are baseless and only uttered by those who don't understand and appreciate the complexities of our profession will only lead to more criticism.

Responding to the Criticism with the Prosecutor's Help

As difficult as it is, we must recognize our contributions to these criticisms. We have influenced this critique by not always being completely prepared and fully aware of judicial guidelines. Some of our actions have led to these censures, whether these actions were intentional or unintentional, even though the motives were honorable at the time. By ignoring such disfavor we will only increase its intensity, which will lead to even more restrictive legislation. In being aware of criticism, we can meet it head on. We can stem criticism if we are properly prepared and understand judicial guidelines. This is why it is of the utmost importance to include the prosecutor as a member of the investigative team. Discussing these drawbacks before the investigation is operational will prevent us from adding to the problem and ensure the storefront's triumphant outcome.

ENTRAPMENT

Entrapment is probably one of the most misunderstood terms in law enforcement today. It must be addressed before opening doors for business. Remember, the prosecutor should be a member of the team. His or her guidance in this complex issue can prevent an unwanted surprise at the conclusion of the storefront—that all your hard work and effort was for naught because the targets got off on a legal technicality.

The information which follows was derived from the notes of Richard G. Lillie, Assistant United States Attorney, Northern District of Ohio, and Rhonda P. Backinoff, Assistant United States Attorney, District of New Mexico. These notes were compiled for all federal prosecutors and law enforcement officers to assist them in the preparation and handling of undercover investigations. When reading this information, keep in mind that your local jurisdiction may have more restrictive guidelines. Each independent jurisdiction can place additional restraints on law enforcement; however, these restraints cannot be less restrictive than the federal guidelines.

Entrapment Defined

1. *Entrapment* means that law enforcement officials, acting either directly or through an agent, induced or persuaded an otherwise unwilling person to commit an unlawful act.

2. The defense of entrapment prohibits law enforcement officials from instigating criminal acts by otherwise innocent people in order to punish them.

3. Thus, the inducement of an individual to commit a crime not contemplated by him or her, for the purpose of instituting a criminal prosecution, constitutes entrapment.

Inducement by law enforcement officials may take many forms:

1. Persuasion
2. Fraudulent representations
3. Threats
4. Coercive tactics
5. Harassment
6. Promises of reward
7. Pleas based on need
8. Sympathy or friendship

A solicitation, request, or approach by law enforcement officials to engage in criminal activity, standing alone, is not an inducement. Law enforcement officials are not precluded from utilizing artifice, stealth, and stratagem, such as the use of decoys and undercover agents, to apprehend people engaged in criminal activities, provided that they merely *afforded opportunities* or *facilities* for the commission of the offenses by one predisposed or ready to commit it.

The defense of entrapment therefore consists of two elements:

1. Acts of persuasion, trickery, or fraud carried out by law enforcement officers or their agents to induce a defendant to commit a crime
2. The origin of the criminal design in the minds of the government officials rather than that of the innocent defendant.

However, when a person is *predisposed* to commit an offense—that is, ready and willing to violate the law—the fact that government officials or their agents merely afforded opportunities to do so does not constitute entrapment.

There are four major Supreme Court decisions which deal with entrapment. The first two decisions deal with entrapment as a matter of law.

1. *Sorrells v. United States*[1]

Supreme Court first recognized and applied the entrapment defense in *Sorrells*.

In *Sorrells,* a federal prohibition agent visited the defendant while posing as a tourist and engaged him in conversation about their common war experiences. After gaining the defendant's confidence, the agent asked for some liquor, was twice refused, but, upon asking a third time, the defendant finally capitulated and was subsequently prosecuted for violating the National Prohibition Act.

The court found that the defendant had not been predisposed to commit the crime and had been entrapped. The validity of the entrapment defense was held to focus on the intent or predisposition of the defendant to commit the crime, and not on the behavior of the government agents.

"If the defendant seeks acquittal by reason of entrapment, he cannot complain of an appropriate and searching inquiry into his own conduct and predisposition as bearing upon that issue."[2]

2. *Sherman v. United States*[3]

The Supreme Court expressly reaffirmed the entrapment defense in *Sherman*.

In *Sherman*, the defendant was convicted of selling narcotics to a government informer. As in *Sorrells*, the government agent gained the confidence of the defendant and, despite initial reluctance, the defendant finally acceded to the repeated requests of the agent to commit the criminal act.

On the basis of *Sorrells*, the court reversed the affirmation of the defendant's conviction, finding that he had been entrapped; and again the court focused on the predisposition of the defendant to commit the crime.

As Chief Justice Warren stated, "To determine whether entrapment has been established, a line must be drawn between the trap for the unwary innocent and the trap for the unwary criminal."[4]

Basically, then, these cases hold that the key issue is whether or not the individual is predisposed to commit the crime. If the defendant introduces evidence of government inducement, the government must establish the defendant's predisposition to violate the law. Finally, it is clear that if the government merely affords the defendant *an opportunity to commit the offense*, his or her defense of entrapment will fail. In adopting this subjective approach to entrapment, a majority of the court rejected the views of the minority, who proposed a more objective test, in which the focus would not be on the defendant's state of mind but rather on the government's conduct. Under this approach, if the government's conduct was regarded as outrageous, then the defendant could not be convicted of the crime.

Outrageous Government Conduct

The following examples deal with the issue of outrageous government conduct. They are provided to give you a sense of the court's view of such activity.

1. *United States v. Russell* [5]

In *Russell,* an undercover agent infiltrated a drug ring, supplied the defendant with the chemical ingredients necessary to manufacture the drug, and participated in the manufacturing process.

The lower court in *Russell* found that the government's methods constituted outrageous government conduct, that the defendant was entrapped, and that his rights to due process had been violated.

The Supreme Court declined to put the government's tactics at issue, stating that the "defense of entrapment was not meant to give the Federal judiciary a 'chancellor's foot' veto over law enforcement practices of which it did not approve." [6]

The court reiterated that the proper focus of the entrapment defense was on the predisposition of the defendant to commit the crime, for if this were not done, and there were no reply to a defendant's claim of inducement, it might then become impossible to secure convictions of any offenses which consist of transactions that are carried out in secret.

The court thus took issue with courts of appeal which had gone beyond *Sorrells* and *Sherman* to bar prosecutions on the basis of overzealous law enforcement tactics.

2. *Hampton v. United States* [7]

In *Hampton* (according to the defendant), a confidential informant supplied the defendant with drugs which undercover agents later purchased from the defendant.

The court affirmed the defendant's conviction and again noted that the entrapment defense "focus[es] on the intent or predisposition of the defendant to commit the crime, rather than upon the conduct of government agents." [8,9]

Thus, the court once again ruled out the possibility that the defense of entrapment could ever focus on alleged governmental misconduct in a case such as *Hampton* in which the predisposition of the defendant to commit the crime was firmly established.

Indeed, the court suggested that where "the police engage in illegal activity in concert with a defendant beyond the scope of their duties, the remedy lies, not in freeing the equally culpable defendant, but in prosecuting the police under the applicable provisions of state or federal law." [10] The *Hampton* court refused to extend the concept of entrapment beyond *Sherman* and *Sorrells.* However, the court stated in *Russell,* [11] "We may someday be presented with a situation in which the conduct of law enforcement agents is so outrageous that due process principles would absolutely bar the government from invoking judicial processes to obtain a conviction,

. . . the instant case is distinctly not of that breed." In *Hampton*, the defendant did not rely on a traditional entrapment defense, but rather, relying on the aforementioned language in Russell, he argued that his conviction should be reversed based on a violation of due process. In affirming the conviction, three justices expressed the view that *Russell* did not expand the defendant's rights beyond the traditional defense of entrapment. Two concurring justices rejected the concept that due process principles could never bar the conviction of a defendant to whom the traditional entrapment defense was not available, no matter how egregious the conduct of the government, but held that the government's conduct in this case did not violate due process. Three dissenting justices, who adhered to the views the dissenters had expressed in *Sherman* and *Sorrells*, held that the focus should be on the government's conduct rather than the defendant's state of mind and concluded that the conviction should be reversed. Thus, a majority of the court in *Hampton* appeared to hold that under appropriate circumstances a defendant's convictions might be subject to reversal on due process grounds, regardless of his or her predisposition.

The Due Process Argument

Although the Supreme Court has not addressed this issue since *Hampton*, the due process defense has been raised by defendants in many cases. Only a few courts of appeals since *Hampton* have found any particular set of facts so indicative of egregious government misconduct as to justify reversal of a conviction. See, for example, *United States v. Twigg*,[12] where, notwithstanding the defendant's predisposition to commit the crime, the court found that the nature and extent of police involvement was so overreaching as to bar prosecution of defendants as a matter of due process.

The *Twigg* case was an investigation conducted by the United States government which delved into the manufacturing of controlled substances. At the behest of the DEA, government agents suggested the establishment of a speed laboratory. The government gratuitously supplied about 20 percent of the glassware and indispensable ingredients. It also made arrangements with chemical supply houses to facilitate the purchase of the remaining materials which would be needed in the manufacturing process. Government agents actually purchased almost all of the supplies. In addition, the government provided an isolated farmhouse well suited for an illegal laboratory. Neither defendant had the independent know-how with which to manufacture methamphetamine.

Evidence of Predisposition

There are two questions of fact:

1. Did the agent induce the accused to commit the offense charged, and if so;
2. Was the accused ready and willing to commit the offense and simply awaiting an opportunity to do so? Provided the inducement exercised by the agents was not outrageous, the only issue then becomes that of the accused's predisposition.

Proving Predisposition

1. Like and similar acts: Under *Sorrells*, once an accused raises the defense of entrapment, he or she cannot then complain of "an appropriate and searching inquiry" into his or her own conduct.[13]
   a. The bad acts should be similar to or "morally indistinguishable" from the charged crime.[14,15]
   b. The bad acts may have occurred before or after the charged crime. When a defendant commits a bad act shortly after the charged crime, it is probative of his or her subjective disposition as well as giving insight into the sort of person he or she is.[16,17,18]
2. Reputation evidence: In the Sixth Circuit, reputation evidence must be proved in the normal fashion (i.e., the agent or witness must have firsthand knowledge). Hearsay may not be used.[19,20] Moreover, only evidence of character which tends to show a predisposition to "willingly engage in the specific criminal conduct involved" in the charge is admissible.[21]
3. Miscellaneous criteria for proving predisposition:
   a. The defendant's initial suggestion of the crime
   b. The defendant's readiness to commit the crime
   c. The defendant's familiarity with the criminal activity
   d. The defendant's possession of illegal contraband prior to the alleged entrapment
   e. The defendant's ready access to the contraband
   f. The defendant's ability to collect a large quantity of contraband in a short time
   g. The defendant's in-court testimony and admissible out-of-court statements.
   See also *United States v. Lasvita*[22] and *United States v. McLernon*[23] for other factors relevant to determining predisposition.

4. Ready acquiescence: A defendant's predisposition to commit the offense can also be inferred from evidence that he or she readily acquiesced in the commission of the proposed offense. (See ABSCAM cases later in this chapter.)

ABSCAM Cases

Although the facts in the ABSCAM cases varied somewhat from one to another, the essential scheme was as follows:

FBI agents set up a fake corporation, Abdul Enterprises, supposedly representing two Middle Eastern sheiks who were interested in investing considerable sums of money in the United States. The Bureau put out the word on the streets that money was available, through the use of a professional con artist, Melvin Weinberg. The Bureau let it be known that the sheiks were interested in emigrating to the United States and that money was available (specifically $50,000 for a senator or $25,000 for a member of Congress) for those who would be willing to help the sheiks with any immigration problem. Several members of Congress and one senator took the bait. Several initially refused the money and had to be persuaded to accept it. Some, in fact, were coached by Weinberg on what to say in their meetings with the sheiks' supposed representatives, who were Bureau undercover agents.

Entrapment defenses were raised in all of these cases, as well as due process arguments based on the language in *Russell* and *Hampton*. In all cases, these contentions were rejected by the several circuits that heard them, and ABSCAM was approved as a valid investigative technique.[24–29] Similar contentions have been raised and rejected in other non-ABSCAM federal cases involving undercover operations.[30,31] The analysis applied by the various courts in these cases is summarized by the court in *Myers:*[32]

> *The appellants' claim of excessive governmental involvement in the instigation of criminal conduct is not supported by the facts. Though the sting was surely elaborate, its essential characteristic was the creation of an opportunity for the commission of crime by those willing to do so. The government produced people with fictitious identities ready to pay bribes to members of Congress. Word of the availability of bribe money was made known. From that point on, the essential conduct of the agents and their paid informants was to see who showed up to take the bribes and videotape them in the act of doing so. Whatever may be the due process limits of governmental participation in crime, it was not reached here (citing Hampton, Russell, and other cases). Even with regard to the coaching of some of the defendants by Weinberg, the Third Circuit held that this hardly constituted an inducement, stating, "If the script was supplied, no one was coerced into playing his part."[33]*

In addition, the ABSCAM courts rejected the contention that the operation should have been limited to members of Congress to whom the government had probable cause to believe had previously engaged in criminal activity.[34,35] Indeed, the court observed in *Jannotti* that "official corruption, in the form of bribery and extortion involving public officials, can, like the narcotics sales involved in *Hampton*, easily elude detection, since both parties to the transaction have an interest in concealment."

In this connection, some comments by the court in the non-ABSCAM case of *United States v. Brown*[36] put the matter in the proper perspective:

Law enforcement officials are often presented with a formidable problem when they become aware of the criminal activity of individuals who are involved in a large criminal enterprise. The alternatives presented to those officials are exceedingly poor. They may arrest known criminals, thus ceasing their particular harmful effect on society; or they may allow them to continue in their violation of the law with the hope that further investigation will reveal a greater number of those involved in the criminal enterprise, the exposure and arrest of whom may effectively eliminate a much broader range and degree of criminal activity.

This is the dilemma confronted by the FBI agents in charge of the HAMFAT investigation. They were compelled to decide whether to arrest Frazier and Campbell when their criminality became known, or to delay those arrests with the prospect of casting a larger net and of eliminating a much broader range of criminality. This problem reasserted itself periodically as evidence accumulated sufficient to arrest and convict other members of the ring.

The difficulty of the problem was exacerbated by the fact that either alternative chosen would result in some harm to society, for the choice of either alternative results in the continuing criminality of some members of the ring. Once the burglary ring began its criminal operations, an event the government had nothing whatsoever to do with, a certain amount of harm to society was an inevitable result. Faced with this situation, the government was forced to choose an alternative that, in its judgment, would result in the least amount of harm. This type of decision is effected by a multitude of varied and subtle considerations with which law enforcement personnel are only to familiar. Nothing in the record before us indicates that the FBI erred so dramatically in their decision in the instant case that the fundamental canons of due process were violated.

Defendant Claiming Entrapment Must Admit Offense

The defense of entrapment relates to the inducement of an accused to commit a crime which he or she was not predisposed to commit. It has been uniformly held in the Sixth Circuit that the defense of entrapment is not available to one who denies the commission of the offense, since the invocation of a such defense necessarily assumes that the act charged was committed. It is inconsistent for an accused to claim that he or she did not commit the acts charged and to simultaneously say that he or she was entrapped into committing those acts.[37–41]

Entrapment Is Not Properly Raised in a Motion to Dismiss

A defendant may not raise the defense of entrapment in a pretrial motion. Whether the defendant was entrapped by actions of the government is a factual issue. The existence of a factual issue precludes the defendant from raising the issue of entrapment in a motion to dismiss.

The defense of entrapment was not permitted to be raised by way of a pretrial motion in *United States v. Leighton*.[42] The court, without extensive discussion, denied such attempt, stating the following:

> *The defense of entrapment is an issue for the jury where an issue of fact is presented (citations omitted); I cannot see how such a defense can be the proper subject of a pretrial hearing, especially since the defendant, even if he were to establish entrapment as a matter of law, would be adequately protected against an adverse jury verdict by the trial court's ability to enter a directed verdict of acquittal. . . .*[43]

Government's Proposed Jury Instruction on Entrapment (with Brief)

Understanding the memorandum on the law in a criminal case could assist you in overcoming any potential conflicts. The following is an example of a brief.

THE ISSUE OF ENTRAPMENT MUST BE SUBMITTED TO THE JURY

The issue of entrapment may only be decided by the trier of law when disputed facts establish a lack of predisposition on the part of the defendant.

> *Entrapment is established as a matter of law only when the lack of predisposition is apparent from the uncontradicted evidence.*[44]

The court further stated in *Sherman* that

> *Unless it can be decided as a matter of law, the issue of whether a defendant has been entrapped is for the jury as a part of its function of determining the guilt or innocence of the accused.*[45]

It has been further held that participation by the government in affording the defendant the opportunity to commit an offense does not establish entrapment as a matter of law.

> *. . . only when disputed facts establish that the criminal design originated with the government agent, that the agent implanted in the mind of an*

innocent person the disposition to commit the offense, and that the de-
fendant then committed the offense at the urging of the government agent,
can we conclude that entrapment was established as a matter of law.[46]

Repeated interactions with a government agent do not prove entrapment as a matter of law. In *United States v. Esquer-Gamez,*[47] a showing of as many as twenty opportunities before the defendant produced a controlled substance did not require a finding of entrapment as a matter of law. The question was for the jury.

The government has shown evidence in the present case of the defendant's predisposition to commit the offenses charged. When evidence of predisposition exists, entrapment cannot be established as a matter of law.[48]

Evidence of predisposition exists in the present case; therefore, the question of entrapment is to be decided by the trier of fact.

THE DEFENSE OF ENTRAPMENT IS TO BE CONSTRUED SOLELY ON THE QUESTION OF PREDISPOSITION

An examination of the defendant's predisposition to commit the offenses charged is the single focus of an entrapment defense. Quoting Justice Stevens in *Hampton v. United States:*[49]

> *I agree with the plurality that Russell definitively construed the defense of*
> *"entrapment" to be focused on the question of predisposition. "Entrapment"*
> *should now be employed as a term of art limited to that concept.*

It is important to note that the predisposition of the defendant may be inferred from the circumstances themselves.[50]

Predisposition on the part of the defendant in the present case may be inferred from his speedy replies to the government's letters. In *United States v. Tobais,*[51] the court considered the defendant's quick response to an inquiry as to his interest.

The most important element of predisposition was noted in *United States v. Kaminski.*[52] The court noted that "the most important element of the equation is whether the defendant was reluctant to commit the offense."[53]

The defense of entrapment focuses on whether the government's actions implanted the criminal design in the otherwise unpredisposed person.[54] What is at issue is the predisposition of the defendant and not the actions of the government agent involved. The entrapment defense "focuses on the intent or predisposition of the defendant to commit the crime,[55] rather than upon the conduct of the government's agent."[56,57]

The only issue of relevance in the instant case is the defendant's predisposition to commit the acts charged.

THE DEFENSE OF ENTRAPMENT IS NOT ESTABLISHED WITH THE SIMPLE SHOWING OF A GOVERNMENT AGENT'S PARTICIPATION IN THE CRIMINAL SCHEME

Governmental participation in the commission of a crime cannot be the basis for an entrapment defense. This was noted in *Sherman v. United States*.[58] The court stated,

> *That government agents merely offered opportunities or facilities for the commission of the offense does not constitute entrapment.*[59,60]

This line of reasoning is echoed in the Sixth Circuit cases of *United States v. Hencair*[61] and *United States v. Eddings*.[62] The court in *Eddings* noted

> *The appellant appears to be under the impression that entrapment is established if the accused shows only that the criminal scheme originated in the mind of the government agent. Such is not the law. In Sorrells v. United States,[63] the court stated that the defense of entrapment is not simply that the particular act was committed at the instance of government officials.*[64]

The primary focus remains on the predisposition of the defendant to commit the acts charged and is not affected by participation of the government through its agents in the criminal scheme.

If there is an adequate showing of predisposition, even repeated attempts to tempt the defendant will not prove to be entrapment. In *United States v. Fletcher*,[65] it was held that when there is an adequate showing of predisposition, there may be a conviction even though government agents make repeated attempts to tempt the defendant.

It remains, then, that the only issue of consequence in the present case is the defendant's predisposition to commit the acts charged, and not the actions of the government agents participating in the criminal scheme. The question of entrapment lies within the domain of the jury.

EXTENSIVE CASE LAW EXISTS DETAILING THE INSTRUCTIONS APPROPRIATE TO GIVE JURORS ON THE ISSUE OF ENTRAPMENT

An examination of case law dealing with jury instructions on the issue of entrapment is appropriate in the present case. Whereas the issue of entrapment must be submitted to the jury, the following case law sets forth previously decided issues in the content of jury instructions on the subject of entrapment. It has been held that the defendant is not entitled to an instruction which would permit the jury to determine the fairness of a government agent's counterfeiting ring.[66]

As applied to the present case, the defendant is not entitled to an instruction which would permit the jury to determine the fairness of the government agent's undercover operation.

It was held in *United States v. Williamson*[67] that a defendant relying on entrapment is not necessarily entitled to a special instruction with respect for his or her reputation for not engaging in the conduct charged against him or her. Nor is such instruction proper in the instant case. By the same token, the defendant is not entitled to an instruction that the government must show prior convictions or prior violations in order to overcome the entrapment defense.[68]

Where the defendant admits all essential elements of the offense, but for his or her claim of entrapment, and rests his or her case on that issue, the jury may be instructed that the only issue is that of entrapment.[69] Furthermore, it was held in *United States v. Paduano*[70] that there was no prejudicial error in telling the jury that the defendant, in defending on a claim of entrapment, had admitted the presence of the essential elements of the offense, when he did so as a matter of trial strategy. Such instructions would be proper in the case at hand.

Regarding government participation in the criminal scheme, case law is extensive. It was held in *United States v. Rubio*[71] that it is proper to tell the jury that the use of informers and undercover agents is not improper. Further, it is not improper to tell the jury the legitimate purposes of law enforcement officers.[72] Nor is it improper to instruct the jury about the need of law enforcement officers for certain undercover activities.[73]

All the aforementioned cases are applicable to the case at hand. The court is not limited to this. The court is acting properly when it advises the jury that the government might use stratagems, artifices, ruses, undercover agents, and fictitious names in order to discover violations of the criminal when the defense indulged in constant suggestions that such practices were improper.[74] This situation exists in the present case, and such instruction would be proper.

All the foregoing case laws may be drawn on for formulation of jury instructions on the issue of entrapment.

GOVERNMENT'S PROPOSED JURY INSTRUCTION

In light of the foregoing case law, the government submits the following as proposed jury instruction for the issue of entrapment in the case at hand.

The following jury instruction is taken from the District of Columbia Criminal Jury Instructions, third edition, in applicable part, and has survived the test of appeal in the case of *United States v. Burkley.*[75]

The government proposes this jury instruction for use in the case at hand.

Note: The following is an example of the instructions given by the court to the jury. When *you* is used, it refers to members of the jury.

JURY INSTRUCTION

Evidence has been introduced that the defendant was the victim of entrapment to the offenses charged. As used in the law, *entrapment* means that law enforcement officials, acting either directly or through an agent, induced or persuaded an otherwise unwilling person to commit an unlawful act. On the other hand, where a person is predisposed to commit an offense, that is, ready and willing to violate the law, the fact that government officials or their agents merely afforded opportunities for him or her to do so does not constitute entrapment.

Inducement by law enforcement officials may take many forms, including persuasion, fraudulent representations, threats, coercive tactics, harassment, promises of reward, or pleas based on need, sympathy, or friendship. A solicitation, request, or approach by law enforcement officials to engage in criminal activity, standing alone, is not an inducement. Law enforcement officials are not precluded from utilizing artifice, stealth, and stratagem, such as the use of decoys and undercover agents, in order to apprehend people engaged in criminal activities, provided that they merely afforded opportunities or facilities for the commission of the offenses by one predisposed or ready to commit them.

If you should find from the evidence in this case that before the alleged offenses occurred, government officers or their agents did no more than offer the defendant the opportunity to engage in criminal conduct, there is no entrapment. On the other hand, if you find evidence in this case that the defendant was induced to commit the offenses charged, you must go on to consider whether or not the defendant was predisposed to commit the offenses, that is, whether he was ready and willing to commit crimes such as are alleged in the indictment, whenever an opportunity was afforded.

In determining whether the defendant had a predisposition to commit the crimes charged, you need not find that he was involved in any prior offenses or criminal conduct. Predisposition may be shown in many ways. The defendant's predisposition or willingness to commit the crimes charged may be shown by evidence of his prior conduct of a similar character or by evidence direct or circumstantial that he was ready and willing to engage in the illegal conduct in question. In evaluating this matter of predisposition, you should look to the totality of the circumstances involved in the alleged offenses with which the defendant is charged.

In summary, then, if you find no evidence that the government induced the defendant to commit the crimes with which he is charged here, there can be no entrapment. On the other hand, if you find evidence that the defendant was induced to commit the offenses with which he is charged, you must then go on to consider if the defendant was predisposed to commit such offenses. If you find beyond a reasonable doubt that the defendant was predisposed to commit such offenses, then you should find the defendant was not a victim of entrapment. However, if the evidence in the case leaves you with a reasonable doubt whether the defendant was predisposed to commit the offenses, then you must find him not guilty.

As demonstrated by the foregoing material, there are a vast number of legal challenges that may arise from a storefront investigation. Having a fundamental understanding of these issues before they are raised will assist you in overcoming these potential legal hurdles. This basic knowledge will also allow for a more productive interaction between you and the prosecutor.

THE REVERSAL IN UNDERCOVER OPERATIONS

In the preoperational meeting with the prosecutor, it may be advantageous to discuss reversal. A reversal is negotiated to sell contraband rather than to buy it. Contraband, when referred to in this context, is usually drugs, but it does not have to be. Any item that is contraband on its own can be used. For example, some firearms and explosives are illegal to possess. These could be used for this purpose. Stolen property, on the other hand, in most instances will not meet the legal requirements for a reversal. Discussing with the prosecutor what contraband can be used is all part of the preoperational briefing.

Why talk about reversals at this meeting? Most storefronts will have an opportunity to carry out this technique. When you prepare for this technique, you will get more from it. We have funded entire storefronts using this method and have organized them specifically for this purpose. Operations such as these have resulted in millions of dollars seized by law enforcement. Storefronts are not only organized to spend money—they can be organized to make money.

The reversal technique sometimes includes furnishing a small amount of contraband as a sample prior to delivery of the full amount. When the full amount is delivered, it is immediately followed by the arrest of the suspects. Most controversy surrounds the fronting of a sample to the target.

Also, since there is a simultaneous arrest, the storefront must be planned for this purpose, be willing to forgo other activity to pursue this case, or plan to use this technique near the end of the operation, which will not interfere with the original objectives.

Of common concern to administrators and some prosecutors is the underlying legality of this approach. Their concern also extends to the protection of officers from criminal liability for their participation in this type of undercover activity. After all, they are selling contraband. This alone causes some administrators to be initially hostile to this enforcement technique.

The following discussion could help you to dissuade this hostility and carry on an informed and productive meeting with the prosecutor.

Delivery of Contraband by Officers

The primary question is, is this activity an unlawful act? Is the offer for sale and/or delivery of a controlled substance or contraband as part of a reversal a violation of the law? The answer is no, it is not an unlawful enforcement technique. There is no criminal intent on the part of the officers. For conduct to be defined as criminal, that conduct must be more than just forbidden by law. The forbidden act must be committed with a criminal state of mind, thus criminal intent.[76] Jury instructions on this general principle have been approved by every circuit.[77]

Certain undercover activities in enforcing the law necessarily involve the commission of forbidden acts. For example, you negotiate to purchase contraband which will be one of your major undertakings at the storefront. The negotiations necessarily include an agreement to commit a criminal offense. You have agreed to purchase contraband. This agreement is an act forbidden by law. But since you make the agreement to thwart the criminal venture, you lack criminal intent and cannot be charged. In another example, when the contraband is delivered, you take possession. Possession of contraband in itself is an act forbidden by law. Yet you cannot be charged with unlawful possession because you took control of the item in question without any criminal intent.

The same applies for distribution of contraband: Criminal intent must be shown. An offer for sale and/or delivery of contraband as part of a reverse undercover operation is made only pursuant to a legitimate investigation into the criminal activities of the target. As such, it is made without the criminal intent necessary to charge you with unlawful distribution of contraband. It has long been held that a suspect cannot be charged with conspiracy when the only other partner to the agreement is an undercover officer. Therefore, you cannot be charged with conspiracy for conducting a reversal. Judge Griffin Bell stated in *United States v. Sears,*[78] "As it takes two to conspire, there can be no indictable conspiracy with a government informer who secretly intends to frustrate that conspiracy."

The United States Supreme Court has repeatedly held that a generally worded statute that imposes restrictions on behavior does not impose those restrictions on the government. This is unless the statute contains some clear expression that it was meant to apply to the government.[79]

Investigator Discretion

When a small amount of contraband is given as a sample, this is a decision to continue the investigation and not arrest the offender at the time. This is a legitimate exercise of mandated investigator discretion. Enforcement of any set of laws includes the setting of goals and the exercise of a certain amount of discretion to meet those goals. This includes the ability to continue an investigation until those goals have been reached, even though probable cause for arrest may already have occurred. This not only applies to reversals, it applies to almost all cases worked by the storefront.

FOR EXAMPLE ──────────────────────────────

You overhear a conversation at the site between two targets that they will burglarize a business and deliver the stolen property to another subject two days later. This subject is a main objective of the operation. You elect to continue the investigation and make no arrest until the delivery is made two days after the theft. The decision not to terminate the investigation by arresting the two targets at the time of the offense is a legitimate exercise of your discretion in conducting an effective investigation. You cannot be charged with aiding and abetting the theft simply because you permit it to occur and make no arrest until after the goal of the probe is reached.

To Seize or Not to Seize

Nothing in the Constitution requires officers to seize people or property immediately. This is emphasized by the United States Supreme Court in *Hoffa v. United States*.[80] Offenders scream at you all the time about their rights, but there is no constitutional right to be arrested. You are under no constitutional duty to call a halt to a criminal investigation the moment you have the minimum evidence to establish probable cause.

Hoffa dealt with the seizure of a person (arrest), but the rule applies to property as well. Letting contraband walk by not seizing it at the first opportunity does not violate the law. Similarly, nothing in the U.S. Constitution prohibits officers from furnishing contraband when it is necessary to infiltrate the target.[81] This practice always creates the risk that the contraband will reach the streets. So, even though the Supreme Court has not addressed this precise issue, the possibility that law enforcement-furnished contraband will reach consumers creates no constitutional problems.[82]

One method that is commonly used to reduce this risk is replacement of a noncontraband item for the bulk of the delivery. A small amount of the real thing must reach its destination if the technique is to be successful. A successful example of this occurred in New York. Investigators substituted 47 pounds of lactose for a shipment of what was originally 48 pounds of heroin.

Establishing Guidelines with the Prosecutor

Certain factors should be discussed with the prosecutor in establishing guidelines for a reversal. Before contraband is allowed to walk, consider these points:

The kind of contraband

The amount that will be fronted

The likelihood of the contraband reaching citizens or consumers

The number of suspects

The suspects' importance

The need for more evidence

Time required to obtain evidence

The likelihood of obtaining evidence.

The first three factors relate to the potential harm to citizens or consumers. The remaining factors relate to the investigative need to let the contraband walk. Guidelines should include that only after proper administrative and prosecutor review, and only when a proper balance of factors has been established, will the investigation continue. However, nothing in the guidelines should prohibit officers from letting contraband walk, provided the procedures outlined in the guidelines are followed and approval is granted.

Letting contraband walk to pursue a reversal should be done only in extraordinary investigations and only after established guidelines have been followed. When this is routinely done and without proper guidance, it could jeopardize reversal as an investigative tool. A reversal in which contraband is shown but not allowed to walk is far more advantageous, and the potential for controversy is reduced. Discuss the reversal technique with the prosecutor in the preoperational briefing, so at the appropriate time it can be properly and confidently employed.

SUMMARY

To obtain the utmost effectiveness from the storefront, include the prosecutor in the entire process of the operation. When the prosecutor is involved in the preoperational briefing, a solid foundation can be established to prevent offenders from eventually getting off on a technicality. The prosecutor will be able to offer invaluable assistance at this stage and throughout the investigation. The prosecutor can

1. Offer guidance in preventing civil litigation
2. Warn of proposed investigative techniques that could lead to judicial conflicts
3. Ensure that proper legal safeguards are being instituted
4. Guarantee that all established judicial guidelines are followed
5. Update investigators about the prevailing tendencies in the courts
6. Inform officers of defense tactics that are likely to be used and methods by which they can be overcome
7. Assist in compiling documents that need approval by the courts, such as search warrants, court orders, arrest warrants, and other orders needed for special electronic surveillance
8. Provide guidance which will instill confidence in investigators to use reversal techniques when appropriate
9. Help ensure that the entire operation, from start to finish, is conducted within established judicial guidelines.

With the ever-increasing complexities in today's judicial issues, the prosecutor should become an even more intricate member of the storefront team. Many jurisdictions already require approval from the prosecutor before initiating an undercover investigation. Even if this is not a requirement of your department, do not overlook this valuable asset.

CASE CITATIONS

1. *Sorrells v. United States*, 287 U.S. 435 (1932).
2. *Id.*, at 451.
3. *Sherman v. United States*, 356 U.S. 368 (1958).
4. *Id.*, at 372.
5. *United States v. Russell*, 411 U.S. 423 (1973).
6. *Id.*, at 435.
7. *Hampton v. United States*, 425 U.S. 484 (1976).
8. *Id.*, at 488.
9. Quoting from *Russell*, at 429.

10. *Id.*, at 490.
11. *Russell*, at 431-32.
12. *United States v. Twigg*, 588 F.2d 373 (1978).
13. *Sorrells*, at 451-52.
14. *United States v. Williams*, 705 F.2d 603 (2nd Cir. 1983).
15. *United States v. Bramble*, 641 F.2d 681 (9th Cir. 1981).
16. *United States v. Moschiano*, 695 F.2d 236 (7th Cir. 1982).
17. *United States v. Carreon*, 626 F.2d 528, 535 n.14 (7th Cir. 1980).
18. *United States v. Jiminez*, 613 F.2d 1373, 1376 (5th Cir. 1980).
19. *United States v. Ambrose*, 483 F.2d 742 (6th Cir. 1973).
20. *United States v. Hairrell*, 521 F.2d 1264 (6th Cir. 1975).
21. *United States v. Ball*, 428 F.2d 26 (6th Cir. 1970).
22. *United States v. Lasvita*, 752 F.2d 249 (6th Cir. 1985).
23. *United States v. McLernon*, 746 F.2d 1098 (6th Cir. 1984).
24. *United States v. Kelly*, 707 F.2d 1460 (D.C. Cir. 1983).
25. *United States v. Williams*, 705 F.2d 603 (2nd Cir. 1983).
26. *United States v. Meyers*, F.2d 823 (2nd Cir. 1982).
27. *United States v. Carpentier*, 689 F.2d 21 (2nd Cir. 1982).
28. *United States v. Alexandro*, 675 F.2d 34 (2nd Cir. 1982).
29. *United States v. Jannotti*, 673 F.2d 578 (3rd Cir. 1982).
30. *United States v. French*, 683 F.2d 1189 (8th Cir. 1982).
31. *United States v. Bagnariol*, 665 F.2d 877 (9th Cir. 1981).
32. *Meyers*, 692 F.2d, at 837.
33. *Id.*, 692 F.2d, at 843.
34. *United States v. Meyers*, 692 F.2d, at 835.
35. *United States v. Jannotti*, 673 F.2d, at 603-7, 609.
36. *United States v. Brown*, 635 F.2d 1207, at 1214 (6th Cir. 1981).
37. *United States v. Lamonge*, 458 F.2d 197 (6th Cir.), *cert. declined*, 409 U.S. 863 (1972).
38. *United States v. Shameia*, 464 F.2d 629 (6th Cir.), *cert. denied*, 409 U.S. 1076 (1972).
39. *United States v. Kilpatrick*, 477 F.2d 357 (6th Cir. 1973).
40. *United States v. Mitchell*, 514 F.2d 758 (6th Cir.), *cert. denied*, 423 U.S. 847 (1975).
41. *United States v. Smith*, 584 F.2d 759 (6th Cir.), *cert. denied*, 441 U.S. 922 (1978).
42. *United States v. Leighton*, 265 F. Suppl. 27 (S.D. N.Y.), *cert. denied*, 390 U.S. 1025 (1968).
43. *Leighton*, at 36.
44. *Sherman v. United States*, 356 U.S. 369, 373 (1958).

45. *Sherman*, at 377.
46. *United States v. Ambrose*, 483 F.2d 742, 746 (6th Cir. 1973).
47. *United States v. Esquer-Gamez*, 550 F.2d 1231 (9th Cir. 1977).
48. *United States v. Wilbur*, 545 F.2d 764 (1st Cir. 1976).
49. *Hampton v. United States*, 425 U.S. 484, 492 (1976).
50. *Walker v. United States*, 334 F.2d 795, 796 (1st Cir. 1965).
51. *United States v. Tobais*, 662 F.2d 381 (5th Cir. 1981), *cert. denied*, 455 U.S. 1108.
52. *United States v. Kaminski*, 703 F.2d 1004 (7th Cir. 1983).
53. *Kaminski*, at 1008.
54. *United States v. Russell*, 411 U.S. 423 (1973).
55. *Russell, supra*, at 429.
56. *Hampton*, at 488.
57. *United States v. Russell*, 411 U.S. 423.
58. *Sherman v. United States*, 356 U.S. 369 (1958).
59. *Sherman*, at 372.
60. *Sorrells v. United States*, 287 U.S. 435 (1932).
61. *United States v. Hencair*, 568 F.2d 489 (6th Cir. 1977).
62. *United States v. Eddings*, 478 F.2d 67 (6th Cir. 1973).
63. *Sorrells v. United States*, 287 U.S. 435 (1932).
64. *Eddings*, at 71.
65. *United States v. Fletcher*, 487 F.2d 23 (5th Cir. 1973), *cert. denied*, 416 U.S. 958.
66. *United States v. Gonzales*, 539 F.2d 1238 (9th Cir. 1976).
67. *United States v. Williamson*, 424 F.2d 353 (5th Cir. 1970).
68. *United States v. Martinez*, 488 F.2d 1088 (9th Cir. 1973).
69. *United States v. Conversano*, 412 F.2d 1143 (3rd Cir. 1969).
70. *United States v. Paduano*, 549 F.2d 145 (9th Cir. 1977).
71. *United States v. Rubio*, 709 F.2d 146 (2nd Cir. 1983).
72. *United States v. Mattoni*, 698 F.2d 691 (5th Cir. 1983).
73. *United States v. Sonntag*, 684 F.2d 781 (11th Cir. 1982).
74. *United States v. Fera*, 616 F.2d 590 (1st Cir. 1980), *cert. denied*, 446 U.S. 969.
75. *United States v. Burkley*, 192 U.S. App. D.C. 294, 291, F.2d 093 (1978), *cert. denied*, 440 U.S. 966.
76. *United States v. Bush*, 599 F.2d 72 (Ca.-5, 1979).
77. *United States v. Greene*, 442 F.2d 1285, 1288 (Ca.-10, 1971).
78. *United States v. Sears*, 343 F.2d 139 (Ca.-5, 1965).
79. *Hancock v. Train*, 96 S. Ct. 2006 (1976).
80. *Hoffa v. United States*, 87 S. Ct. 408, 417 (1966).

81. *Hampton v. United States*, 96 S. Ct. 1646 (1976).
82. *United States v. Campa*, 474 F. Supp. 507 (S.D. Fla. 1979).

CHAPTER 9

How to Select a Site
for a Stationary Storefront
and Prepare It for Operation

Hopefully, by now you have received at least a verbal OK to go ahead with the storefront project. However, now is not the time to start looking for an area of town and site. If you are one of the primary investigators or undercover officers, you should have been at least thinking of areas that would be most conducive to your planned operation. Maybe you have chosen or at least looked at several sites that would fit your storefront.

Probably one of the best ways to get initial ideas for site selection is to sit down with all the investigators that have been involved so far with this project and pull from their experience and expertise.

Let's digress for a moment. Remember in chapter 7, on selection of storefront officers, the discussion on the use of experienced over non-experienced officers? The use of experienced officers, with some exceptions, is preferable. During site selection, you will find that the experienced officer will have a lot more to contribute, and his or her experience will be invaluable in briefing all involved on the sites being considered for the storefront.

Your discussion group should include the undercover officers, the case officer, the evidence officer, the tech officer, and the immediate supervisor responsible for the operation.

Discussion should start with restating the objectives of the storefront. This is necessary to put everyone on the same thought level. Then remind everyone of the type of target the storefront is after and the type of property or contraband that is to be purchased. In addition, everyone must know what facade the storefront will be using. Will it be a small business, industrial in nature, or a service-type business? Will it be fully operational, with the undercover officers doing the work, or will it be just a front? Or will the storefront be a house or apartment? Then take suggestions from the group, first on areas of town, and then on specific sites. Make a list of these suggestions. Then discuss as a group the pros and cons of each area and site listed. Remember, paramount in this selection process is, Will the area and site attract the type of people you have targeted?

FOR EXAMPLE ───

If you have targeted car thieves, you shouldn't expect them to come into a residential area to deliver their ill-gotten merchandise. Or, if your targets are burglars, they are not going to come to a shopping mall carrying VCRs, TVs, or stereos. They are going to come to an area which is close to where they live and feel comfortable about, perhaps an older building in a combination transient residential and industrial area. You have to think as they do and scope out all the ways you, as a crook, could get caught holding contraband, and then decide if the risk of doing business at this location is worth it. If you think this way, you are more likely to come up with a good area and site for your operation.

During this initial meeting, you will probably narrow down the area, but you'll probably have to go shopping for a specific site.

SEARCH FOR THE SITE

After this initial selection meeting, it's time to go shopping. At least you and the tech officer should go. Your supervisor should come along if his or her schedule permits.

You know that the undercover officer must be a primary in site selection because of his or her in-depth knowledge of the operation, but you may be somewhat bewildered about why the tech officer should help choose the site. Your tech officer, whether in house or borrowed from another agency, will look at the site selections in a different perspective. He or she will look at the utilities—in particular, the electric service into the property and its location throughout the site—and the location of the telephone lines.

Tech officers have several responsibilities in site selection. First, they must be able to set up the audio and video surveillance equipment so it obtains the best possible physical evidence of your transactions to ensure a prosecutable case against your targets. This can only be accomplished if there is a nonjeopardizing covert location for the equipment. You'll find out after looking at the possible sites that some do not meet this criteria and will have to be scratched from the list. Others would meet this criteria with some major renovations, but these renovations may not be allowed by the property owner and may not be within your operating budget. Second, tech officers are responsible for the security of the equipment installed, so they may have to install a security system. This installation is highly recommended for obvious reasons.

Third, in considering the location of this equipment on site, tech officers must appraise how easy or difficult it is to reach the equipment once it's in place. They must maintain the equipment to avoid costly malfunctions and repair the equipment should a malfunction occur. In addition, undercover officers frequently need access to the equipment during their daily routine. They'll have to change tapes during the operation.

Your Site and the Neighbors

When you bought your first house or moved into your first apartment, one of the first things you considered was the neighborhood and your potential neighbors. You must do the same thing when searching for a storefront site. However, you must also ask yourself a few questions.

Does the operation that you plan to insert into a neighborhood, whether urban, rural, suburban, residential, industrial, or commercial, fit the surroundings? You must be able to answer this question affirmatively. Does the site meet your operational objectives of being able to attract and do business with the targets? Does the site abide by all state and local zoning laws? Have someone research your potential sites for the type of enterprises that can be inserted. Don't find out the hard way that you've set up your storefront in a no-storefront zone.

Will your storefront interfere with the neighborhood? We discussed this question in chapter 3 when we talked about recognizing the liabilities of operating storefronts. You do not want to be responsible for bringing criminals into a neighborhood. You don't want to cause any problems for two reasons. First, because of the liability aspect, and second, because you want to run a low-key operation that draws little attention—but the right attention from the right people. We're not saying that you can't run an operation in an upstanding, crime-free neighborhood, because you *can* if you control the people you're dealing with by laying a good professional foundation when you start meeting these people.

Will the neighborhood interfere with your storefront? Attracting the wrong type of people to your operation is always a possibility. Depending on the type of storefront you're operating and its location, you'll get a variety of visitors who are not potential targets. Once you've determined that your visitor is not a target, you must get rid of this person as quickly as possible without arousing suspicions. A simple statement that you have all the work you can handle at this time should suffice. You may even refer the person to a similar business (competitor).

Another neighbor problem you may encounter is the "nosy neighbor." This can cause serious problems. It can jeopardize the storefront if this person believes you are doing something illegal based on the amount and type of traffic coming and going and wants to be a good citizen and report this situation to the police. We confronted this situation in a storefront set up in a combination small business and sleazy motel district. We learned that a motel manager was watching our storefront and had contacted the FBI and our department in regard to the situation. He believed that we were buying stolen property. The storefront was an operational auto detailing shop. How he arrived at this conclusion is unknown. He may have had contact with some of the people we dealt with and thought he'd take advantage of the situation, or he may have just watched long enough to see some seedy characters coming and going in vehicles that all the detailing in the world would not help. An investigator from another unit, who knew of the storefront's operation and dilemma, contacted him. The investigator played along and asked him to continue to watch and report this to this investigator in a timely manner. The investigator told him that he would look into the operation and advise him of the situation. This seemed to appease the man, and he felt he was doing the community a service. He continued to make his reports to the investigator for a short time after and then lost interest because he didn't see anything unusual any more. The investigator reinforced his observations by saying that the detailing shop was legitimate.

Will this site offer the undercover officers security? This may be a difficult question to answer for the simple fact that the nature of the storefront puts the officers automatically in some peril. Besides that, the neighborhood where you will find and attract career criminals is not going to be anything like Rodeo Drive. However, you must consider security because you don't want to set up in a neighborhood that's out of control, either. You want your storefront to attract targets; you don't want it to become a target. Your officers must be able to carry on business without having to worry constantly about assaults or robberies or their cars being stripped or stolen while they're in the storefront. If the site is somewhat safe, then you'll find that it will become safer as you start to deal with the criminal element. The word will get out to the others that the storefront is a righteous place to do business and not to mess with it.

The Site and Surveillance

You must consider this aspect of the operation. The storefront must be somewhat easy to conduct surveillance on, for the following reasons.

During the purchase of contraband, stolen property, or weapons it may be necessary to cover the undercover officers if they feel the person(s) they're dealing with poses an unusual threat. This could happen when dealing with a large quantity of narcotics or weapons where a lot of money is involved, or when the undercover officers find themselves dealing with a psycho. In either case, it may be advantageous for these deals to take place at another location where the officers are afforded a better tactical advantage. However, this opportunity may not be available, so the ability to watch the storefront is essential. Another reason to consider surveillance is that it may become necessary to follow the targets from the storefront once a deal has been done to gain more intelligence on the target or to make an arrest.

Without knowing the type of operation you're planning or anything else about your city, it is impossible for us to tell you whether a site will be conducive to surveillance. But surveillance is an important aspect of site selection, and we have therefore devoted a chapter to it (chapter 12).

Exterior Security

The last thing you want to happen to your storefront is a burglary. You might as well pack it in if burglars have attained access to your files, secure room, or tech room. You can and should assume that if this happens your cover and thus your operation is blown.

To prevent burglary, the site you are considering must be burglar proof or designed in such a way that making it secure is possible and within your budget. Exterior fencing, alarms, sturdy locks, and wrought iron on the doors and windows are some of the things you need to consider when looking at a site. If the site doesn't have these items, you must determine what it's going to cost to install these items and make the site secure. Also, if you have to add these items, the landlord or property owner must agree to it.

Besides making the storefront secure for the hours it will be closed, a secure building during operation does two things. It offers undercover officers peace of mind from unwanted entries. Even more important, it offers crooks peace of mind and puts them at ease because they are in a secure building where their detection and identity while doing business are protected.

A word of caution: The storefront must be secure, but it must not look like Fort Knox. This would scare away targets. You must come up with a happy medium that attracts the burglars but deters burglaries.

The Floor Plan

When surveying possible sites for your storefront, after you consider exterior needs, you must consider your needs inside the building. A few things are required.

Secure Room

This is a locked room where you can keep police reports, logs, police equipment, extra weapons (shotgun), playback equipment for reviewing tapes, and a desk for writing reports and filling out logs. This room should be secured such that if a break-in were to occur it would be very difficult to enter this room. On several of our storefronts this room had a steel door and was almost like a safe. During the hours of operation this room was locked even if one of the officers was in it working.

Tech Room

This room may be encompassed into your secure room, but if it is not it must be as secure, for obvious reasons. This room will hold your audio and video recording equipment. In most cases this will include two video-cassette recorders, one for the court copy and the other a working copy, telephone recording equipment, and a supply of video and audio tapes. In addition, this is probably the best place to install your alarm system control box. However, if a room is not available and you don't want to combine your tech room and secure room, you may find that a closet will work just as well for the technical equipment. On one occasion, we had to install our VCRs in a crawl space above the meeting room and use a ladder to retrieve the tapes. What an inconvenience, but there just wasn't any other way to do it without a major renovation.

Office and Meeting Room

This room is your stage, this is where the crimes occur. If this room is not planned properly, this is where your operation will fall apart. This room is not going to be anything special. Any room of a business can be made into the meeting area. If it's a residential storefront, the most likely choice would be the living room, but probably any room would do except the bathroom. If it's a business, an office away from the general customer area would be ideal. This allows crooks to feel more comfortable because they're not going to be interrupted or seen by anyone else. In deciding on a site and looking at a room as the possible meeting room, the arrangement of surveillance equipment (camera and microphones), furniture, security measures, and props should be discussed with the tech officer. We discuss setup of this room later in this chapter.

Waiting Area

The waiting area is just that, a place for potential buyers and sellers to wait. This area can be a room, a garage, or a hallway out of earshot of the meeting room. It is just a staging area where the crook can wait so the undercover officer can prepare for the meeting or finish a meeting with someone else. It should not be an area to discuss business and should not become a gathering place for your clientele to discuss each other's business.

Bathrooms

Notice that the heading is plural. Why? It's not because you must have a boys' and girls' room under law because you are dealing with both male and female crooks. It's because you and your partners don't want to catch anything but crooks. One of our rookie undercover officers let a hype use our bathroom because the other was occupied. After he had left, we learned that he had used the room to fix, left blood in the sink and on the commode, and thrown his used needle in the trash. Needless to say, our rookie became Mr. Clean for the day and scrubbed that bathroom. You should consider having two bathrooms in the storefront, but it is not a necessity.

Utilities and Telephone Lines

In most instances, when you rent or lease a property for a residence or business, all the utilities are present. But make sure. Don't assume that you have water, electric, or gas. We have looked at places that had no utilities or only some, and if we had we not checked we would have been in a fix. If you find a place that is missing something as essential as utilities, I'm sure arrangements can be worked out with the property owner or his or her agent to correct the problem.

The type of services available may be also something to consider when looking at a site. You may need a certain voltage of electricity to run the operation, or you may find that bottled gas is the only way to heat the building and you may not want the delivery of such interfering with the operation.

Regarding telephone service, it's nice to have two phones set up—one for normal business operation and the other a private number given out to active targets so when they call with information on their latest endeavors you are able to record the conversations.

Securing the Lease or Rental Agreement

Let's say that you have found a few possible sites that meet your needs. What do you do next? With a good cover story, you reapproach the property owner or landlord and try to come up with an agreement that is acceptable to both sides. This may take some negotiating if you have to make renovations such as adding wrought iron, installing locks, cleaning and painting, or building walls. Usually, almost any renovation that adds to the value of the building will be acceptable to the property owner, or landlord, and sometimes they'll even foot the bill for materials. If you can come up with an agreement and the price is right, have it put in writing. If you can't, then go to your second choice and try again.

Once you've secured a building, the fun really starts. It's time to roll up your sleeves and get your hands dirty.

SITE PREPARATION

You've all heard the old adage, "If you want a job done right do it yourself." You will find this statement truer than ever when you start preparing the site, and you'll find that doing this job yourself will accomplish several things. First, the more you can do the more money you will save, which means more money for buys. Second, the less outside help you require the less chance of the operation being compromised. And third, this is going to be your home away from home for the next several months. You know what is needed to make the site a workable environment which will be advantageous to the operation and all involved.

General Maintenance and Preparation

This is where you get your hands dirty. It may be necessary to clean and paint the site. If everyone involved chips in, the job can be accomplished in a short time and some costs can be deferred.

Security Installations

This includes security both inside and outside the storefront. Depending on your site, it may include the following:

Fencing: If you're going to run a business that extends outside, such as a used-car lot, then, depending on the neighborhood, you may have to fence in your property. This is a huge expense, so keep that in mind when shopping for a site.

Wrought iron grating: Let's face it, no building is completely secure; if someone wants to get in, they eventually will. To minimize this urge to enter, we suggest that you install wrought iron grating over all your doors and windows. Again, this is an expensive item, but if you shop around you may find someone in your department who does this kind of work, as we did, thus cutting the cost immensely.

Alarms: Here you have a multitude of options and a wide variety of price ranges. Our only suggestion is that you do install an alarm and that it be tied directly to the police department, as opposed to a private alarm service. However, the people at the department who receive the alarm need not know that it belongs to a police operation, just another business.

Locks: Install your own and try not to spare expense on this item, especially on the doors to the tech room and secure room.

Office and Meeting Room: If your meeting room is an office, we have a few suggestions: (1) Be able to lock the office door to prevent unwanted entries during meetings; (2) have targets sit in a chair or sofa that puts them at a disadvantage, for instance a soft, overstuffed chair that they fall down into and have trouble getting out of or moving around in; (3) have a place for a weapon in or under your desk that you can get to quickly in case of trouble; and (4) have some sort of prearranged signal with your partner so that he or she can assist if trouble arises.

If your meeting room is a counter area, as in so many storefronts, you might want to make a portion of the counter bulletproof so you can fall behind it. Install bars so no one can come over the counter. You can also consider installing a button alarm in or under the counter and a two-way mirror behind the counter.

Helpful hint: With all the publicity that storefronts have gotten (including in the movies), it is important that you try not to use the same approach or methods that have been used in the past. Crooks aren't dumb—they watch movies and TV, and some of them have already been victims of a storefront.

Remodeling to Meet Your Needs

You may find that it is necessary to do some minor remodeling such as moving or creating a wall or two, putting in some false air vents or registers, or dropping a ceiling. Again, it shouldn't be a major expense and most likely you can find someone who has the know-how to do such a task. Basically, the reason for such an undertaking would be to accommodate technical equipment (camera, microphones, and recording devices).

Installation of Technical Equipment

This task should be accomplished by your tech officer. Hopefully, he or she is somewhat experienced in this sort of operation and can give you the best possible application. The tech officer's installation is going to have to agree with your daily routine, so work together on the audio and video setup.

We are by no means technical wizards or experts on technical equipment. However, from our experiences we can relay some information that may help you in this aspect of the storefront.

Microphones

These are little electronic devices that pick up sound—not just the spoken word, but *all* sound.

We opened a storefront in the summer months which continued well into the winter. We lost a few good target episodes in the first day of cold weather because we had installed our mikes next to a heating duct, and when the heat came on the conversation was totally blocked out by what sounded like a 747 taking off.

In a similar situation, we sat with a crook in our office with all the doors and windows shut due to traffic noise and the air conditioner shut off because we realized the mike was in the wrong place just before the deal and we didn't have time to change it. The office temperature got up to 110 degrees, and the crook kept telling us to open up the doors or windows if the air conditioner was broke. We ended up having to make up a story to appease him.

Another thing we learned was that the microphones picked up a buzz when they were placed too close to neon lights. I'm sure that there are probably a thousand other things that can go wrong.

Cameras

Cameras make storefront cases unbeatable *if* you get the picture. The key to this, regardless of where you make your covert installation of the camera, is to test, test, test. Set it up and run it under all conditions you can think of. Daytime, lights on, lights off. Different hours of the day. Don't find out, as we did, that in the morning the video was great but at 1:00 in the afternoon the sunlight through the window washed out the picture completely. Test at night with all the lights on and again in low-light conditions. Then one final test: Take your samples and run them on the equipment that is going to be used in court.

Helpful hint: Make sure your date and time indicator is correct at all times. Do not forget daylight savings time and power failures if there is no battery backup.

Recording Devices

Installation of your recording devices should be handled by your tech officer. Both VCRs and the telephone recorder should be in one place so there is easy access to the tapes.

In this high tech world, you can always count on one thing: If something can go wrong, it will. To alleviate the possibility of losing valuable evidence, at least audio, due to an electrical failure, have on hand a backup system. Place a battery-operated tape recorder strategically in the meeting room before the deal. If it happens to be a stormy day, or if this is an extremely important deal, this backup can keep you from losing valuable evidence.

Switches

You must be able to turn equipment on and off at a moment's notice, so your tech officer must install remote switches that are easily accessible and don't look like remote switches. We have found that using ordinary light switches near and around our work area worked just fine. If the storefront is large, you may want to have several switches installed that turn on and off the equipment (camera, VCR).

The telephone recorder should be automatic. Do not forget to have two recordings—original and working copy.

Telephones

The storefront can operate using one telephone, and you may find that the installation of another line is costly. In our area, it cost about $500 for a business line. However, if you can, have two lines, one for normal business and the other hooked up to a recording device for your special calls.

Warning! The misuse of telephone recording devices is a quick way to go to jail. You must know the laws in regard to recording telephone conversations, which are very similar to the laws of recording on audio or video in person-to-person conversations with the consent of one of the people. (More on this in chapter 12.) The term *consenting party* is important to remember when recording telephone conversations. The best way to explain this is by example.

Example 1: You as the undercover officer receive a call from or make a call to a target, and he indicates that he has just committed a burglary and would like to bring the goods by to sell.

Question: Could this conversation have been recorded?

Answer: Yes, you may because you have one party's consent and the crook assumes that you will not relay this information to the police.

Example 2: You have a CI working for you, and he agrees to make a call to a target. During the call, the target implicates himself in a crime.

Question: Could this conversation have been recorded?

Answer: Yes, again because you have one party's consent, but get this consent in writing.

Example 3: You are working with a target in the storefront, and he asks to use the phone to call another target. You consent to the phone call.

Question: Could this conversation have been recorded?

Answer: If you remain in the room with the caller, one side of the conversation can be recorded: that of the target in the room with you. The telephone recorder must be shut down and the recording made on the hard mikes in the room. If the caller wants his privacy for the call and you leave the room, then everything must be shut down, telephone and VCRs. In this scenario, there is an expectation of privacy by the crook and you do not have one party's consent.

If you have any doubts about recording telephone conversations, it is always best to get an opinion from the prosecutor before you make a costly mistake.

FURNITURE AND PROP SETUP

You must treat this task as if you were a producer or director making a motion picture. That's exactly what you are doing, in essence, and the setup of your furniture and props, which may include a multitude of items, should be carefully planned. You must orchestrate your furniture and props so the crooks have to sit in front of the camera. Obviously, you can't tell targets to sit in a certain chair, and you can't put X's on the floor and tell them to stand on the X. You have to keep them from leaning on walls out of camera view, maybe by hanging plants or pictures. Don't have coffee or end tables in a location where targets can sit on them; put items on these tables so using them as a place to sit is impossible. Have your camera positioned so only the crook is viewed and not the officer. Test your setup with other officers and see if they'll automatically sit in front of the camera. If you're using an office as your meeting area, if you have only two other chairs or maybe a sofa in the room so when you sit behind the desk the crook has to sit there, that's where the camera should be focused. If your storefront is residential, this poses a more difficult problem because if you have only two chairs in your living room it's going to look suspicious. It may take some additional thought on your part to get the right picture. Use your imagination.

We conclude this chapter with a checklist of items we have used in our storefronts that may or may not suffice for your operation but will give you an idea of what to use.

SECURITY ITEMS

1. Alarms

2. Wrought iron

3. Locks

4. Fencing

5. Bullet-proof counter

6. Fire extinguisher

7. Flashlights

8. Tinting on windows

9. Curtains (got ours from Goodwill)

POLICE ITEMS

1. Reports and logs

2. Portable police radio with charger

3. Shotgun

4. Personal weapons

5. Binoculars

6. File cabinet

TECHNICAL EQUIPMENT

1. Videocassette recorders (at least two)

2. Camera(s)

3. Microphones

4. Playback equipment (TV)

5. Telephones

6. Telephone recording device

7. Battery-operated body recording device

OFFICE EQUIPMENT

1. Desk

2. Chairs

3. Typewriter

4. File cabinets

5. Ledgers

6. Copier

7. Office supplies (stapler, paper clips, notebooks, etc.)

PROPS

1. Signs

2. Business cards

3. Ad in phone book

4. Ad in trade papers

5. Ad in newspapers

6. Furniture

7. Rugs

8. Lamps

9. Special equipment to fit the facade

10. Family pictures (phony)

11. Trophies and plaques (no marksmanship trophies, please)

12. Trade books and magazines to fit facade (not *this* book!)

13. Scales and drug testing kit (Clorox)

CREATURE COMFORTS
  1. Coffee pot
  2. Microwave oven
  3. Refrigerator
  4. Portable air conditioner
  5. Portable heater
  6. Portable generator in case the site loses power

MISCELLANEOUS SUPPLIES
  1. Cleaning supplies (brushes, brooms, detergents, air freshener)
  2. Paper products (toilet paper, paper towels, disposable coffee cups for crooks)
  3. Hose, lawnmower if needed

I'm sure there's more that can be added to this list, especially if you start to consider the different types of storefronts, but this is a start.

SUMMARY

When considering a location, consider the following:

1. Will the site be conducive to meeting the stated objectives?
    a. Will the area and site attract targets?
2. Does it provide for officer safety?
    a. Will it become a target?
3. Does it fit within budgetary constraints?
4. Is it compatible with technical needs?
5. What is the impact on the neighborhood?
    a. What is the neighborhood's impact on you?
6. Does it lend itself to surveillance?
7. Is there exterior security?
8. Does the floor plan meet your needs?

Site preparation will probably be accomplished by you. Take the time required to ensure that it is completed properly. Remember, this will be your home away from home for an extended period of time. Along with the necessary preparation to create your "film studio," do not forget creature comforts. These simple items make it a more pleasant, and therefore a more productive, atmosphere.

CHAPTER 10

How to Develop an Operational Proposal for Administering a Storefront

An operational proposal should graphically demonstrate a strategic overview of how the storefront operation will be administered. Any applicable departmental or judicial guidelines must be incorporated in this procedure. Its formulation should involve input from your chain of command, administrators of any outside agency that may be involved, and the prosecutor's office. It is intended to give the administration an overall picture of what managerial techniques are to be used.

Why should you be involved with this administrative aspect of the operation—isn't this the job of the upper echelon? You have the most comprehensive grasp of what the storefront is all about and the goals that are to be achieved. Your understanding will be incorporated in the operational proposal. Without your input, a plan could be imposed that does not have the benefit of your insight.

Before you can prepare an operational proposal, you need an awareness of the various aspects involved in administering a storefront. Although the proposal is an overview, it cannot be constructed without first reviewing these facets.

1. What personnel are to be employed, and what are their responsibilities?
2. What is the enforcement policy?
3. How are records to be kept, and who maintains them?
4. How is fiscal management to be achieved?
5. How is unit publicity to be handled?
6. How are the unit's activities to be evaluated?
7. What happens at the conclusion of the operation?

Once this is accomplished and you have determined what will be suitable for your particular investigation, the proposal can be compiled.

Even though many of these components will not be spelled out in the proposal, to maintain the integrity of the probe, they will become part of administering the operation. In this chapter, we discuss the components of a proposal, including:

1. Introduction
2. Organization of personnel
3. Investigative policy
4. Records management
5. Fiscal management
6. Dealing with the news media
7. Preliminary plan for culmination of the storefront.

INTRODUCTION

The introduction to the proposal should include a synopsis of the documentation completed, the objectives to be obtained, and the basic plan to be used in meeting these objectives. This will ensure that all involved in establishing these administrative guidelines have a fundamental concept of the operation. This will also illustrate to the administration that a proper foundation has been established and the objectives of the storefront are feasible.

The introduction does not need to include all the documentation compiled but rather a concise summary of this activity. You may wish to incorporate

1. Why the documentation process was initiated
2. What the documentation revealed
3. How the documentation was compiled
4. How the documentation was analyzed
5. Target(s) identified.

The statement of objectives to be accomplished and the feasibility of meeting these goals should be brief. They could simply be listed. In the introduction, the highlighting of the desired information is favorable to a long, drawn-out narrative. Remember, all you are trying to accomplish here is to ensure that all involved in this process have a basic understanding of the operation.

In writing the introduction, keep in mind who may eventually have access to this information. Be guarded when disseminating the details of the investigation. This is another reason to use a brief and pointed introduction.

ORGANIZATION OF PERSONNEL

You must address how the operation is to be organized. Many storefront investigations are organized or combined with another existing unit within the department. They may be integrated into the vice unit, auto theft unit, burglary unit, etc. However, a special unit may be established for the length of the operation.

Separate units are established so they can be directly responsible to the chief. There are usually two additional reasons for organizing separate units. The first is that an investigation that fails has a direct effect on that office. The second is the sensitive and secretive nature of storefront operations. The potential for compromising the investigation may be lessened when using this approach.

Nevertheless, there could be difficulties. The lack of time due to other responsibilities that could be devoted to the unit could result in a lack of leadership and/or direction. A separatist attitude could also develop among the investigators in the unit. This could affect the attitudes and cooperation of members in other units toward the operation. It could also create the feeling in outside members that the activity of the storefront is none of their concern, thus impairing the communication and assistance often required from outside personnel.

Storefront operations could function more effectively when structured to operate in conjunction with an established unit and as a basic part of the investigative section. The size and specific circumstances of your department and investigation will be factors to consider in organizing the unit. It is best when the storefront operation occurs within an entity that is capable of conducting the operation. This is better than establishing a separate unit for the duration of the storefront. If the investigation was initiated within a unit that is not able to conduct such an operation, incorporate it into one that is. The original unit, however, should be kept informed of the progress and used whenever possible. If there is an outside agency involved, you may need to establish a separate entity. Take steps to minimize the difficulties that may arise in using this method.

To further enhance understanding of the personnel structure, an organizational chart should be included in the proposal. This can be divided into two separate sections. The first is simply the chain of command. Be sure to include the levels of authority for any outside agency involved. The second is the list of all directly involved with the investigation. This usually shows the front line supervisor or his or her immediate superior at the top of the chart, followed by all other personnel involved. The following personnel may need to be included:

1. Undercover operatives
2. Case agent
3. Contact officer
4. Relief officers
5. Surveillance liaison
6. Support personnel liaison (clerical)
7. Outside agency liaison
8. Evidence liaison
9. Technical liaison
10. Prosecutor liaison
11. Media liaison
12. Corrections liaison
13. Chain of command, from the front line supervisor up.

Undercover Operatives

Indicate the primary undercover operatives and a general description of their duties. For example:

Undercover operatives are to conduct the day-to-day activities of the storefront in accordance with established guidelines. Their duties include but are not limited to

1. Ensuring the storefront is readied for daily activities
2. Ensuring the technical equipment is functional
3. Maintaining appropriate logs
4. Conducting interviews and buys from suspects in accordance with objectives established
5. Maintaining offense reports
6. Properly handling evidence obtained
7. Keeping superiors informed of activities at the storefront
8. Maintaining communications with other personnel involved
9. Cooperating with prosecutor to ensure that judicial guidelines are followed.

A brief description of responsibilities is best. Not all the duties listed here may need to be carried out, only those deemed necessary to satisfy the requirements of your administration. The first sentence of the example could be sufficient to meet this requisite.

Case Agent

The case agent's duties will vary widely depending on the scope of the operation. Some of the responsibilities could include

1. Assisting in the identification of offenders
2. Obtaining background information on offenders
3. Maintaining case files
4. Returning stolen property
5. Acting as a relief officer
6. Acting as a liaison with prosecutor and outside agencies
7. Acting as a liaison with records personnel
8. Acting as a liaison with clerical personnel
9. Ensuring that the storefront is supplied with tapes, report forms, logs, etc.
10. Coordinating the activities of support units
11. Preparing cases for presentation to prosecutor.

As is evident in this list of duties, you could simply state that the case agent must be a jack of all trades. With a storefront that has a minimal personnel allocation, the case agent may be required to do everything except those duties assigned to the undercover operatives.

In the proposal, the responsibilities of the case agent could be described as follows:

> The case agent's duties will be of such a nature as to complement those of the undercover operatives and assure a harmonious coexistence between the other units supporting the investigation.

Contact Officer

At times, the contact officer and case agent are one and the same. A contact officer is used as the intermediary between the undercover operatives and the department. This is usually done when the operation is of such a sensitive nature that the investigators are in a deep-cover mode. The contact officer is their link with the real world, relaying information from the operatives to the administration, and vice versa.

This position assures that the undercover operatives have an outlet for communicating their apprehensions and concerns. The contract officer can provide a needed sense of security for those who have been given the responsibility of conducting the investigation. This may require the contact officer's availability twenty-four hours a day. In a deep-cover operation, this availability of communication is essential. Another reason a contact officer may be needed is the safety of the operatives and security of the investigation. The fewer persons who are aware of the activity, the less likelihood there is for compromising the investigators and the storefront.

Still another responsibility of the contact officer may be to communicate between the operatives and their families. In a deep-cover situation, operatives may not be able to communicate directly with their loved ones. The contact officer provides this needed link.

The contact officer's duties could be indicated as follows:

> To afford a direct line of communication between the undercover operatives and the administration, ensuring that the needs of both are met.

Relief Officers

Relief officers are substitutes for the primary investigators. As discussed in chapter 4, there are many reasons a relief officer may be called on. Their duties and responsibilities are basically the same as the undercover operatives. The case agent can and often must meet this challenge in addition to other duties.

The duties of the relief officer could be stated as follows:

> The relief officer will assume the duties and responsibilities of the undercover operatives when they are not available to perform their assigned functions.

Surveillance Liaison

When a separate unit is to be used for surveillance, appoint a liaison within that unit. This person will be contacted when his or her services are needed. The person named to take on this responsibility should have the authority to carry out the task requested. Designating a representative who does not have the authority will only increase the communication chain. The fewer involved in the request, the less likelihood there is for a communications gap or misinterpretation of data.

The surveillance liaison's province could be indicated as follows:

> The surveillance liaison will be utilized for all requests pertaining to this activity. He or she will be accountable for coordinating and providing the desired support.

Support Personnel Liaison (Clerical)

Cooperation of support personnel is essential to the success of the operation. There could be many people involved with the clerical support needed from various units: records section, identification unit, word processing unit, etc. The use of a liaison will enable a more concerted effort. Attempting to deal with a large number of clerical personnel on a one-to-one basis can be frustrating and nonproductive. The liaison will be charged with ensuring that the requested work is accomplished in a competent and timely fashion.

However, do not assume that you don't have to communicate with the clerical personnel. A simple thank you or a "job well done" will enhance support personnel's efforts. We would often bring in a box of donuts or vase of flowers to express our thanks. You would be surprised how this simple and inexpensive gesture can increase production and cooperation. We all like to know we are appreciated.

The following could describe the function of the support personnel liaison:

> The support personnel liaison will be accountable for assuring that requested work is completed in a competent and timely manner. All materials submitted to these units will be directed through the liaison.

Outside Agency Liaison

When a combined venture is planned with an outside agency, the need for a liaison will readily become apparent. The smallest problems can soon become monumental and completely distorted when they have to be relayed several times through various people before reaching the level where they can be dealt with. The liaison should have the authority to act on day-to-day requests or deal with minor problems attributable to the investigation. The potential for misinterpretation is drastically diminished when communications can be funneled through one representative. The liaison should also be able to approach the appropriate administrative tier with problems or requests that are of an exceptional nature. The most logical person to fill this position is the outside agency's front line supervisor assigned to the joint venture.

The outside agency liaison's function could be depicted as follows:

> All requests and communications with the outside agency will be directed through the appointed liaison. He or she will then be charged with replying to these queries in a prompt and proficient manner.

Evidence Liaison

The amount, type, and extent to which evidence is generated may become an area for concern. If the departmental evidence unit is to secure these exhibits, naming a liaison within the unit is the prudent course to take. The liaison can assist with any potentially perplexing situations. These could include the securing of unusually large items or a vast quantity of smaller items. Working with the liaison, you may be able to establish a separate area within the evidence unit to store evidence.

Arrangements could also be made to call on the liaison to secure evidence that has been obtained while that unit is closed. Due to budgetary constraints, many units are not operational twenty-four hours a day, seven days a week. Evidence drop boxes are provided in lieu of this service. The items obtained may be of a size or nature where the use of a drop box is inappropriate. The ability to contact the liaison or his or her representative to open the unit may be desirable in these instances. When the storefront is a joint venture and the other agency has taken on the responsibility of handling the evidence, be familiar with their times of operation and contingencies for handling property obtained after hours. This could prevent you from having to baby-sit evidence until the unit opens.

A description of the evidence liaison's duties could be as follows:

> The evidence liaison will ensure that exhibits rendered to that unit will be maintained in accordance with all established departmental and judicial guidelines; that the exhibits will be secured in such a fashion as to enhance availability to investigators; and that the unit will be accessible on a twenty-four-hour basis when circumstances dictate.

Technical Liaison

When the technical expertise is provided by people outside the unit, the need for a liaison can be critical. This is especially true if the technical assistance is obtained from a unit staffed by various technicians. The liaison will be beneficial in securing the same technician for installing, maintaining, and repairing equipment. This is far more desirable than having numerous repair technicians parading in and out of the storefront. Using the same technician(s) will help to ensure the integrity of the operation and may even contribute to better service.

The technical liaison's duties may be described as follows:

> The technical liaison will supply the necessary services required to ensure the proper installation and maintenance of the electronic equipment, especially those devices intended for use in evidence gathering. This task is to be accomplished in a manner ensuring the integrity of the operation.

Prosecutor Liaison

As previously discussed, the prosecutor should be a member of the storefront team. When the undercover operatives are unavailable for direct contact with the prosecutor, a liaison should be appointed. This is usually the case agent or relief officer. However, if the investigation is of a magnitude, this may not be practical. The liaison will update the prosecutor of the storefront's progress, relay any difficulties with ongoing investigations, and communicate to investigators suggestions from the prosecutor for how to overcome these problems. The prosecutor may even be able to provide a course of action that has been overlooked.

The prosecutor liaison's responsibilities could be written as follows:

> The prosecutor liaison will maintain an open line of communication between the prosecutor and the operation. He or she will ensure that the prosecutor is kept abreast of investigative activities and relay any inquiries made by storefront personnel.

Media Liaison

Within departmental guidelines, someone within the unit should be designated as a media liaison. The need for such a position may not be apparent now but will become very visible near the conclusion of the operation. The liaison's duties should be explicitly detailed in a written directive. All members of the storefront unit must be aware of the directive and abide by it. When one person acts as the media liaison, it will ensure that information received by the media is accurate and appropriate. All inquiries made by the news media should be directed to this liaison.

The information relayed to the press should be as concise as possible. The more that is revealed, the greater the possibility for inaccuracy, conflict, and misinterpretation. The press release can simply give

Dates of the events in question

Times of the events in question

Charges filed

Number of arrests made

Names of those incarcerated.

If juveniles have been arrested, the release of their identity may be in conflict with departmental and/or judicial guidelines. If you are not familiar with these guidelines, it is best not to release this information. Customarily, the press release may also contain the amount and dollar figure of stolen property and/or contraband confiscated (be careful, this information could pose problems), the agencies that participated in the operation, and/or arrests.

Specific details in reference to the operation which should not be released to the news media include the following:

1. How the operation was conducted

2. The amount of time expended on the investigation

3. Names of operatives

4. Number of law enforcement officers who participated

5. Number of buys from each suspect

6. Security used by or at the storefront

7. The importance of those arrested.

8. The amount and/or dollar figure of contraband confiscated

9. The amount of funds spent on the investigation.

Such information should be excluded from a news release. This type of information could have an adverse impact on prosecution efforts. The prosecutor should be provided the opportunity to review the information before it is released to the press. Defense attorneys could claim that such information created a prejudicial pretrial atmosphere for their client. Some of this information could also be of future value to others in the criminal community.

The media liaison's duties can be stated as follows:

The media liaison will ensure that the news media is provided with appropriate information in accordance with the stated directive.

Corrections Liaison

At the conclusion of the storefront, the likelihood that a large number of suspects will be incarcerated in a relatively short time could pose unnecessary difficulties for detention personnel. These problems can be alleviated with proper planning. Easing these potential shortcomings will not only benefit detention personnel but will be advantageous for you as well.

The corrections liaison's duties can be stated as follows:

The corrections liaison will communicate with correctional personnel to ensure that an effective and expedient incarceration procedure will be initiated at the culmination of the storefront.

At this stage in the preparation process, it may not be wise to contact correctional personnel. However, allocating space for their liaison on the organizational chart is appropriate. When the suitable time does arise, near the conclusion of the operation, the name of the liaison can be included in the chart. Incorporating space on the chart now will help prevent an oversight in the future.

Chain of Command

The organizational chart should be formatted to reflect the chain of command. If the operation involves outside agencies, their chain of command must be included. Using this format will eliminate any questions about authority. The administrators of the participating organizations will have to establish their chain of command to be used during the investigation. If there are no other agencies involved, your chain of command will be apparent. (A copy of an organizational chart for a joint venture, as well as a solo undertaking, is found in the appendix.)

INVESTIGATIVE POLICY

Investigative policy is a matter that requires the mutual agreement of all agencies involved. It is a policy established to guide the operation. The primary investigative effort will be directed toward methods that will be best suited to accomplishing the stated objectives. The policy should include

1. Who is to be targeted
2. What is to be purchased
3. How many purchases are to be made from each suspect
4. What is to be accomplished from these buys
5. How offenders are to be dealt with after an optimum number of buys have occurred
6. How spinoffs are to be handled.

Who Is to Be Targeted

This may appear obvious at first. The target of the storefront is the person(s) identified through documentation. But what if the documentation did not reveal the identity of the target? Then anyone engaged in the targeted criminal activity will be the focus of the investigation. This may not always apply. For instance, the activity combated is commercial burglary. This could be specific enough in a small community, but in a larger community this may be too wide of a scope. The specific type or magnitude of the burglaries should be the focus of the investigation rather than the general category.

FOR EXAMPLE _____

Motor vehicle thieves are the target of the storefront. The documentation showed an alarming increase in this activity, but it was unable to reveal specific targets. A subject arrives at the storefront and wants to sell a stolen moped. In conversing with the subject, investigators learn that he is not involved in any other criminal activity. He will only steal these vehicles when the owner has been careless and left the keys in the motorbike.

The thief is not capable of hot wiring. The funds allocated for the investigation may be put to better use if this subject is directed to another unit within the department for investigation. The offense should not go uninvestigated but would be more appropriately handled by another unit.

FOR EXAMPLE

Major narcotics dealers are to be addressed by the storefront. A subject enters and wants to sell a small quantity of marijuana. The sale will constitute a misdemeanor violation. It is revealed through conversation that the subject can only obtain these small quantities and only sells them to supplement his personal use. The subject deals in nothing else and has no interest in dealing larger quantities.

The purchase of the marijuana and subsequent investigation of the subject may not be the most judicial use of funds allocated to the operation.

The investigative policy must contain guidelines on who will become the targets of the storefront. This is accomplished by concentrating on targets who are the most responsible for the criminal activity or those who can lead investigators to those targets. Using the example of a narcotics dealer, the guidelines may appear as follows:

A major narcotics trafficker is one who

1. Is capable of dealing twenty-five dime bags, an ounce, or more of heroin at one time
2. Is capable of dealing one kilogram or more of marijuana
3. Is capable of dealing an ounce or more of cocaine
4. Is capable of dealing any hashish oil
5. Possesses, or is able to possess, clandestine laboratory equipment.

This will give those involved in the investigation a clear understanding of what you mean by a major narcotics trafficker. Of course, this format can be adapted to other forms of criminal activity.

It is important that appropriate priorities and objectives are established. This will help ensure that the operation actively pursues cases involving the target activity. Then a systematic, priority-based investigation can be followed. However, do not allow this investigative policy to be confining. The operation must have the flexibility to deal with the unexpected.

FOR EXAMPLE

One of our storefronts was organized to investigate auto thieves, specifically those stealing Ford or Chevrolet 4 × 4 pickups. The investigative policy clearly stated this. During the operations, a subject came to the attention of the storefront. He did not steal cars; he dealt in small quantities of cocaine, and not very pure cocaine at that. However, the storefront incorporated the subject into its investigation. It was learned through conversations at the storefront that the subject was suspected of committing murder. Drugs were purchased from the suspect, and as a direct result of taped conversation, information about his involvement in the murder was obtained.

The investigative policy we had established was to probe the targeted activity and any other major crime deemed suitable for investigation by the storefront. The policy was specific in giving guidance for the direction of the investigation, but not so restraining that it did not allow for adaptability to unforeseen events.

What Is to Be Purchased

Purchasing contraband just for the sake of obtaining statistics is neither productive nor desirable. Items purchased are for the purpose of obtaining the necessary evidence needed to successfully prosecute the targets of the operation. Buying property or contraband solely to enhance the appearance of success through misleading statistics is a frivolous use of the funds entrusted to the storefront. This is often a concern which detractors point to when criticizing this law enforcement technique. Clearly stating what the operation intends to purchase and the reason for such purchases will limit this criticism. Again, do not be too restrictive in wording this portion of the proposal. Allow for flexibility—you never know who or what may come to your attention.

A sentence such as the following could be incorporated into this section of the proposal:

> Any other items brought to the attention of the storefront will be carefully scrutinized for their suitability in meeting the stated goals and/or the beneficial impact on the community.

How Many Buys

The number of purchases made from each offender can vary depending on various factors. The optimum number of buys from a single individual for the typical case is usually three. This should be discussed with the prosecutor to determine what the optimum number of purchases should be for your particular situation. Buying contraband from a subject after the case has been made is not usually necessary or desirable. However, there may be extenuating circumstances that cause you to make more than the optimum number of buys.

For this portion of the proposal, you could indicate the following:

> After deliberation with the appropriate administrators and the prosecutor, and in keeping with established departmental and judicial guidelines, X number of buys will be the most favorable for obtaining the desired results. Any additional buys will only be completed after carefully considering the consequences and benefit.

What Is to Be Accomplished from Buys

The most obvious accomplishments are

1. To accomplish the stated objectives
2. To obtain the successful prosecution of the target
3. The return of property to its rightful owner
4. To rid the community of contraband.

This should all be integrated into the operational proposal.

There may be other objectives to be gained from buys that you can include, such as the following:

1. Anticipate that the seller will introduce cohorts to the storefront.

Often, the offender needs to become accustomed to the operation before he or she will introduce anyone new.

2. Obtain all the contraband the offender(s) has at his or her disposal.

The offender may have far more contraband stashed than he or she is willing to disclose until becoming comfortable with the operation. This does not mean you keep buying from a dealer because he or she can get more; rather, you keep buying until you get all he or she has, if this is feasible.

3. Obtain intelligence information on other criminal activity affecting your jurisdiction or an outside jurisdiction.
4. Increase cooperation and goodwill among agencies.
5. Instill in the community the perception that the department has successful methods and techniques to combat crime.

This portion of the proposal illustrates what you think will be the achievements of the investigation. It informs all involved that there is a purpose and design to the operation other than obtaining glorified statistics.

How Offenders Are to Be Dealt with after Optimum Number of Buys

After the storefront has obtained the necessary evidence to ensure the successful prosecution of offenders, what is to be done with them? Obviously, the incarceration of offenders by storefront operatives may not be advantageous to the continuation of the operation. There could also be a substantial amount of time before this will occur. To leave the offender unleashed on the streets of your community could be counterproductive to the operation's goals. Formulating a plan to deal with this dilemma before it occurs will prevent confusion and unwanted solutions. Indicating in the proposal that every suitable step will be implemented to alleviate this situation will demonstrate your concern about this potential conflict.

There are a variety of methods that can be used in coping with this problem.

1. Use a surveillance team, armed with the intelligence gathered by the storefront, to tail the subject until he or she is captured in the act.
2. Supplying information collected by the operation—which could involve past or ongoing criminal activity—to the appropriate investigative unit. This could enable the unit to implicate the offender through evidence not directly attributed to the undercover operation.
3. Notify parole officers of the parolee's conduct.
4. If litigation is pending, notify the prosecutor. Trial dates could be moved up and/or bond revoked.
5. Plot for the perpetrator to be apprehended en route to the storefront with contraband.
6. Contrive a plan to have the culprit arrested while taking contraband to another buyer.

When considering any of these methods or one you have devised yourself, bear this in mind: The arrest of the offender before the conclusion of the storefront, even though desirable, may have a detrimental impact on the operation. Consider the consequences to the operatives and operation. The aftermath that could develop from such actions could devastate the integrity of the entire operation and any potential future benefit. (This is discussed further in chapter 14.)

Spinoffs

Almost without exception, a storefront will encounter criminal activity it was not organized to investigate. When this occurs, the personnel involved must understand what appropriate action should be taken.

Spinoff investigations are a plus for any storefront operation. Spinoffs, subsequent to the initial endeavor, can have greater consequences than the original undertaking.

How are these to be dealt with? Let's face it, all criminal activity brought to the attention of the operatives will not be addressed. Some will be too insignificant in nature. On the other hand, some may be of such a magnitude that it is just not practical to deal with them because of the storefront's constraints.

Understanding the limitations and/or restrictions of spinoffs will assist you in determining what appropriate action should be taken. If the spinoff is to be delegated to another unit for scrutiny, maintaining communications between the units is of utmost importance. The probe must be coordinated between the investigating unit and the storefront. If this does not occur, a premature arrest or the release of information that could impair the efforts of the storefront and/or place the operatives in peril is likely. You must consider the significance of the information, the ability of the storefront or another unit to investigate effectively, and the influence, whether pro or con, the information will have on the operation. With a little forethought and communication, spinoffs can be handled effectively and be a big plus for the storefront.

Compiling an Investigative Policy

Now that you understand what is involved in compiling an investigative policy, you can formulate one. The large amount of material pertaining to this topic does not need to be included. The policy itself should be as brief and concise as possible. The following is an example:

> The investigative activities of the storefront will be directed at the documented criminal activity—at those identified, suspected, or as of yet unknown who are perpetrators of the said activity. Transactions will be conducted in accordance with meeting the stated objectives. These will be of sufficient quantity to meet prosecution and applicable department guidelines. Any additional transactions will first be approved by the front line supervisor. They will only be entered into to further the scope of the investigation, in the direction of said objectives, or toward other major crimes deemed compatible with the focus of the operation. When sufficient transactions, that meet the aforementioned criteria, have been accomplished, all attempts will be instituted to effect the incarceration of the perpetrator, while at the same time maintaining the integrity of the storefront. Any other criminal activity brought to the attention of the operation will be scrutinized by the front line supervisor for the adverse impact on the community. If judged to be appropriate for further inquiry, the investigation of this activity can continue.

A policy like this one usually meets the needs of the administration. It does not give specific details of the operation that could become potentially harmful if revealed to the wrong source. However, it does demonstrate that the operation has a direction and safeguards to ensure that it follows that course. You and the other investigators involved understand the policy and how you will implement it.

RECORDS MANAGEMENT

The management of paperwork generated by the operation is a crucial component to the overall success of the storefront. Meticulous documentation and subsequent management of data are the only ways to ensure a triumphant outcome. As the old saying goes, "The job's not over till the paperwork is done." Truer words have never been spoken, especially when applied to the storefront technique.

Our first joint venture was a graphic illustration of this point. The outside agency had taken on the responsibility of records management. To our dismay, their attempt was haphazard at best. Months after the conclusion of the storefront, we were still attempting to collate reports, logs, files, etc. Prosecutors were clamoring for arrest files and giving ominous indications as to the outcome of cases. The administration was bellowing; they were also recipients of the prosecutors' displeasure. They complained that too many hours were being expended unnecessarily. The task at this stage was immense and totally unwarranted. From that point on, records management became a priority.

The sensitive nature of the probe and the need for confidentiality pose unique challenges for the storefront investigation. This applies to records management as well. Security of reports and files, and their accessibility, must be considered. It is recommended that access be restricted to storefront personnel and other departmental personnel the administration deems absolutely necessary. A records system should be established whereby the unit maintains its own files. The central records section can be notified to issue offense report numbers so they can maintain control of the numbers that have been used. The records section can then place a blank offense report using those numbers in their files and indicate "special investigation" or a code name on the form. At the conclusion of the operation, the appropriate paperwork can be forwarded to the records section to be filed under the appropriate case numbers.

If the records section objects to having blank forms in their files, an initial offense report may be completed. The report should contain only the information required for issuance of a case number. This information should be basic and not reveal any data that could be detrimental to the integrity of the storefront. Remember, offense reports filed in a central records section are available to the public. Don't make yourself vulnerable by overlooking this possible compromising situation.

You may wish to maintain the following records and files:

Master index file

General case file

Cooperating individuals file

Address file

Intelligence file

Information dissemination log

Investigator case log.

To satisfy the needs of the proposal, just indicate what files are to be used and who will maintain them. (This is discussed further in chapter 11.)

FISCAL MANAGEMENT

You have been entrusted with funding, possibly from various sources, that *must* be accounted for. Fiscal management can become troublesome if you do not pay strict attention to it. Few things will raise the ire of the community more than discrepancies in the expenditures of public revenue. To protect yourself and the operation, you must develop and follow appropriate guidelines. Although the fiscal management system may vary because of local requirements, each operation should have a written standard operating procedure (SOP) for accomplishing this task. The SOP should outline

1. Who is authorized to receive the funds
2. Who is authorized to spend the funds
3. Who is responsible for recordkeeping
4. A general description of the unit's fiscal system

Each investigator should be required to read the fiscal SOP and sign a statement that it was read and understood. The signed statement should be maintained in the investigator's personnel file that is kept by the unit.

To allow storefront members responsible for fiscal management to carry out their duties, the following records should be maintained:

1. General fiscal records
2. Confidential fund records
3. Other records

For the purpose of the proposal, indicate that a standard operating procedure pertaining to fiscal management has been or will be drafted. Then name the appropriate records that will be used to ensure that the SOP is adhered to. (Chapter 11 contains more details on these files.)

DEALING WITH THE NEWS MEDIA

Earlier, we discussed the appointment of a media liaison and establishing a written directive which explicitly details this person's duties. Dealing with the media in a positive way can contribute to beneficial unit publicity. However, if you do not deal with the media properly, the exact opposite can occur.

On occasion, the news media is allowed to witness the operations of the storefront. This is to gain beneficial exposure of law enforcement's efforts to combat the criminal activity in question. While the media may be allowed inside to obtain a firsthand look of the investigation, their reports cannot be disclosed until after or on conclusion of the probe. The media is customarily invited to go along on the arrest raid at the culmination of the storefront. Again, when you anticipate dealing with the news media, it is advantageous to discuss this activity with the prosecutor beforehand.

There are disadvantages in allowing the news media to observe any portion of the storefront. The most obvious is the likelihood of compromising the investigation. Inviting a member of the media to observe the inner workings of the storefront is not advisable. The media often will not edit their coverage so as not to reveal trade secrets. If the operation is not carried out smoothly and coverage is not objective, the adverse publicity can be enough to counteract months of good work.

During a raid, the initial moments of execution are critical and can be quite complex. The media may only contribute to the confusion. When people not essential to the raid are permitted to accompany investigators, the risk of injury is increased, not only to media but to the investigators whose duties become more complex now that they have to tend to news personnel.

Another factor is that while a camera may not lie, it can distort. It may portray an investigator who is trying to cover a group of suspects at gunpoint while protecting himself and other investigators as hysterical and overzealous. A recent news report reinforces this point. Investigators were conducting a routine search warrant and had brought along a television news team. Upon entry into the house, the offender shot the investigator in the chest with a small-caliber weapon. The investigator fell out the front door onto the porch. Then there was a stampede of other officers into the house followed by yelling and numerous gunshots. The investigator lying on the porch struggled to his feet (fortunately, he was wearing a bullet-proof vest) and tried to clear his head. There were shouts from the house that either the offender was not in custody or there were others hiding inside. The wounded officer then ran from the porch and picked up a long, narrow tree limb that was lying on the ground. He swung the limb at the outside rearview mirror of a pickup truck which was parked outside the house. The mirror was knocked to the ground. He picked up the mirror and ran back into the house. The media reported that this was willful destruction of private property committed by a hysterical and overzealous law enforcement officer.

Those of us in law enforcement understood what this officer was doing, but television viewers had no idea. They more than likely believed the reporters' comments. They could see it for themselves right there in living color. They did not understand or appreciate the calmness and presence of mind that this officer possessed even after going through this traumatic experience. How were they to know he was going to use the mirror to assist in searching the house? The reporters never gave him an opportunity to explain his actions, and they sure didn't understand them. They never had to use a mirror to check around corners or inside a room before exposing themselves to possible gunfire.

These are just a few points to consider when determining what the administrative policy of the storefront will be in regards to dealing with the news media.

EVALUATION OF THE OPERATION

Periodic evaluation of the storefront's performance is important for several reasons. Through evaluation, you and the administration are able to determine what has been accomplished by the operation in terms of meeting stated objectives. Evaluation also focuses the investigation on what has been accomplished and what needs to be accomplished. If you include in the proposal a method by which to evaluate the operation, an incompatible evaluation technique will not be imposed.

There are usually six weak areas in the standard evaluation process of many departments:

1. They tend to rely on basic statistical data that can easily be misinterpreted.
2. Specific objectives are not set.
3. There is no measure of the storefront's impact on the community.
4. There is no justification of the operation's activities on a cost-effective basis.
5. There are no standards for comparing the operation's efforts.
6. There is no classification of offenders so enforcement efforts in each classification can be measured.

In theory, a true evaluation of the storefront's efforts should reflect the degree to which it has and/or will diminish the targeted activity in the community. However, because of the complex nature of many of these investigations, it is almost impossible to obtain a comprehensive understanding of the targeted activity. The evaluation of the storefront's impact on the community often includes subjective data. While the impact can be objectively measured through information on pending arrests, property recovered, seizures, etc., the fact that the targeted activity may have increased during the operation does not necessarily indicate that the investigation is not achieving its objectives or meeting with some measure of success.

Statistics

A weakness in the evaluation of an operation may be relying too heavily on statistics. The variance from operation to operation or between investigations can be misleading and easily misinterpreted. The general arrest figures can be misleading because of the priorities established. A storefront dealing with all types of property crimes and having no restrictions on what is purchased will more than likely have greater statistics than an operation that is more focused on a specific aspect of property crimes, such as major fences. It is necessary to evaluate which had the greatest impact on the targeted activity.

When the targeted activity of the storefront is to focus on a specific controlled substance, such as cocaine, the number of reported incidents related to that substance will increase. The number of cases, arrests, and seizure amounts will go up. However, this statistical data may not indicate the actual amount of cocaine traffic or overall effectiveness of the operation. It is the byproduct of the enforcement strategy.

When concentration is focused on one particular geographical area, the number of arrests, cases, recovered stolen property, and seizure of other contraband in that area will increase. Statistics alone may misrepresent an increase in criminal activity in that area. The statistical data, without evaluation, could be misleading.

Do not rely *too* much on statistics. The success or failure of an operation should not be judged by the statistical data alone. Rely on overall information in reference to all activities of the storefront to obtain a fair indicator of its accomplishments.

Evaluation Areas

In conducting a thorough and comprehensive evaluation of the operation, the following areas should be included:

1. The total number of cases being worked by the operation
2. Expenditure of confidential funds
   a. Buys (include totals and average number of buys per case)
   b. Information expenditures
   c. Nontargeted activity expenditures
   d. Any recovery of confidential funds
3. Number of cooperating individuals
   a. For the purpose of evaluation, these are only individuals who actively engage in assisting the storefront in making buys and/or supplying information on a continuing basis.
4. Number of indictments and/or arrest warrants obtained
5. Total arrests
   a. In the preliminary evaluations, this figure will be pending arrests.

    b. Include arrests resulting from the investigation, but not as a result of targeted activity. Include outstanding warrants, fugitives, etc.

6. Confiscated contraband

    a. Include dollar figure (if an illicit drug, include weight) of all contraband purchased or seized.

7. General disposition of cases

    a. Cases still active

    b. Cases referred to another unit or agency

    c. Cases referred for adjudication

    d. Cases rendered inactive

8. Adjudication of cases

    a. Cases rendered no bill

    b. Cases pending in court

    c. Cases adjudicated not guilty

    d. Cases adjudicated guilty as originally charged

    e. Cases plea-bargained to a lesser charge

    f. Cases receiving probation

    g. Cases resulting in incarceration, and length of sentence

    h. Cases receiving suspended sentences

    i. Cases adjudicated guilty but reversed through appeal

9. Seizures

    a. This is property or cash that has been seized and can be utilized by the investigation and/or the department.

10. Search warrants

    a. Include the number of search warrants obtained and conducted using information obtained by the storefront.

11. Number of complaints lodged against the operation

    a. This will show that this is a beneficial undertaking approved by the community, or vice versa.

12. Information dissemination

    a. Include data given to other units within or outside your department.

    b. This demonstrates that not all activity is reflected in arrest figures.

    c. Include follow-up on information to ascertain if it led to solution of the case and/or arrest.

13. Type of offenders

a. Age (may identify emerging trends)

b. Career criminals

14. Cooperation with other units

    a. Indicates the operation's commitment to the overall crime problem.

15. Number of hours expended per case

    a. This is easily accomplished using daily activity work sheets. (Work sheets are discussed in more detail in chapter 11.)

    b. Shows average time devoted per case.

    c. Can indicate time spent for administrative duties, report writing, court, etc.

    d. Evaluation must be made carefully. Don't draw a wrong conclusion. Difficult cases increase the time of investigation and may result in fewer arrests than easier cases.

    e. Some cases are difficult to evaluate on a time-value basis.

16. Cost factor per case

    a. Include total amount of expenditures per case.

    b. Include average cost per case.

    c. Can indicate if expenditures are excessive when compared with other investigative methods, or vice versa.

17. Highlighting of major cases

    a. Include a brief description.

    b. Show cases in which considerable amounts of time were used and large amounts of property and/or contraband were seized.

    c. Narration can tell the reader certain things statistics alone cannot.

Evaluation Reports

These reports should be furnished to the administration on a timely basis. Their purpose is to demonstrate the activities and workload of the storefront. Without such reporting, it is difficult for the administration to assess the progress of the operation. When appropriate, the evaluation should be presented in a regularly scheduled meeting with concerned administrators. This allows for the personal exchange of data. To compile these reports, it may be helpful to prepare daily, then weekly, reports for your own use. This will facilitate the periodic preparation of the more comprehensive evaluation report, which will be used to complete the overall evaluation of the storefront. For purposes of the proposal, indicate the intervals at which these reports will be furnished.

PRELIMINARY PLAN FOR CULMINATION OF THE STOREFRONT

When the administrative proposal is formulated, a section should be incorporated to indicate the preliminary plan for the culmination of the storefront. This strategy should include

1. Preparation for shutdown of the site
2. Briefing with the prosecutor
3. Plan for the arrests
4. Booking procedure
5. Preprosecution techniques
6. List of possible personnel to notify
7. How to handle the news media

Remember, this is a preparatory procedure and should be indicated as such. Many variables can arise during the storefront investigation that could cause this preliminary plan to become obsolete. All you are trying to accomplish here is to illustrate that forethought has gone into this portion of the proposal.

(A more detailed discussion of the culmination of a storefront appears in chapter 15.)

SUMMARY

In this chapter, we have examined the various components that must be explored to compile an administrative proposal. These include:

1. The organization of the storefront
2. The investigative or enforcement policy
3. How records are to be maintained
4. How fiscal management is to be obtained
5. The storefront's news media policy
6. Evaluation of the operation
7. The preliminary plan for the culmination of the storefront

The exact requirements of each type of storefront will vary. The organization, forms, ledgers, files, and media policy will be determined by the scope and magnitude of the investigation. Remember, if there are any doubts or questions about the legal ramifications of compiling, maintaining, or revealing this material, a meeting with the prosecutor is prudent.

The formulation of this strategy will meet with much more success if it is a combined effort between the investigators, administrators, and prosecutor. Their input, when incorporated into the proposal, will help promote its approval. Such cooperation will also assure that the operation acts in accordance with all established departmental and judicial guidelines. When the proposal has been approved, it becomes the storefront's managerial plan of action.

CHAPTER 11

Administrative Operation of the Storefront

The administrative proposal has been formulated and approved. Now the administrative operation of the investigation can begin. In initiating administrative operation, you must consider:

1. The duties of the supervisor
2. Records management
3. Fiscal management
4. General administrative duties.

In this chapter, we explore these aspects of managing the storefront.

THE SUPERVISOR

The front line supervisor controls and develops the operation, and maintains and enhances the effectiveness of subordinates and the investigation. This involves face-to-face leadership and direction. The primary administrative duties of the front-line supervisor entail

1. Directing work assignments
2. Reviewing offense reports
3. Supervising cases
4. Inspecting equipment
5. Reviewing case files
6. Supervising fiscal management
7. Evaluating the operation
8. Evaluating the operatives

9. Conducting preliminary investigations of external complaints pertaining to the operatives or the operation
10. Maintaining deportment of subordinates
11. Relaying communications
12. Conducting operation personnel meetings
13. Serving as a public relations liaison.

These activities are important and may require that much time be spent confined to a desk. This leaves little opportunity for direct supervision of the operation. Often, this can create a lack of field supervision. Although the supervisor determines cases that are to be pursued and reviews written reports, his or her responsibility to provide direct and active supervision in the field should be balanced with administrative duties.

Time should be spent with subordinates in their daily activities, observing their performance and discussing the case at hand. The supervisor should guard against taking over for the subordinate when errors are being made—unless the errors would affect the outcome of the investigation. The supervisor, if not directly assigned to conduct the investigations of the storefront, should not participate in operational duties. However, he or she should be knowledgeable of this type of activity.

The span of control—the number of subordinates assigned—depends on the complexity and scope of the investigation. It may also be influenced by the type of storefront used, managerial skill, and the capabilities of subordinates. Usually, for a storefront operation, the span of control is three to seven subordinates.

Case Management

The supervisor should actively undertake case management for the unit and outline activities to be undertaken. This outline should cover a time span of seven to fourteen days and be updated as needed. It is difficult to predict accurately what the operation will encounter. Rather, the supervisor should formulate objectives for the unit. The daily occurrences at the storefront could drastically alter the outline. The supervisor should be flexible and strive toward the goals of the operation.

The supervisor must formulate equitable procedures for the assignment of cases to operatives. In most storefronts we have been involved with, the cases are alternated between operatives. The first subject who comes through the door is handled by the first operative, the second subject by the second operative, and so on. Then the operative is charged with conducting that investigation to its conclusion. However, the cooperation of investigators is essential, and this procedure must remain flexible. Storefronts pose unique challenges for case management, and customary practices may not be suitable.

When data is received about a potential target, the supervisor should assign the case agent to verify the information. Then the supervisor assigns the case to an operative. When a relief officer is present and initiates an investigation, the supervisor will determine who continues the probe. Factors the supervisor must consider are the investigative ability and the extent of other responsibilities of each operative and the relief officer. It is important that the supervisor monitors caseloads. Otherwise, those who are resourceful will have a much greater number of cases.

When assigning an operative to a target, a time frame should be allotted in which to develop the case. This will vary depending on the importance of the target and/or specific case. The investigator and/or case agent should make an initial intelligence survey to assist in determining the approximate time frame. Then, during the course of the investigation, if difficulties arise in meeting the deadline, assistance can be provided. Near the end of the time period, the supervisor should review progress and determine the fate of the investigation.

Most cases undertaken by the storefront will not be assigned by the supervisor. They will result from the direct activity of the operation. However, it is important to monitor these cases. A problem may arise when operatives are given the impression that they must "get" the target. Therefore, the supervisor must maintain close supervision to ensure that the probe is conducted in accordance with established departmental and judicial guidelines. The operative who uses questionable methods is a danger to the entire operation.

The supervisor should also evaluate the abilities of personnel and make assignments which fully utilize their capabilities.

FOR EXAMPLE _____

The investigator may be a poor undercover operative because he cannot adapt to the role. He could still be utilized effectively as a case agent or surveillance officer. Each investigator has special abilities. The supervisor must be able to uncover these talents and assign personnel accordingly.

Activity Reports

This form is designed to provide a daily record of the performance of storefront personnel. It can detail the following:

1. Case numbers of investigations conducted
2. Assistance to other units
3. Administrative time
4. Court time

5. Vacation and sick time
6. Overtime
7. Arrests
8. Warrants (arrest and search)
9. Property and contraband recovered
10. Case fund expenditures
11. Information expenditures
12. Miscellaneous expenditures

The form may also indicate

1. Vehicle used
2. Mileage and fuel consumption
3. Duty time commencing and ending
4. Length of time spent on each investigation
5. Names of people interviewed.

The information obtained from the daily report serves as an administrative method of control over the activities of the investigators. It provides the supervisor with a means of determining

1. Personnel usage.
2. Vehicle usage and expense
3. Checklist of reports due
4. Arrest and warrant totals
5. Property and contraband totals
6. Fiscal expenditures
7. Total hours worked by the investigator.

The supervisor should examine and approve these forms. Any discrepancies or questionable items should be discussed with the appropriate investigator. The supervisor may even wish to spot-check entries on these forms against offense reports to ensure that interviews and other activities are accounted for and recorded properly.

The need to control the number of hours worked must also be appraised. The hectic nature of undercover activity in contrast to the relatively small work force must be taken into account. In an attempt to accomplish as much as they can, personnel may expend their energies to a point near depletion. While this is commendable, some structure and routine should be strived for.

Training

The extent of training required will depend on the personnel selected and the nature of the investigation. Therefore, the formulation of a program is derived to suit the needs of the particular type of storefront operation. To accomplish this, the supervisor must determine what will be expected from the unit's personnel, such as the extent of their duties and their expected level of performance. The supervisor must also ascertain the sort of training and experiences personnel may already have.

The general training areas include

1. Undercover techniques
2. The use and handling of informants
3. Surveillance techniques
4. Gathering and utilizing intelligence and information
5. The use and care of equipment
6. Unit policies and procedures
7. Court procedures and demeanor
8. Relevant legal statues
9. Interview techniques.

If training is required, there are two basic types to choose from: internal and external. Internal training, or on-the-job training (OJT) by the supervisor or an experienced investigator, is perhaps the most important, certainly the most common, type of training received. This could also be the only type to which operatives can be exposed. The primary advantage of OJT is that it occurs during a real situation where there is an immediate urgency for comprehension.

Using the services of the supervisor or a knowledgeable investigator is usually the most feasible and cost-effective method. Personnel can be used while learning at the same time. The supervisor can then evaluate the quality of training and rate of retention. Difficulties with particular tasks can be readily perceived.

External training may be required due to the nature of the investigation and lack of qualified instructors within the department. The vast variety of disguises that could be used for the storefront technique often dictates the need for external training to enhance the plausibility of the role portrayed. The supervisor must evaluate the need for such training and determine the most appropriate and cost-effective means by which it can be obtained.

Other Supervisory Duties

The supervisor should also serve as the public relations officer and/or goodwill ambassador. The need for access to other departmental resources is crucial in allowing the operation to meet its full potential. These resources will be more readily accessible if a foundation of cooperation has been laid and is continuously strengthened. This is especially important with the various liaisons from outside the unit. The supervisor should maintain a list of all liaisons and how they can be contacted after regularly scheduled work hours.

A storefront investigation can place unusual demands on investigators. They may be required to work long, intense shifts day after day. This can also place a strain on their families. These conditions can cause tempers to flare on the job and a lack of production. Therefore, the supervisor may be called on to perform psychological duties—calm tempers and uplift morale. The men and women who work the storefront are its most valuable assets, and the supervisor should solicit their input in reference to administration of the operation and, if appropriate, incorporate their ideas. When subordinates are encouraged to participate in administration, everyone reaps the rewards.

RECORDS MANAGEMENT

A crucial component to the overall success of any investigation is how records and information are managed. This is especially true for a storefront operation. There are a variety of techniques which can be used in records management, including

1. Master index file
2. General case file
3. Cooperating individuals or CI file
4. Address file
5. Intelligence file
6. Information dissemination log
7. Investigator's case log.

These were discussed briefly in chapter 10. Now let's take a more detailed look at what these files are comprised of.

Master Index File

This is sometimes referred to as an Alpha file. It includes a list of all people who have had contact with the operation. The file is commonly comprised of 3 × 5 index cards arranged in alphabetical order. The cards list the case and/or intelligence number of reports in which the person is mentioned. Other data to include, when possible, are

Subject's address
Date of birth
Physical description
Driver's license number
Social Security number
Arrest number
Associates
Vehicle description
Hangouts.

See the appendix for an example.

General Case File

This contains the offense and supplementary reports pertaining to the activities of the probe. Reports should be filed by the case numbers that have been issued by central records and then cross-referenced with any other reports that are appropriate. In initiating a numbering system, the case should be given a number in which the first two digits indicate the year and subsequent numbers the ordinal position. Whichever method is used, it should be established to ease the transfer of original reports from files to central records. A copy of the reports should be maintained in the general case file even after the conclusion of the storefront. This is far more convenient than going back and forth to central records whenever information is required.

Cooperating Individuals File

This consists of individual folders on all cooperating individuals involved in the operation. The folders should contain, when possible,

Personal history sheet
Rap sheet
Photograph and/or mug shot
Signature card
List of case numbers, where information was provided
Code name or number.

Not all cooperating individuals do so for personal gain. Those who do need a more complete documentation process.

Personal History Sheet

The personal history sheet should contain as much information as can be obtained on the cooperating individual. The use of a standardized form in obtaining this information is desirable and helpful in preventing oversights. The form could include space in which to answer the following questions.

1. Place of birth
2. Date of birth
3. Marital status of parents and current place of residence
4. Relatives and current place of residence
5. Marital status; if divorced, name and current residence of ex-spouse
6. Education
7. Military service and discharge information
8. Place of employment
9. Financial history
10. Vehicles, owned or at their disposal
11. Associates
12. Hangouts
13. Work done for other agencies.

See the appendix for an example.

Rap Sheet and Photograph

The criminal history of the cooperating individual must be investigated. Any information pertaining to this activity must be incorporated into the file. A current physical description and any new scars, marks, or tattoos should be indicated. If the mug shot is not recent or the CI has never been mugged, a current photograph is desirable.

Signature Card

When a source is monetarily rewarded for his or her services, a signed receipt of this expenditure should be required. The card provides the administration with one method to verify this payment. It should contain the name of the source and the alias he or she may wish to use. The signature of both names is usually desirable. There should also be space on the card to indicate who witnessed the signatures. See the appendix for an example.

List of Case Numbers

For easy cross-reference, include case and/or intelligence numbers of those reports in which the cooperating individual provided information. Indicate next to these numbers if the information given was reliable. This is a quick way to determine the credibility of the individual. Search and/or arrest warrants can then be more easily obtained without having to research each individual case.

Code Name and/or Number

Often, these people are not at ease using their true names. The use of a code name or number can create a more productive atmosphere. These aliases can then be used to create a sense of security through anonymity. Most are more than willing to cooperate as long as they remain anonymous. If the code name will appear on the receipt of payment, that signature should be on the signature card.

Address File

This consists of addresses that have been specifically mentioned by those frequenting the storefront. Be selective and include only those addresses where criminal activity is known or suspected to be occurring. Including every address mentioned could be futile, as some may have no intelligence value. It is advantageous to include case and/or intelligence numbers which refer back to the original report. Thereafter, additional information on that location can be consolidated in that file.

Intelligence File

A file containing all intelligence reports generated by storefront personnel should be maintained. A numbering system that allows for easy access and differentiates them from case reports should be implemented. The purpose of these reports is to document information in reference to a subject or illicit activity for which no case report has been initiated. If a case report is started, a copy of the intelligence file should be included and the case number indicated on the file.

When this file is not maintained, the information is usually stored within the investigator's psyche or discarded. Either way, it is lost to the unit. Some operations initiate a case report on all substantial pieces of intelligences. This can result in many case reports being started that do not lead to an investigation and many pending cases that are not actively pursued. The potential for statistical misinterpretation is obvious. See the appendix for a copy of an intelligence report form.

Information Dissemination Log

This log is maintained to monitor and control information given to other units. Whenever data is given to another investigator, an entry should be made in the log. It should indicate the receipt of information, date and time, a brief explanation of information given, and the reason for divulging data. An example of such a log can be found in the appendix.

Investigator Case Log

You may wish to maintain an investigator's case log, in which every transaction completed is listed. This is an easy reference to use in determining who is dealing with a specific individual. The log is especially useful in an operation that has numerous operatives. It can also assist relief officers in ascertaining how many buys have been completed and who to contact when the subject arrives during that investigator's absence. See the appendix for an example.

Other Files

Due to the particular circumstances of your operation, maintaining other files may be beneficial. Units working near international borders may need to store private aircraft numbers. Those working near large bodies of water may need ship registrations; those dealing with bookmakers may need telephone numbers; and automobile dealers may need license plate files. All these files must be referred back to the master or Alpha file and cross-indexed with other appropriate files.

The more files there are, the greater the effort in maintaining them. The key to having an efficient records system is simplicity. Don't file yourself into inefficiency. When we would dream up all these great files we wanted to keep, our more experienced colleagues would tell us to forget it—keep it simple!

FISCAL MANAGEMENT

The funding entrusted to you must be accurately accounted for. Fiscal management, if not strictly attended to, will become burdensome. There are various methods which can be to accomplish this accountability, including

1. General fiscal records
2. Confidential fund records
   a. Confidential fund expenditure ledger
   b. Transaction card file

c. Receipt file

d. Individual investigator's ledger

e. Cooperating individual ledger

3. Other records.

General Fiscal Records

The operation should have some type of ledger which shows the amounts expended and the remaining funding available in each budget category which is not considered confidential funds. General funds are monies considered for use in purchasing or leasing the storefront site, equipment, supplies, etc. Confidential funds are those monies used to pay for buys and purchasing of information. The distinction is made because general funds records may be inspected by various departmental personnel or city and state fiscal inspectors. Confidential expenditures are more sensitive and therefore should be restricted regarding who may inspect them.

Those records that are required to maintain an audit trail must be kept in such a manner that if released to outsiders they will not compromise the operation. Additional details needed for operational matters should be maintained on separate records properly cross-referenced to code names. This information should never be released except when an investigation into misuse of funds or malfeasance is in progress. However, this type of a probe will not occur if records are properly kept and managed. The whole idea of the storefront is to incarcerate the criminal, not to be indicted for sloppy bookkeeping.

Confidential Fund Records

You must account for all expenditures of confidential funds. This accountability can be maintained using

1. Confidential fund expenditure ledger

2. Transaction card file

3. Receipt file

4. Individual investigator ledgers

5. Cooperating individual ledger.

Confidential Fund Expenditure Ledger

This ledger is maintained to depict either the funds remaining or the money used to date, or both. Include in the ledger an individual reference number for each buy, the date of the transaction, and the amount spent. To simplify bookkeeping, you may also want to include a reference to the investigator conducting the transaction and a brief description of the expenditure. In the appendix there is an example of a confidential fund expenditure ledger.

Transaction Card File

This is a file with an individual card completed for each expenditure. It is intended to provide an original record of expenses which can be audited without searching through the confidential case file. This is important in maintaining the integrity of the operation. Each card should contain the following data, when applicable:

Case number for which funds were spent

Cooperating individual reference number

Buy number as entered on the expenditure ledger

Amount expended

Date of expense

Purpose for expense

Description of articles purchased

Name and signature of the investigator(s) conducting the transaction.

Name and signature of the supervisor who has approved the expenditure.

There is an example of a transaction card in the appendix.

Receipt File

You must maintain receipts for all funds that have been spent by the operation. If the funds cannot be accounted for through the available cash fund or the confidential fund expenditure ledger, a receipt must be on hand to indicate where the money was sent.

Individual Investigator's Ledger

Keep a ledger on each investigator involved in the operation, listing the expenditures of confidential funds. The ledger can be separated into evidence purchased, information expense, and any personal expenses incurred by the investigator as a direct result of the investigation. These personal expenses should have an accompanying receipt. The entry should contain the date and transaction reference number. The ledger can be maintained in the investigator's file or a special file containing all investigators' ledgers.

This file allows for an easy audit showing the amounts, dates, and justifications for all expenditures accountable to an investigator. The ledger can also be important in facilitating general administrative review and in case a discrepancy in an investigator's expenditures is noted. An example of an individual investigator's ledger appears in the appendix.

Cooperating Individual Ledger

Accountability of expenditures for information must be maintained. The ledger offers a quick, easy method to accomplish this. Indicate the date and time of payment. These entries should then be referenced in the confidential fund expenditure ledger, and any receipts should be filed in the cooperating individual's file. Obtaining a receipt for all payments for information is a desirable and sound practice. The person receiving the funds should sign the receipt. When possible, at least one witness and the investigator making the payment should also sign the receipt.

State and Federal Grants

When the storefront is a joint venture and is subsidized in whole or part by a federal or state grant, confidential funds may need to be separated from other funding for the operation. There are usually restrictions on how these funds can be used. Often, they can be used for the following reasons:

1. Payment of cooperating individuals
2. Purchase of evidence
3. Payment of expenses that cannot be made through normal fiscal channels without jeopardizing the operation.

Understand completely how such funds can be used. Any misuse could result in devastating fiscal ramifications. An example of a CI ledger is found in the appendix.

Other Records

You may want to use an individual investigator's file. This could contain

1. Photograph of the investigator
2. List of street names
3. Copy of the investigator's signature for both real and street names
4. Statement of the investigator's familiarity with fiscal procedure and storefront operations
5. Copy of receipt for contingency funds and pocket money

6. Individual expense ledger

7. Description of vehicle assigned

8. Description of equipment assigned.

A file of this type is usually maintained by the unit charged with the responsibility of the investigation.

To ensure the integrity of all files and ledgers, determine what legal claim others may have to inspect them. This can be accomplished by meeting with the prosecutor. You do not want to compile information in a manner that conflicts with established judicial guidelines. At the same time, you do not want to maintain files on sensitive subjects that are going to be open for everyone to view. A little matter such as how the files are classified or used could make a big difference in whether they have to be revealed. This is another area where the prosecutor becomes a significant member of the team.

GENERAL ADMINISTRATIVE DUTIES

There are general administrative duties that must be performed that are unique to a storefront operation, including

1. Site preparation checklist

2. Preparation of technical equipment

3. Communication with support personnel

4. Maintenance of logs, reports, etc.

Checklist for Opening and Closing the Site

At the beginning and end of each day, the operatives should perform certain duties to ensure that the site is prepared for the upcoming activities and closure. Accomplishing these tasks, even though some may seem menial, is important for an efficient operation and the safety of the operatives.

The routine should start with the inspection of the exterior of the storefront. As the site is opened inspect gates, locks, fences, doors, windows, etc. Determine if these have been tampered with and if they are in good working condition. Then inspect for any items that could reveal the true nature of the business—report forms, memos, notes, etc.

We worked at a site with a member of an outside agency. He was a very likable guy, more than capable of preforming the task, but very careless with his administrative material. When checking the exterior of the site, we would always find something—usually black ballpoint pens. The pens had the name of the agency he worked for inscribed on them.

This agency also used routing stickers for memos and such, which we would find lying around in plain view.

When entering the site, disarm the alarm. Ours were silent with a direct line to the police station. Occasionally, as we were relaxing and enjoying the morning's first cup of coffee, SWAT arrived. We have an alarm ordinance. It is very embarrassing when the police department had to pay fines for having too many false alarms.

The closing of the site for the day should involve a similar routine. Often, we were almost home and had to return to make sure that someone had armed the alarm system. Then we'd drive back home and a couple of hours later wonder why the CI phone was so quiet. Then we'd drive back to see if we had placed the site phone on call forwarding. It only took a couple of these trips before we initiated an opening and closing checklist. If you have the tendency to be forgetful at times, as we do, using a list of this type could save a lot of extra miles.

Preparing Technical Equipment

Video and audio recorders have one major drawback: They are not capable of holding a quantity of tape that lasts the entire operation. Therefore, the tape must be replaced. We once forgot to do this! Be sure to include a box on your checklist for this task.

Technical equipment also has a tendency to malfunction. Periodically inspect the equipment to ensure that it is functioning properly. Record the morning coffee session. Then play it back to determine if the quality desired is still present. If your coffee sessions are like ours, be sure to erase the tape after reviewing it. If you don't, it could become very distressing if it fell into the wrong hands.

When you are on your daily inspection tour, check to ensure that all connections are plugged in. If the equipment is on a separate circuit, other than the one that controls the lights, make sure the circuit breaker is on. Check where the camera lenses and mikes are installed to confirm that the disguises used to conceal them are still in place.

Maintaining Communications with Support Personnel

When possible, when it won't harm the operation's integrity, make a conscious effort to maintain communications with support personnel—not only with the clerical personnel, which was discussed earlier, but with others who assist in the investigation.

The beat cops who stopped and identified a subject for you—telephone or buy them a cup of coffee. Express what a fine job was done and how you appreciated it. Do not take for granted what others do for the operation.

These simple gestures will aid in establishing the communications and state of cooperation that will contribute to a more fruitful investigation. We all like to think at times that we are completely capable of handling this job by ourselves, but we know this is not true. Cooperation between law enforcement officers is essential for the success of any investigation.

When information has been relayed to the storefront, contact the source and explain what is being done with it. If a case is made as a result of this, make sure the source receives credit. If you do not, other tips, from sources and other officers, may soon dry up.

We maintained a list of all officers who assisted with the storefront. When it was time to incarcerate offenders, usually using a raid at the culmination of the operation, these officers were invited to participate. You should also make it a point to inform their supervisors of the valuable assistance you received from them. We should all be conscious of the separatist attitudes that can develop in a situation such as this and work hard to dispel them.

Maintaining Logs and Reports

This is everyone's favorite chore. Police work would be so much more enjoyable without all the paperwork. But it is a necessary evil and will comprise most of your administrative tasks. Without the proper recordkeeping system, the storefront will not meet with success. Remember, do not become the target of an investigation because of sloppy bookkeeping and/or records management.

Maintaining reports and files will more than likely be the responsibility of several people within the operation. You should understand what the various systems are and what information they contain, even if it is not your administrative duty to tend to them.

Directive for Robbery Attempts

A written directive should be compiled detailing how a robbery attempt is to be dealt with. The following factors must be considered:

1. Safety of investigators
2. Applicable departmental guidelines
3. Safety of customers
4. Scope of the investigation.

The safety of the investigators is the single most important aspect. If they sense any imminent danger, take action to remove it. Certain precautions should have been instituted during site preparation to deal with this possibility. Funds can be recovered or reissued. New operations can be initiated. But operatives cannot be replaced.

Of course, the directive must incorporate any applicable departmental guidelines. Many departments do not have a standard operating procedure dealing with this topic. Therefore, the directive written for the storefront should obtain administrative approval.

Safety of customers, either legitimate or otherwise, also must be taken into account. The death of a "customer" at the hands of another perpetrator may seem like poetic justice to some. However, this could have serious and lasting ramifications.

The scope of the investigation will also assist in determining this policy. The directive for a storefront that spent a considerable length of time and funds to initiate could differ from one that was more economically launched. The targets of the operation will be another factor to consider. The prudent course of action may be to cooperate with the offender and apprehend this suspect at a later date, even though this takes extraordinary self-control and is very humbling—not to mention the humiliating station-house comments that are sure to follow.

There may be other factors that are relevant and arise from your particular investigation or jurisdiction. These, too, must be evaluated before comprising the directive. A legal review of the directive is advised. This will ensure that the policy is written in such a manner that it cannot be used later against an officer who has otherwise taken appropriate action.

OTHER ADMINISTRATIVE DUTIES

Visits by personnel not directly involved with the day-to-day undercover operation of the storefront should not be allowed. Their intentions may be well meaning and their news worthwhile; however, their presence will pose a danger not only to the integrity of the site but to the operatives as well. When absolutely necessary for other personnel to visit the site, it should be done by appointment. They should be told not to bring along any police items.

We had an administrator who insisted on inspecting one of our sites. He promised to dress down so as not to be too conspicuous. He wore jeans, a sport shirt, and a bolo tie. His belt buckle and bolo tie clasp were a matched set. They both displayed a replica of a police badge. Fortunately, no customers were present. His visit was well intended but could have easily led to dire circumstances. It is the little things that get you.

Other police paraphernalia should also be banned: side-handled batons, items with law enforcement insignias, handcuffs, paychecks, or stubs—anything that could reveal the true identity of the business. If items of this sort are required to be at the site, have a secure area where they can be stored.

The storefront should be referred to as the offsite or the appropriate designated code name. All correspondence and reports should refer to the operation in this manner. The use of the business name or term *storefront* is not advisable in such circumstances. The location of the site should be kept strictly confidential and only released on a need-to-know basis. This also applies to most aspects of the investigation.

When utilizing services from outside units, their reports and logs should be typed by storefront clerical personnel. These documents should then be retained in the operation's files. When a copy is required by the outside unit, it should be censored when possible. All sensitive material should be blackened.

SUMMARY

Supervision is a control and developmental device used to maintain the performance of subordinates. Therefore, the supervisor should be actively involved in the operational planning. The control exercised over subordinates should be tempered so it will not to impair their enthusiasm and creativity. It is true that this type of activity demands that certain regulations and guidelines be strictly adhered to. However, the investigators' freedom to improvise and use their own discretion must also be considered. This, along with proper restraint, will only enhance their performance and the efforts of the storefront.

The management of records, no matter how unpleasant and tedious, must be taken on with zeal and competence. These are the mainstay of the investigation. They not only substantiate the activities of the operation but will become an invaluable resource for prosecution. Their care and organization must be tended to continually.

The area of fiscal management demands rigid scrutiny. The funding bestowed on the investigation must be strictly accounted for. Discrepancies in expenditures cannot be tolerated. The instituting of appropriate documentation and safeguards is essential. They not only protect the integrity of the operation, but investigators as well.

CHAPTER 12

Surveillance Techniques and the Storefront

Surveillance is the secretive, continuous, or periodic observation of people, vehicles, places, or objects to obtain information in reference to the targeted activity. Often, this is the only method available to identify targets and cohorts and to collect intelligence required to complete or enhance the evidence gathered at the storefront. All storefront investigations will use some form of surveillance and usually a combination of techniques. However, relatively few officers have had the opportunity to perform surveillance.

The first two types of surveillance explored in this chapter are

1. Moving surveillance
   a. Foot surveillance
   b. Vehicle surveillance
2. Stationary or fixed surveillance.

We then discuss the mainstay of most storefronts, electronic or audio and video surveillance. This discussion includes:

1. Legal aspects
   a. Public view
   b. Consenting party
2. Establishing a proper foundation for use in court
   a. Using the appropriate equipment
   b. Competent use of equipment
   c. Authentic recordings
   d. Proper maintenance of tapes
   e. Logs.

TYPES OF SURVEILLANCE

As just noted, there are three main types of surveillance which can be beneficial to the storefront operation.

1. Moving: The tracking of a target on foot or in a vehicle.
2. Stationary: The continuous viewing of a place, person, or object from a fixed vantage point.
3. Electronic: The use of mechanical or other devices in recording transactions.

These techniques can provide operatives with valuable intelligence to supplement the information gathered at the storefront. They can also supply other data which will benefit the investigation. The primary objectives of surveillance are as follows:

1. To maintain the safety of operatives
2. To reveal the identity of targets
3. To obtain additional evidence of the crime being probed
4. To aid in determining the reliability of cooperating individuals and information given
5. To establish the associates and hangouts of suspects, which could help in locating offenders at a future date and indicate future targets
6. To locate the stash of a target, additional hidden property, or contraband
7. To gather adequate information to establish probable cause for search and/or arrest warrants
8. To apprehend the target in the commission of a crime
9. To prevent the commission of a crime
10. To compile intelligence that could be used in future interrogations
11. To substantiate information received from a target as to the illicit activities of others.

These techniques can be further categorized according to their function.

1. Information surveillance: Used to learn as much as possible in reference to the target and associates, and their criminal activity.
2. Prepurchase surveillance: Used to gain tactical information that will assist the operatives in conducting the transaction.
3. Cover surveillance: Initiated to provide for further protection of operatives. It can also be helpful in corroborating the investigator's testimony.

4. Postpurchase surveillance: Will establish where the subject goes after the sale. It can also be used in revealing the true identity of the offender and associates.

PREPARATION AND EQUIPMENT

Most investigators are capable of conducting a surveillance when provided with proper equipment and preparation for the activity. However, there are certain desirable qualities officers engaged in these undertakings should possess.

Desirable Qualities of Surveillance Officers

An ordinary appearance is best. Any outstanding physical characteristics, such as exceptional height, either tall or short; obesity; or another personal trait that could draw the target's attention should be considered in the selection of personnel. One of our investigators was 6'7" and weighed about 350 pounds. His use in surveillance was limited. Your attention was automatically directed at him because of his size, and once he was seen, he could not be forgotten. The surveillance officers must also be able to act natural under a wide range of circumstances—fit in as if they belonged. They should have a high degree of alertness and be resourceful. Unanticipated occurrences are the norm rather than the exception. Their powers of observation and memory should be above average. Often, what is seen cannot be written down as it occurs. Patience and endurance are a must. Waiting for a target to arrive or conduct a daily activity, and then following the subject day after day through the same routine, requires a great deal of perseverance.

Preparation for Surveillance Activity

When initiating surveillance, investigators should research all files pertaining to the target and derive as much data as possible on the suspected criminal activities, habits, work and neighborhood environment, associates, and possible vehicles at the target's disposal. They should concentrate on names and aliases used, detailed physical description (obtain a photograph if possible), and any identifying characteristics or mannerisms. Also, knowing whether the subject has been or is suspicious of being tailed could help determine ability to detect or elude surveillance.

Officers should be knowledgeable regarding the scope and extent of criminal activities of the target. A fence may also deal narcotics, a narcotics dealer could also smuggle aliens, and so on. Understanding the various aspects of the target's enterprises will assist in preparing for the surveillance.

Familiarization with the type of neighborhood in which the activity is to take place is also important. Its inhabitants, mode of dress, use of language, and cultural customs must be examined. This will assist in the selection of personnel and vehicles which will blend into the area.

Attire and Vehicles for Surveillance

The equipment to be used is limited only by the officers' ability to improvise and their resourcefulness. For a short-term observation of a construction site, wearing a tool belt and hard hat may be suitable. If the activity is to be conducted on a beach, donning a swimsuit or shorts, rather than a three-piece pinstripe suit, may be more inconspicuous. Clothing should be plain rather than garish and ostentatious. It should also be appropriate for the situation and surroundings. Displaying flashy jewelry is discouraged in most instances. Attire should be chosen to allow officers to blend in, rather than stand out. Carrying a weapon can also become an area of concern; the clothing worn may not be suitable for concealing a weapon. The use of a belly bag, knapsack, or a plain paper bag could be placed into service to conceal a firearm. Cameras, binoculars, telescope, and recording equipment must be included in the preparation when appropriate. Anticipating what could be used to enhance the endeavor is essential.

Vehicles should not be conspicuous. Again, select vehicles that will fit in with the neighborhood. They should be free of any features that make them readily distinguishable. Bright colors, loud exhaust systems, body damage, and unusual accessories could all bring attention to the vehicle. Simple things like bumper stickers, wheel covers, antennas, and window decals can also draw unwanted attention.

When possible, the vehicles should be manned by two occupants—one to drive and one for maintaining notes. The second occupant could also be used for foot surveillance if the need arises. The seating arrangement should be altered periodically to avoid recognition by the target. Hats and/or bandannas and sunglasses can be put on and taken off to give the appearance of different occupants. When one officer is assigned to a vehicle, the use of a small, hand-held tape recorder could be advantageous. Notes could be recorded without having to drive, write, and keep track of the target at the same time. (Remember, all reports and logs should be typed and maintained by storefront personnel.)

Note: When wearing sunglasses, be cautious of their effects on colors. Some alter color drastically. When noting the description of vehicles or clothing lift, the glasses to gain a true perspective.

Other Items to Consider

Creature comforts should also be considered. An assignment that is supposed to last for an hour or two could go on and on and on. A suitable container with snacks, sandwiches, drinks, premoistened towelettes, toilet paper, and other such items can be welcome during an extended surveillance. An empty, rinsed Clorox bottle or other unbreakable receptacle with a screw-on cap should be kept in the vehicle—you never know where you will be when nature calls. Other items appropriate for the circumstances, such as raincoats, sweaters, jackets, and/or hats, should be kept in the vehicle.

It may also be beneficial to carry a different set of license plates that can be changed periodically. Many vehicles readied for surveillance have switches installed to allow for one headlight or the other to be turned off, and one or the other taillight to be turned off. Ploys such as these will give the vehicle a variety of appearances.

Reconnaissance

When the area to be observed is unfamiliar to participating officers, reconnaissance could be necessary. This allows for a study of the peculiarities and possible vantage points. Also, traffic conditions can be viewed and investigators can become familiar with names and locations of streets, including dead-ends, alleys, and one-way roads. These could be used by the target to spot a tail. It is a little unsettling when the target turns a corner and is followed by three or four surveillance units into a dead-end alley. This scouting could also yield information on the neighborhood and inhabitants that would not be found in police files.

Officer in Charge: Tactical Plan

An initial task in planning and conducting a surveillance is the designation of an officer in charge. When a number of officers are involved, a tactical plan outlining the duties of each should be prepared. If it is anticipated to be a lengthy undertaking, suitable relief should be arranged. A prearranged, secure system of communicating with headquarters and car to car must be established. The use of police radio monitors by undesirables is prevalent. You do not want the target privy to your conversations. Explanations for being at a particular place should also be discussed in the eventuality that an officer is approached by the target and accused of following him.

SURVEILLANCE ON FOOT

This type of observation is generally used over relatively short distances to maintain contact with a target. In some areas of high traffic congestion, it could also be advantageous. However, the investigator must be prepared to conduct a lengthy foot surveillance when necessary. There are four principal methods for achieving this: one-person, two-person, ABC, and progressive.

One-Person Method

The one-person method consists of a single officer attempting to follow a target. This usually occurs when the subject has left his or her vehicle and contact is desirable. It is difficult to conduct since you have to keep the suspect in view at all times. It usually requires close proximity to the offender, allowing for observations when a building is entered, a corner is turned, or any sudden movements are made. The effectiveness of this technique is somewhat dependent on pedestrian traffic and physical characteristics of the area. It should be avoided whenever possible.

Two-Person Method

Two-person surveillance affords greater security against detection and reduces the risk of losing the suspect. On streets with heavy pedestrian and/or vehicle traffic, both surveillants should remain on the same side of the street as the target. The first officer trails the suspect fairly closely. The second remains some distance behind. On a less crowded street, one officer should walk on the opposite side almost abreast of the subject. The other tails on the same side. To lessen the chance of detection, the two should periodically change their position relative to the target.

ABC Method

The ABC method uses a three-person team. This further reduces the risk of losing contact and, under most conditions, affords more security against detection. It also allows for a greater variation in the positioning of officers and permits one who suspects he or she has been spotted to drop off. With normal traffic conditions, *A* keeps a reasonable distance behind the target, while *B* follows *A* concentrating on keeping *A* in view. *B* also checks for cohorts who may be there to detect a tail. *C* walks on the opposite side of the street slightly behind the suspect. When there is little or no traffic, two officers could be on the opposite side of the street or one in front of the suspect. On crowded streets, all three should be on the same side. The leading officer follows closely to observe the suspect at intersections or if he or she enters a building. As with the two-person method, positions relative to the suspect should be altered frequently.

When using any method of foot surveillance, try to avoid eye contact. Walk close to buildings or other structures that can afford some cover. Change the eye or eyeball frequently. Try not to peek from doorways or around corners. Act natural, as if you belong.

Progressive Technique

With the progressive technique, the subject is observed intermittently along a certain habitual route. The investigator is stationed at a fixed point until the offender is out of view. The next day, the officer is positioned at the point where sight was lost and watches until the target goes out of view once more. This continues until the desired results are obtained. More than one officer can be used to extend the period of observation.

This method is of value in locating hideouts and meeting places when the risk of tailing the target is too great. It can be time consuming, and the probability of meeting objectives is sometimes poor. There is no assurance that the suspect will go to the same destination or take the same route each day. However, a modified version could be useful when rounds are routine, associates are known, but the base of operation is not known. The subject can be followed until the risk of detection is too great. It is then canceled for that day and reinstituted the next day at the location of the previous day's cancellation.

Detecting Foot Surveillance

There are many ways in which someone can attempt to detect foot surveillance. Some common tactics used are as follows:

1. Stopping to tie a shoestring, while looking for followers
2. Stopping abruptly and turning around to see who is behind him or her
3. Reversing course and retracing steps
4. Stopping abruptly after turning a corner
5. Alternating pace, fast then slow
6. Having associates in a shop or other strategic locations to watch for a tail
7. Riding short distances on a bus or taxi, or circling in a taxi
8. Entering a building and leaving immediately via another exit
9. Watching in wall mirrors or reflections of display windows to see who is coming or going
10. Starting to leave a place quickly, then suddenly turning around and coming back.

Other Problems of Foot Surveillance

There are a multitude of problems that can be encountered in conducting foot surveillance. It is useful to consider some of the more commonly encountered difficulties.

When a subject enters a building, at least one surveillant should follow. This is unless it is a private home, small shop, or if the clientele itself would pose the possibility of exposing the surveillance. In large public buildings with many exits, all team members should enter. It would then be prudent for one member to remain in the lobby or at an anticipated exit point to hopefully observe the target leaving.

Elevators

Elevators can present unique problems. When the offender enters and is the lone occupant, it may not be advisable to follow. Watch the floor indicator and attempt to determine where the target left the elevator. Then proceed to that level and attempt to reestablish surveillance. If you choose to enter the elevator, wait until the subject exits; then ride to the next floor before leaving and trying to regain contact. Whatever method is selected, one officer should remain in the lobby. Often, elevators are used to elude or as a precaution against possible surveillance.

Restaurants

When restaurants are entered, at least one surveillant should follow. Be alert to any contacts that are made inside. Try to anticipate when the target will be leaving. Exit just before, if possible, and wait to resume surveillance outside. Remember, subjects often hurry from their table toward the exit and then turn around quickly to see who is following.

Theater, Racetracks, and Amusement Parks

If a theater, racetrack, or amusement park is entered, most surveillants on the team should follow. The regular admission charge should be paid. Do not badge your way in. The cashier or ticket taker could be in cahoots with the target. It is important to maintain close surveillance in crowds. In darkened theaters, an agent can sit directly behind the suspect and observe any contacts. Sufficient personnel to watch exits is also helpful.

VEHICLE SURVEILLANCE

In most instances this will be the primary type of moving surveillance used by the storefront. There are four basic types which can be used.

One Vehicle

When only one vehicle is available, it should position itself behind the suspect's car. This distance will vary depending on traffic conditions. In most heavy city traffic, two to four car lengths is desirable. As traffic lessens, the demand for greater distance between vehicles increases. Whenever possible, allow a vehicle to be between you and the target. At night, avoid using high beams and have all unnecessary lights inside or outside the vehicle turned off.

Two Vehicle

With a two-car surveillance in city traffic during daylight hours, both vehicles should remain behind the target. Occasionally, one vehicle could travel a known parallel route. When this is done, that vehicle should try to time its arrivals at intersections just before the suspect to observe his or her path at the crossing. This is also a highly suitable method to use at night in a suburban area.

Three or More Vehicles

Three or more vehicles is the primary type of surveillance used. It allows for more usage of parallel routes. Vehicle positions in relation to the suspect can be changed more frequently. This should assist in preventing detection. One vehicle could lead the suspect while observing movements in the rearview mirror. Officers who suspect they have been burned can fall off, and surveillance can still be maintained.

Leap Frog

The leap frog method with vehicles is very similar to progressive foot surveillance. The subject's vehicle is observed intermittently as it proceeds along its suspected route. It is followed for very short distances by members of the team and then allowed to go out of view. The surveillance is picked up from the last observation point the next day. After a number of such attempts, the desired results are gained. This approach is sometimes impractical due to the great distances that can be traveled in a vehicle. For this reason, it would be more beneficial if the surveillance officers followed the target until the risk of detection is great, and then ceased observation for the day. Then the following day or on the next scheduled trip, the surveillance can be initiated at the point where the previous activity was ended.

Detecting a Tail

Targets will use various techniques to detect surveillance, including

1. Alternating fast and then slow vehicle speed
2. Frequent parking
3. Stopping suddenly around curves or corners
4. Speeding uphill and then slowly going downhill
5. Turning down dead-end streets
6. Pulling into driveways and then watching who goes by, or suddenly pulling to the side of the road.

Eluding Surveillance

Once a target has confirmed surveillance, a variety of tactics to elude observation come into play. The most common are

1. Committing flagrant traffic violations
2. Using double entrances to driveways or parking structures—in one, out the other
3. Cutting through parking lots
4. Driving through congested areas
5. Deserting vehicle beyond a blind curve or corner.

FIXED SURVEILLANCE

When this method is used, officers observe from a fixed point such as a room, house, or camouflaged outdoor fixture located near the premises being watched. Typically, this type of surveillance is conducted for the following reasons:

1. To detect illegal activity in the target area
2. To identify people who frequent the dwelling or establishment and determine their role in the illicit activity
3. To provide the probable cause for a search warrant of the targeted area
4. To determine the habits of the people who frequent the location under observation.

Area Reconnaissance: Selecting a Vantage Point

Before fixed surveillance can begin, a careful study of the surrounding area should be made. The officers should note the residents and transients along with the general character of the neighborhood. Only after this is done should the observation point be selected. This position should afford a vantage point covering all entrances and exits to the target location. When using a room or building, there should also be an access by which officers can enter and leave without being seen from the suspect's location. When this type of structure cannot be obtained, a camouflaged outdoor fixture such as a vendor's stand or utility pole tent can be used. An appropriately disguised van or motor home could also be used.

There could be a certain degree of commotion involved in establishing the observation post. Equipment may need to be moved in and relief officers will come and go. These activities should be as unobtrusive as possible. Relief and surveillance officers could enter and leave the post at different times and in separate directions. It is best not to take any of the residents into your confidence. If this is absolutely necessary, the number should be held to a minimum and the purpose of the activity should not be revealed.

Logging Events

Chronological logs of the target activity should be kept, recording pertinent information for surveillance reports. The log should indicate times of arrival and departure of suspects. Descriptive notes of the targets should be made and, when possible, a photographic record of visitors should be maintained. This enables investigators to identify people frequenting the target location and document their involvement with the primary suspect(s). At least one officer should constantly observe the target location while the other takes meticulous notes of all observations.

Equipment

Binoculars could be essential, as they can facilitate positive identification of people and vehicles entering and leaving the location under surveillance. A 35-mm camera with a telephoto lens can also be used effectively in documenting activity. It may prove helpful to have a motor-driven film advance to facilitate rapid shooting and a data-back feature to allow investigators to mark the frame with their initials, time, and date. This is desirable because photographs should be numbered in reference to time.

General Principles of Vehicle Surveillance

There are general principles that pertain to all the aforementioned techniques.

1. Try not to arouse police suspicions; this only brings attention to the surveillance.

2. Avoid unsubstantiated feelings of being burned; do not become paranoid.

3. When you are discovered, do not return directly to the police station or storefront. Make sure you are not being followed to confirm the target's suspicions.

4. Be alert during surveillance to ensure that you are not being followed.

5. The simple deed of losing a target, while frustrating, should not be considered in itself an incompetent act. Those with years of experience and who conduct this activity on a daily basis suffer the same plight.

6. Use subterfuge whenever possible. For example, stop someone on the street to ask questions if the subject stops to talk to someone.

7. The approximate location of the subject's destination can at times be estimated. This is possible when speedometer readings on the target's vehicle can be obtained before and after trips.

ELECTRONIC AUDIO AND VIDEO SURVEILLANCE

While the other forms of surveillance are used to enhance the performance of the investigation, this type of surveillance is more prevalent. One distinctive advantage of using a storefront is the ability to record transactions. This will eventually allow the jury to sit in on the buy. They can see for themselves the attitude and behavior displayed by the defendant during criminal dealings. That is why this form of evidence is so damaging.

Electronic surveillance, as it pertains to the storefront, is the use of audio and video devices to obtain and record criminal activity. There are other forms, such as the interception of wire communications (wiretaps) or oral communications by concealed microphones (bugs), that are not commonly associated with a storefront. The Electronic Communications Privacy Act of 1986, Title III of the Omnibus Crime Control and Safe Streets Act of 1968, Public Law 90-351, and the Fourth Amendment, which prohibits "unreasonable searches and seizures," pertain to these procedures. There could also be applicable state statutes which set forth their own regulations. Keep in mind that state counterparts must be at least as restrictive but can be more restrictive than federal legislation.

Since this type of evidence is going to be the mainstay of the majority of operations, let's take a moment to look into the various legal aspects. There are two relatively distinct situations where video- and/or audio-aided surveillance could be used. Each requires a different constitutional analysis and application. First is the recording of activities that occur in an area that is either viewable by the public or commonly accessible to the public. This could be used to enhance the various types of surveillance that are used in conjunction with the primary investigation. It could also come into play if a deal stemming from the operation takes place outside the site area.

Second is the recording of activity with the consent of a participant in a viewed area, such as the storefront.

Public View

The Fourth Amendment prohibits unreasonable searches and seizures and dictates that warrants be issued on probable cause determined by an individual who is neutral and detached from law enforcement. This is usually a judge or magistrate. Video surveillance evidence obtained in violation of the Fourth Amendment requirements may fall prey to the exclusionary rule and could lead to civil liability for the offending officer and/or department.

Expectation of Privacy

The Supreme Court, in the benchmark case of *Katz v. United States,* interpreted and defined that portion of the Fourth Amendment which prohibits unreasonable searches. The court recognized that the intent of the amendment was to "protect people, not places." Therefore, a search, for Fourth Amendment purposes, occurs whenever there is a governmental intrusion on an individual's justified or objectively *reasonable expectation of privacy.*

The court has also determined that a search must generally be conducted pursuant to a search warrant. This is unless it fits into one of the traditionally recognized exceptions to these requirements. The exceptions include search incidental to arrest, consent, or emergency searches.

Video Surveillance

When members of the storefront conduct video surveillance, they must comply with basic Fourth Amendment standards. A search warrant must be obtained or the surveillance must meet with one of the *specific delineated exceptions* when it intrudes into a reasonable expectation of privacy. However, if the video surveillance will not infringe on the expectations of privacy, it does not constitute a search requiring Fourth Amendment restrictions.

The use of this technique to record and/or observe activity which is viewable to the public does not generally constitute an intrusion into an expectation of privacy. This is because either the public can legally see the activity from a lawful vantage point or has lawful access to the area. An investigator is not normally conducting a search when observing activity which is otherwise open to public view. Therefore, the need to obtain prior judicial approval does not exist. The Supreme Court has stated that the Fourth Amendment "has never been extended to require law enforcement officers to shield their eyes when passing by a home on public thoroughfares."

In respect to this statement, investigators can in most instances use video surveillance to assist in observing certain areas. This is even true when the areas are within one's home, if others can observe the same things from the same lawful vantage point.

Perplexing Questions

What does all this mean, and how does it apply to a storefront investigation? A target arrives at the site. He tells you his partner is in possession of a large amount of contraband. The partner will deal with investigators if they agree to let the target deliver the property to the storefront. Then if everything goes smoothly with this transaction, he will start doing business directly at the site. After intense negotiations, this is the only way this buy can take place. You have been able to ascertain the location of the contraband and when the target will acquire it for delivery to investigators.

Surveillance can be established to record obtaining the contraband from the cohort. A van will be lawfully parked across the street from the residence. This provides an unobstructed view of the front of the location in question. When the target arrives, his associate opens the garage door and the subject drives in. The door remains open as the exchange takes place. The target then leaves and returns shortly. Surveillance units have been alerted that the property in question has been delivered to the storefront. Upon arrival, the offender walks into the house. Through a large glass window you can see the two suspects standing in the front room. Money is passed from the target to his partner. These events were recorded without first obtaining a warrant. Will the tape be admissible in court?

No reasonable expectation of privacy was violated. The activity inside the garage could be viewed by anyone who happened by. The exchange inside the house was also viewable by anyone who may have been on the street or sidewalk and wanted to look inside through the window. The location of the surveillance equipment was in an area commonly used by the public.

Now, let's place some what-ifs into the scenario. What if the property was in the backyard which was surrounded by an 8-foot-high cinderblock wall? To observe the transaction, you had to position the equipment in a public park. The park is located on a hill directly behind the house in question. Have you violated the expectation of privacy? Isn't that why all the expense was incurred to build the wall, to keep nosy people from looking into the backyard? The park is an area commonly accessible to the public. Anyone in the park could have looked upon the same event. No infringement of privacy has occurred.

What if the park was a mile from the house and powerful zoom lenses were required to capture this activity on film? This is most likely going to be construed as an invasion of privacy by most courts. Ordinarily, the public does not have this type of equipment at its disposal. The extraordinary means by which the evidence was obtained must be considered.

What if you had to climb a utility pole which was on public property? This, too, could be ruled as a violation of Fourth Amendment rights. A utility pole is not commonly accessible to the public. Therefore its use, which enabled you to peer over the 8-foot wall, is an intrusion. This differs from using the pole to observe an area that is open to public view, such as the front of the house.

What if the exchange of contraband was to take place inside a store, open to the public, during business hours? You were able to place a pinhole lens through an opening in an adjoining wall. This allowed for coverage of common areas. The space where the video equipment is located is controlled by you. Is this recording admissible? Yes, customers of a publicly accessible store fully expect to be seen by others. Therefore, they do not have a constitutionally protected expectation of privacy.

When considering this often perplexing question, put yourself in the place of the offender. If I were he, would I have a reasonable expectation of privacy? If you answer yes, the suspect probably does also. If you are not sure or have any doubts, do not risk filming. Obtain a warrant or seek legal assistance. Remember, not only is there a danger of the exclusion of evidence, you and the department could face civil liabilities.

Consenting Party

Storefronts are designed to observe and record meetings between an operative, a cooperating witness, and the target. In these situations, the observed subject voluntarily exposes his or her actions to a participant in the activity—the undercover officer or cooperating witness, who has given his or her consent to the video monitoring. Thus, the recorded criminal acts can be made everlasting through the magic of videotape.

Consensual video surveillance can be considered similar to consensual audio surveillance. In this technique, a participant to oral conversations consents to the transmission of the exchange and/or the recording of the conversation. The Supreme Court considered the relevance of the Fourth Amendment to consensual or participant audio monitoring in *United States v. White.*

In reference to this case, Justice White wrote, "If the conduct and revelations of an agent operating without electronic equipment do not invade the defendant's constitutionally justifiable expectations of privacy neither does a simultaneous recording of the same conversation made by the agent or by others from transmissions received from the agent to whom the defendant is talking and whose trustworthiness the defendant necessarily risks." In short, this technique is not a search and does not intrude on defendants' reasonable expectation of privacy when they voluntarily engage in conversation, even if the defendants believe the information will not be revealed.

The courts have reached the same conclusion in regarding video monitoring and recording. In *State v. Jennings*, police officers, with the consent of an undercover operative, observed and audio and videotaped the defendant bring heroin to the operative. The delivery was made in the officer's rented motel room. The State Supreme Court stated in this case

> . . . *we can see no reason why a person's justifiable expectations of privacy would be greater where videotapes are made than where just sound recordings are made. It is not the nature of the recording that is at issue but whether the defendant has an expectation of privacy such that any recording would violate the Fourth Amendment. The defendant is relying on the discretion of the person to whom he is talking, and just as that person can testify as to the statements made by the defendant,* . . . *so can he testify as to physical actions of the defendant. The videotapes, just like the sound recording, simply produce the most reliable evidence of the actual transaction, and there is no apparent reason why a sound recording should be admissible and a video tape inadmissible* . . . *the defendant's expectation of privacy was that [the undercover officer] would not tell the police of the transaction; just as that expectation is not constitutionally protected, so there is no constitutional prohibition against admission of the tape where [the undercover officer] consented to the filming.*

In a similar case, a federal district court ruled that officers conducting an undercover fencing business did not violate any Fourth Amendment standards when they videotaped the defendant selling stolen property to an undercover officer, when the videotaping was conducted with that officer's consent.

Limiting Consensual Monitoring

When using this specific delineated exception, officers must be cognizant to limiting consensual video monitoring. It can only be used in those instances when the consenting party is present at the time of recording. When the consenting party leaves the viewing area, the monitoring and recording must be discontinued until that party returns.

With one of our storefronts, the area where most of the recording was done was a small office inside a larger building. When an officer left the room, the video recording was not always suspended. If you merely walk to the door or just outside the door and can still hear the targets and they and the recording device can still hear you, you do not need to discontinue monitoring. If you were to walk out and close the door or go such a distance that you could not to hear the target, then the suspension of recording is necessary.

PROVING CONSENT

Whenever consensual video surveillance is conducted, you must be able to prove that the consent was voluntary and not the result of coercion.

As a matter of sound practice, obtain written permission to record. This is especially true when relying on the consent of cooperating citizens or informants. This written documentation can be crucial if the consenting party recants permission at trial. It can also play a factor if the defense challenges the voluntary consent.

Consider the possibility that you are conducting a buy with a target and a cooperating individual. The target asks you to leave the room for a moment while he converses with the CI. It is assumed that the CI has given his permission to tape. The evidence obtained during this conversation proves to be pivotal to the case. When it comes time to present this video recording in court, the CI states that he did not consent to the recording. Without a written document to rebuff this claim, the case could be in serious jeopardy.

Establishing a Proper Foundation

With most courts, it is generally agreed that if the following conditions are met, a proper foundation for the admission into evidence of audio and video recordings has been established.

1. The electronic device used is capable of recording the evidence accurately.
2. The operators of the device are competent to use the equipment.
3. The recordings are authentic, accurate, and correct. A fair representation of the recorded event is portrayed.
4. There have been no changes, additions, alterations, or deletions made in the tape.
5. The evidence was properly preserved by the custodians.
6. The participants in the recorded conversation can be properly identified.
7. The conversation took place voluntarily, without improper inducement.
8. At least one party to the conversation consented to its recording.

Therefore, the following safeguards should be instituted. Use quality equipment which is properly maintained and in good working condition. Those operating the equipment should be familiar with its proper functioning and be able to demonstrate this in court if necessary. You do not have to know all the various electronic elements that are needed to bring an image to tape; rather, you must understand of how to turn the machine on and off and insert tapes.

Documenting a Transaction on Tape

On the recording, fully identify the individuals engaged in the conversation, including officers, and any other people present, when possible. This should be done even though these people may not have spoken. Establish the time, date, and location in which the tape was made. It was our practice to make a short introduction on the tapes. It included the aforementioned information and a short statement of the reason for the meeting. It would conclude with a sentence such as, "The recording device will be turned off until the arrival of the target(s)" or would give the name(s) of the subject. When the target arrives, the tape is activated. When possible, indicate on the tape the present time and that the recording device has been turned on in anticipation of meeting with the subject. After the subject has left, indicate on the recording the time and a short statement of who was there and what was accomplished. If an item was purchased, you can describe it on the tape and indicate what was paid to the offender.

Retrieving Tapes from the Recorder: Original and Working Copy

When the tape is retrieved from the machine, it should be labeled and reviewed. The label should contain the date, time, location of events, participants (including officers), and the name of the person removing the tape from the recorder. It should then be sealed in a proper container, tagged, and placed into evidence by the person who removed the tape from the recorder. The seal should not be broken until the recording is presented in court.

It is not advantageous to make copies from the original tape. Therefore, the simultaneous recording of two or more tapes is desirable. The original can be reviewed for the quality of the recording, labeled, and tagged into evidence. The chain of custody for the tapes is like that of any other evidence. It must be strictly maintained for the tape to be exhibited in court. The additional tapes can then be used as working copies. These tapes should bear labels similar to the original with an indication that they are working copies. An indication should also be made on the original tape; this will allow for its positive identification in court. In reviewing the tapes, if any malfunction is detected, indicate this in a written report. This report should detail when the malfunction was discovered, what the problem was, how it was remedied, and a comprehensive description of events not captured on the recording. The mere fact that a recording is not clear and that there may be unintelligible portions does not render it inadmissible in court.

Tape Woes

We were sent to inspect a storefront operation being conducted by another unit within our department. One of the first things they wanted to show us was their innovative technique used to save tapes and compile buys into a concise format. The original recordings had been transferred to a single tape in chronological order. This allowed for showing events without having to change numerous tapes. The editing was superb, and it gave the viewer a real sense of being there, without annoying interruptions. When we asked about the fate of the original tapes, we were told they had been erased and reused. This saved the unit from purchasing six tapes on this one case alone. With the many other cases being investigated, this practice would eventually lead to big savings.

The thought was well intentioned but unfortunately very flawed. Not being able to produce the original tape could spell doom for the investigation. When tapes are compiled into a single format, the originals must be retained and the chain of custody protected. If this is not done, the copied recordings could be excluded as exhibits in court. Even if by some chance they are not, the door is open for the defense to claim that portions of the tapes that were beneficial to the defense have been edited. Do not jeopardize the investigation to save a few dollars. When there are any questions or doubts about any phase of the different surveillance techniques, contact the prosecutor for advice.

Video and Audio Logs

A log should be maintained in reference to the recordings. The following information could be helpful in an audio and video log:

1. Date, time, location, and who placed the tape in the machine
    a. After a tape is placed in a machine, a great deal of time may pass before a transaction is recorded.
2. Date, time, location, and counter number when recording began
    a. The location is usually the storefront, but it can vary if transactions occur away from the site.
    b. The counter number is helpful in locating a particular transaction on a tape that contains several buys.
    c. If there is more than one transaction on the tape, each one would be indicated on the log.
3. Date, time, location, and counter number of when the transaction is concluded
    a. The location would be necessary if the recording is of a moving surveillance—if the buy started at one location and ended at another.
4. Date, time, location, and who removed the tape from the machine
    a. To simplify the chain of custody, the operative who conducts the transaction should insert, remove, review, and tag the tape into evidence. This is not always possible, however.

b. If malfunctions are discovered while reviewing the tape, indicate this on the log.

c. When several operatives are involved in the investigation, it could be advantageous to indicate who turned the machine on and off for each transaction. This is usually the investigator conducting the buy. This can be useful if taping has to be temporarily suspended during consensual monitoring.

5. The names of all participants

a. A space should be allotted on the log to include this information.

6. Narrative

a. Sufficient space should be available for summarizing events. Include a description of what was purchased, the amount paid, and other relevant facts.

7. Tape and transaction number

a. An easy way to cross-reference logs, files, etc.

b. Each tape will have its own number as would each transaction. For example: tape 26, transaction 52. Then when compiling case reports, the various buys, which will more than likely be on different tapes, are easier to locate.

c. A transaction number can also be used on confidential fund expenditure logs to indicate receipt for expended monies.

d. A transaction number can also be placed on initial offense reports required to obtain a case number from central records. This can be in lieu of potentially compromising details.

8. Testing and noncriminal activity

a. With a tape that contains transactions, you must indicate in the log any tests that are conducted to ensure quality or proper working order of the equipment.

b. Any noncriminal meetings that may also appear on the tape must be logged.

c. Any time the tape is turned on, even if accidentally, it must be logged. Include a short note on the log as to the reason the recorder was activated.

9. Other information

a. Include information that would be pertinent to your particular investigation and helpful in tracking and compiling case reports.

The original copy of the log should be tagged into evidence with the original tape. A working copy should be made and filed for any future use.

This prevents the original from having to be checked in and out of evidence, thus aiding the preservation of the chain of custody.

Precautions for Recording

Here are some precautions that should be considered. You may opt to remove the recording tabs when tapes are removed from the machine. This prevents inadvertent recording while the tape is being reviewed. If this occurs, it could ruin your whole day, not to mention what it does to the evidence. Be careful about where tapes are stored. Magnetic fields can erase recordings. Bring this to the attention of the evidence technicians and ensure that a proper area for storage is provided. New tapes are preferable; they should be of good quality. Trying to save a few pennies could cost a lot more in the long run. However, you can utilize used tapes, but check that they are in proper working condition. Whatever type you choose, always inspect tapes before inserting them into the machine. Make sure recording tabs are in place, the case itself is free from damage, and the tape is not twisted or broken. The minimal effort this takes can prevent a lot of aggravation in the future.

With most of our sites the recording area was established to provide a view of people approaching from the street. When a transaction was to occur or we saw a target nearing the site, the recorder was activated. The aforementioned information was then recorded. We also gave a running narrative of what was occurring outside the view of the camera: the direction the offender arrived from, the vehicle and occupant description, where property was obtained from (inside the vehicle, etc.), and any information that would be relative to the case. When the subject left, the same procedure was followed. This portion of the recording, while seldom used in court, was helpful in writing offense reports. This took the place of having to write notes or trying to remember all that took place. When the buy was reviewed, on the working copy, an accurate detailing of these events could be obtained.

Invest the time necessary to tend to tapes and logs. The evidence they could contain is too valuable to be lost because of inappropriate care. A little care now will yield big dividends in the future.

SUMMARY

When the different types of surveillance are used appropriately, in conjunction with other investigative techniques, they contribute to the overall success of the operation. You must ensure proper planning and training. Surveillance is often difficult and could require practice before members become proficient. Adequate time should be set aside for the review of the various legislative statutes that pertain to surveillance. All laws regarding surveillance must be followed. The collection of evidence using surveillance methods is of no value if it cannot be introduced in court.

CHAPTER 13

Cooperating Individuals and the Storefront

The use of a cooperating individual (CI) to facilitate an investigation is often desirable. A CI can be the keystone to a storefront investigation. However, when not properly utilized, there are many potential drawbacks which will not only affect the outcome of the storefront but could have a direct adverse consequence on you. Many officers have not had the opportunity to work a CI before taking on a storefront probe. In using to the fullest all information provided by a CI, you must be aware of the motivation which spurs his or her assistance and how to control his or her actions.

Historically, law enforcement has been less than professional in dealing with available human sources of information. In the case of a CI, we cannot afford less than a professional effort. The more sophisticated the target, the more difficult the penetration. Therefore, if we are to be successful we must approach this potential valuable resource with caution and professionalism.

Using a CI to introduce the target to the storefront is expedient since the CI has already won the confidence of the suspect. However, it can provide less security than other methods when not properly managed. A CI's loyalty or credibility can become questionable at some future date. The CI could easily reveal the true identity of the operatives. Control is therefore a paramount concern.

Often, in our haste to begin storefront operations, we give no consideration to a cover story, how are we going to train and communicate with the CI, and what legal ramifications we are facing. We do not consider whether the CI can do what is asked. We do not think about security measures that will ensure the CI's future usefulness. Some of us have even placed total reliance on the judgment of a CI. This can lead to a disastrous outcome. We sometimes assume that the CI has inbred capabilities to do the job asked without proper guidance and training.

The term *cooperating individual* covers a large variety of human resources available to an investigator. We concentrate mainly on those individuals who supply information for monetary reward or some other form of compensation. There is more to using this source than simply getting the CI out there to learn everything possible. In this chapter, we will discuss

1. Types of CIs
2. Interviewing CIs
3. Special considerations for interviews and handling
4. CI development
5. CI negotiations
6. CI control and protection
7. Training the CI
8. Termination of the CI
9. Civil liability.

TYPES OF COOPERATING INDIVIDUALS

Descriptive titles bestowed on the various human resources which can be used by the investigation vary widely among law enforcement agencies. Frequently, they have a distasteful connotation. *Informant*, for example, is a term that often conjures up a negative image. We unconsciously associate derogatory depictions like snitch, squealer, fink, or rat when we hear the term. We have been taught from childhood not to be a tattletale. If these are your first impressions, what is the image projected to the jury? These latent denigrating labels given to the cooperating individual could be potentially damaging to his or her creditability and/or information provided in court. Why take the risk? Use a title that is benign and not disparaging.

Also, the term *informant* is used to refer to any number of information sources, from the skilled special employee who has been directed to penetrate the target to a reputable citizen who relays information as a civic duty. Therefore, it is important to understand what the terminology represents. To avoid confusion, it will be helpful to describe the CI types in terms of their escalating degree of involvement.

There are five types of CIs that will concern a storefront operation. These are the primary CIs who can provide invaluable assistance when properly handled and for whom special procedures have been established:

1. The occasional CI
2. The arrested CI

3. The constant CI

4. The special CI

5. The controlled CI.

Occasional CIs, as the term implies, supply information on an irregular basis. The investigator must initiate contact before these CIs are willing to reveal their awareness of specific criminal activity. Most are unwilling to provide sworn testimony or appear in court as a witness. They could include known or past criminals, associates of perpetrators, prostitutes, and addicts. The reliability of information given must always be questioned and verified through an independent source if it is to be used as evidence.

Arrested CIs provide information in reference to cohorts to avoid prosecution or reduce the criminal charges filed against themselves. Information furnished is the result of negotiations and is often a one-time opportunity. They could agree to provide testimony against a bigger fish or consent to become a regular CI upon their release. A convicted prisoner would also be included in this category. It would be prudent to involve the prosecutor in these negotiations or keep him or her abreast of any such activity.

Constant or regular CIs are usually members of an illegal group or close associates of those partaking in the criminal dealings. They are likely to be the most valuable for submitting information on the target of the storefront. Contact with investigators is made on a recurrent basis, and the source of the data is to remain anonymous. There can be several motives why they divulge such information, but most often it is for monetary reward.

Special CIs do far more than merely reveal information. They actively assist operatives in penetrating the illicit activity. Their reliability has been established and their credibility continuously monitored. They arrange introductions, buys, and are willing to testify in court if the need arises. They can also be directed to delve into special areas of interest of the investigation. They work under supervision and direction of the operatives. Police protection and relocation assistance should be considered when utilizing these types of CIs.

Controlled CIs are sought out and recruited because of their placement in a group, organization, or business, thus allowing access to desired information. They could also be enlisted for their ability to be placed in a position from which needed data can be acquired. The controlled CIs must be thoroughly evaluated before being approached. Recruitment should be conducted in a cautious and tactful manner, allowing for continual assessment of their value and reliability. They must be stringently managed, specifically directed, and continually tested for their credibility.

INTERVIEWING COOPERATING INDIVIDUALS

To become aware of the potential value of CIs, make an in-person appraisal. Certain special considerations govern interview procedures when dealing with a prospective CI.

Remain sensitive to the possible motives for cooperation, and do nothing to impede the flow of information. As with all undertakings of this sort, you must control the situation and conduct the interview as to gain maximum useful information. Protect your own well-being and guard against revealing information that could compromise the storefront.

The location of the interview should be determined by you. Meetings are usually held somewhere other than the storefront and away from the police department. If at all possible, don't go to the CI's home or place of business for this purpose. Choose a site that will encourage a relaxed, informal conversation. A neutral site will be far more conducive to obtaining the desired results. After the initial contact and the CI has become active, you can use brief telephone conversations. However, a formal person-to-person interview should be conducted with all new CIs.

Note: Administrative requirements such as photographing, fingerprinting, personal history sheet, signature card, and filling out other needed forms should be accomplished now. Take the time necessary to reassure CIs that their identity will be carefully concealed. Also explain why these administrative procedures are required and how they are to be used.

Factors to consider in selecting a place to conduct the interview include

1. Safety of the officer
2. Privacy—the interview cannot be observed or overheard by others
3. Interruptions—there will be ample time to conduct the interview without disturbances
4. Space—enough area to take notes and perform required administrative duties.

The general progress of the interview should stimulate a free-flowing narrative and then a review of details. Then you can ask more specific questions. Do not forget note taking. Indicate any personal idiosyncrasies, the CI's general attitude toward assisting law enforcement, and preferred time and place for future contacts. There are other considerations to bear in mind when conversing with CIs:

1. Sympathize with the CI in reference to any personal difficulties, especially if these difficulties could affect the CI's performance.
2. Encourage whatever reasons the CI may have for providing information.
3. Ask about subjects you are already aware of to verify the CI's reliability.

4. Do not disclose that information given is known to be without value or contradicts known facts. Protect your own secrets during the interview. The CI could be trying to gain information from you about police knowledge of targeted activity.

5. Avoid asking questions that unnecessarily embarrass or offend the CI's sense of decency.

6. Maintain control of the interview; do not argue with the CI.

7. Questions should not be structured so they can be answered with a yes or no.

Additionally, you must be alert not to reveal your own knowledge by the way you phrase questions. For example, you inquire about a specific individual or particular criminal activity. This could indicate that you already have knowledge about that person or endeavor. Develop a talent to proceed from general, purposely vague questions toward the direction desired. You could react with interest to old intelligence and then guide the conversation toward areas where helpful new information could be obtained. You may wish to remain passive when important disclosures are made to safeguard your awareness of the extent of the information already known. If you respond with impatience or anger, this will tell the CI that this information has previously been obtained by investigators.

At the conclusion of the interview, be explicit about what is expected from the CI. Make sure the CI understands basic rules, regulations, and procedures that will be followed. Tell the CI what behavior will not be tolerated. Make clear the consequences of such actions. Discuss other issues such as compensation for services, what procedure is to be followed if arrested, the extent of the CI's participation in the investigation, and what the CI can and cannot do to assist investigators. The latter refers to the types of searches or actual involvement in criminal activity that may legally jeopardize the probe and the degree to which the CI may orchestrate the activities of targets. Do not forget to express your appreciation for the CI's assistance. Make it clear that you value their help. While understanding that the CI could be primarily motivated by revenge, jealousy, or the desire for money, also recognize that the CI is not immune to the effects of common courtesy.

A certain amount of note taking will be necessary at the initial interview. At subsequent meetings, try to limit or avoid note taking; if possible, use a tape recorder. Note taking can inhibit the free flow of information and can indicate to the CI what portion of the conversation you consider important. Immediately after the rendezvous, compile a report detailing the information gained.

Remember, when dealing with any CI, avoid the use of derogatory terms. These have no place in the relationship. Get used to the terms *co-*

operating individual, source, special employee, or any expression that does not invoke unfavorable notions. A slip during an interview could turn off a valuable source of information. A blunder such as this during trial could discredit your efforts as well as those of the CI.

Special Considerations for Interviews and Handling

When the CI is of the opposite sex, you may have to be more careful than usual. He or she could be a reputable citizen, an organized crime figure, a prostitute, or something in between. In any case, you must restrict the relationship to gathering information.

In treating the prostitute with the same considerations and decency extended to any woman, information could be obtained that would otherwise be lost. Depending on the target of the storefront, prostitutes could be a valuable source of intelligence. Men often talk rather freely in their presence about their past and future criminal conquests.

Meetings between male operatives and female CIs are for official business and should take place only after a supervisor has been notified. At each meeting it would be prudent to have two investigators. Whenever possible, contact should be made in a public place. Male CIs may try to befriend the officer; female CIs could attempt to develop friendships by using sex. The unit supervisor must establish strict guidelines prohibiting close relationships or socializing with female CIs. The development of a CI does necessitate a certain amount of personal contact, conversation, and even flattery, but this fraternization with a female CI must be carefully controlled.

Addicts and parolees are potentially an effective source of information. They usually have firsthand knowledge of the targeted activity. They are known and accepted and can introduce operatives without unduly arousing suspicions. When appropriate for the type of investigation being conducted, make a strong effort to recruit and screen potential addict and parolee CIs. When using this process, your judgment as to the CIs credibility and reliability will be based on any prior knowledge, the one-to-one interview, feedback from other officers, and your own intuition.

Unfortunately, addict CIs can pose a very serious threat to an operative's personal safety and the integrity of the storefront. They have been known to set up officers or participate in attempts to frame them. They have provided erroneous information in a deliberate effort to use police as their instrument for personal revenge. They will also try to learn the identity of other undercover officers and exploit this knowledge to further their own objectives. When utilizing addict CIs, remember they will sell their mother to satisfy their habit. They would not hesitate to sell you out.

Parolee CIs pose special problems and should be avoided as much as possible. They are usually not permitted to associate with other ex-convicts or become involved with anyone associated with illegal activity. They may be restricted by curfews, and their participation in the investigation presents grave contradictions to the intent of the parole process. However, exceptions can occur when parolees have already become involved in illegal activity and are subject to being revoked. In these instances, information will usually result from negotiations much like those of an arrested source.

The use of juveniles presents a potentially grave problem. Many jurisdictions restrict the interviewing of juveniles unless conducted by a specially trained juvenile officer. Moreover, courts frown on and may even prohibit an initial or additional exposure of juveniles to criminal activity, even if it is to assist law enforcement. You should refrain from using juveniles to arrange buys or make introductions. However, you can elicit any information they may have on criminal activity when you follow applicable statutes. If it is absolutely unavoidable to use a juvenile CI, obtain written permission from the parents, juvenile officer, and/or probation officer. Again, use extreme caution as you could encounter dire consequences if juveniles are injured as a result of their employment.

You must uphold any promises made during the interview to maintain the confidence of the CI. Never promise anything that cannot be delivered. For example, you cannot promise that the CI will not be tried for certain crimes. However, you can make good the promise to notify the prosecutor of the CI's cooperation. If you are aware that criminal charges are pending, a conference with the prosecutor is advisable.

Some other guidelines include the following:

1. Be on time and keep all appointments even though the CI may be late or not show.
2. Exercise patience and be understanding of the position the CI is in.
3. Investigate all leads.
4. When possible, independently verify information.
5. Information from a CI should be considered valid until proven otherwise.

COOPERATING INDIVIDUAL'S DEVELOPMENT

To handle CIs successfully, you must be tactful and able to inspire the CI's trust. Fairness and living up to the promises are a must. The following attributes are also desirable:

1. A reputation for ethical conduct
2. Good interviewing skills
3. A complete comprehension of the criminal activity to be investigated
4. A keen perception of human nature and motivation

5. Comprehensive knowledge of the target and associates

6. Familiarity with applicable criminal statutes

7. An appreciation of the information received and its value.

These qualities aid in creating an atmosphere in which possible sources of information are able to conquer their inhibitions in reference to relinquishing information. These hindrances include

1. Fear of becoming stigmatized in the community

2. Loss of self-esteem

3. Ridicule from family, friends, and associates

4. General distrust of authority figures

5. Dread of retaliation

6. Repetitious appearances in court.

In the selection process for potential CIs, you should consider the following:

1. Their general state of health

2. Age

3. Educational background

4. Any distinguishing quality of their personalality

5. Present and past employment performance

6. Financial situation

7. Their motives for supplying information and/or assistance.

You must evaluate the CIs who will be used. Consider the whole person when making this judgment.

Motives for Divulging Information

Establishing the motives behind the willingness to reveal information and/or give assistance in the operation is important in obtaining a comprehensive understanding of the CI. The following are some basic motives for a CI's behavior.

Financial Gain

Most CIs will provide information in return for monetary rewards. This desire for money could be mixed with other underlying reasons, but the want of direct financial gain is undeniably significant. Do not be fooled into thinking all CIs who supply information for pay can usually be considered reliable sources, since the quality of their information is their livelihood and they want to stay in business. Be aware of the likelihood of receiving unreliable information particularly when times are slow and CIs want to maintain this means of generating income. This could lead to creative reporting. You must also assess the capability of a potential CI to deliver information as promised. Be cautious of what you reveal in the presence of any CI—one who sells information to one side could just as well sell it to the other.

Fear

The first law of nature is self-preservation. Therefore, fear is a very strong motive. The prospective CI will be far more cooperative when motivated by this powerful emotion which has been generated by something or someone. This is graphically illustrated when the accused deems it is a necessity to provide direct evidence against cohorts or demonstrate how such incriminating information can be gathered. When this need to maintain comfort involves disclosures in reference to big fish or implicates others, it can be advantageous to the storefront. This fear is not restricted to the consequences of being taken into custody for violating the law. A CI's associates could be the source of anxiety. If this is the case, assure the CIs that everything possible will be done to protect them from retaliation.

Revenge

Another all-consuming desire can be revenge: retaliation against an associate(s) who has done the CI wrong. CIs may feel discriminated against by one of their cronies. They do not think they are receiving the preferential treatment desired because of their special talents, or they haven't been given the opportunity to showcase their unique abilities. There could also be other factors that do not directly concern criminal activity. A falling out due to a dispute over a lover can create the bitterest of enemies out of the best of friends. During the initial interview with potential CIs, obtain as much information as possible regarding their motive. When revenge is detected, remember that if the conflict is settled, CIs could once again become chummy with their nemesis. This situation could compromise the storefront.

Self-Importance

Another common stimulus for cooperating with the authorities is the desire for self-importance. The pleasure obtained by some in inflating their knowledge, power, or rank and having an attentive listener is a strong motive. Petty criminals who can achieve the undivided attention of an investigator by revealing a story which supplies ample food for thought can get a real ego boost. This feeling can be enhanced when their own importance or their awareness of criminal activity of more notorious offenders is exaggerated. Those with this motive can supply valuable information, even though their recount can be tedious to endure. However, you must be willing to listen to everything that is said or risk ignoring what is beneficial.

Gratitude

CIs are often willing to assist in the investigation as a way to express their appreciation for an investigator's interest. We have cultivated many such sources of information through simple acts of common courtesy. Showing a concerned interest in CIs and their families can establish a useful rapport. A very productive CI we employed had gone into several drug rehabilitation programs as a direct result of our prodding. When the CI was finally clean, she provided years of beneficial support to many of our operations. Not all offenders will react in the same fashion to the interest you show, but those who do will more than compensate for your effort. There are many CIs today who are aiding in operations because of their gratitude for previous considerations and genuine concern displayed by the investigator.

Reform

CIs may come forward because they are repentant and wish to make restitution for their criminal behavior. They also intend to reform and make a clean break from their past. As with any potential CI, be cautious of this motive. Thoroughly debrief the prospective repenter and verify information given through an independent source, when possible. When it is established that the CI is truly remorseful, he or she can become an excellent continuing source of information.

Special Responsibilities when Using Cooperating Individuals

CIs are not employees of your department. However, their relationship with your agency imposes special responsibilities on you. This is especially true when they have received, or reasonably assume they have received, encouragement or direction for their undertakings. Therefore, it is important to formulate limitations on the activities of CIs and your responsibilities with respect to their endeavors. When considering the use of a CI you should weigh the following factors:

1. Safety of operatives
2. Compromising the operation

3. Acting contrary to instructions
    a. Violating individuals rights
    b. Intruding on privileged communications
    c. Hindering subsequent prosecution
4. Nature and magnitude of the investigation
    a. Is information provided available through other, more secure sources?
    b. Likelihood of information being obtained from more direct means
    c. Information not readily accessible through conventional methods
5. Character and motivation of the CI
    a. Past performance
    b. Potential for benefit in present and future investigations
    c. Reliability
6. Your ability to control the CI's activities
    a. When acting on your behalf
    b. Ensure that conduct is consistent with your instructions
    c. Consistent with departmental and legal guidelines
7. Compensation sought
    a. Potential value of information compared to considerations the CI is seeking.

Instruct all CIs that in accomplishing their assignments they will not:

1. Divulge even the most minute details of the operation to anyone without your prior approval
2. Participate in acts of violence
3. Use unlawful techniques
    a. Breaking and entering
    b. Electronic surveillance
    c. Tampering with the mail
    d. If it is unlawful for you to do it, it is unlawful for them to do it on your behalf.
4. Initiate a criminal conspiracy
5. Participate in criminal activity with person(s) under investigation
    a. Except when you have determined that such participation is necessary in meeting objectives of the investigation
    b. Participation was approved beforehand.

The appendix includes a copy of a contract for the *conduct of cooperating individuals*. It could be advantageous to formulate and institute such an agreement between you and any CI used by the storefront.

COOPERATING INDIVIDUALS NEGOTIATIONS

You should be prepared to negotiate with criminals to obtain the desired information. This aspect of law enforcement is often criticized by the public because it is not well understood. However, it is an important tool, when properly employed, to infiltrate the criminal underworld. When law-abiding citizens observe and/or complain about violators of the law, they expect immediate police action. They do not generally understand why a subject was not incarcerated, even though this strategy could be the best possible approach to alleviating the bigger problem within the community. They lose sight of the fact that greater long-range benefits can be achieved by dealing with small-time offenders to make cases on their more significant counterparts. You should consider those arrested as an opportunity to develop CIs. These low-level villains could be persuaded to aid in the investigation of the target(s) of the storefront. These potential CIs are developed through the process of negotiation.

In some instances, it could be desirable for the defense attorney and/or prosecutor to participate in the negotiations. A general policy is that the cooperation of CIs will be brought to the court's attention when they plead guilty to the original or reduced charges. This, of course, is dependent on their assistance in the investigation. The more significant their contribution, the more enthusiastically prosecutors will reveal to the court their value and request that this be taken into account when passing sentence.

Always consider the possible consequences of negotiating with an arrested offender before initiating the process. You should contemplate the following questions:

1. What type of crime is the potential CI charged with?

2. Is there an expectation that charges will be dismissed, reduced, or a lighter sentence handed down?

3. Does the CI anticipate a monetary reward for his or her involvement?

4. Does the CI think he or she can continue illegal activity with immunity from arrest?

5. Is the information provided reliable?

6. Can it be independently verified?

7. Can a deal be made ethically and legally?

8. What are the feelings of the prosecutor?

9. Must the identity of the CI be revealed in prosecuting the case? If it must:

   a. Is this worth the loss of a valuable source of information?

   b. Can the personal safety of the CI be provided for until the completion of the trial?

   c. Will it be a necessity to fund the CI's disappearance after the trial?

In negotiating with the CI, avoid anything that could be construed as a promise that cannot be delivered. Strict honesty on your part is imperative. If you provide any incentives (you will recommend a reduction of bond, leniency by the court, that charges be reduced or dropped, etc.), take every precaution to ensure that the CI understands that such recommendations may or may not influence the court. The ultimate responsibility of any plea bargaining lies with the prosecutor.

If the negotiation process meets with agreement between the parties and involves cash payments for useful information, a strict policy regarding payment must be established. One major consideration would be to minimize the amount of payment for the initial cooperation. When large payments are made initially, it is extremely difficult to decrease the amounts at a later date. It can also become cost prohibitive to inspire the CI through increased monetary rewards when initial payment was too high. Any payment should only be made at the completion of the CI's appointed task or after information provided has been verified. It is advisable to compensate the CI in stages rather than a one-time full payment. If the CI has agreed to testify in court, you could pay half for his assistance in the investigation and the remainder after the court appearance. Remember, when any payment is made, strictly adhere to the administrative guidelines that have been established. Signed and witnessed receipts must be obtained.

In determining the amounts to be paid, consider the following factors:

1. Value of information given

2. Potential risk to CI

3. Priority given to target suspect

4. Needs of CI and family

5. Potential value over an extended period of time

6. Willingness to testify if needed

7. Time involved in obtaining information

8. CI does not deviate from your direction

9. Availability of funds set aside for this purpose

10. Quality of case(s) made as a direct result of CI's participation.

COOPERATING INDIVIDUAL'S CONTROL AND PROTECTION

The policies concerning who will control the CI differ among departments. The CI can belong to the unit or an individual investigator. When a CI is the property of the unit, the supervisor can designate anyone in the unit to work with and/or control the CI's activity. This method, in most cases, should be considered. The supervisor, who is not personally involved with day-to-day contact, could be in a more objective position to evaluate the usefulness of the CI.

For instance, if the supervisor determines that an agent is not getting adequate cooperation, another agent can be assigned to work the CI. A personality clash that detracts from the potential value of the CI can often be overcome by assigning a new control officer. Let's face it, as hard as we may try, some people just get under our skins. There may be no apparent reason, we just don't like them. This does not lend itself to a productive atmosphere. The reassigning of the CI to another agent could be beneficial to both. Also, in being compassionate and understanding the CI's plight, you can become too friendly. When this is detected, the supervisor may substitute another agent.

Since most storefronts are comprised of small units, the supervisor could control all CIs. All contact with the CI and all payments are made by supervisors. This procedure ensures that strict control is maintained. Although there is some logic to this system, there are distinct disadvantages. The primary drawback is that investigators could feel that they are not trusted to work a CI they have developed. They may also surmise that supervision does not have faith in their investigative talents, which may lead to unproductive low morale and self-esteem. A more favorable procedure is to have the supervisor attend the debriefing of a CI. This provides an opportunity for the supervisor to put forth the hard questions which the investigator could be reluctant to ask. The supervisor could also probe into areas that the agent may have overlooked. When using this method, the supervisor is in a better position to determine the reliability and future potential of a CI.

When the CI is controlled by one officer, an alternate should be assigned. Ideally, the officer who developed the CI should conduct subsequent contacts. The alternate investigator becomes acquainted with the CI by accompanying the assigned officer to meetings and when payments are made. This method facilitates the utilization of the CI if the assigned investigator is not available. It also affords additional protection for the primary contact in respect to personal safety and witnessing of payments made.

The value of having the same investigators (control and alternate) contact the CI is to avoid repetitive demands on the CI's time and aid in avoiding personality conflicts. The investigators are thus more fully aware of any potential pitfalls. This method also affords for a more immediate exchange of information and frugal use of funds. Generally, much more cooperation is attained with this technique. The mutual trust and friendship between the CI and investigators tends to develop more rapidly and naturally. The need for strict adherence to regulations governing CI use still applies. Without this, the relationship will deteriorate.

A principal responsibility of the investigator is to evaluate the CI's performance continually and document his or her reliability. Information received should be scrutinized and analyzed for consistency. This is often accomplished through independent verification of information acquired. The motives and interest for cooperating with law enforcement must also be taken into account in the evaluation. Ensure that the CI is following the course of action laid out and not merely making cases on smaller culprits to appease you.

Policy if the CI Is Arrested

CIs arrested on unrelated charges will often claim they are on assignment for you or will allude to their relationship with you in hopes of avoiding being charged. A policy should be instituted whereby any person making claims of being a CI for the storefront will be processed like all other offenders. The operation supervisor, not the investigator mentioned by the CI, is to be contacted when such an incident occurs. Often, this can lead to disgruntled patrol officers who sense that the CI is being given too much consideration. When your policy is discussed with other supervisors within the department, the storefront can avoid these unproductive conflicts between patrol officers and the operation.

The CI should also be made aware, at the initial meeting, that if this does occur you will do everything possible to assist the arresting officer and to keep the CI incarcerated. CIs should be instructed that if such an unfortunate incident does occur, they are to mention nothing about the storefront or their relationship with you. At the earliest convenience, they are to contact you. Then, depending on the circumstances surrounding the arrest and the nature of the crime, all that is possible will be done to assist. It should also be made clear that their actions may have placed you in a position whereby nothing can be done to assist them. CIs should understand that they cannot run wild and expect you to protect them.

Administering the CI File

The potential for allegations of unethical, immoral, and illegal collusion between law enforcement and a CI underscores the necessity for competent management. For the storefront which chooses to use a CI, to operate effectively the identity of these sources of information must be confidentially maintained. A central file that has complete security and is available only on a need-to-know basis should be kept. The number of people having access to this file should be kept to a minimum.

This file should contain the following:

1. Personal history sheet (include outside income)
2. Arrest record
3. Fingerprint card
4. Current photo
5. Signature card
6. Associates
7. Hangouts
8. Vehicle information.

Other pertinent data include:

1. General attitude toward law enforcement
2. Personal idiosyncrasies
3. Most appropriate time and place for contact.

All financial dealings with the CI must be documented and maintained in the file. This includes:

1. Summary of cases worked
2. CI's disposition
3. Method of payment
4. General up-to-date evaluation of reliability.

A continuous effort must be made to keep the file current. This will ensure that a valuable CI is not lost to the operation.

The true identity of the CI should never appear outside of the central file. Assign a code name or number. This appears in all reports in which reference to the CI is made. Establishing a cross-reference file is useful, but maintain it with the same degree of security as with the central file.

CI Locator File

With more extensive operations, a CI locator file can be compiled and maintained separately from the central file. This file contains general information that is available to all those in need of assistance. The file is cross-indexed using various classifications, such as associates, connections, type of criminal activity, or geographic areas. When investigators are seeking a CI to assist in a probe, they may search the file and determine if one is working in their field of inquiry. The locator file should contain code names or numbers only. If a suitable CI is found, a request for contact arrangements is submitted. Contact should only be made after the control investigator is notified and is present at the meeting. This system allows for greater utilization without compromising identity. Not only can those involved in the storefront use this file, but other appropriate members of the department as well.

Access to Information

A variety of procedures can be tried for the best method to maintain CI files securely and the number of people allowed access to them. In most instances access to the files is only granted after notifying the supervisor. The material within the files cannot be removed from the general area in which they are being stored. This allows for easy monitoring of those using the files and prevents photos, signature cards, personal history sheets, etc. from being misplaced or lost. Those not within the unit should not be allowed into the files. Expert and cautious handling is required to preserve the integrity of the storefront. Security is the paramount consideration for the continued employment of a CI. Mismanagement can result in the CI's demise.

Physical Protection of the CI

It is your responsibility to provide protection and security, both in and out of court, for those revealing information. This is a matter of ethical practice and also relates to the danger of undermining the confidence of the CI. When CIs are directed to be at the scene of a crime during its commission, they become participants under the premise of *res gestae*. This means any witness, including you, who can identify the CI would be required to do so in court. Therefore, every effort should be made to keep the CI away from the scene of buys, arrests, or other activity involving witnesses who know the true identity of the CI and can later be forced to testify to this in court.

CIs who are discovered and have lost their usefulness to the operation may at times need to be relocated. The effort and expense the storefront is willing to put forth in this endeavor should be made clear at the initial meeting. If all the operation can afford is a one-way bus ticket to Palookaville, CIs should be made aware of this.

If the need for relocation arises and the CI is still willing to cooperate with law enforcement, contact another agency that has been cooperative in the past. Advise them of the CI's availability and reliability. If they are willing to work with the CI, they may also be able to assist with the expense of relocating. When this transfer is made, it is important to include complete background information.

TRAINING THE COOPERATING INDIVIDUAL

The CI was selected because of his or her placement and/or access to the target. The CI was carefully assessed and recruited. Why fail now by not providing proper training? This is a resource which cannot be wasted. The potential of CIs can be unlimited if properly guided. You must take the time and effort to see that this potential is used to the fullest extent. There are four areas to consider in training a CI:

1. Communication
2. Security
3. Agent reporting
4. Target exploitation.

A systematic approach was instituted in the CI's selection, assessment, and recruitment. The same type of method should be used for training. This will ensure that nothing in this phase is left to chance or overlooked. In establishing this systematic approach, consider the following factors:

1. Nature of the target
2. Level of placement of the CI
3. Information that is desired
4. Depth of cover that is required
5. Time available for training
6. How CI will communicate with you
7. How you will communicate with CI
8. What security measures are necessary
9. Any special equipment necessary
10. Where you will train the CI
11. How much money will be required
12. How you can evaluate the CI's performance.

When we talk of a systematic training approach, we must also consider the necessity of a training plan. Each storefront where a CI is employed will dictate a different technique. However, having a basic training plan outline can be invaluable. The following outline is for your consideration and is not a hard and fast rule. It will assist you in organizing any training and prevent overlooking any facet that could be important to your particular needs.

Training Plan Outline

A. Concept
1. Identify the problem
2. What type of training is necessary?
3. What will the training accomplish?
4. How will the training be delivered?

B. Time Factor
1. How much time is needed to complete training?
2. When is training to commence?
3. When will it terminate?

C. Training Site(s)
1. Where will you conduct the training?
2. Does the training dictate the use of a specific location?
3. Do you need security for the training site?

D. Security Considerations
1. What can you do to ensure that your operation is not compromised during training?

E. Personnel Requirements
1. Who will participate in the process?
2. Can it be accomplished by yourself or is assistance required?
3. Do you need protective surveillance of the site during training?

F. Transportation Required
1. What kind of transportation is needed?
2. Who requires it?
3. When and where is it required?

G. Cover Requirements
1. Do you need cover for the CI, you, and others during training?
2. Do you need a cover story for the CI during training so the CI can account for his or her absence?
3. Do you need a cover story for using the training site?

4. Is it likely that the cover story will be verified, and can it withstand scrutiny?

H. Areas of Training and Training Aids

1. What are the subjects that you will explore in the training?

   a. Communications

   b. Cover story

   c. Security practices

   d. Target exploitation

   e. Legal aspects

2. What training aids are required?

   a. Camera

   b. Body recorder and transmitter

   c. Tape recorder

   e. Telephone recording devices

I. Fiscal and Logistical Support

1. What will be the monetary requirements?

   a. How much?

   b. For what?

   c. From where?

J. Testing and Evaluation

1. How will you test the CI's complete understanding of his or her training?

2. Testing and review should be continuous from the first contact through the termination of CI employment. However, in this phase never assume that the CI knows; always verify the CI's grasp and understanding.

Properly presented, testing and review not only allow you to measure how effective your training program is but will also enhance your rapport with the CI. They add to your image of professionalism and reinforce the CI's feeling of security in working for you. CIs realize that you will not be satisfied with less than maximum effort. Additionally, testing and review add to your ability to control and direct the CI. It is important that you display a positive and professional, no-nonsense approach.

A comments section at the conclusion of the plan may be helpful. We must all answer to someone. Someone will review the plan and decide whether it can be implemented. This portion enables you to clarify or add needed detail. It also is necessary when you present the sales pitch to convince those in authority that this approach is cost effective, necessary, and beneficial. Point out the wisdom of providing all the elements necessary to execute the whole program and the utilization of the CI.

At this stage it is not unusual for officers to ask, "Why all this preparation? Just turn the CI loose and go do it!" The plan serves many purposes, but there are two very important reasons: First, it provides the guidelines for eliminating difficulties through anticipatory measures. Second, it sets forth in a detailed, organized fashion not only what you propose to accomplish, but how it is to be done. Whether your presentation is written or oral, it will be presented in a systematic fashion. This makes it more readily understandable and when necessary, defensible.

Do not assume that the training of a CI will always have to be formal and the plan extensive. You do not need a classroom with desks, chalkboard, class monitor, etc. The training can be very informal and conducted at any suitable location. You should consider the possible need, take the appropriate steps to implement training, and remember that the process is continual while the CI is employed.

Communication

This is an area of training that has utmost importance. What good is any CI if there is not an exchange of information? The methodology used is predicated by the CI's proximity to the target, his or her motives, and the cover story used. There are three main methods for contact and relaying data:

1. Primary
   a. Routine
   b. Scheduled
2. Alternate
   a. Used when primary methods fail
3. Emergency
   a. Only to be utilized for a true emergency.

Regardless of the types of contact established, impress on the CI the absolute need for security and the consequences of compromising the storefront. All of your hard work can be lost by carelessness or panic.

The methods of communication you choose are limited only by your imagination. The type of storefront and target will usually be the main indicators in providing for effective and timely conversations. Discuss with the CI how contact is to be made before a subject is brought to the storefront: what communications should occur between the operatives and the CI at the storefront; when contact is to be made after the transaction.

You must stimulate the CI's memory to retrieve vital information he or she may not consider important to you. You not only have to draw out this data, you may have to train the CI on how to obtain this information in a manner that will not arouse suspicion. Again, do not assume that the CI will know how to do this; rather, instruct the CI and continually review these techniques.

Security

This is another area of primary concern, and the CI must be trained in these specific procedures. The CI may also need to be provided with protection and security at all times. Stress the do's and don'ts relating to the safety of the CI and the operation. Showing concern for the CI's safety will reinforce his or her confidence in you as a professional. The period of greatest danger of compromise can be during meetings with the CI. It is wise to plan for danger signals when personal contact is to be made or a subject is to be brought to the storefront.

Try to obtain all the information you can on a target before he or she is brought to the operation. This is not always possible and can lead to a very perplexing and dangerous situation. We had a small card placed in the window of many of our storefronts. One side had a star on it, the other a diamond. As the offender was being brought up to the front door, the operative would covertly view him. If he was known to the operative, the card would show the star. The CI knew to make an excuse to leave the site with the offender and then call the operative. If the card showed the diamond, he knew it was safe to come in.

Any number of signals can be arranged to provide for the security of the storefront, CI, and most importantly you.

Of course, you must stress that CIs tell no one what they are doing and for whom they are working. This includes their family, lover, or other law enforcement officers. Constantly remind CIs that their security is their obscurity and that any unusual activity on their part will draw unwanted attention.

In dealing with this section of training, also plan for

1. What to do if the CI is arrested

2. What to do if something big happens or is about to happen

3. What to do if the CI feels he or she has been discovered.

All eventualities concerning the CI and the storefront must be considered and planned for and then implemented in the training.

Cover Story

Consider what type of cover will be necessary during the training of the CI. This might include

1. What is the CI's reason for not maintaining his or her regular habits?
2. Is a cover story necessary if the CI has been recruited because of his or her placement within a group?
3. Will the CI need cover to meet with you and others?
4. Will the CI need cover for what he or she does or does not do?
5. Will the CI need cover for introducing targets to the storefront?

When cover is necessary, the CI must be thoroughly briefed during the training period. Chapter 14 discusses cover stories in more detail.

Reporting Procedures

These will vary with each CI and the targets of the operation. However, it may be necessary to school CIs on the basics of who, what, where, when, why, and how. Whether these reports are written or verbal, these basics of relaying information must be included. Impress on CIs the need to report everything, no matter how trivial it may seem. They must understand that it is your function to put the pieces of the puzzle together and their job to gather the pieces. Allow CIs to relay the information without interruption, and then when they have concluded their report, ask questions. This shows CIs that you are interested in what they are saying and the job they are doing. Also, it reinforces their faith in you and will undoubtedly make them try harder.

Whenever possible, take this opportunity to test the CI. Ask questions you already know the answer to by using previously learned and confirmed facts. This is a very good method to establish the CI's credibility.

Training Limitations

Even though you have selected and recruited CIs, they may not have proven their characteristic disposition or fortitude. Do not reveal more to them than they need to know. This is especially true if they have not been put to the test before. You must protect yourself and the operation against any possible adverse consequences.

A good rule is to avoid the use of police jargon. CIs may have never been exposed to law enforcement. The use of shop talk could confuse and bewilder them. It would also be devastating if these newly learned phrases popped up in the CI's conversations with cohorts. It is a good idea to stop using these expressions long before you start to interview prospective CIs. You don't want these terms to pop up when you are conversing with targets, either.

We were conducting a surveillance of a meeting between two operatives and a target. The meeting was taking place inside a cafe next to a window that looked out onto the highway. About ten minutes into the conversation, there was an automobile accident. It could be plainly heard and then viewed by the participants of the meeting. One operative said to the other, "That's one hell of a 10-44," our ten code for a vehicle accident. The target then excused himself, saying he had to go to the men's room. He was never seen again. The two undercover officers could not understand why the target had left. When they reviewed the taped conversation, they realized they had used police jargon. Get out of this habit as soon as possible; don't be discovered by making this same unfortunate mistake.

Another area to consider is that of identifying the specific target and what information is sought. When possible, apprise the CI of this information only when training is completed. Often, depending on the operation, information such as this is best kept from the CI until a successful test mission has been performed.

The Test Mission

Whenever possible, before dispatching CIs to the target, have them perform an operational test by assigning a test mission. This is a dry run and should always be designed to convince CIs that it is the real thing. It should be totally removed from the actual target. There are three common variations that can be used.

1. Known information mission
    a. Sent to gather information already known to agents
2. Phantom target mission
    a. Sent to gather information on a target that agents have dreamed up
3. Parallel agent mission
    a. Sent to gather information on a target already being worked by another agent. Compare notes.

Other tests that can be used include the following:

1. Polygraph
    a. Not always reliable
2. Electronic

   a. Directional mikes

   b. Body transmitters and recorders

      1) When transmissions or recordings are frequently interrupted or inaudible, at moments when you suspect the conversation would be incriminating, this may be a clue.

   3. Surveillance

   a. Overt, CI knows

   b. Covert, CI does not know

   4. False information.

Whatever methods are used, whether functional to analyze the CI's training and operational procedures or to check his or her veracity, testing should be a continuing process.

TERMINATION OF THE COOPERATING INDIVIDUAL

A problem often not taken into account during the enthusiastic recruitment stage is how to terminate CIs if the need arises. If this must be done, the value of all the things learned about CIs and all the control factors employed become evident. When CIs are terminated, the control officer should have at his or her disposal a wealth of personal facts about them, a variety of documentation related to their police relationship, and a definite psychological advantage.

This decision is usually based on obvious factors. The informant

1. Is not productive

2. Has turned over

3. Is not manageable

4. Has accomplished his or her task and

   a. Will be surfaced to testify

   b. Will be redirected to other targets

   c. Will be deactivated but maintained for future use

   d. Will be terminated completely.

How to terminate is often set out in the operational plan, which is then modified by experience with and knowledge of the CI. Termination is accomplished with security elements given top priority. Depending on the nature of the storefront, the role of the CI, and plans for his or her future use or nonuse, the application of security measures will vary. Circumstances may dictate otherwise, but usually the termination should be accomplished by personal contact with the CI.

This contact should follow a parallel course with the routine procedure established. It should include the following basic elements:

1. Information debriefing

   a. CI is thoroughly debriefed for target-related information and knowledge that may have been overlooked.

2. Operational debriefing

   a. CI is queried about the techniques and procedures employed by the storefront and how they affected his or her operational role. This critique by a CI can be enlightening and, when evaluated, can often serve to improve on your abilities as a control officer.

3. Security debriefing

   a. Review everything that is known in reference to people who may know, think they know, or suspect that the CI worked for the police.

   b. Security measures taken by the CI should be reviewed to uncover possible weaknesses.

   c. Any questions about the CI's security awareness and application of security measures should be covered.

4. Security warning

   a. Keeping in mind the nature of the storefront, the CI's future role (if any), value to the operation, and motivation for assistance, advise the CI of what he or she can and cannot do with the knowledge he or she acquired.

   b. Tell the CI not to discuss the storefront. Whatever is necessary to enforce that warning should be applied. A simple caution with a subtle reminder of all of the information and documentation compiled on the CI could suffice. The CI must understand the dire consequences of violating the rule of security.

5. Test

   a. Test the CI's understanding and solicit a statement from him or her regarding that understanding.

Although actions that are suggested may not always be practical or enforceable, the security warning will have a decided impact. To terminate the CI with techniques which have a good chance of maintaining the desired level of security is certainly better than to terminate without such effort.

CIVIL LIABILITY

No matter what you call your CIs—operator, informer, or snitch—they most probably will be considered an employee of the department. As employees, any harm caused by their actions will create a liability for your public entity and possibly you. Liability more than likely will be based on a legal theory of *respondeat superior* (let the master respond) or on a theory of negligence.

Respondeat superior historically was designed to force the person who benefited (the master) to bear the cost of injuries caused by his slaves. It has evolved to include these costs as a cost inherent in doing business. It is a commercial law concept that has been imposed in an unholy manner on the relationship between the police officer and the CI. Its focus is primarily restricted to the status and acts of the CI.

Scope of Employment

The question of status provides the basis for imposing liability on a public entity for the tortious conduct of its employees. Usually a public entity is liable for injury proximately caused by an act or omission of an employee within the scope of his or her employment. This is when the act or omission would have given rise to a cause of action against that employee (you) or your personal representative (CI).

Let's assume the conduct of the CI constitutes a civil wrong as well as a criminal act. Then the civil liability of the department for this conduct will be decided on a finding of the employment status of the CI and conduct within the course and scope of employment. An employee is defined by most courts as to include an officer, employee, or servant, whether or not compensated. This does not include an independent contractor, which the CI may be. Since most often this is an inclusive definition, and since the independent contractor is excluded, let's look at what common law says. The essential ingredient for an employment relationship to exist is the right of *control* and *direction*. On the other hand, the hallmark of an independent contractor relationship is *control over the result and not over the method of accomplishment.*

The CI who volunteers with no thought of a reward is most likely neither an employee nor independent contractor. The CI who is placed within a criminal group with little or no control, who gives out information as he or she receives it, will more closely resemble an independent contractor. The CI recruited for consideration and direction and controlled by you will be an employee.

A third party seeking damage could sue under the theory of both *respondeat superior* and negligence. Failure to exercise control, while it may weaken the status of an employee under *respondeat superior*, may in itself constitute a negligent act. Because of the unique and dangerous nature of the CI relationship, courts have a tendency to find employment status.

Once this relationship is found, the difficult factual question of "within the scope of employment" presents itself. Conduct carried out under your direction likely would be considered within the scope of employment. As the CI's conduct becomes more collateral to these orders, scope of employment becomes more tenuous.

It is not always necessary that a particular act be expressly authorized by you to bring it within the scope of the CI's employment. The conduct of CIs is within the scope of employment if it occurs while they are engaged in the duties which they were employed to perform and it relates to those duties. Conduct which is incidental to, customarily connected with, or reasonably necessary for the performance of an authorized act is within the scope of the CI's employment.

When CIs are acting on your behalf and within the scope of their authority, and if while so engaged they also and incidentally attend to some matter strictly personal, this does not break the relationship with you to release you from the responsibility for their conduct. On the other hand, when CIs depart or substantially deviate from their duties and pursue some activity not reasonably embraced within their employment, you are not responsible for anything done, or not done, in this activity.

The question of scope will in part be considered in light of the target of the operation, the direction and controls supplied, and the past acts ratified by you. However, it cannot be always said that an act committed despite a contrary command is outside the scope. Many courts today rationalize that the entity's liability should extend beyond actual or possible control over the employee. This to include risks inherent in or created by the operation because they, rather than the injured party, are best able to absorb the loss. This is not merely a justification for reaching a deep pocket. It is grounded in a deeply rooted sentiment that an operation cannot justly disclaim responsibility for conduct which may fairly be said to be characteristic of this activity.

One way to determine whether a risk is inherent in, or created by, an operation is to ask whether the actual occurrence is a generally foreseeable consequence of the activity. However, foreseeability in this context must be distinguished from foreseeability as a text for negligence. In the latter sense, it means a level of probability which would lead a prudent person to take effective precautions. Foreseeability as a test for *respondeat superior* merely means that in the context of the particular operation a CI's conduct is so unusual or startling that it would seem unfair to include the loss resulting from it among other costs of the storefront.

Liability under the Theory of Negligence

This focuses on the relationship (in terms of duties) between all parties from the Chief of Police to the CI. Negligence is the failure to act in a manner that a reasonable person would be expected to act under the same or similar circumstances. The officer using a CI is expected to control the CI's actions, know the CI's propensities, and direct the operation to reasonably ensure his or her safety. Failure to act in accordance could make your actions negligent and you personally liable for any damages caused by CIs to themselves or a third party.

It is imperative that you direct in some specific manner what CIs can and can't do, restrict the use of weapons, and know their criminal history—especially any tendencies they may have toward violent behavior. This can be accomplished in part by use of a CI file and employment agreement. However, this control could very well constitute an employee status.

The actions of the CI can affect not only you but everyone in the chain of command through vicarious liability. In the supervisor-operative relationship, the supervisor must exercise control and supervise the use of the CI. Knowledge of illegal activities may be ratified by the failure to prohibit. In the chief-supervisor relationship, there is a duty to control retention and employment of the CI, even though the chief may have no direct knowledge that the CI is working for the storefront. It is the chief's ultimate responsibility even though this duty has been delegated to a subordinate.

Liability for Injury of the CI

If a CI is accidentally or intentionally injured or killed while gathering information, he or she may be entitled to workers' compensation benefits. The conditions of compensability under most workers' compensation laws are that an injury be

1. Sustained while the CI is performing service growing out of and incidental to employment
2. Sustained while the CI is acting within the course of employment
3. Proximately caused by the employment, either with or without negligence
4. Caused neither by the intoxication of the CI, nor by an intentionally self-inflicted act, nor by an altercation in which the CI was the initial physical aggressor.

Compensability essentially depends on employee status and injury occurring within the course of employment, much the same as vicarious liability in tort. If death occurs and the CI has employee status, he or she could be entitled to the same benefits as you are.

SUMMARY

Using a CI to assist with the storefront investigation can accelerate the progress of infiltrating the target. As we have seen, there is far more involved with this technique than simply telling the CI get busy. As a means of review, let's look at a list of investigator do's and don'ts when working with CIs.

Do's

1. Determine if the CI can deliver. Does the CI have placement and access?
2. Clearly establish and comprehend the CI's motivation for assisting.
3. Obtain an unmistakably clear understanding with CIs in reference to what they are allowed and not allowed to do.
4. Continually question and test information provided and how it was obtained.
5. Maintain operational integrity through meetings and proper reporting procedures.
6. When appropriate, supply necessary training.
7. Always practice need-to-know in discussing your CI with others.
8. When appropriate, direct the CI's efforts to meet the objectives of the storefront.
9. Practice need-to-know in what you reveal to the CI.
10. Establish good communication procedures, CI to you, and you to CI.
11. Maintain a professional relationship.
12. Objectively evaluate information provided.
13. Make the CI understand that you are the decision maker.
14. Tend to the CI's needs, provided the CI is doing a good job.
15. Always consider that the CI may be serving another master—the target.
16. Obtain all information possible on first contact.
17. Continually correlate newly acquired information with old.
18. When possible, use separate sources to verify information and establish credibility.
19. Constantly develop and strive to retain the CI by personality or character improvement rather than by developing an obligated person.
20. Before interviews, take the time necessary to organize your questions, conduct, and attitude. There is always time for mental organization.

Don'ts

1. Bring the CI to the police facility at any time or to the storefront until reliability is established.
2. Meet with CIs where their association with you can be compromised.
3. Tell CIs anything other than what they need to know.
4. Allow CIs to run the show.
5. Get too chummy.
6. Establish patterns of meetings and/or communication. (Be aware of countersurveillance and change procedure periodically.)
7. "Fall in love" with the CI and accept information at face value.
8. Rely on hearsay if you can get information from an original source.
9. Give out more information than you get.
10. Make promises you cannot keep.
11. Allow the CI to continue any illegal activity.
12. Believe the CI over another officer.
13. Continue to use the CI if he or she has gone sour.
14. Have the CI do what you cannot legally do.

When properly recruited, trained, and controlled, the CI can be a valuable asset to the storefront investigation. Invest the time and energy necessary to use this source fully and properly. When this is accomplished, it will return big dividends.

CHAPTER 14

Tactical Operation
of the Storefront

The time is almost here. Before the doors of the storefront can be opened and the shingle hung, there is one more step: devising a cover story for the operatives. Once this is accomplished, you are ready for business. Offenders will have to be beaten off with a stick—figuratively speaking, of course.

In this chapter, we examine what is required of a cover story and the various aspects involved with the tactical side of the storefront:

1. Meeting the target
2. Legal considerations when conversing with sellers
3. Who to buy from
4. What to buy
5. Paying for items purchased
6. Documenting your activities: investigation reports
7. Postbuy debriefing with the prosecutor.

COVER STORY

You have gone to great lengths to create the desired facade using the disguise of a storefront. Now that illusion must be completed: You must establish the cover story for the operatives. One without the other is like a firearm without bullets—it may appear impressive, but it does not function as intended. The same applies to the storefront. The visual impression created will not enable operatives to meet stated objectives when it stands alone. The investigator must to augment the pretense through a cover story.

The complexity of the story will depend on the sophistication of the targets and magnitude of the investigation.

A cover story is created for two purposes:

1. Status

2. Action.

It is used to offer something attractive to the targets of the probe. We have already discussed choosing a type of storefront the investigators can make believable. You do not want to open a welding shop if you have no idea of what a welder does. Do not select a profession to impersonate unless you are familiar with all operations and terminology involved. When tools of the trade are required, ensure that they appear used. If tools and any carrying cases are new and remain that way throughout the operation, it will arouse undue suspicion. Also anticipate questions that will be asked about other aspects of the operatives' personal lives.

The operatives must abandon their official identity. Badges, police credentials, cards, letters, notebooks, clothing, and all others items that might cause suspicion must be relinquished. This may seem obvious. However, the thought of going to work without carrying one's badge can be unsettling to some. This is their symbol of authority, and without it they feel naked and uneasy. Some personal items may actually verify cover. When real names are to be used, credit cards or identification bracelets can be verification of identity. Just the opposite applies if this is not the case.

The fictitious role assumed must allow for compatibility with both the targets and neighborhood of the operation. A competent background story should include names, addresses, associates, and neighborhoods. The fictitious information should be of such a nature that it cannot be easily checked by the targets. The background city should be one with which the investigator is familiar. When possible, the location should not be familiar to the targets. Newspaper clippings from that city which "just happen" to be in your possession can be used to aid in establishing the undercover identity.

At one time, that a buyer was armed was a good indication that he or she was the heat. Times have changed, unfortunately. Now people engaged in criminal activity are not suspected of being the law if they carry a weapon.

The type of weapon carried will depend on your preference and departmental guidelines. Automatic pistols, because they are flat, more easily concealed, and usually not readily identified with law enforcement, could be desirable. Many departments today are selecting this type of weapon for their officers. If this is so, choose an undercover weapon that differs from the ones issued to patrol officers. Remember, it is essential to be properly trained with any and all weapons carried. This could preclude you from being sued under civil liability for injuring or killing someone with a weapon you were not trained and qualified to use. It also ensures your ability to use the weapon properly under stressful and often deadly circumstances. Having a fellow officer killed because we were not completely familiar with the workings of the firearm chosen is unthinkable.

Personal possessions such as clothes, wallets, rings, watches, and the amount of money carried should be appropriate to the character chosen. Clothes and the method of dress should conform to appropriate conditions and degree of cleanliness. Any laundry marks or clothing labels must be obliterated or agree with the cover story. Altered identification cards and letters bearing an assumed name and address will help in establishing the legitimacy of the story.

Pretended deformities or infirmities can be dangerous. They are difficult to maintain over the length of the probe. One of the stories that circulated around our department involved just such a circumstance. An officer had a plaster cast installed on one arm as a ruse. The investigation he was involved in took place over a four-month (summer) period. By the end of the assignment, his arm had become severely infected. He had been using anything, and we mean anything, to get inside the cast to scratch those itches.

Background for Status

This background story is the state or condition of a person: position or status, an explanation of what he or she is, way of life, and image. Developing this story is analogous to painting a picture or creating an image, much like that accomplished by the storefront facade. The operative must create a new person, a new identity. This should be designed to follow a course with which the operative is familiar in real life and with which he or she feels comfortable. If you were born and raised in Chicago, use this life experience. Do not claim to be from Chicago if you are unfamiliar with the city. If the place in which you were raised is sparsely populated, choose a familiar metropolitan area as your origin. When assuming an identity and background, be aware of the counterintelligence capability of the target.

One officer we knew decided that being an ex-con would be an advantageous cover. He had worked with an agent who used this story. That agent had previously been employed at a penitentiary for many years. He was familiar with the inner workings and behavior of those at an institution of this sort. The other officer was not and only possessed a very basic knowledge. When he and his fellow ex-cons got together, it didn't take long for them to discover he did not belong to their fraternity.

Once the identity and background is selected, you may need to fill in the new character with a number of paper details. The following can provide you with identification papers sufficient to satisfy any inquiry from official or unofficial sources:

1. Operator's license
2. Residence
3. Telephone
4. Vehicle
5. Occupation
6. Credit cards or bank account.

Operator's License

The operator's license can usually be obtained at the nearest motor vehicle department by filling out an application under the assumed name. A temporary license is often issued, and a permanent license will follow in the mail within a short time. This provides a new name, photograph, birth date, and address. If the identity of a real person is chosen, an associate or childhood friend, preferably in another city, use the same birth date. If the target has the ability to check with the bureau of vital statistics, they find the same name and birth date.

The advantages to assuming the identity of a real person are: (1) You can refer to your background with a maximum degree of confidence if it is queried by anyone, and (2) assuming the name of a real person provides a built-in file in the public schools, department of motor vehicles, and other such public agencies. There are disadvantages, however, such as (1) danger of physical harm when the target comes looking for you, and (2) administrative harm such as motor vehicle records, credit records, etc. We usually created a new person to avoid these problems.

In creating a new person, there is less likelihood of involving an unwitting victim. There are several ways to do this. One, of course, is with the assistance of the proper authorities. In most cases, this will be the desired course to follow. In some instances, the fear that these authorities themselves could compromise the investigation precludes this avenue.

One of our storefronts was organized to investigate improprieties involving the motor vehicle department. This involved the issuance of phony driver's licenses and automobile titles. Not knowing the extent to which this activity had infested this government bureau, we decided to use another approach in obtaining an undercover driver's license. There are people within every community who supply phony documentation. We paid a visit to just such an individual. We used the phony papers he provided to obtain the ID we required. We subsequently directed other investigators to this subject to affect his arrest. This allowed for the integrity of the storefront to remain intact. We then used these phony documents, baptismal certificates, Social Security cards, high school diplomas, etc. to obtain a driver's license.

When any phony ID is acquired, by whatever method, be certain that proper administrative documentation is maintained. This allows for monitoring the use of such ID and ensures against allegations of misconduct. At the conclusion of the storefront, any such ID should be destroyed using established administrative procedures.

When choosing a name, keep it simple. Usually your coworkers are accustomed to calling you by your first name. This should be the first name chosen for the assumed identity, unless the first name is so distinctive and unique that it would be inappropriate. In using your own first name, those that work undercover with you do not have to get accustomed to using a new name. There will be less chance of a slip-up. When a new name is selected, start using it as soon as possible. This allows fellow investigators to get in the habit of addressing you correctly.

Residence

Establishing a residence can often be a concern. Many motor vehicle departments mail the permanent driver's license to the residence. Therefore, it is necessary to have a mailing address. When applying for business licenses, bonds, permits, or other such forms for a storefront, this could also be a requirement. A post office box is suitable for this purpose, but it can often raise suspicion. A more desirable approach is to use a private mail facility. These are nothing more than post office boxes that use a street name and number to identify the occupant rather than a box number, and thus seem to be a home address. These are widely used by people trying to con or hide.

Establishing a residence to work in conjunction with the storefront can be helpful. It is not unusual for fringe people (i.e., not established in the community, no relatives, and no ties that can be traced) to have an inexpensive apartment that is paid for on a weekly or monthly basis. In addition, if the targets make a cursory inquiry, the operative's name will be on the mailbox. If this technique is used and meetings are to be held there, install the necessary technical apparatuses, enabling transactions to be recorded.

We usually preferred to use the disguised post office box. This eliminates the need for someone to be at the residence and the additional expense. If a check is made and a suspect discovers the home is a post office box, there are many explanations that can be given. This is not ordinarily necessary, though, because the suspects will assume they know why this was done. Many of their counterparts do the same thing.

Telephone

A telephone, other than the one at the site, can also provide another piece of credibility. It provides for identification with a number and means of additional communication with the targets. It will place your name in the telephone directory and further legitimize your identity. The disguised post office box can be listed in the directory, and calls can be forwarded to any location. The telephone bill can be strategically used to promote the desired illusion.

Telephone answering services are quickly becoming passé with the ever-increasing use of pagers and mobile phones. If you choose to use an answering service, be aware that they could provide injurious information about the operation to the target. Therefore, messages left by police personnel must be in code. In addition, be aware of those operating and/or employed by the service. Those not appreciative of law enforcement's endeavors could reveal their true identity.

Vehicles

Consider carefully the vehicle you drive for the operation. It should be registered under your new name and address. This provides another piece of credibility. However, merely reregistering a vehicle owned by the department may not suffice. Often, motor vehicle departments can trace the history of a car back to its original owner. If the target has access to these files, they will reveal the department's ownership. Depending on the trust and relationship with motor vehicle personnel, a stop can be placed on this paper trail. When this information is sought, the registration history ends with your assumed name. A skip can also be placed on the information, but this is a less desirable method. Those familiar with this practice know or will suspect that this means cop.

Another method which can provide more security but is more expensive is leasing. This is a common practice among criminals and usually will not raise suspicion if the vehicle was leased using the new identity. When employees of the leasing agency are let in on the secret, it can place the integrity of the storefront and your safety in their hands.

Occupation

When your occupation is not obvious through the storefront, it must be considered. Often, an operation is organized in which the operatives are not employees, rather people who just hang around.

A video arcade we used was organized in just such a fashion. The operator of the business, who was a police officer, would direct clients to us. We would, in turn, take prospective customers to an adjoining room, which had been electronically prepared for transactions, to do business. This permitted those conducting the buys to leave the confines of the video arcade to pursue other avenues of the investigation.

It also required us to explain our occupation. When someone (even a target) asks, "What do you do for a living?" you can't reply, "I'm a crook." This is too obvious and will make suspects shy away. Being self-employed as a consultant, efficiency expert, or a salesperson between jobs is a far more advantageous answer. It provides to the legitimate world a reasonable explanation for why you have money but do not have a job. It also provides the opportunity for fringe people and targets to develop certain favorable perceptions about you. It is not uncommon for them to conclude that you are a good thief or hustler if you do not work but always have a pocketful of money and a car.

Credit Cards and Bank Accounts

Obtaining credit cards and/or a bank account under the new identity can be helpful. This can be accomplished with or without the assistance of a friendly banker. Credit cards and bank accounts supply another piece of credibility when the target sees you writing a personal check or using a credit card. Also, having large deposits and withdrawals indicated on the bank statement, and then leaving it where the target can see it, can lead the target to think you're worth doing business with.

A bank account should be maintained with a minimum of funds. As with all monies, the accountability must be precise and meticulously documented. All credit card charges and checks written should be explained and justified in a written report.

Cover for Action

This is a reasonable explanation of what you do or do not do and lends plausibility to whatever action you take. During the course of the storefront, you will have the opportunity to engage in criminal and noncriminal activities which could jeopardize your safety and/or the operation. These situations must be anticipated and a believable story prepared to explain nonparticipation. For instance, you are cordially invited to join in on a burglary. A counter to such an invite could be that you prefer buying and burglary is not your thing. Someone inquires about your absence from the storefront. A reply could be that you have a girlfriend or boyfriend out of town or have been gone on business.

A technique to use when anticipating being away from the storefront is to inform one of the targets of your absence. Tell the target if you are not back by a certain day to have a bail bondsman check the jails in and around the community specified. This allows you to get away from the storefront for a few days, creates a plausible reason for your absence, and aids in developing a relationship of trust.

You must build a cover story that is easy to remember and believable and with which you are comfortable. You must be able to say to yourself, "I am this other person."

MEETING THE TARGET

When all the necessary preparation has been completed, it is time to concentrate on becoming acquainted with the targets. This is accomplished by various methods. The most common and easiest is to use a CI to introduce the target to the storefront. Other undercover operatives can be used to bring suspects to the operation or spread the word on its activity. There could also be walk-ins who will unwittingly assist in increasing clientele. Whatever the approach, it is time to befriend the targets.

Once contact is made, it is essential to obtain the confidence of the suspect as soon as possible. This must be accomplished in a manner that will not create suspicion. You must act as natural as possible. Showing too much enthusiasm toward the pending transaction could queer the deal. A certain amount of questioning will be inevitable. Remember, asking too many questions, especially on first encounters, can cause undue suspicion. On the other hand, the suspect may also want to ask too many questions. Act suspicious of the target and his or her inquiries. Crooks are usually not willing to divulge much information on first contact. Remember, in every respect, you must live the role. Talking too freely or giving too many explanations will be contrary to what is expected. Do not bluff or give any more information than is not absolutely necessary. As the relationship and trust is established, you can ask the target more direct questions and become more open with your answers.

It is usually unwise to display much interest in the spouses and lovers who could accompany a target. A simple expression of interest may result in jealousy, thereby jeopardizing the success of the transaction.

When a suspect appears to be suspicious in reference to your identity and starts to demand information, demonstrate anger, contempt, sarcasm, or dismay. Place the suspect on the defensive by insisting that you are not completely satisfied with his or her identity and demand more proof. This will often cause the suspect to backtrack and refrain from this line of questioning. Indifference is another technique. Act as if you do not care what the target thinks, and ask whether the target will do business or not. This could induce the suspect into making the sale. Remember, the suspect is suspicious of almost everyone. It is an occupational hazard. The biggest factor working against suspects is greed. This will make many of them deal even though it may be against their better judgment.

Also bear in mind that lying, deception, and double crossing are normal conduct for many of the people dealing with the storefront. Be cautious and try to avoid creating disfavor or being placed in a defensive position. Be skeptical; never trust or rely on a suspect; and cautiously assess all developments. The exchange of information is what meeting with the targets is all about. It is a one-way exchange; them to you. One method to initiate a one-sided conversation is to praise their skills and cunning. We have all heard that flattery will get you everywhere; in most instances that is true. When the situation allows, play dumb, ask how they are able to accomplish their tasks, compliment their bravery. When some offenders have a captive audience who shows interest in their exploits, they cannot resist blowing their own horn. Most will go on and on until stopped. They will reveal almost everything without too many questions being asked.

We had a subject who was bringing stolen cars to the storefront. He was very quiet and hesitant to talk. He answered questions with a yes or no, and occasionally with a guttural sound. We walked out to the garage area where he had delivered one of the vehicles. As we were inspecting it, we commented on the skill it must take to hot-wire a car without doing extensive damage. These remarks were like opening the floodgates on a dam, for the next thirty minutes, information poured out.

Establishing Rules for Sellers

With most of our storefronts, it was necessary to establish a procedure the sellers had to follow to do business. When CIs are used, they should be aware of this procedure, and you must ensure that they follow it. On first contact with the targets, we were very straightforward and forceful in detailing what was to be done. We explained that these rules were for their protection as well as ours. The rules instituted will depend on the particular circumstances of the individual storefront. With most of our operations, the same basic guidelines were established.

Telephoning before Delivery

The first rule: Telephone the storefront to arrange delivery. This can be explained by saying that you do not keep money around the business and would only have money there if they called first. This is a precaution against rip-offs. Even when the offender does show up announced, try to have another operative retrieve the funds from some "unknown location." This should be done after a display of the merchandise and the deal is negotiated. In most neighborhoods where a storefront operation is established, it is easy for the target to understand these safeguards. This phone call would also allow you to make sure other customers are not there at the same time. Explain to targets that this keeps others from knowing their business and protects them from a possible snitch. Most offenders will appreciate this concern for their well-being.

The telephone call permits last-minute preparation of the meeting area, making sure it is "clean" and technical equipment is operational. These calls are not usually tape-recorded. They should be very short and usually consist of "Hi, this is me. I've got something for you." Tell the targets when to come to the storefront, usually a short time after the call. Do not keep targets waiting too long. Document the call on the investigative and offense report. If targets revealed more than their pending arrival, ask them during the meeting what they had said when they telephoned. This conversation is recorded and collaborates what you reported.

Two telephones can be installed in the storefront—one for everyday use and one equipped with a recording device. If targets feel they must provide more than basic information, have them call on the "private" phone. If every telephone conversation is recorded, transcribing all those calls can become a nightmare. Reduce the workload whenever possible.

When it is established that offenders are of no further value to the operation, the requirement to telephone before delivery can be used to an additional advantage. As the relationship is established, targets will become more and more free with information. Ask them what they have and where they are. Have them wait there and call at a later time. Any number of excuses can be used for this delay. Surveillance is then established at the offenders' location. At the appropriate time, they are arrested before arriving at the storefront, usually before they make the second call. This should be accomplished with one thought in mind: maintaining the security of the operation.

The subjects will then usually call from jail. Yell and scream that you have been waiting and had to turn other business away because of them. When informed of their arrest, express sorrow and then concern for your own fear of arrest. Demand that the target not snitch off the operation. If they request bond, assure them that you will try to bond them out. That you do not do so usually turns them off, and they do not revisit the storefront. If they do return, express the anxiety of dealing with them now and that activity should be suspended for a while to ensure that the cops are not watching them. If this practice is used selectively and with the thought of maintaining the integrity of the operation, it can be very effective in curtailing an offender's activities.

Curtailing Activity of Offenders

A paradise of sorts has been created for the targets. Once they realize you will purchase their goods at a fair price, they can overrun the operation. We have had offenders who wanted to visit the storefront two and three times a day. You must consider how the offenders will be dealt with after their usefulness has passed. Having them arrested using surreptitious methods is favorable but not always practical. When dealing with a close-knit group, they soon come to realize that after the third transaction they are all arrested, and this could drastically impede the progress of the operation. It could also seriously jeopardize your safety.

Assess, as quickly as possible, the potential benefit the offender could have in assisting the investigation. If the benefit is minimal and successful prosecution can be obtained with fewer than the optimal number of buys, this would be prudent. If three buys were determined to be the optimal number and the same result can be obtained on a particular offender with two buys, then this should be the practice. Once the necessary evidence is obtained and there is no anticipation that the offender can assist in furthering the investigation, conducting more buys will be counterproductive.

In evaluating the worth of offenders, consider who else they are able to introduce to the operation. Often, buys are made from fringe offenders with the expectation that they will bring or spread the word to primary targets. Encourage this type of activity. Explain to targets that their value to the storefront is of such importance that it should not be jeopardized by arrest. You do not want them to commit any more crimes, but to introduce associates who are committing the crimes. Promise that they will be rewarded for their effort. Direct unwitting CIs toward career criminals who meet with the established objectives. However, do not allow them to create criminals. When transactions with these new recruits are conducted, use audio and video recordings to ensure that the criminal activity being conducted is of their own design—that no collusion or coercion is involved.

One of the most obvious methods for handling this problem is simply to tell offenders that you do not want to do business with them anymore. Again, this can be counterproductive when investigating a tightly knit group. They will soon become aware that after three buys, they are out. Plan a variety of methods for curtailing unwanted or made offenders. Indicate that they will receive half payment now and the remainder at a later date. Of course, the later date never comes. Take possession of contraband and do not pay for it. Tell them the word is out; therefore, you do not want to deal with them anymore. Never explain exactly what you meant by this. Or drastically lower the price paid for goods, thus making the storefront a less desirable place to deal.

When using these techniques, be aware of possible retaliation. Cons should only be employed against offenders when the reasonable expectation is that they will not react too violently. You cannot keep buying and buying from the same offender throughout the course of the operation. Carefully consider all the options and consequences involved in curtailing offenders.

Introducing Unannounced Associates

The second rule to establish is that targets cannot bring unannounced cohorts to the storefront. Do not discourage the introduction of possible new offenders; just emphasize that they be announced before being brought to the operation.

The introduction of new people to a criminal undertaking is a time for suspicion and concern. The storefront is posing as a criminal undertaking and should express the same cautions. If you appear too anxious to meet new people, it would be contrary to the offender's criminal upbringing. While encouraging targets to do this, let them understand it is only because you trust them and are sure they would never bring a cop, or anyone who would deal with cops, to the storefront. Tell them that they are one of the very few who are trusted in this fashion and are allowed to do this. Express the same anxieties the target would.

When new clients are brought to the operation, insist on conducting the transaction with them. Whoever else is present should be strongly persuaded to leave the meeting. This affords a greater opportunity to evaluate new targets. They will not be limited or intimidated by the presence of a mediator. You can capture their words and actions on tape without interruption or direction from the one who made the introduction. This also permits you to establish that what you have been told is true—that the recruit is a proven professional and the desire to deal with the storefront is theirs and theirs alone.

Other Rules

Other rules may have to be established due to the particular circumstances and type of storefront chosen. Whatever standard operating procedure is implemented, always consider, from the target's point of view, why these rules have been established. They should be explained in a manner that is consistent with the suspect's other criminal experiences. In doing so, the target will more easily comprehend the rules and will be less suspicious.

Any rules that are enacted should be strictly enforced. An offender showed up at one of our storefronts unannounced with a stolen pickup. We told him that was contradictory behavior and we would not buy the truck. After a long and heated discussion, we agreed to buy the vehicle. Since the offender had not telephoned first, we did not have any money at the site. It was agreed that he would be paid at the next delivery. When the next delivery was made, after all the rules were followed, we rewarded him only for that pickup. We told him he was being chastised for not following the rules on the previous occasion. We explained that the rules were for all of our protection and we had to compel obedience to ensure that no one would end up in jail. After considerable grumbling, the offender departed. He followed the rules from then on, and so did the others he introduced to the operation. Insisting, without exception, that the rules be followed does not always have a happy ending. However, when you have established rules, they must be followed. If not, the operation could soon become unmanageable.

LEGAL CONSIDERATIONS WHEN CONVERSING WITH SELLERS

Officers are often confused about the impact telling minor lies to the offender will have on the outcome of the case, and about how concealing one's true occupation as a police officer or giving others a false impression of criminal connections might compromise the operation. This specific conduct by law enforcement officers has been held to be lawful.[1]

Some uninformed or misinformed people still think this is entrapment. This is especially true of some offenders. This belief is so prevalent that we constantly heard the same oration upon meeting an offender the first time. They would ask, "Are you affiliated in any way with any law enforcement agency either federal, state, city, or county? If you are and you do not reveal this fact, you cannot prosecute me for my actions. This is because you lied, and that is entrapment!" Many have told us their lawyers had told them to ask that question. When we would respond that we were not affiliated with law enforcement, we could see the relief on their faces—not necessarily because they believed us, but they truly believed they were now immune from prosecution. They believed that all they needed to do was ask us if we were cops, because cops have to tell the truth. We even started to give the same spiel to those who came to the storefront. Usually, after we asked the question, they would smile and say, "I was just about to ask you the same question."

Entrapment, as we know, is the procurement of one to commit a crime that he or she did not contemplate or would not have committed, for the sole purpose of prosecuting that person. The storefront merely *affords the opportunity to someone predisposed* to commit an offense. The idea to commit the crime originated with the offender. (This topic was covered in more detail in chapter 8.)

There are some other commonly misunderstood aspects in reference to conversing with a seller. Using the "jargon of the trade" to enhance cover is not unlawful.[2] Dressing the part to place the offender at ease and facilitate conversation is not unlawful.[3] Using an alias, being introduced to the defendant by one of his or her friends, or misrepresenting the purpose for which contraband is sought is also not considered unlawful.[4]

The use of profanity, even though it usually is not a legal consideration, should be limited. We listened to a taped conversation of a transaction, and we all commented on how the judge and jury were going to react unfavorably to the foul language and off-color remarks being made by the offender. We all thought how damaging this would be to the offender's courtroom image. Then, to our amazement, we realized that it was the undercover officer. The offender's language was not offensive at all. Keep in mind that the conversation is being recorded and will eventually be played back in court. Do not jeopardize the case using excessive profanity or racial or religious comments.

Through conversations with offenders, establish that they are *predisposed*. Comment on the quality of contraband and say that they must have done this before. Maybe comment on their bearing and calmness during the transaction and indicate that they must be pros—anything to have them reveal that they have previously been engaged in this type of criminal activity and they were not induced to commit this act. You are trying to demonstrate on tape that the offender was ready and willing to commit the crime and was simply awaiting an opportunity to do so. If there are any lingering questions concerning predisposition, you may want to review that portion of chapter 8. As with any legal consideration, the best source of information is the prosecutor. Do not hesitate to contact him or her and express any concerns.

WHO TO BUY FROM

This may appear obvious at first. Buy from the targets of the operation or those who meet the objectives of the storefront. However, there are fringe people who need consideration. These are people who could lead you to the targets or to people who were previously unknown to you. These offenders may or may not be engaged in the targeted activity. Buys are made in anticipation of using them as a conduit to the primary targets.

This can be accomplished in several ways. Acting as an unwitting CI, they could introduce the target or arouse the target's curiosity, compelling him or her to pay a visit to the storefront. If you can establish a connection between fringe people and the target, and they can facilitate movement of the target toward the storefront, it would be advantageous to deal with them.

As with all offenders who visit the storefront, they should be run on NCIC as soon as their true identity is established. There is usually no reason to conduct transactions with them if they have an outstanding felony warrant. Once this situation is uncovered, conduct a subsequent meeting. They then can be arrested after leaving the vicinity of the storefront. This, of course, would be done in a manner that would not compromise the operation. Additionally, it has become the policy of many departments that if the target has an outstanding warrant, an arrest must be made as soon as possible.

An arrest warrant is a court order directing any officer of the court to take an offender into custody without undue delay. When you are aware and absolutely sure the person named on a warrant and the person you are dealing with is one and the same, you should arrange for his or her arrest. However, if there is any question, and the subject may have some value to the storefront, contact the prosecutor and discuss possible remedies.

Some suspects are also aware of entrapment, predisposition, and other such legal aspects. This is due to their firsthand experience with the legal system. They try to incorporate these safeguards into their illicit activity. They are confident that if they are dealing with the police, they will eventually get off on a technicality.

When you perceive a scheme such as this, do not deal with the offender until this attempt at deception can be unmasked. Often, such offenders claim to be at the storefront only at the direction of a friend. When brought to court they will assert that they did not know that the items sold were contraband. They will also profess that the contraband was found and only sold after an owner could not be located. These are examples of just two of the many schemes used in trying to avoid prosecution. Beware of attempts such as these and take the necessary precautions.

Again, through taped conversations, establish that offenders know what they are doing and are doing it of their own free will. The latter point is especially important when using CIs to introduce targets to the storefront. Their involvement should be no more than just that. When a seller says he is doing this at the direction of the CI or the CI has told him what to do, the investigation is in for trouble. Document, through conversations recorded on video and audio tape, that the CI's involvement was no more than making the offender aware of a potential buyer. This will dispel any notions of a discrepancy or coercion.

If you detect obvious diminished mental capability in a seller, do not make the buy. The seller could have consumed an intoxicating substance or have a permanent mental impairment. In the first case, instruct the seller to leave and return when he or she has more control. In the second instance, do not conduct any transactions at all. When you learn that a person with a mental handicap has committed a crime, have them arrested.

Do not use the storefront to create crooks. There are plenty to go around without adding to the problem. If a suspect comes into the storefront who is contemplating, for the first time, committing a criminal act, try to discourage him or her. We have had numerous people enter our storefronts to talk to us about committing crimes and ask how much we would pay for different items they might steal. They have heard from one of their friends how lucrative the criminal lifestyle is. Stress the downside and serious consequences. A storefront is designed to deal with career criminals. It should maintain that focus. Document your efforts on video and audio tape. This recording can be used for two purposes: The first is to show that not everyone who comes into the storefront is a customer. One defense often incurred is that the deal offered was too good for anyone to pass up. Second, if the subject does return with contraband, you can show the efforts made to dissuade this act.

How Many Buys

Once you have decided who to buy from, the next question is, How many buys? The number of buys required for a particular case will depend on a number of variables, including

1. Prevailing attitude of local courts
2. Relative size of the buy, and financial considerations
3. Likelihood that the seller may move away
4. The desire of the operation to remove a CI from any connection with the sale
5. The possibility of apprehending the seller with a large cache of contraband
6. The possibility of introducing others to the operation
7. Time—additional buys shortly before warrants are issued could keep cases current.

As a general rule, three buys are made. This allows for the offender to become comfortable with agents and information on other criminal activity and/or offenders to be revealed. It also shows that this was not a one-time thing and helps establish a pattern of criminal activity.

WHAT TO BUY

The items to be purchased should be consistent with the stated objectives. Additionally, the main purpose of the buy is to obtain evidence of a criminal act. Different items will create various problems, and there are times which the property purchased will not be used in court. It is bought to place the offender at ease so bigger and better deals will hopefully occur in the future.

Realistically, you will also be bound by the problem of insufficient funds. Make the utmost of what is available. Act as if it were your money being spent. Always haggle for a better price and demand more for your dollar. Be dissatisfied with every transaction made, and ask for more the next time. This not only saves funds; the seller expects it. Those in a hurry to buy everything and who pay too much are only one thing, COPS!

Do not be afraid to be selective. No fence will jump at every opportunity. When you buy junk, offenders will only bring in more junk. If you are unfamiliar with dickering over prices, take an item to a pawnshop. Listen and learn while the clerk tries to take the property for next to nothing. Then use this experience to wheel and deal with storefront customers. You have to play the role to be believable.

Test Buy

Due to potential clients' suspicions, you may need to conduct test buys. Offenders often test agents to see if they are cops and/or what they can get away with. Suspects will come to the storefront with shoplifted goods. It is obvious the merchandise is stolen, but it is very hard to prove. The rightful owners usually cannot be located. Even if an owner is located, statutes for shoplifting are often misdemeanors. Offenders are quick to learn what constitutes a felony. When the law states that shoplifting property valued at $100 or more is a felony, you can safely bet that $99.99 worth of property will be brought to the storefront.

Test buys can become very expensive for an operation; they should seldom be entered into. When subjects came into our storefront with property such as this, we simply told them we did not deal in such items. We then told them, in a general manner, what we did deal in. There is nothing wrong with telling a crook, "We deal in stolen cars." Maybe you don't want to be as direct as that, but you want the suspect to get the idea. Being too specific about what you want to buy can create problems. The assertion will be that the offender was directed by you. Use a general, nonspecific approach such as, "We buy pickups if the price is right. No paperwork required."

Identifiable Property

Property such as jewelry, small appliances, automotive parts, furs, cameras, tools, etc. can be very hard, if not impossible, to trace back to the rightful owner. Televisions and larger appliances can also fall into that category. Most have small, easily removable stickers which contain the serial number. The offender will remove or obliterate the number before bringing the property in. Even when there are serial numbers, victims don't know them. Do you know the serial number of your television? Property is of no value if the rightful owner cannot be located.

After a quick evaluation of the seller we would often ask, "Where did you steal this?" The suspects' expressions were quite amusing. If the suspect hesitated or balked at the question, we would explain it further. We did not want an exact address, although that was nice, just the area from which the theft occurred. That way we did not take the property back to that general location to unload it. You would be surprised at how many told us. This makes it easier to research police reports. We would also ask about what method they used to gain entry into the home, business, or car, and any other property they might have taken and kept for themselves or gave to a friend—anything that would assist us in locating the victim. It is better to lose some potential customers because you are too inquisitive than to end up with a warehouse full of property and no victims.

At the conclusion of some of our storefronts, we conducted walk-throughs for the public. Property which had been purchased, and for which a victim had not been located, was placed on view for all interested. Many cases were made this way. However, buying property in the hopes that it can be returned in this fashion is a crap shoot at best.

Most firearms have serial numbers on them. You would think this would make them easy to trace. This is not not necessarily the case. We purchased most firearms brought to the storefront if for no other reason than to get them off the street, although this practice is becoming cost prohibitive. Being aware that guns will eventually show up at most storefronts, we made arrangements with the Bureau of Alcohol, Tobacco and Firearms (ATF) to prosecute convicted felons in possession of a firearm. We did not have a state statute dealing with such an offense. Even though an agreement was entered into beforehand, very few were charged with this offense. We had the most success with offenders who could be tried on several different counts, including the firearm violation.

Criminal Statutes

Understanding the criminal statutes and the elements of the crimes will also dictate what to buy. For instance, if property is brought into the storefront with a value that constitutes a misdemeanor under the receiving, concealing, or disposing of stolen property statute, you may not want to buy it. If, through recorded conversation, it can be proven that the subject actually stole the property, it could now become a felony, and you could reconsider the purchase.

Statutes could require you to show that the subject was in possession of the property. That is one reason why the subject brings the property to the storefront rather than having it picked up at another location.

FOR EXAMPLE _____

The subject enters the storefront and says he has a car to sell. Investigators ask where the car is, and he points to a red Ford sitting in the parking lot across the street. Investigators then go across the street and examine the car. The wing vents have been cleaned out, and it is obvious the car has been hot-wired. They go back to the storefront, assuming the subject stole the car, and he is paid. The investigator then takes the car from the parking lot to evidence.

With this scenario, prosecuting the offender will be very difficult. The taped conversation does not lend itself to proving he stole the car; he simply said, "I have a car to sell."

Showing that the vehicle was even in his possession, that he transported it or received it, is not likely. His defense could be that he just happened by the vehicle, saw it had been hot-wired, and knew some people who might buy the car. Friends had told him they were shady characters. Assuming they might buy stolen cars, they could also steal them. So he went and told them about it. He just took advantage of his good fortune. The cops stole the car then drove it away.

Understanding what constitutes the crime in question and what elements need to be proven to prosecute the offense will assist you in determining not only how items should be purchased but what to buy.

Controlled Substances

When you purchase controlled substances at the storefront, a lab test should always be requested to determine the quality of the drug. This is because there will usually be at least two additional buys. If the suspect has sold a diluted narcotic, bunk, and there is no dissatisfaction expressed by the buyer, the pusher could become suspicious. We never set ourselves up as a user. We always played the role of middleman. This prevents having to simulate use or making excuses for not using. We told those visiting the storefront who brought the conversation around to drugs that we were hustlers, not junkies. Even when using this ploy, the pusher still assumes someone will use the drugs. They, in turn, will report back on their pleasure or dislike of the product.

If the lab test results, indicating purity factors, are not known before the next meeting, go on the offensive. Accuse the dealer of selling weak stuff. Express outrage and how you lost out on the deal. The consumer was a good customer who had made a lot of money for you. A refund had to be paid on a portion of the proceeds just to keep him happy. Demand better quality and a better deal next time. Bear in mind that the dealer could be testing the water and did sell bunk to solicit a reaction. Even if he did not, you are always looking for ways to get a better deal; you are a hustler.

Street Value

Check with other investigators, both within and outside the department, to learn about street value. If the opportunity presents itself, question CIs, offenders in custody, known culprits, or fringe people to establish the going rate for the contraband the operation is concerned with. Again, as a basic rule, new property brings 10 percent or less and used property 5 percent or less.

We frequently called agents with ATF to ascertain the street value of weapons and explosives. This was an area in which we were weak. Some weapons, especially those converted to fully automatic, can demand a higher price than the retail value. If you have not bought machine guns or plastic explosives lately (and how many of us have?) it would be advantageous to ask for assistance. When street value is determined, always negotiate for a lower price.

The geographical area of the particular operation will also have an effect on price. In one area a stolen vehicle could command a much higher price than in another. The old economic principle still applies—supply and demand. At one time, CB radios were in demand. Offenders could get top dollar for them. Now CBs are a dime a dozen. Dope has fluctuated in price, both up and down. Televisions at one time could bring a handsome profit. That is no longer true in our area. Another location could be just the opposite. Just because investigators on the West Coast paid far less for the same type of item than the East Coast investigators does not mean they got the better deal. The West Coast could have paid far too much when compared with other similar buys in that area. The East Coast might have negotiated the better bargain. Street value is the price paid in a particular geographical area, dictated by the supply and demand of that specific locale.

PAYING FOR ITEMS PURCHASED

The last option to consider is using cash. Yes, cash will more than likely be the number one commodity used. However, exhaust all other alternatives first. There are many other forms of compensation that can be used, including:

1. Personal service
2. Property
3. Promises
4. Checks.

Personal Service

The facade used for the storefront can be a functioning business. If this is so, a service by this enterprise could be offered to the target in exchange for his or her services. We have repaired cars, detailed cars, done odd jobs, and provided chauffeured limousines, just to name a few of our efforts. The last thought that would come into most people's minds, even crooks, is that the plumber is a cop, especially when the plumber is under their sink unplugging the pipes. Use this tactic to carry on the illusion you have tried so hard to create.

We drove one target of ours around for three months in a chauffeur (police)-driven limousine. When he first came to the storefront and engaged in a transaction, we told him we lacked cash. He not only agreed to supply contraband to us but accepted our services for payment. What a status symbol; for a while he was the envy of the neighborhood. Of course, driving him around from associate to associate allowed us to become acquainted and invite his associates to the shop. Being a chauffeur for such an individual can be humiliating at times until you remember how injurious it is going to be to the offender's self-esteem, not to mention freedom.

Service, as any form of payment, should not be offered to get the target to do something. Do not say, "I'll fix your car if you steal me a television." That could be construed as directing the subject to commit a criminal act. All you want to do is afford an opportunity without inducement or persuasion. If the subject enters the site and asks, "What will you do for me if I do this for you?", tell him or her. Ask yourself, "Is what I'm doing prodding the subject to commit a crime?" If you answer yes, so will others.

Property

Barter with the target and use property for payment. We had a subject who traded three new vehicles he had stolen for one used clunker. The cost to us was far less than if we had paid cash. Transportation can become a problem even for auto thieves. Their credit history can be less than acceptable to a lender. The ability to buy on credit may not exist. With most large purchases being made on the promise of monthly payments, they have limited buying power. Use this to the operation's advantage.

Property released from police evidence can also be used. (We discussed this earlier.) We have traded jewelry, tools, furniture, and small appliances for contraband. Since these items can be obtained without having to incur a monetary loss, the available funding can be conserved.

Some merchants in the area are often sympathetic to law enforcement's plight. They will donate or sell, at a substantial discount, items that can be of use. In conversation with the target, try to uncover their wants. Do they want a new television, car, or jewelry? Then supply these items in lieu of cash and usually at a savings to the operational fund.

Any time property from evidence is used, document it. Then indicate on the inventory list the case number in which it was used. Do not bring problems on yourself with sloppy bookkeeping.

Promises

The optimum amount to give for any contraband is zero. There is nothing at all wrong with making promises in lieu of payment. Pay half now and indicate the rest will come later; better yet, pledge it all later. Cash does not need to pass hands to prosecute the vast majority of offenders. When this is not a required element for violating the statute, why do it unless it is unavoidable? Offenders make promises all the time; give me money now and I'll bring you something later. They want you to front them money. Reverse it; have them front the contraband.

On the first transaction with most offenders, asking them to front the goods will meet with limited success. Try, however; all they can say is no. It will not raise suspicion; just the opposite, they play this con all the time. As trust develops, the ploy is more likely to work. If items are fronted on the first transaction and subsequent buys are desired, maintain the practice. On the second buy, pay for the first items, and so on. Then when the last transaction occurs put off the target; payment will come later.

Keep in mind that broken promises can lead to retaliation. Take the necessary precautions. When it got to the point that a disgruntled target was about to raise havoc, we gained a reprieve by keeping as small a portion of the pledge as possible. String them along as they would like to string you along.

Checks

Paying by check has its advantages: bookkeeping and intelligence. It provides a record of expenditures. The need to have large amounts of cash on hand is also eliminated. The canceled check is an additional piece of evidence. Offenders usually balk at this until it is explained that this is being done for their protection. It is a means by which they can explain how they always have money without a visible means of support. We would make the check appear as if it were for wages. Then when the cops hassled them, they could show their check stub or have them go check with their "boss."

The canceled check also allows for positive identification of offenders. It is returned to the operation. The offender's bank account number and signature will appear on it. Targets would often use the excuse for not accepting this form of payment that there is no place they can cash it. Anticipating this, make arrangements with a nearby bank that handles the account. We would take the offenders to our bank—a gesture of goodwill to prove the check would not bounce. When offenders presented a check, the teller would take all the pertinent information from the target's ID and write it on the back of the check. Subjects are often not aware they are being identified.

It is not at all unusual for a small business to have a checking account. This is the norm rather than the exception. Solicit assistance from a friendly banker in establishing this account. When the offender knows money is not kept on the site, there is less potential for a robbery attempt. When you explain why payment is made this way and you demonstrate to offenders that they will receive their money, most will agree to this form of payment.

There is nothing wrong with giving the offender a "bad" check. We would usually use this tactic near the end of an operation. By then, most of the offenders were accustomed to being paid in this fashion. They no longer asked for someone to escort them to the bank to ensure that the check was good. A lot of property was purchased with a piece of paper. When considering using "bad" checks, brief the banker on this activity. It is not necessary, just a courtesy. You never know when you may need to ask for the banker's assistance again. If the administration raises questions about the legality of this technique, assure them it is acceptable. Obtaining a brief written opinion from the prosecutor could also place administration at ease.

Flash Roll

The cash used at the storefront and all funds used for a flash roll should be photocopied, if for no other reason than identification in the case of a rip-off. Flash rolls are used to impress a prospective seller or as a way of showing the seller you are more than just talk. We have all heard the expression on the street, "Money talks, bullshit walks." There are times you have to put up or shut up. The flash roll can be an important tool used to induce a target into making a sale.

The source of a flash roll may vary since it often consists of large sums of money. In some jurisdictions, money is borrowed from the city treasury or a banking institution that will lend without interest, on the signature of law enforcement officials. Occasionally, when the funds required are too large for one department to provide, an outside agency is asked to assist. When this is required, this agency will automatically become involved in the transaction. The agency is also responsible for its funds and wants to protect them. The agency could also impose situational controls in keeping with its policies and procedures.

Police officers have been killed for a flash roll, so you must have a comprehensive understanding of the target's criminal background and potential for attempting a robbery. Determine if the target is capable of doing what he or she has stated. Outrageous claims are often made in an attempt to set up officers. In preliminary meetings with the suspect, note if he or she is habitually armed. Use caution if the suspect is adamant about setting up the deal under conditions conducive to a rip-off. On the other hand, the same concern must be shown when suspects are too willing to agree to terms which are clearly not advantageous to them. You must sometimes rely on your gut feeling that conditions are right.

In making arrangements to display a flash roll, consider the following characteristics of the meeting place:

1. Is it well lit?
2. Do surveillance officers have ready access to the scene and a vantage point from which observations can be made?
3. Can escape routes be blocked?
4. Can involvement of unknowing citizens be minimized?
5. If a motel is used, can rooms with adjoining doors (allowing rapid access by surveillance and undercover officers) be obtained?
6. Will the area or room be easily accessible or visible to the subject's associates?

If the meeting is taking place away from the storefront, an electronic recording and listening device should be used. This could be either a room/car listening microphone or a body transmitter. Whenever possible, insist on the meeting taking place at the storefront. This will probably be the most advantageous location. If at any point the suspect appears to be placing too many conditions on the meeting, back off. There is no reason why the operation should take an unwarranted risk of losing money, or more importantly, getting you or someone else killed. The thought of making that big deal stimulates all of us. This enthusiasm must be controlled with proper planning and restraint. Do not allow the excitement of the moment to cause you to rush headlong into a deal.

DOCUMENTING YOUR ACTIVITIES: INVESTIGATION REPORTS

An important aspect of any tactical operation is the documentation of its activity. You must produce an investigative report which contains the pertinent facts of each case you are involved in. These written narratives complement the audio and video recordings, describing the transaction and observations of witnesses and of you that might not have been captured on tape. They are essentially the same as a follow-up investigation report or supplementary report produced by officers in some other police specialty.

You will usually work from incident reports initially filed by field officers. Most of the activity at the storefront will involve purchasing property which is listed on these original reports as being stolen. Occasionally, you will author all preliminary reports relating to a case. This usually involves crimes that do not have a "victim"—drugs, gambling, etc. In all cases, you must be able to communicate clearly and accurately in writing. These reports ultimately become the foundation on which the prosecution will build its case.

In addition to its use by the prosecutor, the investigative report serves a number of other functions:

1. It informs fellow officers of what work has been performed.
2. It permits superiors to make informed decisions concerning
    a. Coordination of investigative efforts
    b. Direction of the probe
3. It prevents a duplication of effort.
4. It suggests areas where relationships with other departments might be strengthened.
5. It is a learning tool.
6. It serves as an evaluation of effectiveness
    a. Of the investigator
    b. Of the investigation.

Material that is maintained in an investigative case file, compiled during the progress of an investigation that has not yet produced an arrest, can become a critically important progress report if the original operative becomes sick, injured, or for some other reason is unable to complete the investigation.

Production of a competent report requires that certain basic guidelines for report writing be followed. These are the ABCs; Accuracy, Brevity, and Completeness. This is the goal of every report. The means to accomplishing this are:

1. Research
2. Organization
3. Attention to detail
4. Simplification
5. Checking and rechecking to ensure accuracy.

It is said, "An army travels on its stomach." If that is true, then cops travel on their reports. Without skillful and precise reporting, the efforts of the storefront will go for naught. Invest the time necessary to showcase your good work through a superbly crafted investigative report.

POSTBUY DEBRIEFING WITH THE PROSECUTOR

After the completion of the first or a few buys, it could be prudent to schedule a meeting with the prosecutor. In this meeting, the recorded transactions (working copy of the tape) and investigative reports can be reviewed. If any problems are detected, a solution can be discussed. It is far easier to solve problems now rather than at the end of the operation; by then it could be too late. It is hard to think of anything much worse than at the culmination of the storefront discovering your efforts were in vain because of a legal technicality.

At this time in the investigation, you also have a more complete sense of any special needs that should be resolved: questions that have come up since the last meeting; situations that have presented themselves that you were not quite sure of; items overlooked at the first conference. Each storefront is unique, and every storefront you operate will present its own special problems. Do not shy away from legal guidance. The outcome of the entire operation could depend on it.

SUMMARY

Undercover work is an investigative process in which disguises and pretexts are used. This is to gain the confidence of a target for the purpose of determining the nature and extent of criminal activity. The cover story is an intricate part of the ruse. It should offer something attractive to the suspect. The cover story must

1. Facilitate the objectives of the operation
2. Be appropriate
3. Be comfortable for operatives
4. Be thoroughly memorized
5. Anticipate questions and formulate answers in advance.

You must abandon your official identity and assume a character compatible with the target and the neighborhood.

In meeting with the target, elicit the desired information. In accomplishing this,

1. Talk no more than necessary to keep the suspect talking.
2. Listen to all the suspect has to say.
3. Presume the suspect is as cleaver as you are.
4. Carefully observe all activity.
5. Remember that asking too many questions arouses suspicion.

The exchange of information should be from the target to you, rather than you to the target. There are essential procedures and precautions to follow:

1. Cases should generally be initiated only after the authority has been granted by a supervisor.
2. Make arrangements in advance to communicate with fellow officers.
3. Do not take part in any criminal act without first obtaining approval from a superior and prosecutor.
4. Do not develop a romantic involvement with anyone associated with the target.
5. Remember that lying, deception, and double-crossing are normal conduct for criminals.
6. Be skeptical: Never rely on or trust the target.

Be aware of entrapment and other legal considerations when conversing with the target. Remember:

1. Do not induce criminal activity.
2. Ensure that the target is predisposed to commit a crime.
3. Disguises and aliases are legally permitted.
4. Telling white lies is legally permitted.

Purchases should be made in compliance with stated objectives. Transactions are entered into for the purpose of meeting the goals of the storefront. The price to be paid for contraband should always be negotiated. Do not buy everything brought to the operation, and avoid using cash to purchase items. Document the buys with an investigative report. And, last but not least, hold a postbuy meeting with the prosecutor.

CASE CITATIONS

1. *State v. Sanchez*, 448 P.2d 807 (N.M. App., 1968).
2. *People v. Johnson*, 222 P.2d 58 (Cal. App., 1950).
3. *McVean v. State*, 227 P.2d 535 (Fla. App., 1969).
4. *Peters v. State*, 450 S.W.2d 276 (Ark., 1970).

CHAPTER 15

Culmination
of the Storefront

The storefront is nearing the end of its run; the question now is, What to do with all those offenders? Due to the relatively close association of those frequenting the operation and eventual media coverage of the investigation, the subjects may have to be taken into custody in a short time span. This is to prevent them from scattering and/or going into hiding once the word is out. A situation such as this requires an arrest raid. Initial planning must be coordinated with the prosecutor to determine how the offenders are to be placed into the legal system: (1) Arrest warrants can be issued in conjunction with grand jury indictments, (2) warrants can be obtained prior to the grand jury indicting, or (3) a warrantless arrest can be executed. We chose the second option most frequently. The third option should only be considered with approval of the prosecutor. There is an old saying in police work: If there is time to get a warrant, get one!

Taking into account the needs of your particular situation and coordination with support personnel (listed in chapter 10), formulate an apprehension plan. There is far more involved than simply stating, "OK, let's go get them!" Since most officers have not had an opportunity to participate in, or have limited exposure to, this type of undertaking, proper preparation and training is necessary, the limits of which will be dictated by the magnitude of the investigation, departmental resources, number of offenders, officer experience, personnel, and other specific restrictions that apply to your unique operation.

The raid should have a two-fold purpose: first, incarceration of targets; and second, to seize additional evidence. Therefore, not only do arrest warrants have to be obtained but search warrants, when applicable. Once the suspects are taken into custody, interviews should be conducted. Depending on the number of operatives in your investigation, you may be limited in how many of these you can conduct. A contingency plan must be established to overcome this weakness in the process.

Not knowing the sophistication of the offenders or type of evidence to be seized for your individual operation, we discuss arrest raids from more to less complex. We also examine dealing with offenders once they are in custody.

ARREST RAID

Conducting a raid is one of the more dangerous aspects of law enforcement. It is frequently done at the conclusion of a storefront operation. The extent to which this method is used and its complexity will be dictated by the magnitude of your particular storefront. You must develop, in yourself and other investigators, the skills required to conduct an arrest raid before you attempt to do it. In carrying out an arrest raid, officers knowingly enter into a situation which could result in casualties. Improper planning or failure to recognize and appreciate the various factors involved have resulted in ridicule to police agencies. A more grievous outcome of inadequate preparation is serious injury or the death of a fellow officer.

Raid can conjure up many different mental images based on your personal experience and law enforcement background. Within the context of a storefront investigation, it is the invasion of a building or locality for lawful purposes. These purposes, or objectives, are usually the apprehension of offenders, seizure of evidence, or the recovery of stolen property. When the purpose is for the arrest of a subject, an estimation of the resistance to be encountered is important. Fortunately, with a storefront investigation, efforts are directed toward a known subject. Officers are able to make some judgments as to the potential opposition.

The second objective of a raid is the seizure of evidence. During the course of the operation, offenders may have revealed that stolen property has been converted for their own personal use or is being stored at their residence; or controlled substances are kept at their home. There are also other items you could be searching for when affecting the arrest—items such as tools of the trade, a personal journal, storefront funds, etc. Since some of this evidence can easily be destroyed or altered, it is often necessary to surprise the offender. It is important to know the type and amount of evidence you are seeking, and, when possible, the location within the building in which these items are kept. This information is needed to secure a search warrant and to effect a speedy seizure. If you are seeking controlled substances that could pose a danger, ensure that you are aware of proper handling techniques.

Storefront units which work closely with narcotics units could also conduct raids to recover narcotics. These offenders, by the nature of their illicit profession, often deal in stolen goods. While working with offenders, you often receive information in reference to drug traffic. Consequently, a raid could be conducted for the primary purpose of recovering stolen items.

Raid Personnel

On many occasions, raid teams are made up of representatives of different law enforcement agencies. This is common in this type of investigation because of overlapping jurisdictions and the need for additional personnel due to the number of arrests being made simultaneously. This multiagency composition presents special problems in the planning and execution of the raid.

Initially, it must be determined which agency will have the primary responsibility for the raid operation. In a vast majority of cases, this will be your department. This is because the accountability for the raid should rest with the agency which has determined that the raid is required. Once the lead agency is selected, it must be fully supported by the other participating parties. The primary agency should establish specific duties for the outside departments, lines of authority, and a means of communication. It must also plan for the

Execution

Securing of the target location after the raid's completion

Maintaining of the chain of evidence for items seized

Prebooking

Transportation of those in custody.

The operation should be under the authority of one officer, sometimes referred to as the raid commander. He or she is charged with supervising the entire operation from planning to execution. Apart from the considerations which must be given to the various agencies involved, the selection of this officer should not be based on rank or seniority alone. Emphasis should be placed on

1. Prior experience
2. Ability to conduct such an activity
3. Knowledge of offender(s)
4. Knowledge of the target location(s).
5. Knowledge of legal guidelines.

The raid commander should have the confidence of team members. He or she should also have confidence in, and knowledge of, the capabilities of the team. With most undertakings of this sort, the front line supervisor of the storefront is the raid commander.

An arrest raid stemming from a storefront is usually a large operation which involves many police officers assigned to different areas. Therefore, unit leaders should be designated by the raid commander. If these units are to be further divided into subunits or teams, then each team will have a supervisor. This organizational structure allows all operational personnel to know precisely whose instructions are to be followed. Additionally, this gives the commander a span of control which facilitates directing the actions of every person assigned. Even if the raid involves only three to four officers, one should still be in charge of the entire operation.

The raid commander should strive to outnumber the opposition. When offenders see that they are outnumbered, they may not resist. The location of the offenders will assist in determining the number of team members required to control the situation. Sufficient personnel to secure the entire area of the raid, to block escape routes, and to control onlookers should be assigned. Consider the reputation and tendency toward violence of each person to be apprehended. The neighborhood and its general attitude toward law enforcement must also be taken into account. Caution should be used in any arrest raid situation, but more personnel should be assigned when apprehending a subject with an explosive temper and a propensity toward violence, or if an arrest is to take place in a hostile area.

There may be times when the presence of too many team members is not prudent. When appropriate, any reserve personnel should stand ready near that location. They should not come to the scene unless called on. In some circumstances, an overwhelming presence of law enforcement personnel can create its own problems. Sometimes in hostile neighborhoods, too many police draw an unwanted and potentially explosive crowd.

In the selection of team members, rank and seniority should not be primary considerations. As with the selection of the raid commander, experience and ability should be the guiding force. Whenever possible, the team leader should choose team members. Qualities to consider in selecting team members include

1. Experience

2. Good judgment

3. Mental stability

4. A personality that is not easily excited

5. A willingness to follow directions

6. Legal knowledge

7. Knowledge of evidence handling

8. Ability to communicate with others

9. Sensitivity to the situation.

Within this framework, personnel should be selected for their capabilities and special skills. These are some of the areas that should be considered:

1. Large-bodied officer for
   a. Breaking down doors
   b. Heavy lifting
2. Those who excel in the use of firearms
3. Those directly involved in the case
4. Technicians
   a. Photographs
   b. Fingerprints
   c. Explosives
   d. Evidence
   e. Chemist
   f. Pharmacist
5. Officers with good report-writing skills
6. Officers with special skills
   a. Dog handler
   b. Foreign language capability
   c. Scuba diving
   d. Appearance (subterfuge)
7. Technical equipment operators.

It is important to maintain team members at a manageable level. This refers to span of control—too many members on one team could be uncontrollable for one team leader. Responsibilities can be combined if the situation dictates. It is most desirable to select members who are known to one another. When this is not possible, the team leader should ensure that all members become acquainted before taking on the task.

There are occasions when outside support could be required. This type of assistance can include

1. Medical personnel
2. Rescue unit
3. Ambulance
4. Fire department
5. Paddy wagon
6. Uniformed police (used as backup)

7. Public service (electric)

8. Water department

9. Telephone service technician

10. Sewer technician.

Outside support personnel are not considered members of the team. They are there to assist with any special needs that could be encountered. Uniformed officers are especially important when team members are not in uniform. They can provide perimeter and roadblock functions, identify activity to the public, and at times be used as part of distraction to effect entry into target locations.

Assignments for Team Personnel

Members should be deployed to perform four basic unit functions:

1. Perimeter unit

2. Cover unit

3. Apprehending unit

4. Support unit.

The size of these units will vary according to the magnitude of the undertaking. However, regardless of size, all four functions must be carried out in a raid. When considering people for any of these units, remember those who assisted in the storefront. When appropriate, invite them along. This demonstrates your appreciation for their help and shows that you have not forgotten. However, do not be offended if they turn you down—some of us would rather not volunteer for this pursuit.

The Perimeter Unit

The perimeter unit will usually use the largest number of officers. This will be especially true in heavily populated areas when crowds are likely to gather. This unit's purpose is to seal the outer boundary of the raid location. With this accomplished, the possibility that team members will be hindered or endangered by the curious public is reduced. Onlookers who could interfere with the operation and bystanders who might be placing themselves in danger must be controlled. It is advantageous to use uniformed officers for this function. Officers with less experience in arrest raids should also be used on this detail. Moreover, perimeter personnel should be prepared to remove people from the area and to establish additional crowd control if necessary.

The Cover Unit

The cover unit must contain the offenders within a specified area or capture them if they flee from the apprehending unit. Personnel should position themselves so they are not easily observed and in a way that secures all possible exits. They should not enter or actively search the structure. They must exercise restraint and caution so they do not mistakenly fire on other officers.

The Apprehending Unit

The apprehending unit or entry unit effects the entry into the building and the arrest of the offender(s). These unit members will usually be exposed to the greatest danger since they come in contact with the target. Due to the risk involved, officers within the unit should be accustomed to each other. In addition, they should know apprehension techniques and be specially equipped. They should wear clothing that makes it apparent that they are police officers—raid jackets, caps, badges, etc. They should also wear protective gear. As few members as possible and practical should be assigned for this function.

The Support Unit

The support unit reinforces the apprehending unit and should follow that unit into the building after the location has be secured. This team is responsible for taking custody of prisoners and conducting a thorough and systematic search. A team member should be in possession of the warrant(s). Personnel of this unit should also provide the following:

1. Accurate log of events
   a. Date and time of entry and of securing the scene.
   b. Officers assigned
   c. People arrested/present in the building
   d. Location of evidence
   e. Damage officers caused to structure
   f. Witnesses
2. Tape recorder
   a. Excitement and the rapid pace of events do not always allow for proper note taking.
   b. Statements of witnesses, offender(s), and/or others in the building
   c. Recorder usually remains on during entire operation

3. Photographer

   a. The site condition before and after the raid/search.

   b. Offender(s) and others in building

   c. Evidence and where it was found

   d. Any damage caused by officers

   e. Any other appropriate items or events

4. Evidence/property handler

   a. Receive, assemble, and tag all goods

5. Custodian

   a. Process people taken into custody.

Gathering Information

The success of any raid is a direct consequence of the attention given to its preparation. Time limits will determine the depth to which intelligence on the target can be gathered. In most instances, operatives have had several months to prepare. However, there are latecomers to any operation who could limit preparation to a week or even days.

In obtaining planning data, three activities should be performed:

1. Background information on offender(s)
2. Surveillance

   a. Behavior patterns

   b. People frequenting the building

3. Reconnaissance of the neighborhood.

The reconnaissance of the raid area should include the structure to be entered and the surrounding neighborhood. Study the building to be entered for its construction and layout. Locate doors, windows, common exits, fire escapes, and communications facilities. When possible, note placement of lights and switches. If the building is an apartment, hotel, or motel, the design of an individual room can often be determined by examining a similar room. This technique can also apply to houses in a subdivision. Otherwise, details about the layout can be obtained by questioning neighbors or someone familiar with the property. When a business office is the target, a blueprint or floor plan can be obtained from the manager or owner. As always, be careful not to reveal the nature of the inquiry.

Adjoining buildings should be surveyed to determine their accessibility from the target site. These could be used as escape routes, or the raid team could use them as an avenue of approach. The physical terrain of the neighborhood should be studied to establish means of approach or various paths of escape. Any obstruction, viewing points, pedestrian and traffic patterns should be noted. A videotape of the neighborhood and raid site is a realistic method of showing the area to team members. This technique is not used as frequently as it could be. A diagram depicting essential information could also be given to personnel.

Residents of the neighborhood should be observed to anticipate any alarm they could give of pending activity. Note individual behavior characteristics of those in the immediate target area. Determine their likelihood to interfere with police. Raid plans should ensure that bystanders cannot be used by the offender(s) as hostages or otherwise endangered.

The following is a checklist of those areas which should be the focal points of information gathering:

1. Geographical location

2. Interior layout

3. Maps, photos, and/or drawings of target location (do not forget video recording, when appropriate)

4. Approach and escape routes

   a. Fire escapes/stairs

   b. Elevators, dumbwaiters, or laundry chutes

   c. Void air shafts

   d. All doors, windows, and skylights

   e. Access to and from adjoining buildings through roofs, basements, holes in walls, etc.

5. Construction and peculiarities of location

   a. Can it be penetrated by gunfire?

   b. Does it pose a fire hazard?

   c. Are there underground parking facilities or an attached garage?

   d. Is there a doorman, porter, or superintendent?

   e. Are windows barred and doors reinforced, or is there a sophisticated locking system?

   f. In what direction do doors and windows open?

   g. Are there guard dogs or other such animals present?

6. Location of all utility shutoffs, both internal and external

7. Location of internal utilities

   a. Sinks

   b. Toilets

   c. Drains

    d. Fireplaces

    e. Garbage disposal

  8. Attitude of people in immediate area

    a. Possible reaction to police

    b. Warn of pending raid

    c. Assist offender(s) escape

  9. Dangers posed to innocent residents in or near target location.

When anticipating how a subject(s) could react, consider the legal penalties of the offense. Do not assume that those charged with lesser crimes will not react violently. Information on offenders should include their physical condition, state of mind, the possibility of surrender, any history of resisting arrest or abuse of narcotics, and the firearms available and skill with weapons. The offenders' precise location within a building should be determined whenever possible, and whether they are likely to be asleep or awake at the time of the raid. Also ascertain if others in the building and/or target location are likely to support the offender.

The following factors, in reference to a suspect, should be assessed when planning a raid.

  1. Name/description of offender

    a. Have photograph whenever possible

  2. Makeup of people involved

    a. Male/female

    b. Will there be children present?

    c. Ages of occupants

  3. Number of suspects at the location at any particular hour

    a. Identity and background of leader

  4. Capabilities of suspect(s)

    a. Magnitude of violation

    b. Suspect's classification, parolee, AWOL, etc.

    c. Previous police record

    d. Likelihood of resistance

  5. Physical and mental condition

    a. Repeat offenders, junkies, psychotics

    b. Copfighters

    c. Known militants

    d. Specialists in martial arts

6. Weapons background

    a. Information obtained through conversations at the storefront

    b. Police record for firearm violations

    c. Military background

    d. Access to weapons (types and numbers)

    e. Knowledgeable in use of explosives

7. Modes of transportation

    a. Obtain all registration numbers and descriptions of autos, planes, boats, etc.

    b. Locate all vehicles for the purpose of guarding them during the raid.

8. Anticipation of media reaction to arrest, injury, or death of offender.

A fixed surveillance could be necessary to observe and understand habits of the offender(s). Also learn the identity of people frequenting the building or surrounding area. A continuous surveillance could be used during the period immediately before the raid to provide last-minute information: specifically, to determine if the suspect is present and if any unusual circumstances are occurring. More importantly, surveillance officers are attentive to indications that a suspect could be arrested leaving the building or entering his or her vehicle. This could alter the need for a raid and thus the danger associated with this type of activity.

The following sources can also be used to gather information:

1. Case file on the investigation

    a. Could contain intelligence on suspect's habits, accomplices, contacts, vehicles, and/or residence

2. CI who has proven reliability

    a. Can offer invaluable information on offender, associates, layout of building, and personal habits

    b. Whenever possible, information should be independently verified

3. Subterfuge

    a. Getting team members into the area for surveillance

    b. Gathering information on the raid site

    c. Access to target area

    d. Disguises could include building inspector, fire inspector, clergy, or even a uniformed officer if circumstances permit and presence is not unusual.

Positive Identification of the Physical Target

Positive identification is a very important legal consideration. It should be accomplished during the ongoing investigation by the operatives and/or support personnel. It must be firmly established before organizing the raid. When intelligence is not updated, mistakes can occur. Incidents in which gross errors were made have resulted in (1) violations of the rights of innocent people, (2) the loss of cases at judicial levels, and (3) the death or injury to law-abiding citizens and police officers. You are not only subject to departmental discipline for such errors in judgment, but you can also be held legally responsible in civil suits.

Today, with tract homes, look-alike garden apartments, high-rise complexes, and identical layouts, it is very easy to err if you do not pay proper attention to detail. Although the location to be raided must be fully described on the affidavit for the warrant, mistakes are still made. Therefore, it is incumbent on the team leader to verify the target location. In addition, after team members are selected, they should be allowed to clarify and/or confirm the positive identification of the target location if any doubt exists.

Preraid Briefing

During the course of planning, there will be numerous meetings among operatives, members of the raid team(s), the team leader(s), supervisors, and support personnel. Initial planning should be conducted among the immediate members, and information concerning the proposed raid should be disseminated on a need-to-know basis. All the planning activity that precedes the raid culminates in this briefing. Therefore, it is important the following be carried out:

1. The raid commander, who conducts the meeting, is identified.
2. Team members should be familiar with each other and present at the briefing.
3. If an extremely large raid group is used, team leaders should be briefed by the raid commander. They, in turn, brief their team in detail on specific assignments. If a small group is used, all members are briefed by the raid commander.
4. Ensure that all members are aware of the specific nature of the operation.
5. All members must know the tactics to be used to gain entry.
6. Information on timing should be specific. The briefing officer should give the exact time that members will meet at the preselected assembly point. Also allow for a specific amount of time for the team to get from this point to the target area and into position.

A raid folder should be compiled and given to each team leader. The following material would be included in the folder:

1. A mock-up diagram of the objective
   a. Should be as detailed as possible
   b. When available, complemented by photographs, maps, and sketches
   c. This allows for potential problems to be discerned and eliminated during briefing.
2. Identification of offender(s)
   a. Current photograph
   b. Rap sheet
   c. Personal history sheet
   d. Observations of operatives, especially on temperament and statements about expected violence
   e. Any information on associates or family who may be present
3. Accurate, detailed description of vehicles used by the target
   a. If vehicles are to be seized
4. Nature and description of evidence sought
   a. Will assist in determining amount of surprise necessary to prevent destruction
   b. Will help in planning for where evidence could be concealed
5. Arrest/search warrant and affidavit
6. List of postentry assignments
   a. Custody and handling of prisoners
   b. Custody and handling of evidence
   c. Custody and handling of seized vehicles
   d. Handling of additional suspects who arrive on the scene
   e. Transportation of the team from raid site back to assembly point
   f. Procedures for searching the location
   g. Postraid surveillance (if required)
7. Copy of advise-of-rights form
8. Location of booking area (if not at customary location)
9. List of names and phone numbers of support people who may need to be contacted

    a. Supervisor

    b. Detention personnel

    c. Probation/parole officers

    d. Prosecutor

    e. Media liaison

    f. Police garage/towing (for seized vehicle).

Allow time to discuss special instructions and assignments when circumstances dictate. Although the what-ifs for such occurrences are inexhaustible, the following are some examples:

1. If an operative is going to be present at a target location, be sure raid team members are aware of it. Instruction on how the operative is to be treated should be given (suspect or actively assist).
2. If a CI is to be present, it would be advisable to make his or her identity known to members on a need-to-know basis, as well as how the CI is to be treated (suspect or allowed to walk).
3. Any special equipment required should be used by those trained to do so.
4. Develop a system of hand or light signals in case of communication failure or if circumstances prohibit using established communication modes.
5. If raiding a clandestine laboratory, a qualified lab raid team should accompany search detail.
6. Health precautions need to be considered—rubber gloves, masks, and protective clothing and shoes should be worn or available.
7. Juveniles need special arrangements for processing.
8. Female suspects or those at the target area could need to be searched. Arrange for a female officer.

Raid Equipment

When discussing the equipment needed for a raid, it is important to consider that each operation will have its own special requirements. These can be based on the nature of the raid, resistance expected, method of entry, and availability of intelligence. The storefront's unit commander should recognize that necessary equipment will often need to be borrowed. Most units are limited in available funding and cannot or do not desire to purchase these items, since these items are often not cost effective (due to infrequent use).

All raid team members should be armed with their personal firearm as dictated by departmental policy. The use and/or display of the right weapons at the appropriate time will often prevent conflicts or casualties on both sides. The following factors should be considered in selecting appropriate firepower:

1. Fully automatic weapons have a great psychological effect, although in some locations they are impractical due to the possible infliction of casualties on citizens. They can be very inaccurate when not in the proper hands and are controversial.

2. High-powered rifles are very good when used for an antisniper role. However, due to the range and impact of these weapons, their use in raids in urban areas is severely restricted.

3. Shotguns are considered by most as the best all-around weapon in a raid situation due to the firepower they can provide and their psychological effect. Their uses are all but limitless because of the various types of slugs or shot that can be used. They are easy to maintain, and most officers have been trained in their use.

4. Attempt to standardize weapons and ammunition. This affords for an easy supply effort. Furthermore, the exchange of ammunition between team members could be critical during an assault. In all cases, personnel should abide by departmental guidelines.

There are several advantages in requiring that all police officers who participate in this activity be easily identified:

1. The likelihood that officers might mistake one another for a suspect is reduced.

2. People will not have grounds to doubt their official identity.

3. Those observing the raid will be aware it is a law enforcement operation.

Investigators participating should be provided with some means of identification which is instantly recognized from a distance. This could include

1. Coveralls

2. Lightweight jackets

3. Baseball caps

4. Head/arm bands.

All these items should be of a distinctive color and bear a proper insignia. When appropriate, the word *police* should also appear in large, bold letters on the front and back of the garment. Badges or shields should be worn where they can be seen. They can be worn alone, although a combination of items provides the best visibility.

Equipment considerations should include the need for vehicles for transportation of raid teams and equipment, suspects who have been arrested, and/or evidence seized. Decide beforehand if

1. Team personnel will use marked or unmarked vehicles or a combination of both.
2. There is a need for sound, lighting, or communication-type vehicles.
3. High-pursuit vehicles will be on hand in case of a breakout.
4. Standby medical and fire units will be needed in the area.

Effective communication between team members is a major factor in the success of the operation. This will provide comprehensive control of the raid's activities. In addition to hand-held radios, there are devices that provide hearing and transmitting functions without restricting your mobility. Reliance on shouted verbal commands should be avoided. Hand and arm signals may be the oldest form of communication, but they can still play an important role in providing an alternative means of communication. During the preraid briefing, establish a system of signals to be used in case of radio failure or other problems. Public address systems could also be required for crowd control and at times to communicate with the offender.

Entry tools should be included in the usual complement of equipment—tire iron, large metal crowbar, slide bar, bolt cutters, etc. These can be augmented by special tools—jaws of life, cutting torch, battering ram, wrecker, etc.—when the nature of the operation dictates. Many of these items, if not available through normal channels, can be borrowed from the local fire department.

Raid Execution

The raid should begin as soon as possible after the preraid briefing, while information is still fresh in the minds of team members. The first phase will consist of all raid team members and support personnel reporting to a preselected assembly area at the assigned time. This location, which could be a public building, school, warehouse, etc., should have been selected for its usefulness in concealing the operation and/or proximity to the target.

At the assembly point, any last-minute updating of intelligence can be accomplished and unforeseen problems corrected. All vehicles and equipment that will not be initially required at the target location should remain here. Do not forget to leave car keys with officers assigned to remain behind and watch the vehicles. There should be direct communications between these officers and the raid team in case any equipment is needed promptly.

Perimeter team members will then proceed to their assigned locations to seal off the area. Roadblocks, if deemed necessary, should be set in place. When there is an anticipated need for pursuit vehicles, they should be manned and ready. Take caution with any equipment used by the perimeter unit—an unfriendly or sticky-fingered crowd could damage and/or steal unattended items.

The cover detail, support detail, and entry detail should then move directly on the target location. Use as much cover and concealment as is available, adhering (as much as practical) to the planned method of approach. The raid team should avoid using red lights and sirens, screeching brakes, slamming doors, or shouting directions—anything that makes their arrival conspicuous. Remember the unfriendly and sticky-fingered neighbors: Lock and secure vehicles, or you could come back out to an unwanted surprise!

The cover detail should take up assigned positions, surround the immediate area of the target location, and proceed with their assignments. These duties could include

1. Covering all escape routes
2. Establishing an observation post
3. Preventing anyone from entering or leaving the building
4. Securing the offender's vehicle (prevents usage in an escape attempt)
5. Eliminating disadvantageous lighting
6. When planned for, securing all external utility connections (telephone and water)
7. Locating doormen or other building personnel who could disclose the team's presence
8. Notifying the team leader when the detail is in position and objectives are accomplished.

The support detail (acting as an inner perimeter team), accompanied by the entry detail, should then enter the target building. They should observe the target's residence for any signs of activity. During such observations, the support team should not cluster together, as this makes them an easy target. The officers, with weapons ready, should allow time for their eyes to adjust to interior lights. The use of more than one entry point should be avoided especially during a night operation. All means of escape from within the building should be sealed by the covering detail, who are strategically located adjacent to the target site.

The support detail must immediately take up their assigned positions within the building and initiate their assigned duties. These duties include securing internal stairways, elevators, and egress routes such as dumbwaiters and laundry chutes. They should secure the immediate outside area of the apartment or room to prevent people from entering this location from adjoining apartments or floors. Their task is also to darken the hallways, specifically the one leading to the door of the target room or apartment. The support detail's position should be one with a good view of this doorway. After the support detail has taken its position, it should notify all other details, inside and outside the building, that it is in position. The raid team leader will normally be with the support detail.

After the raid commander has determined that all teams are in position, he or she will give the entry detail the signal to proceed as planned. Entrance must be made quickly and forcefully, allowing the suspects a minimum amount of time to react. The immediate situation confronting the entry detail will, of course, depend on the actions of the suspect(s). For example, the suspect could offer no resistance, fire on officers, attempt to escape, physically resist, or attempt to destroy evidence. The assigned duties of the entry detail will be to

1. Effect entry to the target's residence.
2. Identify themselves and state the purpose of the entry.
3. Gain control of the suspect(s).
4. Secure all weapons found at the scene.
5. Prevent the destruction of evidence.
6. Establish order inside the dwelling.
7. Search all suspects and place them under guard.
8. Advise all members of the raid team as to the status of the operation.

After the entry and support teams have secured the area, the team leader can call for a search of the premises to begin. The area is sealed off until processing is completed. Processing includes

1. General photographs or video recording of dwelling before search
2. Recording, photographing, tagging of evidence
3. Identifying and evacuating apprehended suspects
4. Moving property or goods that have been confiscated or recovered
5. General photographs or video recordings of the scene after the search.

After the suspects and all evidence are removed and the raid team leader determines that the operation is concluded, all units should be notified. Beginning with the inside units, the raid team can begin to depart. This, too, should be accomplished using prearranged procedures. Team personnel should report back to the assembly point, where a head count is taken and all equipment is inventoried and checked.

Entry into an offender's residence can be very eventful. Assignments must be carried out rapidly yet cautiously. Controlled confusion and panic can be the name of the game. The adrenaline rush combined with hesitation about what exactly is to be done can result in deadly consequences. If unit members are not accustomed to this task, practice of simulated entries is advisable. There will be more than enough to worry about without having to ponder over your assignments. They should be carried out on instinct, no matter what unforeseen events occur.

These suggested procedures merely offer a guideline and will, of necessity, change to conform with the method of entry and the nature of the target. For example, in the case of a private home, entry could be made directly into the specific target location. This could exclude the necessity for an internal support unit.

Other Strategies and Tactics

A number of strategies and tactics can be deployed by an entry unit. Four of these are

1. Warning
2. Surprise
3. Subterfuge
4. Knocking.

Warning

In some situations, the tactic of warning the suspect that a raid is imminent could be the most effective approach. This can be given with an unaided voice, over the telephone, or using a public address system. When asking an offender to give up, be certain that he or she hears and understand the instructions clearly. The warning must first establish that the speaker is a police officer, that it is not a joke, and the purpose of the raid. Then request surrender and tell the suspect that law enforcement has control of the area; all avenues of escape have been cut off, and resistance is futile. Then give specific instructions about how the offender should surrender. If there is more than one subject in the building, the most potentially dangerous one should be ordered out first. If there is the possibility of another subject, do not leave your cover to take the first offender into custody. When the suspect is ordered out on the threat of using an irritant gas, the raid commander should be ready to follow through, if the subject does not comply. Team members should not fire on the building unless the offender takes direct detrimental action to the safety of officers.

Warning shots should not be used. If the telephone is used to communicate, the conversation should be recorded.

Surprise

The tactic of surprise is often successful in an investigation of this sort. Offenders can be invited to a party hosted by operatives. Promises of free-flowing booze, drugs, and sex can be made. The invitations would have offenders arriving at various times. When they enter the gaily decorated hall, they are given an adorned package—just a small token of appreciation for their business with the operation. When they rip open the gift, it reveals a copy of the arrest warrant, and you say "Surprise!"

Other similar schemes can be used. The suspects can receive a telephone call stating that they have won a trip, Super Bowl tickets, or cash. If the prize is to be claimed, they must appear in person for publicity photos and to fill out required forms. Your imagination is the only limitation on the surprise. When the surprise is used, proper planning and briefing of support personnel are still necessary. Raid folders should be compiled on each offender, with appropriate information and paperwork enclosed. Instructions must be given on how offenders are to be taken into custody and where they are to be detained out of sight of other "guests," and transportation to a detention center must be arranged. A contingency raid plan may also have to be developed for no-shows.

Subterfuge

The tactic of subterfuge can also be used to gain entry into a building without encountering resistance or having to use force. With this method, an officer can pose as a member of an occupational group and thereby not arouse the suspicion of the individuals sought. Whatever pretext is used, it should seem logical to the subject. Officers must be able to act the role chosen and gain the upper hand before the suspect becomes suspicious. The exact nature of the ploy will, naturally, vary with each situation. Officers should be aware of pretexts used by other units. When used too often they lose their originality, and this can create serious dangers for investigators.

Knocking

We often overlook the most obvious: simply knocking on the offender's door and announcing your presence. The target knows and trusts the same people he or she dealt with at the storefront. The raid team could consist of a fellow officer and yourself. You gained a comprehensive understanding of the target through personal contact during the investigation. If, in evaluating the suspect, this method seems feasible, use it. A "big production" is not always needed. However, be aware of how to carry out a more complex plan, if that is called for.

Since the methods that are open to a raid unit to effect entry are infinite, it is impossible to discuss all contingencies in this phase of the operation. The specific tactic of gaining entry, whether surprise, subterfuge, knocking, or warning, must be well established before the raid team arrives at the target location. Recognize that some latitude must be given in the plan to allow for an on-site change, should the need arise.

Postraid Debriefing

As soon as possible after the conclusion of the raid, a debriefing should be held, during which all members of the team are questioned for pertinent information relating to the undertaking. Notes should be made of their observations. All reports should be submitted shortly after the conclusion of the meeting. Raid folders should be turned into the raid commander and necessary forms checked for accuracy and completeness.

A critique of the raid should also be compiled. Attempt to identify both strengths and weaknesses in the plan and possible improvements for coming activities of this nature. Problems encountered in the field should be analyzed and noted on a copy of the overall tactical plan. This can provide valuable assistance in future operations.

IN-CUSTODY INTERVIEW

In-custody interviews (also referred to as formal interviews or interrogations) historically have not been used as extensively in storefront operations as they have in other forms of police work. This is because of the almost exclusive use of undercover officers and CIs in storefronts. Once the buys have been completed and substantiated by electronic surveillance and contraband evidence, there seems to be little reason to further add to the case with a confession. However, the storefront's investigation does not always end with the arrest of the violators. There could be a need to look further into the extended criminal activity and associates of certain offenders. It may also be possible to turn these subjects into CIs and direct their attention toward people operating at higher levels. The in-custody interview, in some instances, can become an important tool in completing the work of the storefront. These special interviews should be conducted by the operatives or other storefront personnel familiar with the case.

Advise-of-Rights Form

In each raid folder, there should be an advise-of-rights form. At the bottom of this form appears a list of questions constructed by the operatives and/or the prosecutor that are relevant to the particular storefront investigation. A standard advise-of-rights form can be used with these specific questions typed on the bottom or back of the form. The questions are structured to aid against foreseeable defense tactics. For example, one question could be: "Have you ever done business with (name of storefront), located at (street address)?" If the subject answers no, and then later claims entrapment, the question can be used to disprove the claim. You cannot be entrapped by a storefront you supposedly never did business with. Other such questions geared toward predisposition and other legal considerations should be included.

Due to the potential number of arrests being made at approximately the same time, operatives will not be able to interview all of the subjects. The questions are placed on the advise-of-rights form so even those not familiar with the investigation can obtain answers to these basic queries.

Helpful Hints: Most forms have a waiver-of-rights section for the offender's signature. The statement before this signature line will usually say, "I have read and understand my rights." If the word *read* appears, make sure subjects can indeed read. Have them read out loud a portion of the text. If they cannot read, indicate this on the form. Also, at the end of the prepared questions there should be another similar space for the subject's signature. It basically says, "I have read the statement and it is the truth as I have told it." As an indicator that this was actually done, use obvious typographical errors. Then have subjects change and initial corrections. The final question that appears on the prepared list should be similar to this: "Do you have anything else to add or say?" This shows that the offender had an opportunity to do more than just respond to your questions. (A copy of an advise-of-rights form can be found in the appendix.)

Systematic Inquiry

The in-custody interview is a systematic inquiry to ascertain the extent of involvement in criminal dealings. Full Miranda warnings must be read and explained to the offender at the start of the process. Preparing for the interview would be much like that of any other queries made of CIs or witnesses. You must consider exactly what information would be most beneficial in continuing the investigation. Plan a series of questions that can be referred to during the interview.

Two officers are commonly used for the in-custody interview. Both will assist in the interview and serve as witnesses to the proceedings. They should decide, before initiating questioning, on their respective roles. It is often advantageous for them to adopt contrasting styles. The reaction of the offender could be to favor one approach over the other. Selection of initial techniques will depend on the officers' impression of the subject's personality and knowledge of the case. A variety of styles and techniques can be used:

1. Logical
2. Sympathetic
3. Aggressive
4. Indifferent
5. Face-saving
6. Egotistical
7. Exaggeration.

Logical Technique

Often, in storefront cases, the evidence is overwhelming; thus, subjects may appear unemotional about their predicament. The investigator may choose to appeal to the subject's respect for logical reasoning. This approach is directed at presenting entirely logical reasons why the subject should cooperate. Play to the subject's self-interest and demonstrate that assisting law enforcement is the only logical alternative. Use a businesslike tone of voice and posture that displays confidence. Remember, no promises of leniency can be made; nor can it be suggested in any fashion that the subject will be better off if he or she decides to help with the investigation. However, it can be stated that the subject's cooperation will be brought to the attention of the prosecuting attorney at the time of trial.

Sympathetic Technique

When it is determined that the subject will be affected by an emotional appeal, the sympathetic approach could be prudent. Conduct the interview in low tones and include expressions of compassion and understanding for the subject's plight. This can be expanded to other topics as well: the subject's spouse, parents, children, health, business, religion, etc. While talking, sit reasonably close, and when appropriate touch the subject's arm or shoulder in a friendly manner. Attempt to generate feelings of guilt and self-pity. The subject will usually blame others for his or her problems. A sympathetic reaction encourages the subject to further relieve feelings of guilt by assisting in the investigation.

Aggressive Technique

An aggressive technique is basically a threatening overture, conveying the impression of hostility toward the subject. Act as if struggling to restrain from physically attacking the suspect. At times you do not have to act, but this method will be far more successful if your emotions are under control. This remnant of a bygone era is becoming more and more difficult to portray without risk of violating the suspect's civil rights. Therefore, only a limited amount of dislike and disgust can be communicated. This is best exhibited by disagreeable and impatient facial expressions and fluctuations in voice tone rather than an actual threat. This approach could be incorporated as part of a total interview strategy in which conflicting styles are displayed. The anxiety created by one interviewer could encourage a more cooperative attitude toward the sympathetic, friendlier member of the team.

Indifferent Technique

The indifferent technique could be described as a modified aggressive posture. It emphasizes a fundamental indifference on the part of the interviewer. Suggest that it does not really make a difference to you, and you do not care if the subject cooperates. However, the opportunity to do so must remain an option. Give the impression that you are merely going through the motions. The idea is to express a feeling that severe treatment for the crimes committed is preferred to any consideration that may be given for assistance. As with the aggressive approach, this technique is most advantageous when used with a contrasting style, such as sympathy. When both interviewers display this attitude, it could adversely affect the eventual outcome of the questioning.

Face-Saving Technique

This provides a psychological way out that justifies participation in the crime. It is hinted at, but never actually stated, that a thorough comprehension of the subject's motivation could affect the degree to which he or she is responsible for the criminal activity; much as children claim that the only reason for their actions is that someone else had done it first or had talked them into it. When systematically rationalizing the subject's motivations up to the point of the crime, describing them as natural consequences of other difficulties or problems, try to get the subject to explain the cause of his or her illegal behavior. As the process progresses, occasionally make comments that have the appearance of diminishing the importance of the subject's personal involvement in the crime. These could stimulate the offender into revealing further details.

Egotistical Technique

The subject's pride and sense of accomplishment is the focus of this technique. Express an appreciation for the intelligence required in such a criminal undertaking. Act impressed by the efficiency of the operation and the managerial ability displayed and amazed at the wealth amassed in just a short period of time. Note the skillfulness and dexterity that must be possessed to carry off such a feat. Express respect for anyone who could organize and place into action such a complicated and daring plan. These types of accolades encourage the subject to boast about his or her accomplishments and, in so doing, provide additional details to further impress the interviewer.

Exaggeration Technique

This technique is often used against an uncooperative suspect who has otherwise been unaffected by other strategies. Exaggerate the charges that could possibly be brought against the subject. Suggest that the subject's role is much bigger and important than is actually the case; that the charge is merely the tip of the iceberg compared to the subject's true involvement. State that when the truth is revealed the subject's legal problems could grow dramatically. These exaggerations are made in the hope that the offender will admit his or her exact participation in the violations to protect himself or herself from other allegations. It works well when cohorts are in custody simultaneously—telling one that the other is claiming he or she is the brains behind the illicit activity or that one is revealing other criminal acts that the subject might have been involved in.

Using the Techniques

The foregoing are only some of the more common interviewing styles. Others exist, and many of the described methods are known by different labels. These techniques do not always require two interviewers to be effective. One investigator can employ several styles in the same interview. The essential point is that numerous possible approaches can be used. The selection of one over the other should be made on the basis of the circumstances surrounding the case and personality of the offender—not on the basis of a personal preference because the investigator feels more comfortable using a specific style. It is true that some officers can use some techniques far better than others. However, it is the ability to vary techniques and use the most advantageous style that makes a skilled interviewer.

There are two other skills to be cultivated: The ability to recognize when a suspect is reaching an emotional peak, and the ability to detect when a suspect is most likely to respond to a particular style of interviewing. This comes from experience in the interviewing room. However, there are some basic guidelines.

Watch carefully for the body responses of the subject. Body language such as running fingers through the hair, finger tapping, covering the mouth with hands, nervous laughter, hand wringing, and other movements could indicate rising tension. Skin color changes can be caused by fear, anger, or embarrassment. Facial expressions can be involuntary signals of the emotional condition. Stuttering, voice fluctuations, and repetitiveness can be caused by apprehension and reflected in one's speech. Note these responses at the beginning of the interview and watch for changes during its course. Often, subtle movements are detected that can be used to facilitate the questioning. Learn to read these signals accurately and to respond with the appropriate technique.

Draw on your own experiences to select the right style in bringing the interview to its decisive moment. This may require focusing with increased intensity on the subject. Enumerate the various lies and attempts at deception that have been tried during the interview; the lack of response to someone who is trying to understand; family embarrassment and suffering; the lack of remorse. Use whatever particular style you deem necessary at that moment. It is important that some technique be tried to extract the greatest possible reaction from the subject. Even if the ploy does not work, your skills as an interviewer are sharpened by this experience.

At the conclusion of an interview, it is important to maintain the role. Do not indicate that the whole thing was an act and all along the cooperation of the subject was ensured because of it. Project a professional demeanor. If the questioning was a success, celebrate after the subject has left the area. Remember that expressing concern and understanding toward an offender can pay off in the future.

IN-CUSTODY CONFESSIONS: LEGAL ASPECTS

As we all know, a confession must be voluntary to be admissible in court. Simply reading a subject his or her rights under Miranda may not be sufficient. It must be shown that the confession was given by the subject's own free will. There are three types of police behaviors which would adversely affect a confession's admissibility:

1. *Coercion:* The use or threat of physical methods to induce a confession
2. *Duress:* The imposition of restrictions on physical behavior such as a prolonged interview, deprivation of food, water, or sleep, or excessive physical discomfort
3. *Physical constraint:* Restraining of free will by threats or other methods of instilling fear, such as indirectly suggesting harm to suspects, their family, or their property.

Statements stemming from an in-custody interview are not admissible unless it can be demonstrated that procedural safeguards to ensure the subject's privileges against self-incrimination were taken. This must be proven through your own testimony and/or that of witnesses; for example, that you informed the accused of his or her rights under Miranda. Moreover, you should be able to show that the confession was voluntary. This is accomplished by showing that

1. The statement was a spontaneous or self-induced utterance of the accused and was not obtained by urging or by request.
2. The statement was obtained without coercion and not during an official investigation.
3. The statement was obtained during an official investigation without coercion, after the accused had been informed of the nature of the offense and his or her rights under Miranda and after waiving whose rights.

A number of steps can be taken to minimize the likelihood of being accused of placing undue duress on the suspect. For instance, if arrangements are made for appropriate intervals of rest, you could question the suspect over a reasonable period of time depending on the amount of information sought. Several days or weeks could be required. During such lengthy in-custody interviews, offenders should be informed of their rights under Miranda from time to time.

In regard to psychological constraints, the following statements have been held by some courts to constitute a threat:

1. "It would be better for you to confess."
2. "You had better tell the truth."
3. "The truth or else."
4. "Do not make me do this the hard way."

However, it is permissible to

1. Tell the suspect that the truth will be discovered anyway.
2. Display impatience with a subject's story.
3. Give the underlying impression that you consider the suspect to be guilty.

Refrain from using deception, promises, threats, or tricks to obtain a waiver of rights. The safest policy is to avoid all deception and promises. This minimizes misunderstandings and misinterpretations that could later render a confession inadmissible. The following types of promises can render a confession inadmissible:

1. Release if the truth is told

2. Stopping of prosecution

3. Pardon

4. Lighter sentence

5. Granting of immunity

6. Remission of sentence

7. Prosecution for only one of several crimes.

The culmination of the storefront is a very eventful occasion; time will be at a premium. Do not invest in and endure the headaches of in-custody interviews only to find that the confessions are inadmissible. As with all aspects of storefront investigation, a little time spent in preparation and an understanding of legal guidelines will only add to success.

SUMMARY

The complexity of the procedure to be used in apprehending offenders at the culmination of the storefront will be dictated by several factors. Among those are the magnitude of the investigation, sophistication of the targets, departmental resources, and the experience of the officers. Once a decision is reached on the method or methods to be used, a plan of action must be formulated. Apprehension of offenders can be one of the most dangerous aspects of the entire undertaking. Therefore, prepare as much as possible and develop the necessary skills.

Coordination with the prosecutor is necessary in determining the most advantageous approach for placing the accused into the legal system. Arrangements must also be made to obtain search warrants if they are required. Due to the length of most operations, it is not advisable to arrest offenders without obtaining a warrant. Specific questions to be asked of suspects should be discussed and then incorporated on the advise-of-rights form.

Once the accused are in custody, the need for interviews arises. This phase of the investigation is often overlooked. Interviews can range from support officers presenting prepared questions to a more in-depth endeavor conducted by storefront personnel. Decide beforehand which primary offenders will receive your attention. Then, based on the knowledge acquired through contact at the storefront and the attitude displayed by the subject while being detained, select the appropriate interviewing techniques.

Adhere to all legal guidelines concerning this type of activity. Rights of the accused, under the Miranda ruling, must be respected. Take necessary steps to ensure that there are no discrepancies or misunderstandings. Without attention to legal aspects, continuation of the investigation could be in jeopardy.

CHAPTER 16

Case Preparation
and Testifying in Court

The offenders are in custody, and it's time to sit back and relax. The tedious and often boring documentation at the onset of the probe is far past. Lobbying for funds is over. Scrounging for items to make the storefront functional is at last an experience that can be laughed at. Many months of dealing day after day with unsavory characters seems like only a bad dream. All the hustle and bustle of the operation took its toll on you. Now you just want to sit back and take it easy for a while and enjoy the fruits of your labor.

However, you keep thinking that something is not quite right. "I know I forgot to do something, but what?" What's left is the final objective of the operation. Goals of the storefront included obtaining the necessary evidence required for successful prosecution. The evidence has been collected, and now it's time for the final step: the prosecution of the offenders.

In today's legal system, most cases do not end up in court. They are plea-bargained. Therefore, many officers do not have the opportunity to participate actively in this portion of the legal process. However, you might not be so fortunate. You must be fully prepared to do your part in taking the case through the entire system.

The participation of storefront personnel is more involved in this stage than in a routine investigation. This is because many cases come to court at relatively short intervals. We often had two to three cases being tried at the same time in different judicial jurisdictions. Also, operatives are the main witnesses and often the only witnesses for the prosecution. Therefore, their participation in the process becomes much more involved.

You have worked too hard to fail at this stage of the game. Actively involving yourself in this final phase will ensure that your diligent efforts pay off.

In this chapter, we discuss case preparation as well as the actual trial itself. Topics include

1. Case preparation
   a. Prosecution report
   b. Pretrial conference
   c. Preparation of witnesses
   d. Investigator's preparation
2. Testifying in court
   a. Personal appearance
   b. Pretrial activities
   c. Basic trial procedure
   d. Investigator's testimony
   e. Prosecutor's strategy
   f. Errors in testimony
3. Common defense tactics
   4. The jury
   5. Posttrial
6. Preservation of evidence.

CASE PREPARATION

This is a topic that many officers have little experience with. It is not the result of any deficiency, but rather the lack of opportunity. Officers are seldom required to prepare a felony case for presentation in court on a regular basis. They make the arrest and submit their police report. The case is then likely handled before a court proceeding occurs. This too can be the circumstances for cases generated by the storefront, but don't count on it. Usually the cases which appear first on the court docket will go to trial. Then, when the defense counselors realize their motions and tactics are not resulting in acquittals, the trailing cases will be adjudicated without the necessity of a jury trial. The important factor here is the success of the first cases. If the motions and tactics used by the defense counselors result in acquittals, a jury trial on every case submitted is almost assured.

In the many storefronts we have operated or been involved with, only once did every case submitted go before a jury. There were fifty-eight cases and fifty-eight trials. All the trials resulted in guilty verdicts. The tactics and motions on every case were almost identical. At the conclusion of the proceedings, the defense counsel received a scathing review from the courts for not judiciously using precious judicial time. This scathing review was in part a direct result of the preparation by the members of the storefront and the prosecutor.

Case preparation in its broadest interpretation is said to begin the moment an operation is initiated. Here, for our purposes, it describes only those actions taken by officers after making the arrest and completing the investigation. Before the court appearance, officers prepare themselves, the prosecutor, and the witnesses for the presentation of the case in court. Preparing an adequate case for court commonly consists of documenting all significant events which resulted in the arrest of the offender. A prosecution report should be completed for each case. It consists of material from the case file that is condensed into an easily understood format.

The Prosecution Report

This provides a procedure for officers to organize cases for prosecution. It assists the prosecutor by outlining each case, listing witnesses, and describing evidence involved. It also shows (1) how the incident was brought to the officers' attention, (2) more important investigative activity and its results, and (3) the circumstances surrounding the arrest. A summary is useful since it is not uncommon for a trial to be held several months or even a year after the arrest. With the potentially large number of offenders and this time span, facts pertaining to a specific case can become vague. Because of these factors, it is important that the report remain as comprehensive as possible in reference to pertinent information. Keep in mind that it must organize material briefly and succinctly.

A prosecution report form should be formulated for this task if one is not available through the department or the prosecutor. Regardless of the form used, it should include this basic information:

1. Space provided for the defendant's name
   a. Last name, first name, middle initial. This simplifies filing and handling.
   b. Space provided for sex, race, DOB
   c. Codefendants are listed in the same fashion, usually at the beginning of the narrative section.
   d. A check box can be used at the top of the form to show if there are codefendants listed elsewhere.
2. A box to indicate the police department case number
   a. To assist in filing, usually two boxes are used—one in the upper right corner and the other in the lower right corner.
3. Space to indicate the charge against the offender
   a. If there is more than one, the most serious should be listed at the top of the form and the others listed in the narrative section.

4. Space to indicate the jurisdiction in which the charge is filed

5. Space for the arrest number

6. Space for the date of occurrence

   a. When the offense occurred, not the arrest date

7. Check boxes to indicate if there are documents and reports accompanying the report

   a. Arrest report

   b. Offense report

   c. Supplemental/investigative reports

   d. Local arrest record

   e. FBI rap sheet

   f. Statements

8. Space for the date and time of the arrest

9. Location of the arrest

   a. Describe in detail the intersection, house address, name of establishment, etc.

10. Space for the original charge at the time of arrest

    a. It could have changed by the time of trial.

11. Space for the officers' names

    a. Those who can provide the best testimony of both the investigation and arrest.

12. Space for listing the names and addresses of victims and witnesses

    a. Include residential and business phones (if applicable).

13. Space for a narrative section

    a. List any additional pertinent information.

    b. Brief, organized description of events

    c. Description of probable cause used to obtain a search warrant, when applicable

14. Space at the bottom for

    a. Who prepared the report (include ID number/badge number)

    b. Supervisor approving the report

    c. The date the report was compiled

    d. The number of pages in the report.

This report is completed to assist the prosecutor. However, it also provides you with an opportunity to stimulate your memory and organize your notes before the court appearance. A copy of a prosecution report can be found in the appendix.

Pretrial Conference

Close cooperation between the investigators and the prosecutor should have been ongoing throughout the operation. It would make little sense to conduct such a lengthy and complicated investigation if the attorney does not intend to prosecute the cases. In combining efforts, both avoid wasting time on cases in which the charges are dropped due to insufficient evidence or other legal ramifications.

A pretrial conference is essential in continuing this cooperation. Technically, the prosecutor will initiate this meeting. Keep in mind that the prosecutor is often very busy, especially since the operation has increased the case load. It would be easy to neglect this aspect of case preparation until the last minute. A prudent practice is to contact the prosecutor's office routinely to inquire about a preferred time and place for the conference and to ensure that there is nothing else you can do to assist with the case.

At this meeting, the case can be discussed in a less formal manner than was possible in the brief prosecution report. Officers may be able to assist the prosecutor in a number of ways to make the case stronger. In the exchange of information, the prosecutor will become aware of exactly what testimony can be provided by the investigators. Any aspects of the case that are obscure or unclear can be clarified. Operatives, due to contact through the storefront, are more familiar with the people involved in the case and can provide useful information in reference to personalities of the defendants. The pretrial conference is a collaborative effort used to place the prosecutor in a forceful posture to prosecute the case effectively when it comes to trial.

Preparation of Witnesses

The pretrial conference is often used by the prosecutor to interview key witnesses. However, with many storefront operations, the preparation of witnesses is a task given to the investigators. It is the officer who must adequately prepare them for their courtroom experience. This task must be accomplished without doing anything that could embarrass the prosecution at the time of trial.

FOR EXAMPLE ⸻

Witnesses should be informed that they are not legally obligated to discuss the case with the defendant or defense attorney before trial. Do not say, "You cannot talk to the defendant or defense attorney before court" or, "Avoid talking to either one before the proceedings." Merely tell the witnesses those things they are required to do and those things they are not required to do. It should be their decision if they want to discuss the case with the defense.

Most civilian witnesses have no previous courtroom experience. The investigator must prepare them for their day in court. They could be very anxious about this upcoming event, partly because they do not know what to expect. Take the time necessary to explain basic courtroom procedures. A brief explanation of the respective roles of the prosecutor, defense attorney, judge, and jury should suffice. A concise description of normal trial progression (opening statements, introduction of evidence, calling of witnesses, closing statements, etc.) can also help alleviate the jitters. A relaxed witness can deliver higher quality testimony, and a more favorable impression is therefore made on the jury.

Witnesses should anticipate being cross-examined by the defense. Make them aware of certain courtroom tactics often used to discredit testimony—specifically, those used to embarrass, anger, or confuse in the hope of extracting an emotional outburst or making it appear that the witness is perplexed. The expectation of the defense is that other testimony from this witness will be similarly impaired.

Often, other witnesses in this type of a case are police officers. They could include the case agent, surveillance officers, or officers who participated in the raid. The primary investigator(s) should contact these people prior to the trial to ensure that they are prepared. A review of the case file, specifically those reports written by them, before their appearance is most advantageous.

Investigator's Preparation

The final pretrial task is to prepare yourself for the courtroom. Review all personal notes, police reports, video and audio tapes, and other evidence dealing with the case at hand. Be certain that your answers to the who, what, where, when, why, and how questions that could be asked are readily available.

When thorough notes have been compiled, the span of time between the investigation and an appearance in court will not detract from your testimony. Most of us cannot recall facts such as dates, times, weather conditions, and other information without referring to notes. Most courts realize this and permit officers to use their original notes to refresh their memory while testifying.

Notes should be on looseleaf paper contained in a small, plainly covered binder. Only those notes to be used in the trial should be brought to court. The defense has a right to inspect them if they are used during testimony.

Unnecessary information, doodling, and "personal" reminders must not be overlooked. There have been instances in which the defense attorney has found such inscriptions and used them to embarrass the officer, confuse the case, and impeach the officer's testimony.

In preparation for a court appearance, thoroughly review the following aspects of the case:

1. Elements and details of the offense
2. Probable cause for arrest and, when applicable, a search
3. The defendant's story
4. The defendant's confession, when applicable
5. Any prior statements and testimony of witnesses
6. Reliability and credibility of the CI
7. Warrants and affidavits
8. Physical evidence, including audio and videotapes
9. Exhibits, sketches, and diagrams.

Review and practice presentation of all physical evidence. The verdict of the jury often hinges on the quality and quantity of physical evidence. The recordings made at the storefront are often the most damaging evidence of all. Therefore, it is absolutely imperative that you invest whatever time is necessary to ensure that the equipment used to present this evidence is in proper working order. Also, be able to recall all the circumstances regarding the collection and preservation of all evidence.

Finally, the mental preparation for testifying in court is no less important than knowing the facts. Anticipation of giving testimony in front of a courtroom filled with people can produce anxiety and nervousness. These are normal emotions that can be controlled and to some extent prevented. Self-confidence stems from the thorough investigation that was conducted, facts well arranged, and completion of all steps needed for proper case preparation. This almost certainly will demonstrate a command of the material. In taking a professional approach to case preparation, you assure your competent appearance in court.

TESTIFYING IN COURT

What is the most crucial part of the criminal justice process? This question can raise a myriad of responses. Your testimony in court, if not first on the list, will run a close second. No matter how much case preparation you have done, the failure of the jury to believe your testimony leads to a partial or total defeat. Of course, without proper pretrial preparation, testimony will not be as effective as it should be.

The most appropriate time to start preparing for your appearance in court is during the initial meeting with the prosecutor. Waiting until the last minute to prepare for court can have disastrous consequences. The process should start early on and be continually reviewed during the course of the storefront.

Personal Appearance

We all know you should not judge a book by its cover, but unfortunately it is done all the time. The jury should not judge the credibility of a witness's testimony by personal appearance, but they sometimes do. We have all come to court and had to look twice to make sure the defendants are the people we apprehended. At the time of arrest they had long dirty hair, were unshaven, emitted an offensive body odor, and their clothes appeared to have been slept in for several days. Now, in court, they are all spruced up. Defense attorneys understand the psychological impact personal appearance can have on members of the jury. They know personal appearance can be manipulated to give the jury a false impression. There is no doubt that the appearance of a witness influences a jury's opinion of testimony.

Your appearance should be nonoffensive and conservative. We had an officer who wore the loudest ties he could find to court. They had pictures of fish, elk, clowns, and other such things painted on them. His reasoning for this was that it drew the jury's attention to him while he testified. Yes, we want the jury to be attentive while we present the facts, but how attentive will they be if they're laughing at Bozo the Clown's flashing red nose? Is this the type of attentiveness desired, and how is this going to affect the credibility of our testimony?

The prosecutor will most often request that civilian attire be worn by uniformed officers who are to testify. This attire should consist of a clean, well-pressed business suit, a plain tie for male officers, and a conservative shirt. This will make the best impression. Shined shoes and color-coordinated socks or stockings will add to the positive appearance. Pockets should not be filled with papers, cigarettes, facial tissue, or other objects.

When possible, weapons should not be worn when testifying. Many courtrooms today will not allow a witness to be armed. They have metal detectors and security guards to prevent this from occurring. If it is absolutely necessary to carry a firearm, wear it so it is not visible. How many times have you seen an officer sit on the witness stand and then, ever so casually, push back his suit coat revealing a pistol hanging from a shoulder holster? We have overheard jurors saying they didn't believe a word the witness said after this has transpired. They felt the witness was trying to intimidate them by conveying "believe me or else."

Your hair should be neatly trimmed and your hands and fingernails clean. Male officers should be cleanshaven. However, this may not always be possible. There have been occasions when we had to testify and then, almost immediately, participate in a deal. Cutting our hair and shaving our beards could have jeopardized the ongoing investigation. But our hair was clean and combed and our beards were trimmed for court. The prosecutor could address, in court, the reason for this appearance if it was deemed necessary. Addressing the issue before the jury tends to aid in obtaining their understanding for this unconventional look.

Pretrial Activities

It is best to arrive at the assigned court early. This gives you time to attend to any remaining details. Upon arriving, meet with the prosecutor to discuss any last-minute questions. Try to locate and greet each witness and victim, and introduce them to the prosecutor. Have a list of the names, addresses, and phone numbers of every witness. Attempt to contact any who are not present. Remember, this is your storefront on trial. Take an active interest to ensure its positive outcome.

Be careful of the impression made before the trial convenes. A light comment such as, "I hope this thing gets over with fast, I've got more important things to do" could lead others to believe the court hearing is not significant. Avoid gathering in the hallway in front of the courtroom and socializing with other officers. Due to the nature of most police officers, these get-togethers can often unwittingly leave an undesirable impression on others who might overhear the conversation.

Basic Trial Procedure

To gain the confidence needed to give an effective courtroom presentation, you should be familiar with the basic trial procedure. This will also be necessary if you are charged with the task of preparing witnesses. Often, the prosecutor asks the operatives or the case agents to sit at his or her table. They will then assist the prosecutor during the course of the hearing.

Courtroom procedures throughout the country are basically the same. There may be some small variations in your particular jurisdiction. Being completely familiar with trial procedure will add to your effectiveness in the courtroom.

The right to a speedy, public, and impartial trial by jury is guaranteed to every citizen of the United States. This right is a guarantee spelled out in the Constitution. In almost every state, a defendant is entitled to a trial by jury except in those cases involving a petty misdemeanor. As a general rule, if incarceration is the possible punishment for the defendant's criminal act, he or she is entitled to a trial by a jury of peers.

Some cases can be tried without a jury if that is the defendant's wish. In these cases, the judge performs the jury's function of weighing the evidence presented, determining the credibility of a witness, finding fact, and ultimately issuing a verdict. In a trial by jury, the selection of jurors is regulated by rules designed to protect the rights of both the defendant and the government from parties who may be prejudiced against either.

The following is an outline of a criminal judicial proceeding:

Opening statements

Introduction of the government's case

Presentation of evidence

Defense counsel cross-examination

Prosecutor redirect examination

Defense direct examination

Prosecution rebuttal

Final arguments.

Opening Statements

Most trials begin with an opening statement. The prosecutor outlines what he or she intends to prove beyond a reasonable doubt with the evidence to be presented. The defense may then choose to summarize its view of the case or delay giving an opening statement until the prosecution has presented its case. The latter tactic is used by the defense in order to conceal its strategy until after the government's case has been presented.

Introduction of the Government's Case

The prosecution introduces the government's case and will present its evidence first. It is burdened with the responsibility of proving the defendant's guilt *beyond a reasonable doubt*. The mere probability of guilt is not sufficient, nor is the defense required to prove the defendant's innocence.

Presentation of Evidence

This begins with the direct examination of the government's witnesses. The purpose of this examination is to produce evidence that proves the government's case against the defendant. You will be the star witness for the prosecution. Your testimony will lay the foundation for the introduction of the electronic and other physical evidence which is to be presented. Your testimony is the key to the success of the prosecution.

Defense Counsel Cross-Examination

The defense has the right to cross-examine witnesses presented by the prosecution. This is where the defense tactics discussed earlier will come into play. The purpose of this cross-examination is to discredit the testimony given by witnesses for the prosecution or to impeach their credibility. In some jurisdictions, defense counsel is not limited only to questions pertaining to issues raised by the prosecutor. It may cross-examine the witness concerning any issue which is relevant to the case.

Prosecutor Redirect Examination

At the conclusion of cross-examination, the prosecutor may wish to conduct a redirect examination. This is to clarify evidence that may have become distorted or muddled during cross-examination. The scope of redirect questioning is limited to issues brought out in the previous inquiry by the defense. New issues cannot be explored in redirect questioning, unlike cross-examination. The same applies if the defense counsel decides to conduct re-cross-examination.

Defense Direct Examination

The defense counsel may also call witnesses for direct questioning. The prosecutor, in turn, may then wish to cross-examine these witnesses in the same manner as the defense attorney cross-examined the government's witnesses. Defendants do not have to testify. They have a constitutional right protecting them from self-incrimination. They can choose to testify if they desire. When defendants do testify, they will be treated like any other witness.

Prosecution Rebuttal

At the conclusion of the case delivered by the defense, the prosecution may present rebuttal testimony for consideration. This is intended to contradict evidence presented by the defense. Rebuttal testimony is limited in focus to new matters raised during the presentation of the case for the defense. You may be recalled to testify further at this point. The prosecution will attempt to correct any errors or misleading impressions which resulted from the defense counsel's presentation.

Final Arguments

After all the evidence has been brought before the court, both the prosecutor and defense counsels have the opportunity to make a final argument. These arguments are for the purpose of convincing the court of the validity of their respective positions. The prosecutor will address the court first. The defense counsel will follow. At the conclusion of the defense's final argument, the prosecutor is allowed to give a brief closing rebuttal. In these final arguments, both attorneys call on their wit and imagination to convince the jury of their point of view. The arguments must be related to the evidence presented and reasonable inferences which could be derived from the evidence displayed.

Investigator's Testimony

There are certain distinct factors that repeatedly influence the outcome of a jury trial. Some of these factors you will have no control over, such as the conduct and abilities of counsel and rulings by the bench. There are other factors that you can control, and these must be understood for you to provide maximum effectiveness in the courtroom.

Effective courtroom testimony is primarily a matter of confidence. Start to build this confidence at the preoperational briefing with the prosecutor. Also, if you are completely familiar with the facts of the case as well as general courtroom procedure, you will find testifying to be a positive experience. When you leave the courtroom, you will know that you accomplished your job. Regardless of the outcome, you will not be plagued with doubts or second thoughts concerning your role in the proceeding.

Your role as a witness is to respond to questions posed by the prosecution and defense. It is your reaction to these questions as well as what is said that will affect the outcome of the trial. In our discussions with prosecutors and defense attorneys regarding courtroom psychology, they pointed to several factors that play an important role in what the human mind consciously or subconsciously chooses to believe. These factors include

Body language

Eye contact—with others in the courtroom, especially jurors

Voice and tone

Red flag words and baiting

Memorized or scripted testimony

Cop talk.

Body Language

Body language can convey positive or negative signs to the jury. Crossing your arms in front of your body can suggest to some a negative or contrary feeling. We have all seen pictures of the big bully, with his arms crossed in front of his body, gloating over a scrawny victim. What image does this project in your mind? You can bet at least one of the jurors sees it the same way. Placing your hand in front your mouth, a repeated "cough," itching your nose or scalp, playing with your hair, or a nervous twitch can convey that what you are saying is contrary to your feelings or the truth. A conscious effort at posture, when testifying, can negate emitting unwanted messages that may have a lasting impact on the case. Don't forget your entrance and exit. The jury will be watching you as you enter and exit the courtroom. The first impression they will have of you is upon your entry into the courtroom. When you are called to testify, approach the witness stand in a businesslike fashion. Take the oath in an attentive manner. Position yourself so a full view of the jury and attorneys is afforded. Sit erect with both feet on the floor and hands on the chair arms or on your lap.

Eye Contact

Eye contact is very important and has a tangible effect on the jury. Eye contact should be maintained with someone constantly. Look at the judge, prosecutor, defense lawyer, defendant, and don't forget the most important people in the room, the jury. You observe people walk into court and they are staring at the floor. They take the stand and maintain a fixed gaze at their lap. They leave the courtroom in the same manner as they entered. Would you believe their testimony beyond a reasonable doubt? Jurors we have talked to indicated that they found particular witnesses more credible because "that person looked right at us." When responding to questions, don't be afraid to look at the jury.

Voice and Tone

Many of us often overlook the ability to use our voice to impart psychologically more than just facts. Monotone presentations are far less effective than presentations which contain variations in volume, speed of delivery, and injection of polite smiles or scowls, when appropriate. Your voice and style or speech should convey the same image as your dress and demeanor. Speak in a moderate tone, loud enough for all the jurors to hear easily. Be courteous when addressing the judge, attorneys, or jury. Use "Your Honor" when responding to the judge and "Sir" or "Ma'am" when answering the prosecutor and the defense attorney. Do not display prejudice against the defendant or animosity toward the defense counsel.

Red-Flag Words and Baiting

Red-flag words tend to make the jury believe a response is less than definitive; for example:

I believe . . .
I'll try to explain . . .
I think . . .
In my opinion . . .
To the best of my recollection . . .
To my knowledge . . .
As far as I know . . .
It could have been . . .

Defense counsel will often phrase questions in hopes of receiving this type of response. They are aware of the psychological implications. When questions call for these qualified responses, pause and wait for the prosecutor to object. If no objection is forthcoming, request a conference with the prosecutor. Then explain the concern that the question requires a conclusion to be drawn or an opinion to be rendered that your are not qualified to give. The one who guesses in court not only offers frivolous information but also demonstrates a lack of concern for the proceedings. This could lead to grounds for a mistrial or reversal by an appellate court.

The psychological impact on the jury through the use of red-flag words will vary with circumstances. The impact can be heightened if the exchange between the witness and counsel becomes heated. Counsel may try to bait you into making sarcastic or derogatory remarks. When this tactic is used, maintain control of your emotions. Remain calm and respond in a straightforward manner. Do not deviate from what you intended to impart to the jury. Keep in mind it is not you *against* the defense counsel, rather you *with* the jury. Getting even or attempting to give back what you got can be devastating to the case—just what the defense counsel hoped for.

Memorized or Scripted Testimony

When summoned to testify, be prepared; understand fully the facts and events of the case. Know the facts so you can related them to the jury without having to remember in exact words the course of events being described. Nothing will annoy a jury more than their perception that the witness is being coached or has memorized testimony. Memorized testimony plays into the hands of the defense counsel. It is easier to fluster witnesses and gain unproductive testimony if their presentation of the facts seems scripted.

FOR EXAMPLE

Investigators were involved in a drug buy that went sour. When the offenders fled the scene, a 5-mile, high-speed chase ensued. The attempted buy, car chase, and apprehension of the offenders took approximately twenty-five minutes. At the trial, the officers involved were asked to relate the events of the case. Each took approximately five minutes to describe the offense. When defense counsel cross-examined the officers, they simply read a transcript of the officers' testimony given in Grand Jury. The testimony was verbatim. The defense lawyer then said, "Good job officer!" and excused the witness. This scene was replayed at the conclusion of each officer's testimony. The jury took little time in finding the offender not guilty. After the trial, jury members commented that they thought the officer's testimony was memorized and scripted and therefore unbelievable. The defense had not been able to dispute the facts in the case but did destroy the credibility of those revealing the facts. The jury had concluded that since the officers had to memorize the events, there must be some flaw or fabrication in them that they were trying to conceal.

Cop Talk

Cop talk, or police jargon, should be avoided when testifying. If this jargon is used, care should be taken to explain its meaning to the jury. We all use jargon; cops are famous for it. We often talk in numbers. If asked if we are OK, we will reply with "I'm 10-40." In our code, a mentally disturbed person is 10-40. An officer on the witness stand was asked to give his opinion of the defendant's actions. You guessed it—he replied that the defendant was 10-40. All the cops knew what he meant, but no one on the jury had any idea what *10-40* was.

Also avoid using the street names that we sometimes use to label members of the criminal element. The use of this jargon can be embarrassing for you, and the jury may consider it derogatory toward the defendant. These "derogatory" remarks may be all that is needed to sway the jury over to the side of the defense. Be professional on the stand and use terms and language the jury will easily understand.

Prosecutor's Strategy

A competent prosecutor will enter into a trial with a detailed plan for achieving a conviction. This strategy is derived in part to project the most effective presentation of the case. Part of this strategy also includes methods to combat the defense. The specific plan might not be known to the officers. They must allow the prosecutor to guide them through their testimony. This will enable the testimony to influence the court favorably and avoid weaknesses that the defense counsel could use to its advantage. The prosecutor could opt to avoid certain points during cross-examination, perhaps because this testimony is being saved for rebuttal or in hopes that the defense will address the issue first during cross-examination. Don't volunteer information or assume that the prosecutor has overlooked significant facts. The prosecutor has trusted you to gather the facts; now you must trust the prosecutor to present these facts.

Errors in Testimony

There will be occasions when you are asked a question for which you do not know the answer. Never hesitate to admit that you do not know the answer. To attempt to respond under such circumstances will inevitably lead to a disastrous consequence. Concocting a reply is an error that should never be made.

Police officers may err during testimony, as may any witness. The natural reaction of many witnesses who err on the stand is to try to conceal or ignore it. This will only compound the mistake and could place the outcome of the trial in jeopardy. Police officers cannot attempt to conceal or ignore a mistake in testimony. As soon as you realize that an error has occurred, and you are still on the witness stand, inform the judge that you would like an opportunity to correct the error made in prior testimony. If you have already left the witness stand, notify the prosecutor immediately of the discrepancy. The prosecutor will then evaluate the error and may wish to recall you to the stand to correct the mistake.

COMMON DEFENSE TACTICS

Be aware of what you are likely to encounter on cross-examination. Defense tactics can be nullified when they are recognized and understood. The following is a list of these tactics with examples, their purpose, and how you could respond.

1. *Patronizing counsel:* Kindhearted in approach, oversympathetic in questions, to the point of ridicule. This approach is used to give the impression that you are inept, lacking confidence, or may not be a reliable witness. You can confront this tactic with a firm, decisive answer, soliciting that the inquiry be restated if it is improperly phrased.

2. *Friendly counsel:* Very courteous, polite, questions which tend to take you into the attorney's confidence. This can lull you into a false sense of security in which you will give answers favoring the defense. Stay alert; bear in mind that the purpose of the defense is to discredit or diminish the effects of your testimony.

3. *Badgering, belligerent counsel:* The defense attorney stares you in the face and yells, "This is so, isn't it, officer?" This is an attempt to anger you so your sense of logic and calmness is impaired. This approach can

also involve rapid repetitive questioning. You must stay calm and speak in a deliberate voice, giving the prosecutor time to make appropriate objections.

4. *Restrictive questioning:* "Did you discuss this case with anyone, officer?" A response of no will place you in a position of denying any pretrial conferences. A yes response could be used to indicate that you have been coached on how to testify. Answering "I have discussed the case with the prosecuting attorney and other officers assigned to the case" is prudent.

5. *Suggestive questioning:* This tends to be leading questioning, allowable on cross-examination. "Was the color of the car blue?" as opposed to "What was the color of the car?" This is done to suggest an answer to the question in an attempt to confuse or lead the witness. Concentrate carefully on the facts of the case and disregard any suggestions.

6. *Counselors who demand a yes or no response:* This is usually to a question that needs further explanation. "Did you lie to the defendant when he inquired as to your true identity?" This tactic prevents all pertinent and mitigating details from being considered by the jury. Explain the answer to the question. If stopped by the defense counsel, pause; this will give the prosecutor time to object and/or the court time to instruct you to answer in your own words.

7. *Reversing your words:* You respond, "I purchased 72 ounces of 97 percent pure cocaine from the defendant." The defense counsel then says, "You purchased 97 ounces of 72 percent pure cocaine from the defendant?" This is an attempt to confuse and fluster you in the hope that it will demonstrate a lack of confidence in your testimony. Listen intently whenever counsel repeats something, especially numbers, you have stated. If an error is made, correct it.

8. *Repetitive questioning:* The same question asked several times which has been rephrased slightly. Defense counsel is trying to coax inconsistent or conflicting responses from you. Listen carefully to the questions and reply, "I have just answered that question!"

9. *Conflicting answers:* "But Officer Bill, Detective Bob just said . . . " This is done to show inconsistencies in the investigation. This tactic is usually used on testimony concerning measurements, dates, times, weights, etc. You should remain calm; conflicting statements have a tendency to make a witness extremely nervous. Be guarded in your answer in reference to measurements, dates, times, weights, etc. Unless you have exact knowledge, use the term *approximately.* You can also refer to police reports or your notes. The use of notes to aid in testimony is a topic to be discussed with the prosecutor. This practice is often discouraged and can prove harmful if used improperly. The defense counsel has the right to review any notes used by you.

10. *Staring:* After you have responded to the question, the defense counsel just glares at you as though there is more to come. This can make you feel that the long pause must be filled; thus, you say more than is necessary. The defense is trying to provoke you into offering more than the question calls for. Remain quiet and calm and wait for the next question.

THE JURY

At the conclusion of the judicial proceeding, the jury is given the task of rendering a fair and unbiased verdict. The jury determines the outcome of the case. Thus, it is important to examine the "typical" jury. This will provide you with a more complete understanding of the judicial procedure.

"Typical" jurors in all likelihood have had little or no exposure to the criminal justice system. Most of their knowledge is derived from a hazy or vague interpretation of media reporting, movies, and prime-time television. They may have formed their conception through dialogue with an acquaintance who professes to be an expert on the subject. These conversations often lead to prejudicial and derogatory notions.

Then there are the pretrial instructions given by the judge and counsel. These instructions are often so laden with legal jargon that the jurors understand little. During the trial, the jury must ingest and evaluate what is probably a bewildering clash of both fact and wits between the prosecution and defense. This confusion can cause jurors to become susceptible to external influences. This occurs most frequently during high-visibility trials that generate extensive media coverage and public debate—the type of trial that could result from the efforts of the storefront.

The socioeconomic status and geographic location of the jurors may also taint their perception toward law enforcement. These feelings may exist even before any testimony is given. It is your responsibility as a witness, often the star witness, to overcome these misconceptions and present the facts that represent the complete story. Using the proper methods to project these facts to the jury will heighten their credibility.

POSTTRIAL

Giving competent testimony in court is an art that must be acquired, practiced, and continually improved on. After each session in court, evaluate your performance. The prosecutor, because of his or her knowledge and experience in the courtroom, is the person to seek advice from. The prosecutor's critique of your presentation can often pinpoint deficiencies or weaknesses in your testimony. The prosecutor can make constructive suggestions which will enable you to enhance your future appearances. We have testified in court hundreds of times. Each time was a learning experience. The assistance we have received from the prosecutor in these posttrial critiques improved our confidence and knowledge, thus allowing for an even more effective delivery of our testimony in future cases.

PRESERVATION OF EVIDENCE

If the defense presumes that the government's evidence was insufficient or that the indictment did not present adequate facts to substantiate the criminal offense under the law, it can file a motion seeking a judgment of acquittal. The defendant can also file a motion for a new trial.

The most routine grounds for granting a defendant's request for a retrial is the insufficiency of the evidence presented to support the verdict. Other grounds for granting a new trial may be errors of law and/or improper conduct of trial participants. A motion can also be filed claiming that new evidence, which will affect the verdict, was uncovered. To justify this claim, it must be shown that

1. The new evidence will more than likely alter the outcome of the trial.
2. The evidence could not have been uncovered prior to the trial through the exercise of due diligence.
3. The evidence is material to the issue.
4. The evidence is not merely cumulative or of an impeaching nature.

Even if all the defendant's posttrial motions have been quashed by the bench, the right to appeal still exists. This appeal procedure is not a retrial process. It is not ordinarily a re-examination of factual issues. The basic function of the appellate court, in an appeal of this nature, is to review the legal issues raised by the case. *Miranda*, a case we are all familiar with, is an example of this type of appeal.

With the possibility of an appeal being successful or a motion for a new trial being granted, you must be careful to preserve all notes, reports, evidence, or other items relating to the case. This is necessary to ensure their availability if a second trial is ordered. Before destroying any materials that pertain to a case, seek advice from the prosecutor.

SUMMARY

Considering the many offenders who have come and gone through the doors and the length of time the operation covered, the need to review events should be quite evident. Including the period of time from arrest to court, up to two years could have passed since the first case was made. Preparing a prosection report under these circumstances is not a luxury, it is a necessity. You cannot expect to give competent testimony without first preparing.

Using procedures similar to the ones described in this book gives you an opportunity to bring all the various aspects of the investigation together. Using a format that allows for an organized and concise overview of facts strengthens your case, refreshes your memory, and builds your confidence in your ability to relay information to the jury clearly and precisely.

For storefront officers, testifying in court involves more than just showing up. Taking an active role in the process and doing just a little more than is absolutely required will help to ensure the desired outcome. The amount of time and energy invested in the storefront has been considerable. The problems that had to be overcome seemed endless. The politicking required to get the investigation off the ground goes against most of our natures. It was all done so the final important objective could be met. Do not fall short now by simply placing all your perseverance and hard work in someone else's hands and saying, "Here, it's yours now!" Take that active role, do just that little extra, and the total success of the operation will be guaranteed.

Now that it is all over, you have time to reflect on the many times you wanted to quit and all those promises you made to yourself about never doing this again. You are now thinking, "It really wasn't that bad, it was almost fun. It was fun!! I wonder what I should use for my next storefront facade?"

WORK SHEETS
AND
FORMS

WORK SHEET #1

	CONTACTED	DATE	PERSON CONTACTED	INFO. YES	NO	OFFICER
RECORDS	LOCAL					
	SHERIFF					
	STATE POLICE					
	F.B.I.					
	OTHER					
PROSECUTOR	STATE					
	FEDERAL					
INTELLIGENCE UNITS	LOCAL					
	SHERIFF					
	STATE POLICE					
	F.B.I.					
	OTHER					
OTHER AGENCIES	N.C.I.C.					
	E.P.I.C.					
	N.A.T.B.					
	OTHER					
CRIMESTOPPERS	LOCAL					
	STATE					
OFFICERS	FIELD					
	DETECTIVE					
	OTHER					

WORK SHEET #1
(Example)

	CONTACTED	DATE	PERSON CONTACTED	INFO. YES	NO	OFFICER
RECORDS	LOCAL	1-1	Mrs. Jones	X		J. Law
	SHERIFF	1-1	Det. Smith	X		J. Law
	STATE POLICE	1-1	Sgt. Brown	X		B. Good
	F.B.I.	1-1	Agt. White		X	B. Good
	OTHER					
PROSECUTOR	STATE	1-2	ADA Jones	X		T. Jones
	FEDERAL	1-2	AUSA Wall		X	T. Jones
INTELLIGENCE UNITS	LOCAL	1-2	Det. Snow	X		J. Law
	SHERIFF	1-1	Dep. Ray		X	J. Law
	STATE POLICE	1-1	Off. Rye	X		B. Good
	F.B.I.	1-1	Agt. Pete	X		B. Good
	OTHER					
OTHER AGENCIES	N.C.I.C.	1-3	Ms. Hall	X		T. Jones
	E.P.I.C.	1-4	Mr. Lyle		X	B. Good
	N.A.T.B.	1-2	Mr. Webb		X	J. Law
	OTHER					
CRIMESTOPPERS	LOCAL	1-6	Off. Fay		X	T. Jones
	STATE	1-4	Off. Bill	X		T. Jones
OFFICERS	FIELD	1-5	Off. Blue	X		B. Good
	DETECTIVE	1-6	Det. Black		X	J. Law
FBI	OTHER	1-7	Agt. Redd	X		T. Jones

WORK SHEET #2

Category of crime being analyzed   _____

Time frame being analyzed   ___/___/___ to ___/___/___

Total number of crimes reported   _____

Frequency rate:

      Month: Jan _____   Feb _____   Mar _____

               Apr _____   May _____   Jun _____

               Jul _____   Aug _____   Sep _____

               Oct _____   Nov _____   Dec _____

      Day: Sun_____ Mon_____ Tue_____ Wed _____

               Thur_____ Fri_____ Sat_____

      Time: _____a.m.   _____p.m.

Geographical area crimes reported

      Quadrant: SE _____   SW _____   NE _____   NW _____

Clearance Rate   _____%

Recovery Rate   _____%

Recovery Condition: Striped _____   Drivable _____

(cont. on next page)

Recovery area: Quadrant: SE _____ SW _____ NE _____ NW _____

Monetary loss $_____

M.O.:

Suspect Information:

Comments:

WORK SHEET #2
(Example)

Category of crime being analyzed   <u>Auto Theft</u>

Time frame being analyzed   <u>01/01/99</u> to <u>12/31/99</u>

Total number of crimes reported   <u>1074</u>

Frequency rate: Month: Jan <u>76</u>   Feb <u>64</u>   Mar <u>79</u>

      (Number of reported   Apr <u>81</u>   May <u>90</u>   Jun <u>86</u>

        incidents per month)   Jul <u>88</u>   Aug <u>95</u>   Sep <u>99</u>

                                Oct <u>103</u>   Nov <u>112</u>   Dec <u>101</u>

                Day: Sun <u>62</u> Mon <u>74</u> Tue <u>85</u> Wed <u>153</u>

(# of crimes reported for   Thur <u>206</u> Fri <u>246</u> Sat <u>248</u>

  each day of the week)

              Time: <u>0130/0230</u> a.m. <u>2230/2330</u> p.m.

  (Time activity most prevalent)

Geographical area crimes reported

        Quadrant: SE <u>86</u>   SW <u>384</u>   NE <u>91</u>   NW <u>513</u>

Clearance Rate   <u>35</u>   %

   (Include all, unfounded, repossessed, arrest)

Recovery Rate   <u>23</u>   %

Total Recoveries   <u>247</u>   %

(cont. on next page)

WORK SHEET #2
(Example cont.)

Recovery Condition: Striped ___191___ Drivable ___56___

Recovery area: Quadrant: SE __136__ SW __12__ NE __78__ NW __21__

Monetary loss $ _9,684,000_

M.O.: (List any Modus Operandi information your documentation may
      have revealed.)

Suspect Information: (List all suspect information including
                     vehicle information.)

Comments: (This portion is used to expound on any area you
          determine needs further interpretation.)

WORK SHEET #3

Vehicle:

        Obtained from:_____
        Cost: $_____

Comments:

Maintenance:

        Serviced by: _____
        Operational Readiness: $_____
        Preventive: $_____

Insurance:

        Obtained from: _____
        Cost: $_____

Comments:

Special Equipment Needed:

    Mobile Phone: Obtained from: _____
                    Cost: $_____

    Alarm: Obtained from: _____
                    Cost: $ _____

    Recording Equipment: Obtained from: _____
                    Cost: $_____

    Video Equipment: Obtained from: _____
                    Cost: $_____

Advertising: Cost: $_____

(cont. on next page)

License: Obtained from:_____
                            Cost: $ _____

Bonds: Obtained from:_____
                            Cost: $ _____

Training: Obtained from: _____
                            Cost: $_____

Props: Cost: $_____

Comments:

Total Operating Cost Per Month $ _____

Total Operating Cost for Period of Storefront $ _____

WORK SHEET #3
(Example)

Vehicle: (Give complete description of vehicle.)
                           Obtained from:_____
                           Cost: $_____

Comments: (Indicate any stipulations that may be attached in
          acquiring the vehicle. If vehicle is rented or
          leased indicate total cost as well as monthly cost.)

Maintenance:
                        Serviced by: _____
                        * Operational Readiness: $_____
                        Preventive: $_____
   * Operational readiness is the expense to make the vehicle
     operational.

Insurance:
                        Obtained from: _____
                        Cost: $_____

Comments: (Use this section to explain coverage.)

Special Equipment Needed:

    Mobile Phone:
                     Obtained from: _____
                     * Cost: $_____

    Alarm:
                     Obtained from: _____
                     * Cost: $ _____

    Recording Equipment:
                     Obtained from: _____
                     * Cost: $_____

    Video Equipment:
                     Obtained from: _____
                     * Cost: $_____
     * If equipment is being rented or leased indicate total
     cost as well as monthly cost. Any installation cost
     also needs to be included.

Advertising: * Cost: $_____
  * Any advertising to be placed on the vehicle. Cost of
  materials if work is to be done in house, materials and
  labor if work is to be done outside of the department.

(cont. on next page)

349

License: Obtained from:_____
                                  Cost: $ _____

Bonds: Obtained from:_____
                                  Cost: $ _____

Training: Obtained from: _____
                                  Cost: $_____

Props: * Cost: $_____
         * Any props that may be needed to enhance the facade of
           the storefront.

Comments: (Use this section to indicate any special observations
           you may have made while compiling this work sheet.)

Total Operating Cost Per Month $ _____

Total Operating Cost for Period of Storefront $ _____

WORK SHEET #4

Site:

        Prospective Landlord:_____
        Date Available: _____
        Cost: $_____ Mo. _____Total
        Deposit: $_____

Questions:

Comments:

Utilities:

Natural Gas:	Available	YES	NO
	Installation Cost: $_____		
	Deposit Cost: $_____		
	Cost: Per Mo.$_____ Total $_____		
Electricity:	Available	YES	NO
	Installation Cost: $_____		
	Deposit Cost: $ _____		
	Cost: Per Mo. $_____ Total $_____		
Water:	Available	YES	NO
	Installation Cost: $ _____		
	Deposit Cost: $ _____		
	Cost: Per Mo. $_____ Total $_____		
Telephone:	Available	YES	NO
	Installation Cost: $ _____		
	Deposit Cost: $ _____		
	Cost: Per Mo. $_____ Total $_____		

(cont. on next page)

Comments:

Insurance: Available Through _____
                    Cost: Per Mo. $_____ Total $_____

Comments:

Security: Fence: YES   NO
                    Cost to Install: $_____

                    Dead Bolts   YES   NO
                    Cost to install: $_____

                    Wrought Iron: YES   NO
                    Cost to Install: $_____

                    Alarms: YES   NO
                    Cost to Install: $_____

Comments:

Total Cost Per Month: $_____

Total Cost for Period of Storefront $_____

Site: (List address and description of proposed site.)

                     Prospective Landlord:_____
                     Date Available: _____
                     Cost: $_____ Mo. _____Total
                     Deposit: $_____

Questions:

    Can a month to month agreement be secured? . . . . YES   NO
    Can a rental agreement be broken? . . . . YES   NO
    Can a rental agreement be extended? . . . . YES   NO
    Is remodeling permitted? . . . . YES   NO
    Is a security deposit required?. . . . . YES   NO
    Is a damage deposit required? . . . . YES   NO
    Are deposits returnable? . . . . YES   NO
    Is the site furnished? . . . . YES   NO

Comments: (List any additional information you deem is
           necessary that pertains to the above questions. You
           may want to indicate the attitude of the prospective
           landlord in regards to your particular requirements.
           Does the prospective landlord seem to be agreeable
           and easy to work with?)

Utilities:

    Natural Gas: Available   YES   NO
                 Installation Cost: $_____
                 Deposit Cost: $_____
                 Cost: Per Mo.$_____ Total $_____

    Electricity: Available   YES   NO
                 Installation Cost: $_____
                 Deposit Cost: $ _____
                 Cost: Per Mo. $_____ Total $_____

    Water: Available   YES   NO
                 Installation Cost: $ _____
                 Deposit Cost: $ _____
                 Cost: Per Mo. $_____ Total $_____

    Telephone: Available   YES   NO
                 Installation Cost: $ _____
                 Deposit Cost: $ _____
                 Cost: Per Mo. $_____ Total $_____

(cont. on next page)

Comments: (Indicate any additional cost for utilities here.)

Insurance: Available Through _____
                              Cost: Per Mo. $_____ Total $_____

Comments: (List coverage of policy here.)

Security: Fence: YES   NO
                              Cost to Install: $_____

                              Dead Bolts   YES   NO
                              Cost to install: $_____

                              Wrought Iron: YES   NO
                              Cost to Install: $_____

                              Alarms: YES   NO
                              Cost to Install: $_____

Comments: (Indicate any problems you may conceive in reference
           to the security at this site.)

Total Cost Per Month: $_____

Total Cost for Period of Storefront $_____

WORK SHEET #5

TTOP = Total Time Of Proposal

Undercover Officers: Number of Officers Needed:_____
                       Salary: Per Mo. $_____ TTOP $_____
                       Overtime: Per Mo.$_____ TTOP $_____

Relief Officer: Number of Officers Needed: _____
                       Salary: Per Mo. $_____ TTOP $_____
                       Overtime: Per Mo.$_____ TTOP $_____

Training: Available Through _____
                       Cost Per Officer: $_____ Total $_____

Case Agent: Number of Officers Needed: _____
                       Salary: Per Mo. $_____ TTOP $_____
                       Overtime: Per Mo.$_____ TTOP $_____

Supervisor: Number Needed: _____
                       Salary: Per Mo. $_____ TTOP $_____
                       Overtime: Per Mo.$_____ TTOP $_____

Clerical Personnel: Number Needed _____
                       Salary: Per Mo. $_____ TTOP $_____
                       Overtime: Per Mo.$_____ TTOP $_____

Clerical Equipment: Available Through _____
                       Cost: Per Mo. $_____ TTOP $_____

Electronic Technicians: Available Through _____
                        Cost: Per Mo. $_____ TTOP $_____

Electronic Equipment:

        Audio: Available Through:_____
                       Cost: Per Mo. $_____ TTOP $_____

        Video: Available Through:_____
                       Cost: Per Mo. $_____ TTOP $_____

        Hardware: Available Through: _____
                       Cost: Per Mo. $_____ TTOP $_____

        Maintenance: Equipment: _____
                       Available Through:_____
                       Cost: Per Mo. $_____ TTOP $_____

(cont. on next page)

355

Surveillance Officers: Number Needed:_____
          Cost: Per Mo. $_____ TTOP $_____
          Overtime: Per Mo.$_____ TTOP $_____

Evidence Expenditures: Cost: Per Mo. $_____ TTOP $_____

Source Expenditures: Cost: Per Mo. $_____ TTOP $_____

Special Equipment Needed: Available Through _____
          Cost: Per Mo. $_____ TTOP $_____

Props: Available Through _____
          Cost: Per Mo. $_____ TTOP $_____

Evidentiary Storage: Available Through _____
          Cost: Per Mo. $_____ TTOP $_____

Furniture: Available Through _____
          Cost: Per Mo. $_____ TTOP $_____

Inventory: Available Through _____
          Cost: Per Mo. $_____ TTOP $_____

Supplies: Available Through _____
          Cost: Per Mo. $_____ TTOP $_____

Advertising: Available Through _____
          Cost: Per Mo. $_____ TTOP $_____

Licenses: Available Through _____
          Cost: Per Mo. $_____ TTOP $_____

Bonds: Available Through _____
          Cost: Per Mo. $_____ TTOP $_____

PROJECTED OPERATIONAL EXPENSE:

    Cost Per Month $_____

    Total Cost $_____

IN HOUSE INVESTIGATION CHAIN OF COMMAND

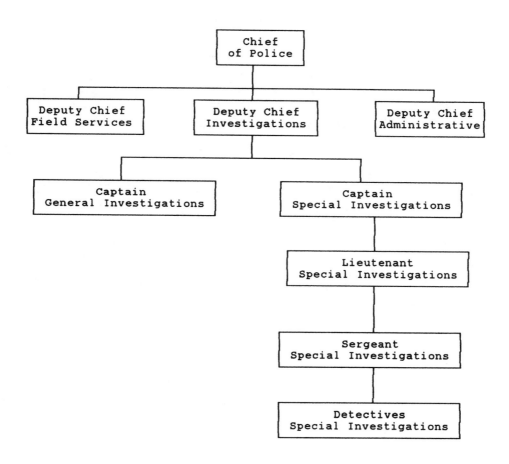

MULTI-AGENCY INVESTIGATION CHAIN OF COMMAND

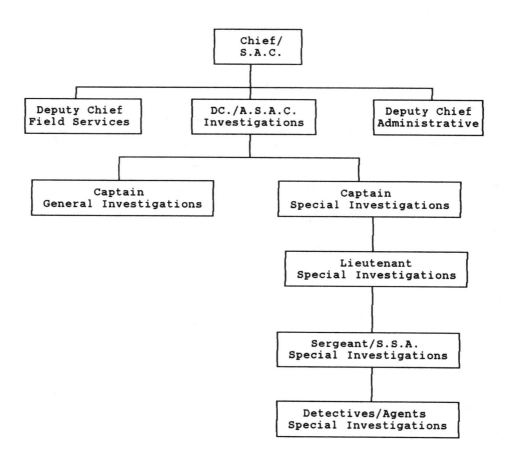

NOTE:
S.A.C.   = Special Agent in Charge
D.C.   = Deputy Chief
A.S.A.C.   = Assistant Special Agent in Charge
S.S.A.   = Supervising Special Agent

ORGANIZATIONAL LIST STOREFRONT PERSONNEL

LIEUTENANT
SPECIAL INVESTIGATIONS
Name:
Phone:

SERGEANT
SPECIAL INVESTIGATIONS
Name:
Phone:

SUPERVISING
SPECIAL AGENT
Name:
Phone:

CASE AGENT
Name:
Phone:

OPERATIVES/OUTSIDE AGENT
Name:
Phone:

Name:
Phone:

Name:
Phone:

RELIEF OFFICER
Name:
Phone:

CONTACT OFFICER
Name:
Phone:

CORRECTIONS LIAISON
Name:
Phone:

EVIDENCE LIAISON
Name:
Phone:

MEDIA LIAISON
Name:
Phone:

OUTSIDE AGENCY LIAISON
Name:
Phone:

PROSECUTOR LIAISON
Name:
Phone:

SUPPORT LIAISON (CLERICAL)
Name:
Phone:

SURVEILLANCE LIAISON
Name:
Phone:

TECHNICAL LIAISON
Name:
Phone:

NOTE: The distribution of this list should be monitored closely.

FORM FOR CONDUCT OF COOPERATING INDIVIDUAL

I, _____ the undersigned understand that while I
am cooperating with and assisting the _____, I am
<u>forbidden</u> to do any of the following:

   A. Sell or deliver any contraband or controlled substance
      (illegal drug) to anyone.

   B. Never sell or deliver or cause to be sold or delivered
      any contraband or controlled substance to any person who
      would then in turn sell or deliver said
      contraband/controlled substance to any member of the
      unit or any other person.

   C. Never use my sex, sexuality, or sexual activity to
      induce or persuade any individual to sell or deliver
      contraband/controlled substance to any member of the
      unit.

   D. I further understand that I may never search any
      suspect, person, house, papers, or personal effects.

   E. I may never become involved in any activities that would
      constitute entrapment.

   F. I further understand that I may not engage in any
      illegal or improper conduct so long as I am working with
      the _____ unit.

   G. I understand that I am not authorized to carry a firearm
      or any weapon while working for _____ unit.

   H. I understand the need for maintaining the
      confidentiality of my association with the
      _____ unit and promise to do so.

   I. Further, I understand that any violations arising from
      my actions in violation of the above circumstances will
      result in an investigation of matters and if the charges
      are substantiated, appropriate action (including the
      possibility of criminal prosecution) will be taken.

(cont. on next page)

J. I am agreeing to cooperate with the _____
unit of my own free will and accord, and not as a result
of any intimidation or threats.

In agreeing to work with the _____ unit, I
understand that no unit agent may make any explicit or
implicit promises or predictions regarding the likely
disposition of any criminal proceedings that are pending
against me, but that unit agents will make their best
efforts to arrange a meeting with prosecutorial authorities
at which time such matters can be discussed.

SIGNED:_____

WITNESS #1: _____

WITNESS #2: _____

PLACE: _____
DATE: _____
TIME: _____

FORM FOR CONDUCT OF COOPERATING INDIVIDUAL
(Example)

I, <u>John B. Jones</u> the undersigned understand that while I am cooperating with and assisting the <u>Central Police Dept</u> , I am **forbidden** to do any of the following:

A. Sell or deliver any contraband or controlled substance (illegal drug) to anyone.

B. Never sell or deliver or cause to be sold or delivered any contraband or controlled substance to any person who would then in turn sell or deliver said contraband/controlled substance to any member of the unit or any other person.

C. Never use my sex, sexuality, or sexual activity to induce or persuade any individual to sell or deliver contraband/controlled substance to any member of the unit.

D. I further understand that I may never search any suspect, person, house, papers, or personal effects.

E. I may never become involved in any activities that would constitute entrapment.

F. I further understand that I may not engage in any illegal or improper conduct so long as I am working with the <u>Special Investigations</u> unit.

G. I understand that I am not authorized to carry a firearm or any weapon while working for <u>Special Investigations</u> unit.

H. I understand the need for maintaining the confidentiality of my association with the <u>Special Investigations</u> unit and promise to do so.

I. Further, I understand that any violations arising from my actions in violation of the above circumstances will result in an investigation of matters and if the charges are substantiated, appropriate action (including the possibility of criminal prosecution) will be taken.

(cont. on next page)

FORM FOR CONDUCT OF COOPERATING INDIVIDUALS
(Example cont.)

J. I am agreeing to cooperate with the <u>Special Investigations</u> unit of my own free will and accord, and not as a result of any intimidation or threats.

In agreeing to work with the <u>Special Investigations</u> unit, I understand that no unit agent may make any explicit or implicit promises or predictions regarding the likely disposition of any criminal proceedings that are pending against me, but that unit agents will make their best efforts to arrange a meeting with prosecutorial authorities at which time such matters can be discussed.

SIGNED: _John B. Jones_

WITNESS #1: _J. Law_

WITNESS #2: _B. Good_

PLACE: _106 Main St. Central City_
DATE: _01-01-99_
TIME: _1300 Hrs._

MASTER INDEX FILE CARD

(FRONT OF CARD)

NAME:_____   AKA:_____
DOB:_____   ARREST/ID #_____   SOC SEC #_____
ADDRESS_____   PHONE_____
DESCRIPTION
SEX:_____ RACE:_____ AGE:_____ HGT:_____ WT:_____ BUILD:_____   EYES:_____
HAIR:_____ SCARS/TATOOS:_____
VEHICLE
YR:_____ MAKE:_____ MODEL:_____   COLOR:_____
LIC #:_____ STATE:_____ OUTSTANDING FEATURES:_____
PERSONAL INFORMATION
DL#_____ STATE:_____ OCCUPATION:_____
PLACE OF EMPLOYMENT:_____   ADDRESS:_____
PHONE:_____ EDUCATION:_____ LAST SCHOOL ATTENDED:_____

(BACK OF CARD)

ASSOCIATES
NAME:_____   ADDRESS:_____   PHONE:_____
_____   _____   _____
_____   _____   _____

RELATIVES
SPOUSE NAME:_____   ADDRESS:_____   PHONE:_____   ARREST/ID #:_____
PARENTS NAME:_____   ADDRESS:_____   PHONE:_____   ARREST/ID #:_____
                             ADDRESS:_____   PHONE:_____   ARREST/ID #:_____
BROTHERS/SISTERS
    NAME:_____   ADDRESS:_____   PHONE:_____   ARREST/ID #:_____
    _____   ADDRESS:_____   PHONE:_____   ARREST/ID #:_____
    _____   ADDRESS:_____   PHONE:_____   ARREST/ID #:_____

            CASE #_____   INTELLIGENCE #_____
            CASE #_____   INTELLIGENCE #_____
            CASE #_____   INTELLIGENCE #_____

364

MASTER INDEX FILE CARD
(Example)

(FRONT OF CARD)

```
NAME:        Jones, John B.                    AKA:        Jones, John P.
DOB:     05/17/55      ARREST/ID #    98-0578963    SOC SEC #    936-81-3628
ADDRESS     16453 W. 33rd St. Central City         PHONE    (825) 263-4695
DESCRIPTION
SEX: M  RACE:  White  AGE: 44  HGT: 66"  WT: 175  BUILD: Stocky  EYES: Brown
HAIR: Brown   SCARS/TATOOS: Mother on left forearm, devil on upper right arm
VEHICLE
YR: 1997  MAKE: Chevy    MODEL: Monte Carlo    COLOR:    Candy apple red
LIC #: 237-DYR  STATE: California  OUTSTANDING FEATURES: Low-rider, silver interior
PERSONAL INFORMATION
DL# 3659825290  STATE: California  OCCUPATION:         Professional C.I.
PLACE OF EMPLOYMENT:        None         ADDRESS:         None
PHONE: None  EDUCATION: Nine Years  LAST SCHOOL ATTENDED:    Wegot High School
```

(BACK OF CARD)

```
ASSOCIATES
NAME:      Ivy S. Long        ADDRESS: 3284 People St. Central City  PHONE:    None
_____  _____  _____
RELATIVES
SPOUSE NAME:    None     ADDRESS:_____ PHONE:_____ ARREST/ID #:_____
PARENTS NAME: Davey Jones ADDRESS: Same as above PHONE: Same ARREST/ID #: 86-376479
              Deceased   ADDRESS:_____ PHONE:_____ ARREST/ID #:_____
BROTHERS/SISTERS
    NAME:     None       ADDRESS:_____ PHONE:_____ ARREST/ID #:_____
_____          ADDRESS:_____ PHONE:_____ ARREST/ID #:_____
_____          ADDRESS:_____ PHONE:_____ ARREST/ID #:_____

          CASE #  92-8356573      INTELLIGENCE #  I92-25426
          CASE #  93-3626300      INTELLIGENCE #  I93-11430
          CASE #  96-4865032      INTELLIGENCE #  I96-41752
```

365

COOPERATING INDIVIDUAL PERSONAL HISTORY SHEET

CI #_____   Arrest/ID #_____   Work done for other agency _____

Name:_____
                (last, first, middle initial)

AKA:
    #1_____, #2_____, #3_____

PERSONAL INFORMATION:
DOB:_____, Place of Birth:_____, SOC SEC #_____
Address:_____, Phone:_____
Occupation:_____, Place of Employment:_____, Phone:_____
DL #_____, State:_____

DESCRIPTION:
Sex:_____, Race:_____, Age:_____, HGT:_____, WT:_____,
Eyes:_____, Hair:_____,
Scars/Tattoos:_____

VEHICLE:
Year:_____, Make:_____, Model:_____, Color:_____
License Plate #:_____, State:_____
Outstanding Features:_____

EDUCATION:
Amount of:_____, Last School Attended:_____

Military Service:
Branch:_____, # of years:_____, Type of Discharge:_____

FINANCIAL HISTORY:
Bank:_____, Account #:_____, Type:_____
Bank:_____, Account #:_____, Type:_____
Credit Card Name:_____, Account #:_____
            Name:_____, Account #:_____
Other Creditors Name:_____
            Name:_____

FAMILY:
Spouse:_____, DOB:_____, ADD:_____, PHO:_____, Arrest/ID#:_____
Parent:_____, DOB:_____, ADD:_____, PHO:_____, Arrest/ID#:_____
            _____, DOB:_____, ADD:_____, PHO:_____, Arrest/ID#:_____

(continued on next page)

ASSOCIATES:
Name:_____, DOB:_____, ADD:_____, PHO:_____, Arrest/ID#:_____
_____, DOB:_____, ADD:_____, PHO:_____, Arrest/ID#:_____
_____, DOB:_____, ADD:_____, PHO:_____, Arrest/ID#:_____

KNOWN HANG OUTS:
Name:_____, Address:_____, Phone:_____
_____, Address:_____, Phone:_____
_____, Address:_____, Phone:_____

COMMENTS:

COOPERATING INDIVIDUAL PERSONAL HISTORY SHEET
(Example)

CI # ___00456___ Arrest/ID # ___98-36974___ Work done for other agency ___Yes___

Name: _____Crook, Ira NMI_____
                    (last, first, middle initial)

AKA:
  #1___Crook, Ben A.___, #2_____, #3_____

PERSONAL INFORMATION:
DOB: __10/09/77__, Place of Birth: ___Sin City, USA___, SOC SEC # ___012-99-3456___
Address: _____895 Main St. Central City_____, Phone: ___957-2416___
Occupation: __Ditch Digger__, Place of Employment: _Sandhill Construction_, Phone: _957-6306_
DL # ___None___, State: _____

DESCRIPTION:
Sex: _M_, Race: ___White___, Age: __22__, HGT: __70"__, WT: __150__,
Eyes: __Blue__, Hair: __Blond__,
Scars/Tattoos:_____

VEHICLE:
Year: __1990__, Make: ___Ford___, Model: __Escort__, Color: ___Green___
License Plate #: __URA-666__, State: __Anywhere__
Outstanding Features:_____

EDUCATION:
Amount of: ___12 Years___, Last School Attended: _____Outlaw High School_____

Military Service:
Branch: __US Forced__, # of years: __4__, Type of Discharge: _____Medical_____

FINANCIAL HISTORY:
Bank: __Overdrawn National__, Account #: __9847503-836__, Type: ___Checking___
Bank:_____, Account #:_____, Type:_____
Credit Card Name: ___Payulater___, Account #: ___736402-86459-2835493___
        Name:_____, Account #:_____
Other Creditors Name: _____Gooddeal Auto_____
        Name:_____

FAMILY:
Spouse: __Bea__, DOB: 8/22/80, ADD: _____Same_____, PHO: __Same__, Arrest/ID#:99-865890
Parent: __Deceased__, DOB:_____, ADD:_____, PHO:_____, Arrest/ID#:_____
        _____, DOB:_____, ADD:_____, PHO:_____, Arrest/ID#:_____

(continued on next page)

COOPERATING INDIVIDUAL PERSONAL HISTORY SHEET
(Example cont.)

ASSOCIATES:
Name: __I.R. Weasel__, DOB:03/12/69, ADD: ___502 Pen Ave.___, PHO: __None__, Arrest/ID#:87-953176
_____, DOB:_____, ADD:_____, PHO:_____, Arrest/ID#:_____
_____, DOB:_____, ADD:_____, PHO:_____, Arrest/ID#:_____

KNOWN HANG OUTS:
Name:_____Con Bar and Grill_____, Address:_____9637 Con Blvd._____, Phone: _897-7539_
_____, Address:_____, Phone:_____
_____, Address:_____, Phone:_____

COMMENTS:
Prior arrests of Grand Theft, Armed Robbery, Trafficking of Controlled Substance (Heroin)
Worked with Det. Goodguy on Narcotics cases, reliable information.

COOPERATING INDIVIDUAL SIGNATURE CARD

```
CI #_____
Name:_____
          (last, first, middle initial)
AKA:
  #1_____
  #2_____
  #3_____

Signature:_____
                      (real name)
Signature:_____
             (name to be used on receipts)

Witness:_____
Witness:_____
```

COOPERATING INDIVIDUAL SIGNATURE CARD
(Example)

```
CI #     00456
Name:              Crook, Ira  NMI
            (last, first, middle initial)
AKA:
  #1              Crook,  Ben  A.
  #2
  #3

Signature:              Ira  Crook
                      (real name)
Signature:              Ben  A.  Crook
                  (name to be used on receipts)

Witness:      John Law
Witness:          Ben  Good
```

INFORMATION/INTELLIGENCE REPORT FORM

DATE:_____   NUMBER: I_____

SUBJECT:_____
                              (person, business, organization)

ALIAS:_____
ADDRESS:_____
OCCUPATION:_____

DESCRIPTION
SEX:_____, RACE:_____, AGE:_____, HGT:_____, WT:_____ EYES:_____, HAIR:_____

VEHICLE
YEAR:_____, MAKE:_____, MODEL:_____, LICENSE #_____

ASSOCIATES: (persons & places)   CRIMINAL ACTIVITY: (known or suspected)

_____   _____
_____   _____
_____   _____

FBI #:_____, STATE ID #:_____ OTHER ID #:_____

PLACES FREQUENTED:_____
_____
_____
_____

ADDITIONAL INFORMATION:

Received By:_____ Date Received:_____

Received From:_____
                                              (address)
Actual Name:_____   Assumed Name:_____ (check one)

Reliability of Source:(check one) Reliable:_____ Unknown:_____ Doubtful:_____

372

INFORMATION/INTELLIGENCE REPORT FORM
(Example)

DATE: ___11/19/99___   NUMBER: ____I99-6354895____

SUBJECT: _____ ___Con Bar and Grill_____
                       (person, business, organization)

ALIAS:_____
ADDRESS: _____9637 Con Blvd. Central City_____
OCCUPATION:_____

DESCRIPTION
SEX:_____, RACE:_____, AGE:_____, HGT:_____, WT:_____ EYES:_____, HAIR:_____

VEHICLE
YEAR:_____, MAKE:_____, MODEL:_____, LICENSE #_____

ASSOCIATES: (persons & places)   CRIMINAL ACTIVITY: (known or suspected)

____Irving (Izzy) A. Scammer (Owner)_____   _____Manufacturing Methamphetamine_____

_____   _____

_____   _____

FBI #: ___895267-8648___, STATE ID #:___71-37549___ OTHER ID #:_____

PLACES FREQUENTED: ___Gooddeal Auto, 14873 Auto Park Rd. (Owner: Heisa Nogood)_____
_____
_____

ADDITIONAL INFORMATION: Lab is supposed to be located in separate building in back of bar.
Deals with motorcycle gangs and prostitutes.

Received By: _____Detective I. R. Law_____ Date Received: ____11/19/99___

Received From: ___Ben A. Crook CI# 00465_____
                           (name & address)
Actual Name:_____ Assumed Name:__X__ (check one)

Reliability of Source:(check one) Reliable:_X_ Unknown:_____ Doubtful:_____

INFORMATION DISSEMINATION LOG

Date of Inquiry	Agent Handling Request	Time	Requesting Agency	Subject & Reason for inquiry by Requesting Agency	Source of Info. Conveyed	Information Disseminated Via			* Date of Return
						Phone	Person	Written	

* When Applicable

INFORMATION DISSEMINATION LOG
(Example)

Date of Inquiry	Agent Handling Request	Time	Requesting Agency	Subject & Reason for inquiry by Requesting Agency	Source of Info. Conveyed	Information Disseminated Via			* Date of Return
						Phone	Person	Written	
1-1-99	J. Law	1303	F.B.I.	J. Bad Guy subject of robbery investigation	Intelligence file #I-6301	XX			
1-6-99	B. Good	1407	State Police	P.P. Bad Distribution of Controlled Substance	Case # 00-00000		XX		
1-12-99	J. Jones	1106	County Sheriff	Al Hurt Criminal Background	Arrest File # 00-00000			XX	1-13-99

* When Applicable

INVESTIGATOR CASE LOG

INVESTIGATOR:						
Date	Case #	Expenditure #	Purchase of Evidence	Payments to Informants	Expenses	Running Total

INVESTIGATOR CASE LOG
(Example)

INVESTIGATOR: I. R. Law							
Date	Case #	Expenditure #	Purchase of Evidence	Payments to Informants	Expenses	Running Total	
Jan 10	00-0023	00-0001	$ 100.00	$ 50.00		$ 150.00	
Jan 19	00-0144	00-0002	$ 100.00			$ 250.00	
Jan 20	00-0289	00-0003	$ 50.00		$ 20.00	$ 320.00	

CONFIDENTIAL FUND EXPENDITURE LEDGER

Date	Expenditure	Purchase of Evidence	Payment to Informant	Expenses	Running Total

378

CONFIDENTIAL FUND EXPENDITURE LEDGER
(Example)

Date	Expenditure	Purchase of Evidence	Payment to Informant	Expenses	Running Total
Jan 1	Buy #00-000000 (case #00-0000) 2nd buy on John Doe 1 FAX machine Model #2000 by Agent 32	$ 75.00			$ 75.00
Jan 2	Buy #00-000000 (case #00-0000) Pd. to CI # 125 by Agent #12 for information		$ 25.00		$ 100.00
Jan 3	Meeting (case # I-0006) with CI #009			$ 5.00	$ 105.00

TRANSACTION CARD

```
┌─────────────────────────────────────────────────────────────┐
│                    TRANSACTION CARD                           │
│                                                               │
│ Case No._____  Expenditure No._____   │
│ Date of Expenditure:_____ Amount:_____    │
│ Cooperating Individual No._____          │
│ Subject:_____        │
│                                                               │
│ Purpose:_____        │
│        _____         │
│        _____         │
│                                                               │
│ Property/Contraband:_____        │
│                    _____         │
│                                                               │
│ Agent:_____ Date:_____      │
│                                                               │
│ Approved by Unit Commander:                                   │
│ _____ Date:_____      │
└─────────────────────────────────────────────────────────────┘
```

TRANSACTION CARD
(Example)

```
┌─────────────────────────────────────────────────────────────┐
│                      TRANSACTION CARD                         │
│                                                               │
│ Case No. ____99-007536____   Expenditure No. ____99-6534____  │
│ Date of Expenditure: _05/23/99__ Amount: _$_1,200.00_____    │
│ Cooperating Individual No. ___602____                         │
│ Subject: _____John Lawbreaker_____                │
│                                                               │
│ Purpose: __$ 1,000 paid for vehicle listed below to subject   │
│          listed above. $ 200 paid to CI #602 for assistance   │
│          in deal_____          │
│                                                               │
│ Property/Contraband: 1999 Ford F-250 P-U Lic.# 603-201 VIN    │
│                      # 1234567891011 Value $ 25,000           │
│                                                               │
│ Agent: _____J. Law_____ Date: _05/23/99__      │
│                                                               │
│ Approved by Unit Commander:                                   │
│ _____I. B. Upchain_____ Date: __05/24/99__   │
└─────────────────────────────────────────────────────────────┘
```

INVESTIGATOR LEDGER

NAME:_____   DATE:_____ to _____

EXPENDITURES

Date	Paid for Evidence	Paid for Information	Paid for Other	Comments
				GRAND TOTAL
TOTALS	$	$	$	$

SIGNATURE:_____

INVESTIGATOR LEDGER
(Example)

NAME: _____J. Law_____   DATE: __01/01/99__ to __01/30/99__

EXPENDITURES

Date	Paid for Evidence	Paid for Information	Paid for Other	Comments
01/01	$ 100			Expenditure # 99-00001
01/02		$ 50		CI #125
01/09	$ 100		$ 20	Expenditure # 99-00010 Potables During Deal
01/21	$ 300	$ 100		Expenditure # 99-00015 CI #96
01/27			$ 25	Meeting with J.B. Guy Potables
01/29	$ 400			Expenditure # 99-00035
				GRAND TOTAL
TOTALS	$ 900.00	$ 150.00	$ 45.00	$ 1095.00

SIGNATURE:_____J. Law_____

COOPERATING INDIVIDUAL LEDGER

COOPERATING INDIVIDUAL #					
Date	Case #	Expenditure #	Received for Information	Received for Expenses	Running Total

COOPERATING INDIVIDUAL LEDGER
(Example)

		COOPERATING INDIVIDUAL # 043			
Date	Case #	Expenditure #	Received for Information	Received for Expenses	Running Total
Jan 10	00-00060	00-00020	$ 50.00		$ 50.00
Feb 15	00-00072	00-00050	$ 100.00		$ 150.00
Mar 10	00-00229	00-00167		$ 20.00	$ 170.00
Jun 02	00-01085	00-00231		$ 30.00	$ 200.00

ADVISE OF RIGHTS FORM

Location:_____

            Date:_____

            Time:_____

_____, you are now in_____ I
am _____ of the _____ and this is
_____ of the _____. We would like you
to tell us what you know about _____ and
answer any questions we want to ask you about it. You have an absolute right to remain silent. You do not have to
tell us anything, or answer any questions that we ask you. If you do not want to say anything, we will respect your
right not to talk with us. If you want to make a statement and answer our questions, anything you do say can be
used against you in a court of law. You also have the right to be alone with a lawyer and to talk to him and to
be advised by him. After talking to a lawyer, you can also have him present during any time you want to give us
a statement and while we are questioning you. If you are not able to afford a lawyer, but you want one before
speaking to us, a lawyer will be appointed for you. If you decide to talk to us without a lawyer present, but
during our questioning you want to stop and get a lawyer, you have the right to do so and to say nothing more. You
are not being promised anything to make a statement or to answer questions and no threats are now, or will be, made
against you to have you tell us anything.

Q. Do you understand what I have just told you?
A.

Q. Are you willing to make a voluntary statement after being advised of your rights?
A.

Q. Do you understand that by making this voluntary statement you are waiving your right not to talk to
us and to have a lawyer present?
A.

Q. What is your full name?
A.

Q. What is your age and date of birth?
A.

Q. What is the highest grade you completed in school and what school did you attend?
A.

Q. Can you read and write?
A.

Q. Are you presently under the influence of alcohol or narcotic drugs?
A.

(cont. on next page)

Q. Do you know what day of the week this is?
A.

Q. Do you know where you are now?
A.

Q. Have you been advised of your rights?
A.

Q. Will you tell us in your own words exactly what you know about _____
_____.

BODY OF STATEMENT

Q. Have you ever been to _____?
A.

(cont. on next page)

Q. Do you know _____?
A.

Q. Have you ever sold anything at _____?
A.

Q. Have you ever sold anything to _____?
A.

Q. What?
A.

Q. Has anyone beaten, threatened, or intimidated you in any manner in order to obtain this statement?
A.

Q. Has anyone made you any promises, offers of reward, or immunity, in order to obtain this statement?
A.

Q. Then, has this statement been given voluntarily and of your own free will and accord?
A.

Q. Has this statement been read to you?
A.

Q. Have you read this statement?
A.

Q. Having read it (or having had it read to you), do you want to make any changes or corrections in it?
A.

Q. Is this statement the truth as you have told it?
A.

(cont. on next Page)

ADVISE OF RIGHTS FORM
(cont.)

Q. Will you sign your name to it?
A.

This statement was terminated at _____ .
This statement, consisting of (   ) pages, which I have initialed,
is the truth as I have told it and I sign my name to it.

Signed:_____

WITNESSED:

_____
(officer)

_____
(officer)

ADVISE OF RIGHTS FORM
(Example)

Location: (location of building where interview is conducted)
           Date: _____ (of interview)
           Time: _____ (of interview)

_____(name of suspect)_____, you are now in _____(room location of interview)_____
I am __(rank and name of officer)__ of the _____(organization)_____ and this is
___(rank and names of others present)___ of the _____(organization)_____. We would like
you to tell us what you know about _____(state nature of crime being investigated, including date and time)_____
and answer any questions we want to ask you about it. You have an absolute right to remain silent. You do not have
to tell us anything, or answer any questions that we ask you. If you do not want to say anything, we will respect
your right not to talk with us. If you want to make a statement and answer our questions, anything you do say can
be used against you in a court of law. You also have the right to be alone with a lawyer and to talk to him and
to be advised by him. After talking to a lawyer, you can also have him present during any time you want to give
us a statement and while we are questioning you. If you are not able to afford a lawyer, but you want one before
speaking to us, a lawyer will be appointed for you. If you decide to talk to us without a lawyer present, but
during our questioning you want to stop and get a lawyer, you have the right to do so and to say nothing more. You
are not being promised anything to make a statement or to answer questions and no threats are now, or will be, made
against you to have you tell us anything.

Q. Do you understand what I have just told you?
A.

Q. Are you willing to make a voluntary statement after being
advised of your rights?
A.

Q. Do you understand that by making this voluntary statement
you are waiving your right not to talk to us and to have
a lawyer present?
A.

Q. What is your full name?
A.

Q. What is your age and date of birth?
A.

Q. What is the highest grade you completed in school and what
school did you attend?
A.

Q. Can you read and write?
A.

(cont. on next page)

390

ADVISE OF RIGHTS FORM
(cont.)

Q. Are you presently under the influence of alcohol or
narcotic drugs?
A.

Q. Do you know what day of the week this is?
A.

Q. Do you know where you are now?
A.

Q. Have you been advised of your rights?
A.

Q. Will you tell us in your own words exactly what you know about _____(nature of crime, including _____date and place)_____ .

BODY OF STATEMENT

NOTE: Let the suspect make the statement in his own words, without interruption. After
he finishes, then he can be asked specific questions. If, for any reason, a
break is taken in the statement, it should be noted.

Q. Have you ever been to _____(name and location of storefront_____ ?
A.

Q. Do you know _____(cover names of operatives at storefront)_____ ?
A.

Q. Have you ever sold anything at _____(name and location of storefront_____ ?
A.

Q. Have you ever sold anything to _____(cover names of operatives)_____ ?
A.

Q. What?
A.

Q. Has anyone beaten, threatened, or intimidated you in any manner in order to obtain this statement?
A.

Q. Has anyone made you any promises, offers of reward, or immunity, in order to obtain this statement?
A.

Q. Then, has this statement been given voluntarily and of your own free will and accord?
A.

(cont. on next page)

ADVISE OF RIGHTS FORM
(cont.)

(Read this statement to suspect and then let suspect read it.)

Q. Has this statement been read to you?
A.

Q. Have you read this statement?
A.

Q. Having read it (or having had it read to you), do you want to make any changes or corrections in it?
A.

Q. Is this statement the truth as you have told it?
A.

Q. Will you sign your name to it?
A.

This statement was terminated at _____(date and time)_____.
This statement, consisting of ( ) pages, which I have initialed,
is the truth as I have told it and I sign my name to it.

Signed:_____
                    (suspect)

WITNESSED:

_____
            (officer)

_____
            (officer)

PROSECUTION REPORT

1. DEFENDANT'S NAME	2. SEX	RACE	D.O.B.	3. CASE NO.

4. CHARGE (IF MULTIPLE LIST COMPLAINT NOS. BELOW)	5. CITY ☐ STATE ☐	6. ARREST NO.	7. DATE OCCURRED

8. ATTACHMENTS: ☐ ARREST REPORT	☐ OFFENCE REPORT	☐ SUPPLEMENTAL REPORT(S)	☐ LOCAL ARREST RECORD	☐ FBI RAP SHEET	☐ STATEMENT

9. DATE/TIME ARRESTED	10. LOCATION OF ARREST

11. ORIGINAL CHARGE	12. OFFICERS WHO MAY TESTIFY

13. CO-DEFENDANTS ☐ NONE	NAME	CHARGE	SEX	RACE	D.O.B.

CODE: C - COMPLAINANT   P - PARENT/GUARDIAN   V - VICTIM (if different from Comp.)   W - WITNESS

14. NAME	CODE	RESIDENCE ADDRESS CITY	RES PHONE	BUS PHONE

15. NARRATIVE

16. PREPARED BY	NO.	17. APPROVED BY	NO.	18. DATE	PAGE NO. OF

NOTE: (1) Additional parties - list additional witnesses, etc., additional charges, additional co-defendants. (2) The crime - give brief summary description of crime, list property stolen and recovered and disposition. (3) Testimony- briefly indicate what testimony may be provided by each witness. (4) Evidence - Briefly describe each item of physical evidence, its present location, who will present at court. (5) Elements of offense - List the legal elements of the offense(s) charged and indicate who can testify or present evidence as to each one. (6) Remarks -Provide any additional information officer considers helpful to prosecutor. Use supplemental report if additional space is required.

Index